Henry Stevens

Historical nuggets. Bibliotheca americana

A descriptive account of my collection of rare books relating to America

Henry Stevens

Historical nuggets. Bibliotheca americana
A descriptive account of my collection of rare books relating to America

ISBN/EAN: 9783337278038

Printed in Europe, USA, Canada, Australia, Japan

Cover: Foto ©ninafisch / pixelio.de

More available books at **www.hansebooks.com**

HISTORICAL NUGGETS

BIBLIOTHECA AMERICANA OR A
DESCRIPTIVE ACCOUNT OF MY
COLLECTION OF RARE
BOOKS RELATING
TO AMERICA

HENRY STEVENS GMB FSA

I will buy with you, sell with you.
Shakespeare.

LONDON
PRINTED BY WHITTINGHAM AND WILKINS
TOOKS COURT CHANCERY LANE
MDCCCLXII

BIBLIOTHECA AMERICANA.

LABAT (JEAN BAPTISTE). Nouveau Voyage aux Isles de l'Amerique. Contenant l'Histoire Naturelle de ces Pays, l'Origine, les Mœurs, la Religion & le Gouvernement des Habitans anciens & modernes: Les Guerres & les Evenemens finguliers qui y font arrivez pendant le long féjour que l'Auteur y a fait. Le Commerce et les Manufactures qui font établies, & les moyens de les augmenter. Avec une Defcription exaĉte & curieufe de toutes ces Ifles. Ouvrage enrichi d'un grand nombre de Cartes, Plans, & Figures en Taille-douce. A *La Haye*, P. Husson, etc. M.DCC.XXIV. *Six Volumes.* Tome Premier. 15 prel. *leaves*; viz. *Collective title, Title, Table des Chapitres, and Preface.* Text 504 pp. *Map at p.* 1 *and plates at pp.* 45, 75, 200, 269, 297, 312, 315, 343, 376, 379, 380, 402, 432, 475. Tome Second. 4 prel. *leaves, and* 576 pp. *Plates at pp.* 9, 12, 15, 29, 39, 46, 48, 54, 200, 212, 251, 257, 326, 349, 379, 380, 387, 398, 414, 463, 553. Tome Troisième. 3 prel. *leaves, and* 528 pp. *Plates at pp.* 21, 32, 57, 63, 65 (2), 68 (2), 69, 74, 79, 86, 93, 98, 104, 109, 114, 116, 132, 178, 181, 222, 223, 234, 246, 255, 275, 278, 333. Tome Quatrième. 4 prel. *leaves, and* 539 pp. *Plates at pp.* 36, 37, 54, 59, 202, 203, 207, 346, 356, 387, 420, 504, 510. Tome Cinquième. 4 prel. *leaves, and* 504 pp. *Plates at pp.* 1, 35, 55, 262, 380. Tome Sixième. 3 prel. *leaves, and* 514 pp. *Table des Matieres,* 58 pp. *Plates at pp.* 1, (3), 110, 143, 312, 382, 404, 406. *Old calf.* 12*mo.* (1*l.* 11*s.* 6*d.* 1613)

LABAT (JEAN BAPTISTE). Nouveau Voyage aux Isles de l'Amerique. Contenant l'Histoire Naturelle de ces Pays, l'Origine, les Mœurs, la Religion & le Gouvernement des Habitans anciens & modernes : Les Guerres & les Evenemens finguliers qui y font arrivez pendant le long féjour que l'Auteur y a fait : Le Commerce et les Manufactures qui y font établies, & les moyens de les augmenter. Ouvrage enrichi d'un grand nombre de Cartes, Plans, & Figures en Taille-douce. A *La Haye*, P. Husson, *etc.* M.DCC.XXIV. *Two Volumes.* Tome Premier. 11 *prel. leaves; viz. Collective Title*, 'Voyage du Pere Labat, aux Isles de l'Amerique. Contenant Une exacte Defcription de toutes ces Ifles ; etc. En II. Volumes.' *Title;* ' Epitre,' 3 *pp.* 'Preface,' *viii. pp.* 'Avis au Relieur,' 2 *pp. containing a list of the maps and plates in the 2 volumes; viz.* 'Tome I. Premiere Partie, 11 *maps and plates*. Seconde Partie, 13 *plates*. Troisieme Partie, 23 *plates*. Tom. II. Quatrieme Partie, 9 *plates*. Cinquieme Partie, 6 *plates*. Sixieme Partie, 4 *plates*. 'Table,' 3 *pp. Text Premiere Partie,* 175 *pp. Seconde Partie,* 360 *pp.* Tome Second, 4 *prel. leaves; viz. Collective title, Title,* 'Table,' 3 *pp. Text* 520 *pp.* 'Table des Matieres,' 20 *pp. With the maps and plates. Old calf.* 4to. (1*l.* 4*s.* 1614)

LABAT (JEAN BAPTISTE). Nouveau Voyage aux Isles de l'Amerique, Contenant l'Histoire Naturelle de ces Pays, l'Origine, les Mœurs, la Religion & le Gouvernement des Habitans anciens & modernes. Les Guerres & les Evenemens finguliers qui y font arrivez pendant le féjour que l'Auteur y a fait. Par le R. P. Labat, de l'Ordre des Freres Prêcheurs. Nouvelle Edition augmentée confidérablement, & enrichie de Figures en Taillesdouces. A *Paris*, Ch. J. B. Delespine, M.DCC.XLII. *Eight Volumes.* Tome Premier, xxxvi *pp. und* 7 *prel. leaves, Text* 472 *pp. Portrait,* 20 *maps und plates.* Tome Second, 3 *prel. leaves, and* 444 *pp.* 17 *maps and plates.* Tome Troisième, 3 *prel. leaves, and* 475 *pp.* 31 *plates.* Tome Quatrième, 2 *prel. leaves, and* 533 *pp.* 12 *plates.* Tome Cinquième, 3 *prel. leaves, and* 418 *pp.* Tome Sixième, 2 *prel. leaves, and* 502 *pp.* 14 *plates.* Tome Septième, vi. *and* 516 *pp.* 5 *plates.* Tome Huitième, 3 *prel. leaves,* and 437 pp. *Privilege du Roi.* 7 pp. 4 *plates. Old calf.* 12*mo.* (1*l.* 11*s.* 6*d.* 1615)

LAET (JEAN DE). Befchrijvinghe/ van/ West-Indien/ door/ Ioannes de Laet/ Tweede druck:/ In ontallijcke plaetfen ver=/betert, vermeerdert, met eenige/ nieuwe Caerten, beelden van/ verfchyden dieren ende/ planten verciert./ Tot *Leyden,* bij de Elzeviers. A°. 1630./ 14 *prel. leaves, including half-title, Engraved title, and Register of Maps (of which there are* 14), *on the reverse Errata; Text* 622 *pp.* 'Register.' 17 *pp. Fine copy. Half calf. Folio.* (2*l.* 2*s.* 1616)

LAET (JEAN DE). Novvs Orbis/ feu/ Descriptionis/ Indiæ Occidentalis/ Libri XVIII./ Authore/ Ioanne de Laet Antverp./ Novis Tabulis Geographicis et variis/ Animantium, Plantarum, Fructumque/ Iconibus illuftrati./ Cvm Privilegio./ *Lvgd. Batav.* apud Elzevirius. A°. 1633./ 16 *prel. leaves, including the Half-title, Engraved title, and list of Maps (of which there are* 14). *Text* 690 *pp. Index,* 17 *pp. Folio.* (1*l.* 11*s.* 6*d.* 1618)

LAET (JEAN DE). L'histoire/ dv/ Nouvean Monde/ ou/ description/ des Indes/ Occidentales,/ Contenant dix-huiƈt Liures,/ Par le Sieur Iean de Laet, d'Anuers;/ Enrichi de nouuelles Tables Geographiques, & Figures des/ Animaux, Plantes, & Fruiƈts./ A *Leyde,*/ Chez Bonauenture & Abraham Elfeuiers, Imprimeurs/ ordinaires de l'Vniuerfité./ cIɔ Iɔcxl./ 14 *prel. leaves, including Title, list of Maps, (of which there are* 14), *Preface, Table of Chapters and List of illustrations; Text* 632 *pp. and Index* 6 *leaves. Old calf. Folio.* (1*l.* 10*s.* 1619)

LAFITAU (JOSEPH FRANÇOIS). Histoire des Decouvertes et Conquestes des Portugais dans le Nouveau Monde, Avec des Figures en taille-douce. Par le R. P. Joseph-François Lafitau de la Compagnie de Jesus. A *Paris,* Saugrain, & Jean-Baptiste Coignard. MDCCXXXIV. *Four Volumes.* Tome Premier. *Frontispiece,* 3 *prel. leaves, xl and* 432 *pp. Copperplate map and plates, at pp.* 1, 38, 74, 302, 320. Tome Second. *Title and* 381 *pp.* 'Table, I & II Tomes.' 79 *pp. Plates at pp.* 52, 206, 254.

Tome Troisième. *Title and* 512 *pp. Plates at pp.*
66, 334. Tome Quatrième. *Title and* 388 *pp.*
'Table,' III & IV Tomes, *Approbation, Privilege,
and Errata,* 149 *pp. Plates at pp.* 16, 32, 190, 200,
379. *Uncut. Small* 8*vo.* (1*l.* 5*s.* 1620)

[LAFITAU (Joseph François)]. Algemeine Gefchichte der Länder und Völker von America. Nebſt einer Vorrede Siegmund Jacob Baumgartens der h. Schrift Doctors und öffentl. Lehrers, auch des theologifchen Seminarii Directors auf der königl. preufzl. Friedrichs univerſität in Halle. Mit vielen Kupfern. *Halle,* bey Johann Juſtinus Gebauer. 1752. *Two Volumes.* Erſter Theil. *Frontispiece and* 23 *prel. leaves; Text* 688 *pp. Copperplate Map at p.* 13, *and plates numbered* I *to* XLI. Zweiter Theil. 11 *prel. leaves, and* 905 *pp. Register* 63 *pp.* 25 *Copperplate maps and plates. Vellum.* 4*to.* (15*s.* 1621)

LA HONTAN (Baron de). New Voyages to North-America. Containing An Account of the feveral Nations of that vaſt Continent; their Cuſtoms, Commerce, and Way of Navigation upon the Lakes and Rivers; the feveral Attempts of the Englifh and French to difpoffefs one another; with the Reafons of the Mifcarriage of the former; and the various Adventures between the French, and the Iroquefe Confederates of England, from 1683 to 1694. A Geographical Defcription of Canada, and a Natural Hiſtory of the Country, with Remarks upon their Government, and the Intereſt of the Englifh and French in their Commerce. Also a Dialogue between the Author and a General of the Savages, giving a full View of the Religion and ſtrange Opinions of thofe People: With an Account of the Authors Retreat to Portugal and Denmark and his Remarks on thofe Courts. To which is added, A Dictionary of the Algonkine Language, which is generally fpoke in North-America. Illuſtrated with Twenty Three Mapps and Cuts. Written in French By the Baron Lahontan, Lord Lievtenant of the French Colony at Placentia in New-foundland, now in England. Done into Englifh. In Two Volumes. A great part of which never Printed in the Original. *London:* H. Bonwicke, 1703. Vol. I. 12 *prel. leaves* and 280 pp. 13 copperplate maps and plates. Vol. II. wanting. Old calf. 8vo.   (7s. 6d. 1622)

LA HONTAN (Baron de). Nouveaux Voyages de Mr. Le Baron de Lahontan, dans l'Amerique Septentrionale, Qui contiennent une Relation des différens Peuples qui y habitent; la nature de leur Gouvernement; leur Commerce, leurs Coûtumes, leur Religion, & leur manière de faire la Guerre. L'intérêt des François & des Anglois dans le Commerce qu'ils font avec ces Nations; l'avantage que l'Angleterre peut retirer dans ce Païs, étant en Guerre avec la France. Le tout enrichi de Cartes & de Figures. Tome Premier. A la Haye, Chez les Fréres l'Honoré, Marchands Libraires. M.DCC.III. Two Volumes. Tom. I. 12 prel. leaves, and 279 pp. 15 copperplate maps and plates. Tom. II. 'Memoires de l'Amerique Septentrionale, ou la suite des Voyages de Mr. Le Baron de Lahontan. Qui contiennent la Defcription d'une grande étenduë de Païs de ce Continent, l'intérêt des François & des Anglois, leurs Commerces, leurs Navigations, les Mœurs & les Coutumes des Sauvages, &c. Avec un petit Dictionaire de la Langue du Païs. Le tout enrichi de Cartes & de Figures. Tome Second. A La Haye, Chez les Fréres l'Honoré, Marchands Libraires. MDCCIII. 220 pp. Table 16 pp. Copperplate map and 13 plates. Old Calf. 12mo.   (18s. 1623)

LA HONTAN (Baron de). Dialogues De Monfieur le Baron de La Hontan Et d'un Sauvage, Dans l'Amerique. Contenant une defcription exacte des mœurs & des coutumes de ces Peuples Sauvages. A Amsterdam, Boeteman, M.DCCIV. 8 prel. leaves, and 103 pp. Copperplate at page 1. 12mo.   (1l. 1s. 1624)

LA HONTAN (Baron de). Voyages du Báron de La Hontan dans l'Amerique Septentrionale, Qui contiennent une Rélation des différens Peuples qui y habitent; la nature de leur Gouvernment; leur Commerce, leurs Coûtumes, leur Religion, & leur manière de faire la Guerre: L'Intérêt des François & des Anglois dans le Commerce qu'ils font avec ces Nations; l'avantage que l'Angleterre peut reteirer de ce Païs, étant en Guerre avec la France.

Le tout enrichi de Cartes & de Figures. Tome Premier, Seconde Edition, revuë, corrigée & augmentée. A *Amsterdam*, Chez François l'Honoré, vis-à-vis de la Bourfe. MDCCV. *Two Volumes.* Tom. I. 10 prel. leaves *including Frontispiece, and* 376 pp. 2 copperplate maps and 11 plates. Tom. II. ʻMemoires de l'Amerique Septentrionale, ou la suite des Voyages de Mr. Le Baron de La Hontan: Qui contiennant la Defcription d'une grande étenduë de Païs de ce Continent, l'intérêt des François & des Anglois, leurs Commerces, leurs Navigations, les Mœurs & les Coutumes des Sauvages, &c. Avec un petit Dictionaire de la Langue du Païs. Le tout enrichi de Cartes & de Figures. Tome Second. Second Edition, augmentée des Conversations de l'Auteur avec un Sauvage diftingué. A *Amsterdam*, Chez Francois l'Honoré & Compagnie. MDCCV. *Title, and pp.* 5-336. *Table* 2 pp. *Small copperplate map and* 9 *plates. Old calf.* 12mo. (18s. 1625)

LA HONTAN (Baron de). New Voyages to North-America. Containing An Account of the feveral Nations of that vaft Continent; their Cuftoms, Commerce, and Way of Navigation upon the Lakes and Rivers; the feveral Attempts of the Englifh and French to difpoffefs one another; with the Reafons of the Mifcarriage of the former; and the various Adventures between the French, and the Iroquefe Confederates of England, from 1683 to 1694. A Geographical Defcription of Canada, and a Natural Hiftory of the Country, with Remarks upon their Government, and the Intereft of the Englifh and French in their Commerce. Alfo a Dialogue between the Author and a General of the Savages, giving a full View of the Religion and ftrange Opinions of thofe People: With an Account of the Author's Retreat to Portugal and Denmark, and his Remarks on thofe Courts. To which is added, A Dictionary of the Algonkine Language, which is generally fpoke in North-America. Illuftrated with Twenty-Three Maps and Cuts. Written in French By the Baron Lahontan, Lord Lieutenant of the French Colony at Placentia in Newfoundland, at that Time in England. Done into Englifh. The Second Edition. In Two Volumes. A great Part of which never

Printed in the Original. *London:* J. and J. Bonwicke, M,DCC,XXXV. *Two Volumes.* Vol. I. 12 *prel. leaves, and* 280 *pp.* 10 *copperplate maps and plates.* Vol. II. 'New Voyages to North-America. Giving a full Account of the Cuftoms, Commerce, Religion, and ftrange Opinions of the Savages of that Country. With Political Remarks upon the Courts of Portugal and Denmark, and the Prefent State of the Commerce of thofe Countries. The Second Edition. Written By the Baron Lahontan, Lord-Lieutenant of the French Colony at Placentia in Newfoundland: Now in England. *London:* J. Walthoe, 1735.' 304 *pp.* 10 *Copperplates. Old calf.* 8*vo.* (18*s.* 1626)

LAMB (R.) An Original and Authentic Journal of Occurrences during the late American War, from its commencement to the year 1783. By R. Lamb, late Serjeant in the Royal Welch Fuzileers. *Dublin:* Wilkinson & Courtney, 1809. 6 *prel. leaves, and pp.* 5-438. ' Order,' 1 *page, at page* 158. *Calf.* 8*vo.* (10*s.* 6*d.* 1627)

LAMBRECHTSEN (N. C.) Korte Beschrijving van de ontdekking en der verdere lotgevallen van Nieuw-Nederland, weleer eene volkplanting van het gemeenebest der vereenigde Nederlanden in America, door Mr. N. C. Lambrechtsen van Ritthem, ridder der orde van den Nederlandschen leeuw, President van het Zeeuwsch Genootschap der Wetenschappen. *Te Middelburg,* bij S. Van Benthem, MDCCCXVIII. 2 *prel. leaves, and* 102 *pp. With Map. Uncut.* 8*vo.* (10*s.* 6*d.* 1628)

LARRANAGA (BRUNO FRANCISCO). Prospecto de una Eneida Apostólica, ô Epopeya, que celebra la predicacion del V. Apóstol del Occidente P. Fr. Antonio Margil de Jesus: Intitulada Margileida. Escrita con puros versos de P. Virgilio Maron, y traducida a verso Castellano: La que se propone al público de esta America septentrional por Subscripcion: Para que colectados anticipadamente los gastos necesarios, se proceda inmediatamente á su impresion. Su Autor Don Bruno Francisco Larrañaga. Impresa en *México* en la Imprenta nueva Madrileña de los Herederos del Lic. D. Joseph de Jauregui. Calle de S. Bernardo. Año de 1788. 2 prel. leaves and 28 pp. Half morocco. 4to. (1l. 1s. 1629)

LAS CASAS (BARTHOLOME DE). ⁂Aqui ſe contiene/ vna diſputa, o controuerſia : entre el/ Obiſpo dō fray Bartholome de las/ Caſas, o Caſaus, obiſpo q fue de la/ ciudad Real de Chiapa, que es en=/ las Indias, parte de la nueua Eſpa=/ña : y el doctor Gines de Sepulueda/ Coroniſta del Emperador nueſtro ſe/ñor : ſobre q el doctor contendia : q las/ conquiſtas de las Indias contra los/ Indios eran licitas : y el obiſpo por/ el cōtrario d'fendio y affirmo auer ſi/ do y ſer ĩpoſſible no ſerlo : tiranicas,/ injuſtas ⁊ iniquas. La qual queſtiō/ ſe vētilo ⁊ diſputo en preſencia d'mu/ chos letrados theologos ⁊ juriſtas/ en vna cōgregacion q mando ſu ma=/geſtad juntar el año de mil ⁊ qniētos/ y cincuēta en la villa de Valladolid./ Año. 1552./ [Colophon] ⁋Aloor y gloria de nueſtro ſe/ñor Jeſu Chriſto y dela ſacratiſſima virgen ſancta/ Maria ſu madre. Fue impreſſa la preſente obra/ enla muy noble ⁊ muy leal ciudad de Seuilla :/ en caſa de Sebaſtian Trugillo impreſſor de/ libros. Frōtero de nueſtra ſeñora de Gra/cia. Acaboſſe a. x. dias del mes de Se=/tiembre. Año de mil ⁊ quinien/tos ⁊ cincuenta y dos./ ✤/ (Here is contained a dispute or controversy between the Bishop Friar Bartholomew de Las Casas, or Casaus, formerly Bishop of the royal City of Chiapa which is in the Indies a part of New Spain, and the Doctor Gines de Sepulveda Chronicler to the Emperor our Lord, in which the Doctor contended that the conquests of the Indies against the Indians were lawful, and the bishop on the contrary defended and affirmed them to have been and to be impossible to be so, but tyrannical, unjust and iniquitous. Which question was examined and disputed in the presence of many learned theologians and jurists in a meeting which his Majesty ordered to be held in the year one thousand five hundred and fifty in the City of Valladolid. In the year 1552. [Colophon] To the honor and glory of our Lord Jesus Christ and of the most holy Virgin Saint Mary his Mother. The present work was printed in the very noble and very loyal City of Seville ; at Sebastian Trugillo's, printer of books, and Opposite Lady of Grace. Finished the 10th day of the month of

September. In the 1552. *62 leaves, signatures* a to g *in eights and* h *in 6 leaves, the last being blank.* 4to. (2*l.* 2*s.* 1629*)

LAS CASAS (BARTHOLOME DE). ⁋ Aqui fe cõtienẽ tre/ynta propoficiones muy juridicas: en/ las quales fumaria y fuccintamente fe/tocā muchas cosas perteneciẽtes al de/recho q la yglefia y los principes chri=/ftianos tienen, o puedẽ tener fobre los/ infieles de qual quier efpecie que fean./ Mayormente fe affigna el verdadero/ y fortiffimo fundamento en que fe affi/enta y eftriba: el titulo y feñorio fupre=/ mo y vniuerfal que los Reyes d'Cafti/lla y Leon tienen al orbe de las que lla/mamos occidẽtales Indias. Por el ql/fon conftituydos vniuerfales feñores y/Emperadores enellas fobre muchos re-/ yes. Apuntā fe tambien otras cofas cõ/cernientes al hecho acaecido en aql or/be notabiliffimas: y dignas d'fer viftas/ y fabidas. Colijo las dichas treynta p/ poficiones El obifpo dõ Fray Bartho-/ lome de las Cafas, o Cafaus: Obifpo/ q fue d'la ciudad Real de Chiapa: cier/to Reyno de los de la nueua Efpaña./ Año. 1552./ [*Colophon*] ⁋ Impreffo en *feuilla* en cafa de febaftiã trugillo./ (Here are contained thirty most lawful propositions, in which are summarily and succinctly treated of, many things appertaining to the right which the church and the christian princes have, or may have over the infidels of whatever kind they may be. Chiefly the true and strongest foundation is assigned on which is based and supported the title and supreme and universal lordship which the kings of Castile and Leon hold over the world of what we call the West Indies. By the which they are constituted universal lords and emperors in them, over many kings. Other most remarkable things are also pointed out relative to the transaction which has taken place in that world, and worthy to be seen and known. The Bishop Don Friar Bartholomew de Las Casas or Casaus, formerly Bishop of the royal City of Chiapa a certain kingdom of the new Spain, collected the said thirty propositions.—In the year 1552.) 10 *leaves, signature* a. 4to. (2*l.* 2*s.* 1630)

LAS CASAS (BARTHOLOME DE). ⁋ Aqui fe cõtienẽ vnos/ auifos y reglas para los confeffores q/ oyeren

confeſſiones de los Eſpaño/ les que ſon, o han ſido en cargo a/ los Indios de las Indias del/ mar Oceano : colegidas por/ el obiſpo de Chiapa don/ fray Bartholome d'las/ caſas, o caſaus dela/ orden de Sancto/ Domingo./ [*Colophon*.] ℭ Aloor y gloria de nueſtro ſe/ñor Jeſu Chriſto y dela ſacratiſſima virgen ſancta/ Maria. Fue impreſſa la preſente obra en la muy/ noble ⁊ muy leal ciudad de Seuilla, en caſa/ de Sebaſtian Trugillo impreſſor de li/bros. Frõtero de nueſtra ſeñora de/ Gracia. Acaboſſe a. xx. dias del/ mes de Setiembre. Año de/ mil ⁊ quinientos ⁊ cin/cuenta y dos./ ✤ / (Here are contained some devices and rules for the confessors who have heard the confessions of the Spaniards who have or have had the charge of the Indians of the Indies of the Ocean Sea; collected by the Bishop of Chiapa Don Bartholomew de Las Casas, or Casaus, Friar of the Order of Saint Dominick. [*Colophon*] To the honor and glory of Our Lord Jesus Christ and of the most Holy Virgin Saint Mary. The present work was printed in the very noble and very loyal City of Seville, at Sebastian Trugillo's, printer of books. Opposite Our Lady of Grace: finished the 20th day of the month of September. In the year one thousand five hundred and fifty-two.) 16 *leaves, signature* a, *the reverse of the last leaf blank.*
4to. (2*l.* 2*s.* 1631)

LAS CASAS (BARTHOLOME DE). ℭ Breuiſſima rela/cion de la deſtruycion de las In=/dias : colegida por el Obiſpo dõ/ fray Bartolome de las Caſas, o/ Caſaus de la orden de Sãcto Do/mingo./ Año. 1552./ [*Colophon*] ℭ Fue impreſſa la preſente o=/bra enla muy noble ⁊ muy leal ciudad de *Seuilla*/ en caſa de Sebaſtian Trugillo impreſſor de/ libros. A nueſtra ſeñora de Gracia./ Año de M. D. L ij./ (A very brief account of the Destruction of the Indies; collected by the Bishop Don Bartholomew de Las Casas, or Casaus, Friar of the Order of Saint Dominick. In the year 1552. [*Colophon*] The present work was printed in the most noble and loyal city of Seville at Sebastian Trugillo's, printer of books. At our Lady of Grace's. In the year 1552.) 54 *leaves, signatures* a *to* e *in eights,* f *ten, and* g *in four leaves being a separate tract commenc-*

ing ¶ Lo que se sigue es vn pedaço de vna carta, *etc.* 4to. (2*l.* 2*s.* 1632)

LAS CASAS (Bartholome de). ✤ Entre los re=/medios q dō fray Bartolome de las casas :/ obispo d'la ciudad real de Chiapa : refirio/ por mandado del Emperador rey nro se=/nor: en los ayuntamiētos q mādo hazer su/ magestad de perlados y letrados y perso/nas grādes en Valladolid el año de mill τ/ quiniētos y quarēta y dos : para reforma=/ciō de las Indias. El octauo en ordē es el/ siguiēte. Dōde se asignā veynte razones :/ por las qles prueua no deuerse dar los in=/dios a los Españales en en-comiēda: ni en/ feudo: ni en vassallaje: ni d'otra manera al/gūa. Si su majestad como dessea quiere li/brarlos de la tyrania y perdicio q padecē/ como de la boca de los dragones : y q total=/mēte no los cōsumā y matē y q de vazio to=/do aql orbe d'sus tā infinitos naturales ha/bitadores como estaua y lo vimos poblado/ [*Colophon.*] ¶Fue impressa la pre-sente obra en/ la muy noble y opulentissima y muy leal ciudad/ de *Seuilla*, en las casas de Jacome Crō/berger. Acabose a diez τ siete dias/ del mes de Agosto, año de mill/ τ quinientos τ cinquen=/ta y dos años./ (Among the remedies which Brother Don Bartholomew de Las Casas Bishop of the Royal City of Chiapa reported by order of the Emperor, the King, our Lord, in the meetings which his Majesty ordered to be held by the pre-lates and learned men and grandees of Valladolid, in the year one thousand five hundred and forty two, for the reformation of the Indies ; the eighth in order is the following, wherein twenty reasons are assigned, by which it is proved that the Indians should not be given to the Spaniards, neither in commission, nor in fief, nor in vassalage, nor in any other way whatsoever, if His Majesty accord-ing to his desire would free them from the tyranny and perdition which they suffer, as from the mouth of the dragons, and that they may not totally con-sume and kill them, and devastate that world of its so infinite natural inhabitants, with whom it was, and we saw it, peopled. [*Colophon.*] The present work was printed in the very noble and most opulent and very loyal city of Seville at Jacob Cromberger's ; finished on the seventeenth day of

the month of August in the year 1552.) 54 *leaves,
signatures* a to f *in eights, and* g *in six leaves, the last being blank.* 4to.   (2l. 2s. 1633)

LAS CASAS (BARTHOLOME DE). ⁋ Efte es vn tratado q/ el obifpo de la cuidad Real de Chiapa dō/ fray Bartholome de las Cafas, o Cafaus/ compufo, por comiffion del Confejo Real/ de las Indias : fobre la materia de los yn=/dios que fe han hecho en ellas efclauos. El/ qual contiene muchas razones y aucto=/ridades juridicas : que pueden apro/uechar a los lectores para deter=/minar muchas y diuerfas/ queftiones dudofas/ en materia de re=/ftitucion : y de/ otras que al/ qfente los/ hōbres/ el tiēpo de agora tratan./ Año 1552./ [*Colophon*] ⁋ Aloor y gloria de nueftro fe/ñor Jefu Chrifto y dela facratiffima virgen fancta/ Maria. Fue impreffa la prefente obra en la muy/ noble τ muy leal ciudad de *Seuilla*, en cafa/ de Sebaftian Trugillo impreffor de li/bros. Frontero de nueftra feñora/ de Gracia. Acaboffe a doze/ dias del mes de Setiem/bre. Año de mil τ qui/nientos y cincuē/ta y dos./ (This is a treatise which the Bishop of the Royal City of Chiapa, Friar Don Bartholomew de Las Casas or Casaus composed by commission of the Royal Council of the Indies: upon the subject of the Indians who have been made slaves there; which contains many reasons and lawful authorities, which may profit the readers for the determination of many and different doubtful questions in the matter of restitution, and of others which now the men of the present day treat of. In the year 1552. [*Colophon*] To the honor and glory of Our Lord Jesus Christ and of the most Holy Virgin Saint Mary. The present work was printed in the most noble and most loyal City of Seville, at Sebastian Trugillo's, printer of books. Opposite Our Lady of Grace. Finished the twelfth day of the month of September. In the year one thousand five hundred and fifty-two.) 36 *leaves, signatures* a to c *in eights*, d *in* 12 *leaves, the reverse of the last leaf blank.* 4to.   (2l. 2s. 1634)

LAS CASAS (BARTHOLOME DE). ⁋ Principia quedā ex quibus/ procedendum eft in difputatione ad manifeftan/dam et defendendam iufticiam Yndorum :/ Per Epifcopū. F. Bartholomeū a Ca/faus ordinis predicatorū, collecta./ [*Colophon*] ❡ Impreſſum Hiſpali in edibus Sebaſtiani Trugilli./ (Certain principles from which we are to proceed in disputation to the manifestation and defence of the jurisdiction of the Indians. Collected by bishop Bartholomew de Las Casas, Friar of the Order of Preachers. [*Colophon*] Printed at Seville, at Sebastian Trugillo's, [1552].) 10 *leaves, signature* A. 4*to*. (3*l*. 3*s*. 1635)

LAS CASAS (BARTHOLOME DE). ❡ Tratado cōpro/batorio del lmperio ſoberano y/ principado vniuerſal que los Re/yes de Caſtilla y Leon tienen ſo=/bre las indias : compueſto por el/ Obiſpo don fray Bartholome d'/ las Caſas, o Caſaus de la orden d'/ Sancto Domingo. Año. 1552./ [*Colophon*] ❡ A loor y gloria de nueſtro ſe/ñor Jeſu Chriſto y de la ſacratiſſima virgen ſancta/ Maria ſu madre. Fue impreſſa la preſente o=/bra en la muy noble τ muy leal cuidad/ d' *Seuilla* en caſa d Sebaſtiā Tru/ gillo impreſſor de libros. Aca/ boſſe a ocho dias d'l mes/ de Enero. Año./ 1553./ 84 *leaves, signatures* a *to* k, *in eights*. 4*to*. (3*l*. 3*s*. 1636)

LAS CASAS (BARTHOLOME DE). Tyrannies/ et Crvavtez/ des/ Espagnols,/ perpetrees/ és/ Indes Occidentales,/ qu'on dit Le Nouueau monde ;/ Brieuement deſcrites en langue Castillane par l'Eueſque/ Don Frere Bartelemy de Las Casas ou/ Casavs, Eſpagnol, de l'ordre de S. Dominique; fide-/lement traduiɛ̄tes par Iaqves de Miggrode :/ Pour seruir d'exemple & aduertiſſement/ aux XVII Prouinces du païs bas./ Heureux celuy qui deuient ſage/ En voyant d'autruy le dommage./ A *Anvers,*/ Chez François de Ravelenghien ioignant le por-/tail Septentrional de l'Egliſe noſtre Dame./ M.D.LXXIX./ (Tyrannies and cruelties of the Spanish, perpetrated in the West Indies which are called the New World; briefly described in the Castilian tongue, by the Bishop Don Bartholomew de Las Casas or Casaus, Spaniard, Friar of the Order of St. Dominick; faithfully translated by James de Miggrode; to serve as an example and warning to the seventeen provinces of the Low Countries. Happy is he who becomes wise in witnessing another's disadvantage. Antwerp, at Francis de Ravelingen's, adjoining the northern

entrance of the Church of our Lady. 1579.) 8 *prel.*
leaves, and 184 *pp.* 8vo.   (2*l.* 2*s.*   1637)

LAS CASAS (BARTHOLOME DE). The/ Spanish Colonie,/ or/ Briefe Chronicle of the Acts and/ gestes of the Spaniardes in the West In-/dies, called the newe World, for the/ space of xl. yeeres: written in the Ca-/stilian tongue by the reuerend Bi=/shop Bartholomew de las Casas or Casaus, a Friar of the or-/der of St. Dominicke./ And nowe first translated into/ English, by M. M. S./ ¶ Imprinted at *London* for/ William Brome./ 1583./ [*Colophon*] Imprinted at London at the three/ Cranes in the Vintree by Thomas/ Dawson, for William Broome./ 1583./ 8 *prel. leaves; viz. Title in a broad type metal border, the reverse blank;* 'To the Reader.' 7 *pp.* 'The Argument of this present/ Summarie.'/ 2 *pp.* 'The Prologue of the Bishop Frier/ Bartholomewe de las Casas or Casaus,/ to the most high and mightie prince,/ Our Lord Don Philip Prince/ of Spaine.'/ 4 *pp. in roman type. Text* 52 *leaves in Black letter; Signatures A. to N. in fours.* 'To the Reader.' 14 *leaves in roman type; signatures* O. *to* Q. *in fours,* R. *in two.* [*Colophon*] Imprinted at London at the three/ Cranes in the Vintree by Thomas/ Dawson, for William Broome./ 1583./ *Russia extra.* 4to.   (10*l.* 10*s.*   1638)

LAS CASAS (BARTHOLOME DE). Newe Welt./ Warhafftige Anzeigung/ Der Hispanier grewli=/chen, abschewlichen vnd vnmenschlichen Ty=/ranney, von ihnen inn den Indianischen Ländern,/ so gegen Nidergang der Sonnen gelegen, vnd die/ Newe Welt gennet wird, begangen./ Erstlich/ Castilianisch, durch Bischoff Bartholomeum de las Casas oder/ Casaus, gebornen Hispaniern, Prediger Ordens, beschrieben: Vnd/ im Jahr 1552 in der Königlichen Staat Hispalis oder/ Sevilia in Spanien gedruckt:/ Hernacher in die/ Frantzösische Sprach, durch Jacoben von Miggrode, den 17/ Provincien desz Niderlands, zur Warnung/ und Beyspiel, gebracht:/ Jetzt aber erst ins/ Hochteutsch, durch einen Liebhaber desz Vatterländs, vmb ebenmässiger/ vrsachen wissen, vbergesetzt./ Jm Jhar/ 1597./ 8 *prel. leaves and* 158 *pp. Register* 12 *pp. unbound.*
4to.   (3*l.* 3*s.*   1639)

LAS CASAS (BARTHOLOME DE). Spieghel der Spaenſcher ty=/rannye, in Weſt-Indien. Waer inne verhaelt wordt de moorda=/dighe, ſchandelijcke, lende grouweijcke feyten, die deſelve Spaen-/jaerden ghebruyckt hebben inde ſelve Landen./ Mitſgaders de beſchryvinghe vander ghelegentheyt, zeden/ ende aert van de ſelfde Landen ende Volcken./ In Spaenſcher Talen beſchreven, door den E. Biſſchop Don Fray Bartholome de las Caſas, van S. Dominicus Oorden./ t'*Amstelredam,*/ By Cornelis Claeſz. Boeckvercooper woonende opt Water,/ int Schrijfboeck. Anno 1607./ 44 *leaves including title, with map of America engraved on the title, the reverse blank. Black letter. Signatures A. to L. in fours, the last blank.* 4to. (1*l.* 10s. 1640)

LAS CASAS (BARTHOLOME DE). Den/ Spieghel/ Vande Spaenſche Tyrannie beeldelijcken af=/gemaelt, leeſt breederen in-hout door het schrijven van den E. Biſſchop/ van Chiapa in nieu Spaengien, ghenaemt Don Fray Bartholome de/ las Caſas, van S. Dominicus Oorden, aen den grootmach-/tigen Coninck van Spaengien Philips de tweede./ Ghedruckt tot *Amstelredam* by Cornelis Claeſz. 1609./ *Title with copperplate engraving the reverse blank, and copperplates numbered* 1 *to* XVII, *with letter-press description at foot of each. Black letter.* 4to. (1*l.* 10s. 1641)

LAS CASAS (BARTHOLOME DE). Le Miroir/ De la/ Tyrannie Eſpagnole/ Perpetree aux Indes/ Occidentales./ On verra icy la cruaute plus/ que inhumaine, commiſe par les/ Eſpagnols, auſsi la deſcription de/ ces terres, peuples, et leur nature./ Miſe en lumiere par un/ Eveſque Bartholome de las Caſas,/ de l'Ordre de S. Dominic./ Nouvellement refaicte, avec les/ Figurs en cuyvre./ tot/ *Amsterdam*/ Ghedruckt by Ian Evertſs,/ Cloppenburg, op't Water,/tegen over de Koor-Beur/ iñ vergulden Bijbel./ 1620./ 68 *folioed leaves including title within an engraved border of Figures, and copperplates with the text on folios* 5, 6, 8, 11, 14, 18, 20, 21, 24, 27, 29, 30, 33, 49, 53, 55, 65. *Old calf.* 4to. (1*l.* 11s. 6d. 1642)

LAS CASAS (BARTHOLOME DE). Istoria/ ò breuiſsima relatione/ Della Distrvttione/ dell' Indie Oc-

cidentali/ di Monsig. Reverendiss./ Don Bartolomeo dalle Cafe, ò Cafaus, Siuigliano/ Vefcouo di Chiapa Città Regale nell' Indie./ Conforme al svo vero originale/ Spagnuolo, già ſtampato in Siuiglia./ Con la traduttione in Italiano de Francefco Berfabita./ Dedicata all' Amicitia./ In *Venetia* Preſſo Marco Ginammi. M.DC.XXVI./ Con licenza de' Superiori, & Priuilegio./ (History or very short account of the destruction of the West Indies; by My Lord the most reverend Don Bartholomew de Las Casas, or Casaus, of Seville, Bishop of Chiapa, a royal City in the Indies. According to his true original Spanish, formerly printed in Seville, with the translation in Italian of Francis Bersabita. Dedicated to Friendship. Venice, at Mark Ginammi's, 1626. With license of the Superiors and privilege.) 8 *prel. leaves and* 154 *pp. Libri Stampati & Errori* 2 *pp. Vellum.*
4*to.* (1*l*. 1*s*. 1643)

LAS CASAS (BARTHOLOME DE). Tyrannies/ et/ Crvavtez/ des/ Espagnols,/ Commises es Indes/ Occidentales, qu'on/ dit le Nouueau Monde./ Briefvement descrite en/ Espagnol, par Dom Frere Barthelemy de/ las Casas de l'Ordre de S. Dominique, &/ Euefque de la ville Royalle de Chiappa./ Traduitte fidellement en François par Iacques de Miggrode/ sur la Coppie Espagnolle : Imprimée à la ville de Seuille./ A *Roven,*/ Chez Iacques Cailloüé à la Court du Palais:/ M.DC.XXX./ Iouxte la Coppie Imprimée à Paris, par Guillaume Iulien./ Avec Privilege dv Roy./ (Tyranny and Cruelties of the Spaniards, committed in the West Indies, called the New World. Briefly described in Spanish by Don Fr. Bartholomew de Las Casas of the Order of St. Dominic and Bishop of the Royal City of Chiapa. Faithfully translated into French by James de Miggrode from the Spanish original, printed in the city of Seville. At Rouen, at James Cailloüé's, in the Palace Court. 1630.) 11 *prel. leaves* ; *viz.* Title, *the reverse blank,* ' Advertissement av Lectevr tovchant le present Livre.' 12 *pp.* 'Sonnet.' 1 *page.* ' Argvment dv prefent Liure.' 2 *pp.* ' Prologve de L'evesqve dom Frere Barthelemy de las Casas,' *etc.* 5 *pp : Text* 214 *pp. Old calf extra.*
4*to.* (1*l*. 11*s*. 6*d*. 1644)

LAS CASAS (BARTHOLOMEO DE). La Libertà/ Pretesa/ Dal fupplice Schiauo Indiano/ di Monsignor Reverendiss./ D. Bartolomeo dalle Cafe,/ ò Cafaus, Siuigliano, dell' Ordine de' Predicatori, & Vefcouo/ di Chiapa, Città Regale dell' Indie./ Conforme al fuo vero Originale Spagnuolo già ftampato in Siuiglia./ Tradotto in Italiano per opera di Marco Ginammi./ All' Altezza Sereniſſima di/ Odoardo Farnese/ Dvca di Parma, et Piacenza, &c./ In *Venetia*, Preſſo Marco Ginammi. M DC XXXX./ Con Licenza de' Superiori, & Priuilegio./ (The pretended liberty of the suppliant Indian slave, by My Lord the most reverend D. Bartholomew de Las Casas, or Casaus, of Seville, of the order of Preachers and Bishop of Chiapa, a royal city of India. According to the true Spanish original, formerly printed at Seville. Translated into Italian by the industry of Mark Ginammi. To His Most Serene Highness Edward Farnese, Duke of Parma and Piacenza, etc. Venice. At Mark Ginammi's, 1640. With license of the Superiors, and privilege.) 158 *pp*. *Vellum*. 4*to*. (1*l*. 1*s*. 1645)

LAS CASAS (BARTHOLOME DE). Histoire/ des Indes/ Occidentales./ Ov l'on reconnoit/ la bonté de ces païs, & de leurs/ peuples; & les cruautez Tyran/niques des Espagnols./ Décrite premierement en langue Caftillane par/ Dom Barthelemy de las Casas,/ de l'Ordre de S. Dominique, & Euefque/ de Chappa; & depuis fidellement/ traduite en François./ A *Lyon*,/ Chez Iean Caffin, & F. Plaignard,/ en ruë Merciere, au Nom de Iesvs./ M.DC.XLII./ Auec Approbation, & Permiſsion./ (History of the West Indies. Where are recognised the excellence of those countries and of their people, and the tyrannical cruelties of the Spaniards. First described in the Castilian tongue by Don Bartholomew de Las Casas, of the Order of Saint Dominic, and Bishop of Chiapa, and since faithfully translated into French. Lyons. At John Caffin and F. Plaignard's, in Mercer Street, at the name of Jesus. 1642. With approbation and permission.) 4 *prel. leaves; viz. Title on the reverse, Approbation, and Permission.* 'Preface av Lectevr.' 6 *pp*. *Text* 299 *pp*. *Vellum. Small* 8*vo*. (1*l*. 1*s*. 1646)

LAS CASAS (BARTHOLOME DE). Istoria,/ ò Breuiſsima Relatione/ della Diſtrvttione/ dell' Indie Occidentali/ di Monsig. Reverendiss./ Don Bartolomeo dalle Caſe, ò Caſaus, Siuigliano dell' Ordine/ de' Predicatori; & Veſcouo di Chiapa./ Conforme al ſuo vero Originale Spagnuolo già ſtampato in Siuiglia./ Tradotta in Italiano dall Eccell. Sig. Giacomo Castellani,/ già ſotto nome di Francesco Berſabita. Al Molt' Ill.ᴿᴱ, & Ecc.ᵐᵒ. Sig.ᴿᴱ Sig.ʳ mio Col.ᵐᵒ Il Sig./ Nicolo' Persico./ In *Venetia* Preſſo Marco Ginammi. M.DC.XLIII./ Con Licenza de' Superiori, & Priuilegio./ (History or very short account of the destruction of the West Indies. By My Lord the most reverend Don Bartholomew de Las Casas, or Casaus, of Seville, of the order of Preachers, and bishop of Chiapa. According to the true Spanish original formerly printed in Seville. Translated into Italian by His Excellency Signor James Castellani, formerly under the name of Francis Bers-abita. To the most Illustrious and most excellent Signor, my most Honored Lord, Signor Nicholas Persico. Venice, At Mark Ginammi's. 1643. With license of the Superiors, and privilege.) 3 *prel. leaves and* 150 *pp.* 4*to.* (1*l.* 1*s.* 1647)

LAS CASAS (BARTHOLOMEO DE). Conqvista/ dell' Indie/ Occidentali/ di Monsignor/ Fra Bartolomeo dalle Case,/ ò Caſaus, Siuigliano, Voſcouo di Chiapa./ Tradotta in Italiano per opera di Marco Ginammi./ All' Ill.ᵐᵒ & Ecc.ᵐᵒ Sig.ᴿᴱ Sig.ᴼᴿ/ & mio Padron Col.ᵐᵒ/ Il Sig.ᴼᴿ Pietro Sagredo/ Procvratore di S. Marco./ In *Venetia*, M DC XXXXV./ Preſſo Marco Ginammi./ Con Licenza de' Superiori, & Privilegio./ (Conquest of the West Indies by My Lord, Brother Bartholomew de Las Casas or Casaus, of Seville, Bishop of Chiapa. Translated into Italian by the labours of Mark Ginammi. To the most Illustrious and excellent Lord, My Lord and most honoured patron the Lord Peter Sagredo, Procurator of Saint Mark. Venice, 1645. At Mark Ginammi's. With the license of the Superiors and privilege.) 184 *pp.* *Vellum.* 4*to.* (1*l.* 1*s.* 1647*)

LAS CASAS (BARTHOLOME DE). The Tears of the Indians :/ Being/ An Hiſtorical and true Account/

Of the Cruel/ Maſſacres and Slaughters/ of above Twenty Millions/ of innocent People;/ Committed by the Spaniards/ In the Iſlands of/ Hiſpaniola, Cuba, Jamaica, &c./ As alſo, in the Continent of/ Mexico, Peru, and other Places of the/ Weſt-Indies,/ To the total deſtruction of thoſe Countries./ Written in Spaniſh by Caſaus,/ an Eye-witneſs of thoſe things;/ And made Engliſh by J. P./ *London,*/ Printed by J. C. for Nath. Brook, at the Angel/ in Cornhil. 1656./ 15 *prel. leaves; viz.* 1*st blank*, Title the reverse *blank*, 'To His Highneſs, Oliver Lord Protector of the Commonwealth of England, Scotland and Ireland, With the Dominions thereto belonging.' 7 *pp. Signed* 'J. Phillips.' 'To all true Engliſh-men.' 18 *pp. Text* 134 *pp. Copperplate by* 'R. Gaywood.' *Old calf. Small 8vo.* (1*l.* 1*s.* 1648)

LAS CASAS (Bartholome de). Popery/ Truly Diſplay'd in its/ Bloody Colours :/ Or, a Faithful/ Narrative/ of the/ Horrid and Unexampled Maſſacres, But-/cheries, and all manner of Cruelties, that Hell and/ Malice could invent, committed by the Popiſh Spaniſh/ Party on the Inhabitants of West-India :/ Together/ With the Devaſtations of ſeveral Kingdoms in America/ by Fire and Sword, for the ſpace of Forty and Two/ Years, from the time of its firſt Diſcovery by them./ Compoſed firſt in Spaniſh by Bartholomew de las Caſas, a Biſhop/ there, and an Eye-Witneſs of moſt of theſe Barbarous Cruelties;/ afterward Tranſlated by him into Latin, then by other hands, into/ High-Dutch, Low-Dutch, French, and now Taught to ſpeak/ Modern Engliſh./ *London*, Printed for R. Hewſon at the Crown in Cornhil,/ near the Stocks-Market. 1689./ 4 *prel. leaves and* 80 *pp.* 4*to.* (2*l.* 2*s.* 1649)

LAS CASAS (Bartholome de). La Decouverte/ des/ Indes Occidentales,/ par/ les Espagnols./ Ecrite par Dom Balthazar de Las-/Casas, Évêque de Chiapa./ Dedié à Monſeigneur le Comte/ de Toulouse./ A *Paris,*/ Chez Andrè Prelard, ruë Saint Jacques, à l'Occaſion/ m.dc.xcvii./ Avec Privilege du Roi./ (The Discovery of the East Indies by the Spaniards. Written by Don Balthasar de Las Casas, Bishop of Chiapa. Dedicated to my Lord, the Count of Toulouse. Paris, At

Andrew Prelard's, St. James Street, at the Opportunity, 1697. With the King's privilege). 6 *prel. leaves including engraved title; Text* 382 *pp; Table* 2 *pp. Old calf.* 12*mo.* (12s. 6d. 1650)

LAS CASAS (BARTHOLOME DE). Relation/ des/ Voyages/ et des/ découvertes/ Que les Efpagnols ont fait dans les/ Indes Occidentales ;/ Ecrite par Dom B. de Las-Cafas, Evê-/que de Chiapa./ Avec la Relation curieufe des Voyages du/ Sieur de Montauban, Capitaine des/ Filbuftiers, en Guinée l'an 1695./ A *Amsterdam,*/ Chez J. Louis de Lorme Libraire fur le/ Rockin, à l'enfeigne de la Liberte.'/ M.DCXCVIII./ 6 *prel. leaves, including Frontispiece; Text* 402 *pp. Catalogue,* 2 *pp. blank leaf; Followed by* L'Art/ de/ Voyager/ Utilement./ Suivant la Copie de Paris./ A *Amsterdam,*/ Chez J. Louis de Lorme Libraire fur le/ Rockin, à l'enfeigne de la Liberte.'/ M.DC.XCVIII./ 2 *prel. leaves and* 52 *pp. Old calf.* 12*mo.* (10s. 6d. 1651)

LAS CASAS (BARTHOLOME DE). An/ Account/ Of the Firft/ Voyages and Discoveries/ Made by the Spaniards in America./ Containing/ The moft Exact Relation hitherto pub/lifh'd, of their unparallel'd Cruelties/ on the Indians, in the deftruction of a-/bove Forty Millions of People./ With the Propofitions offer'd to the King of Spain,/ to prevent the further Ruin of the Weft-Indies./ By Don Bartholomew de las Cafas, Bifhop of Chiapa,/ who was an Eye-witnefs of their Cruelties./ Illuftrated with Cuts./ To which is added,/ The Art of Travelling, fhewing how a Man may/ difpofe his Travels to the beft advantage./ *London,*/ Printed by J. Darby for D. Brown at the Black Swan/ and Bible without Temple-Bar, J. Harris at the/ Harrow in Little Britain, and Andr. Bell at the/ Crofs-keys and Bible in Cornhil. M.DC.XC.IX./ 4 *prel. leaves; viz. Title, Preface, and Contents: Text* 248 *pp.* 'The Art of Travelling to Advantage.' 40 *pp.* 2 *copperplates, each in two leaves at page* 1. *Old calf.* 8*vo.* (12s. 6d. 1652)

LAS CASAS (BARTHOLOME DE). Breve Relacion de la Destruccion de las Indias Occidentales, Presentada a Felipe II siendo Principe de Asturias por D. Fr. Bartolomé de las Casas, Del Orden de

Predicadores, Obispo de Chiapa. Impresa en Sevilla en 1552. Reimpresa en *Londres* Por Schulze y Dean, 13, Poland Street. 1812. *Half-title, title, and* 140 *pp. Uncut.* 12*mo.* (10*s.* 6*d.* 1653)

LASO DE LA VEGA (ANTONIO DE CORDOVA). ✤/ Por/ D. Antonio de Cordova/ Laſo de la Vega, Capitan de las Guardas/ de el Governador, y Teniente Gene-/ral de la Cavalleria del Reyno/ de Chile./ Con/ El Señor Fiscal del/ Conſejo de Indias, y el Promotor Fiſcal/ de Cobranças de él./ [*Lima* 1620?] 4 *unnumbered leaves, unbound. Folio.* (1*l.* 1*s.* 1654)

LASSO DE LA VEGA (GABRIEL). Elogios/ en loor de/ los Tres Famosos Varo-/nes Don Iayme Rey de Aragon, Don Fernan-/do Cortes Marques del Valle, y Don/ Aluaro de Baçan Marques de/ Santa-cruz./ Cõpueſtos por Gabriel Laſſo dela Vega Cõtino del R. N. S./ Dirigidos a Don Gaſpar Gal-çaran de Caſtro y Pi-/nos, Cõde de Guimaran, Vizcõde de Ebol, &c./ Año 1601/. Con priuilegio, En *Caragoça* por Alonſo Rodriguez./ 8 *prel. leaves and* 144 *folioed leaves. Fine copy. Old calf.* 16*mo.* (3*l.* 13*s.* 6*d.* 1655)

LAST (THE)/ Eaſt-Indian/ Voyage./ Containing Mvch/ varietie of the State of the ſeuerall/ king-domes where they haue traded :/ with the Letters of three ſeuerall Kings/ to the Kings Maieſtie of England,/ begun by one of the Voyage: ſince continued/ out of the faithfull obſeruations of/ them that are come home./ At *London*,/ Printed by T. P. for Walter Burre./ 1606./ *Title, reverse blank;* 'To the Reader.' 1 *page, Signed* 'W. B.' *Text, sig.* B *to* K *in fours. Half mor.* 4*to.* (3*l.* 3*s.* 1656)

LATHROP (JOHN). A Discourse Preached, December 15th 1774. Being the day recommended By the Provincial Congreſs, To be Observed In thankſgiving to God for the Bleſſings enjoyed; and humiliation on account of public Calamities. By John Lathrop, A.M. Pastor of the Second Church in Boston. *Boston:* Printed by D. Kneeland; and Sold by Samuel Webb, in Queen-Street. 1774. 39 *pp. Uncut.* 8*vo.* (4*s.* 6*d.* 1657)

LATHROP (JOSEPH). Two Sermons, on the Chriſtian Sabbath, for Distribution in the New

Settlements of the United States. By Joseph Lathrop, D.D. Paſtor of the firſt Church in Weſt-Springfield. *Northampton*, (Maſſachuſetts.) Printed By William Butler, (For the Hampſhire Miſſionary Society.) 1803. 28 *pp. Uncut.*
8*vo.* (2*s.* 6*d.* 1658)

LATOUR (A. LACARRIERE). Historical Memoir of the War in West Florida and Louisiana in 1814-15. With an Atlas. By Major A. Lacarriere Latour, Principal Engineer in the Seventh Military District United States' Army. Written Originally in French, and translated for the Author, by H. P. Nugent, Esq. *Philadelphia:* Published by John Conrad and Co. J. Maxwell, printer 1816. *xx and* 264 *pp.* 'Appendix,' *crc pp. With 7 colored maps and plans. Boards, uncut.*
8*vo.* (15*s.* 1659)

LAW (WILLIAM). An Extract from a Treatise By William Law, M.A. Called, The Spirit of Prayer; or, The Soul riſing out of the Vanity of Time, into the Riches of Eternity. Diſcovering the true Way of turning to God, and of finding the Kingdom of Heaven the Riches of Eternity in our Souls. *Philadelphia:* Printed by B. Franklin, and D. Hall. 1760. 47 *pp.* 8*vo.* (10*s.* 6*d.* 1660)

LAWSON (DEODAT). Christ's Fidelity/ the only/ Shield/ against/ Satan's Malignity./ Asserted in a/ Sermon/ Deliver'd at Salem-Village the/ 24th of March, 1692. Being Lecture-/day there, and a time of Publick Examination, of ſome Suſpected/ for Witchcraft./ By Deodat Lawson, Miniſter/ of the Goſpel./ The Second Edition./ Printed at Boſton in New-England, and Reprinted/ in *London* by R. Tokey for the Author; *etc.* 1704./ 6 *prel. leaves, and* 120 *pp. Fine copy, half calf.*
12*mo.* (2*l.* 2*s.* 1661)

LAWSON (JOHN). A New Voyage to Carolina; Containing the Exact Deſcription and Natural Hiſtory of that Country: Together with the Preſent State thereof. And A Journal Of a Thousand Miles, Travel'd thro' ſeveral Nations of Indians. Giving a particular Account of their Cuſtoms, Manners, &c. By John Lawson, Gent. Surveyor-General of North-Carolina. *London:* Printed in the Year 1709. *Title, reverse blank; Dedication to Lord Craven* 2 *pp; Preface* 2 *pp; Introduction & Journal,* 60 *pp; Description of North Carolina, pp.* 61 *to* 258; *Lately published etc.* 1 *page. Map at p.* 61. *& plate of animals at p.* 125. *Fine copy. Calf.* 4to. (2l. 12s. 6d. 1662)

This copy is as it was originally published in numbers, having the several titles to the April, May, June, and July numbers, 1709.

LECHFORD (THOMAS). Plain Dealing:/ Or,/ Nevves/ from/ New-England./ A ſhort view of New-Englands/ preſent Government, both Eccle-ſiaſticall and Civil,/ compared with the anciently-received and eſta-/bliſhed Government of England, in/ ſome materiall points; fit for the graveſt/ conſideration in theſe times./ By Thomas Lechford of Clements Inne,/ in the County of Middleſex, Gent./ *London,*/ Printed by W. E. and I. G. for Nath: Butter, at the ſigne/ of the pyde Bull neere S. Auſtins gate. 1642./ 4 *prel. leaves; viz. Title, on the reverse Royal Arms;* ' To the Reader.' 5 *pp.* ' A Table' *etc.* 1 *page; Text* 80 *pp. Fine copy, calf extra by Bedford.* 4to. (5l. 5s. 1663)

LEDERER (JOHN). The/ Discoveries/ of/ John Lederer,/ In three ſeveral Marches from/ Virginia,/ To the Weſt of/ Carolina,/ And other parts of the Continent:/ Begun in March 1669, and ended in September 1670./ Together with/ A General Map of the whole Territory/ which he traverſd./ Collected and Tranſlated out of Latine from his Diſcourſe/ and Writings,/ By Sir William Talbot Baronet./ *London,* Printed by J. C. for Samuel Heyrick, at Grays-/Inne-gate in Holborn. 1672./ 3 *prel. leaves; viz. Title reverse blank,* ' To the Right Honourable Anthony Lord Ashley,' *etc.* 2 *pp, signed* ' William Talbot.' ' To the Reader.' 2 *pp, signed* ' William Talbot.' ' A Map of the whole Territory Traversed by Iohn Lederer in his three Marches.' *Text* 27 *pp. Fine copy. Green morocco extra.* 4to. (3l. 3s. 1664)

LEE (CHARLES). Memoirs of the life of the late Charles Lee, Esq. Lieutenant Colonel of the Forty Fourth Regiment, Colonel in the Portuguese service, Major General, and Aid du Camp to the King of Poland, and Second in Command in the Service of the United States of America during the Revolution: To which are added his Political and Military Essays; also, Letters to, and from many distinguished Characters, both in Europe and America. *Dublin:* P. Byrne, *etc.* 1792. *xii and* 439 *pp. Old calf.* 8*vo*. (10*s.* 6*d.* 1665)

LEE (CHARLES). The Life and Memoirs of the late Major General Lee, Second in Command to General Washington, during the American Revolution, to which are added, his Political and Military Essays. Also, Letters to and from many distinguished Characters both in Europe and America. *New-York;* Richard Scott, 1813. 4 *prel. leaves and pp.* 13-352. *Calf.* 12*mo*. (7*s.* 6*d.* 1666)

LEEDS (DANIEL). An Almanack For the Year of Christian Account 1687. Particularly respecting the Meridian and Latitude of Burlington, but may indifferently serve all places adjacent By Daniel Leeds, Student in Agriculture. Printed and Sold by William Bradford, near *Philadelphia* in Pennsylvania, pro Anno 1687. *A broadside.* *Folio.* (2*l.* 2*s.* 1667)

This sheet Almanac is said to have been the first piece printed at Philadelphia. The present copy is only a fragment of about three-eighths of the whole, but it has the lower right-hand corner, with the date 1687.

LEEDS (DANIEL). *The same, a reprint. A broadside.* *Folio.* (2*s.* 6*d.* 1668)

LEEVEN EN DADEN/ der Doorluchtighſte/ Zee-Helden/ en/ Ontdeckers van Landen,/ deser eeuwen./ Beginnende met/ Christoffel Colombus,/ Vinder van de Nieuwe Wereldt./ En eyndigende met den Roemruchtigen Admirael/ M. A. de Ruyter, Ridd, &c./ Vertoonende veel vreemde Voorvallen, dappere Verrichtingen,/ ſtoutmoedige Beſtieringen, en ſwaere Zee-ſlagen, &c./ Naeukeurigh, uyt veele geloofwaerdige Schriften, en Authentijcke/ Stucken, by een gebracht, en beſchreven,/ Door V. D. B./ t'*Amsterdam,*/ By Jan Claesz. ten Hoorn, en Jan Bouman,/ Boeckverkoopers. Anno 1676./ Met Privilegie voor 15. Jaren./ 5 *prel. leaves; viz. Engraved title* 'Leeven. en Daden./ der Doorlughtige/ Zee-Helden./' *title on the reverse* 'Privilegie.' *Portrait of De Ruyter.* 'Op-dracht' 2 *pp.* 'Aen den Lezer.' *and* 'Register.' 2 *pp. Text* 350 *pp. Copperplates at pp.* 1, 20, 45, 79, 89, 108,

128, 153, 183, 210, 235, 258, 280. Tweede Deel.
2 and 303 pp. 'Register.' 7 pp. Copperplates at pp. 1, 7, 43, 50, 71, 85, 92, 121, 166, 173, 179, 185, 251, 271, 281, 295, 299. Calf extra by Clarke and Bedford. 4to. (1l. 11s. 6d. 1669)

LEEVEN EN DAADEN/ der Doorluchtigfte/ Zee-Helden,/ Beginnende met de Tocht na/ Damiaten,/ Voorgevallen in den Jare 1217./ En eindigende met den beroemden Admirael/ M. A. de Ruyter, Hartog, Ridd, &c./ Vertoonende alle de voorna-emfte Zeedaden die de Hollanders en Zee-/landers &c. van haer begin aen, loffelijck tegens hun vy-anden ver-/richt hebben; nevens veel vreemde Voorvallen, dappere Helde-/daden, ftoutmoedige Beftieringen, en fwaere Zee-flagen, &c./ Naeukeu-righ, uyt veele geloofwaerdige Schriften, en Authentijcke/ Stucken, by een gebracht, en befchre-ven,/ Door V. D. B./ Met veele curieufe koopere Plaeten verciert./ t'*Amsteldam*,/ By Jan ten Hoorn, en Jan Bouman,/ Boekverkoopers, in Compagnie. Anno 1683./ 8 prel. leaves; viz. Engraved title, ' Leeven. en Daden./ der Doorlughtige/ Zee-Hel-den./ T'*Amsterdam*/ By Jan ten Hoorn, en Jan Bouman,/ Boekverköpers in Compani 1683./ *Title*, on the reverse ' Privilegie.' ' Opdracht' 2 pp. ' Aan den Leezer.' 2 pp. ' Register Der Hooft-Deelen ' 8 pp. Text 784 pp. ' Register.' 7 pp. Copperplates at pp. 3, 39, 93, 123, 127, 150, 193, 203, 224, 282, 293, 326, 412, 482, 489, 512, 519, 548, 558, 587, 593, 601, 633, 721, 749, 773, 778, 781. Vellum. 4to. (1l. 11s. 6d. 1670)

LEIGH (EGERTON). Extracts from the Proceedings of the High Court of Vice-Admiralty, in Charles-town, South Carolina, upon Six several Informa-tions, adjudged by The Honourable Egerton Leigh, Esq; Sole Judge of that Court, and His Majesty's Attorney-General in the faid Province, In the Years 1767 and 1768. With explanatory Remarks, &c. And copies of two extraordinary Oaths. To which are subjoined, Recapitulation, reflections arising from a retrospect of a late Case, and some General Observations on American Custom-House Officers, And Courts of Vice-Admiralty. The Se-cond Edition, with an Appendix. *Charlestown*: Printed by David Bruce. MDCCLXIX. iv and 64 pp. Folio. (2l. 12s. 6d. 1671)

LEJARZA (JUAN JOSE MARTINEZ DE). Análsis Estadístico. De la Provincia de Michuacan, en 1822. Por J. J. L. *Mexico*: 1824. 2 prel. *leaves, ix and* 281 pp. *Tabla Num.* 1-7. 4to.   (15s. 1672)

LEO AFRICANUS (JEAN). Historiale/ Description/ de l'Afriqve, Tier=/ce partie dv/ Monde,/ Contenant fes Royaumes, Regions, Viles, Citez,/ Chateaus & forterefles: Iles, Fleuues, Ani-/maus, tant aquatiques, que terreftres: coutu-/mes, loix, religion & façon de faire des habitûs,/ auec pourtraits de leurs habis: enfemble autres/ chofes memorables, & fingulieres nouueautez :/ Efcrite de nôtre temps par Iean Leon, African,/ premierement en langue Arabefque, puis en Tof-/cane, & à present mife en François./ En *Anvers*./ Ches Iean Bellere./ 1556./ 16 prel. *leaves*: *Text* 412 *folioed leaves.* 'Indice des principales matieres' etc. 48 pp. Calf extra. 8vo.   (1l. 1s. 1673)

LEON (ANTONIO DE). Epitome/ de la/ Biblioteca/ Oriental i Occidental, Nautica/ i Geografica./ Al Excelentiff. Señor D. Ramiro Nuñez/ Perez Felipe de Guzman, Señor de la Cafa/ de Guzman, Duque de Medina de las Tor=/res Marques de Toral i Monafterio, Conde/ de Parmaccello i Valdorce, Comendador/ de Valdepeñas, Gran Canciller de las In=/ dias, Teforero General de la Corona de Ara/=gon i Confejo de Italia, Capitan de los cien/ Hijosdalgo de la guarda de la Real per=/fona i Sumiller de Corps./ Por el Licenciado Antonio de Leon/ Relator del Supremo i Real/ Consejo de las Indias./ Con Priuilegio./ En *Madrid*, Por Iuan Gonzalez./ Año de M.DCXXIX. *Engraved title and* 43 *prel. leaves; Text* 186 pp. 'Appendice.' *xii pp, and Colophon leaf. Half calf.* 4to.   (2l. 2s. 1674)

LEON (ANTONIO DE). Politica/ de las Grandezas/ y Govierno del Svpremo/ y Real Consejo de/ las Indias./ Dirigida/ Al Rey Nvestro Señor en el/ mifmo Real Confejo, Prefidente el Licenciado D. Iuan de Vi-/lela del Abito de Santiago; Gran Can ciller el Côde Duque dõ/ Gafpar de Guzman, Comendador mayor de Alcantara; Confe-/jeros, el Lic. don Francifco Arias Maldonado, Maeftre-efcuela/ de Salamanca, Lic. Iuan Gonçalez de Solorçano, Lic. don Ro-/drigo de Aguiar y Acuña, Lic.

Alonſo Maldonado de Torres,/ Lic. Fernando de Villa ſeñor, Preſidente de la Contratacion,/ Lic. Sancho Florez del Conſejo de Cruzada, Lic. don Diego de/ Cardenas, Lic. don Franciſco Manſo y Zuñiga, Lic. don Pedro/ de Bibanco, del Abito de Santiago, Lic. don Diego Gonçalez/ de Cuenca y Contreras, Lic. don Franciſco Antonio de Alarcŏ/ del Abito de Santiago ; Fiſcal el Lic. don Antonio de la/ Cueva y Silva, Secretarios, Pedro de Ledeſma, y/ don Ferdinando de Contreras ; Teniente de/ Gran Canciller D. Antonio de/ Aguiar y Acuña, del Abito/ de Santiago./ Por el Licenciado Antonio de Leon./ [*Lima*, 1658 ?] *Title and 20 folioed leaves. Vellum. 4to.* (1*l*. 1*s*. 1675)

LEON PINELO (Antonio de). [*Printed Title*] Vida/ del Ilvstr. i Reverend./ Don Toribio/ Alfonso Mogrovejo/ Arzobispo de Lima./ [*Engraved Title*] Vida/ del Ilvstrissimo/ i Reverendiſſimo D. Toribio/ Alfonso Mogrovejo./ Arcobispo de la Civdad/ de los Reyes Lima/ Cabeza de las Provincias del Piru./ Dedicase./ Al Eminentissimo S.ʳ/ Don Baltasar de Moscoso/ y Sandoval, Presbitero Cardenal de la/ S.ᵃ Igleſia de Roma del Titulo de S.ᵃ Cruz/ en Gerusalen Arcobiſpo de Toledo Pri/-mado de las Eſpañas Chanciller/ mayor de Caſtilla del Con-/ſejo de Eſtado. &/ Por el Licenciado Antonio/ de Leon Pinelo, Relator del Conſejo Supre-/mo de las Indias, y del de la/ Camara dellas./ [*Lima*] 1653. *24 prel. leaves and* 421 *pp. With Portrait of Toribius Alfonsus Mogrovejo. Calf. 4to.* (2*l*. 2*s*. 1676)

LEON Y GAMA (Antonio de). Disertacion Fisica sobre la Materia y Formacion de las Auroras Boreales, que con ocasion de la que aparecio en Mexico y otros Sugares de la Nueva España el dia 14 de Noviembre de 1789. Escribió D. Antonio de Leon y Gama. Con las Licencias Necesarias. *Mexico:* Por D. Felipe de Zuñiga y Ontiveros, calle del Espíritu Santo, año de 1790. *Title and* 37 *pp. Half mor. 4to.* (10*s*. 6*d*. 1677)

LEON Y GAMA (Antonio de). Descripcion Histórica y Cronológica de las dos Piedras que con ocasion del nuevo Empedrado que se está formando en la Plaza Principal de México, se hallaron en ella el Año de 1790. Explícase el sistema de los Calendarios de los Indios, el método que tenian de dividir el tiempo, y la correccion que hacian de él para igualar el año civil, de que usaban, con el año solar trópico. Noticia muy necesaria para la perfecta inteligencia de la segunda piedra: á que se añaden otras curiosas é instructivas sobre la Mitología de los Mexicanos, sobre su Astronomía, y sobre los ritos y ceremonias que acostumbraban en tiempo de su Gentilidad. Por Don Antonio de Leon y Gama. *México.* En la Imprenta de Don Felipe de Zúñiga y Ontiveros Año de M.DCC.XCII. *3 prel. leaves and 116 pp. Lista, etc. 2 pp. and 3 plates. Calf. 4to.* (15s. 1678)

LE PAGE DU PRATZ (M.) Histoire de la Louisiane, Contenant la Découverte de ce vafte Pays; fa Defcription géographique; un Voyage dans les Terres; l'Hiftoire Naturelle; les Mœurs, Coûtumes & Religion des Naturels, avec leurs Origines; deux Voyages dans le Nord du nouveau Mexique, dont un jufqu'à la Mer du Sud; ornée de deux Cartes & de 40 Planches en Taille douce. Par M. Le Page du Pratz. *A Paris,* M.DCC.LVIII. *Three Volumes. Tome Premier, xvj and 358 pp. 2 copperplate maps at pp. 138, 139. Tome Second, Half-title, title, and 441 pp. 34 copperplates. Tome Troisieme, Half-title, title, and 451 pp. Approbation and Privilege 3 pp. Errata 1 page. 4 copperplates. Old calf. 12mo.* (15s. 1679)

LE PAGE DU PRATZ (M.) The History of Louisiana, or of The Western Parts of Virginia and Carolina: Containing A Defcription of the Countries that lye on both Sides of the River Miffifipi: With An Account of the Settlements, Inhabitants, Soil, Climate, and Products. Tranflated from the French, (lately publifhed,) By M. Le Page Du Pratz; with Some Notes and Obfervations relating to our Colonies. In Two Volumes. *London,* T. Becket and P. A. De Hondt. MDCC LXIII. *Two Volumes. Vol. I. Half-title, title, l pp. vii and 368 pp. 2 maps. Vol. II. 4 prel. leaves, and 272 pp. Old calf. 12mo.* (15s. 1680)

LE ROY (P. L.) A Narrative of the singular Adventures of Four Ruffian Sailors, Who were caſt away on the deſert Iſland of East-Spitzbergen. Together with some Observations on the Productions of that Iſland, &c. By Mr. P. L. Le Roy, Profeſſor of Hiſtory, and Member of the Imperial Academy of Sciences at St. Peterſburg. Tranſlated from the German Original, at the deſire of ſeveral Members of the Royal Society. [*London*, 1774?] *Title and pp*. 43-118. *Half morocco.* 8vo. (4s. 6d. 1681)

LERY (JEAN DE). Histoire/ d'vn Voyage/ fait en la terre/ dv Breſil, avtre-/ment dite Ame-/rique./ Contenant la nauigation, & choſes remar-/quables, veuës ſur mer par l'auɛ̂teur: Le compor/ tement de Villegagnon, en ce païs là. Les meurs/ & façons de viure eſtranges des Sauuages A-/meriquains: auec vn colloque de leur langage./ Enſemble la deſcription de pluſieurs Animaux,/ Arbres, Herbes, & autres choſes ſingulieres,/ & du tout inconues par deça, dont on verra les/ ſommaires des chapitres au commencement du/ liure./ Non encores mis en lumiere, pour les cauſes/ contenues en la preface./ Le tout recueilli ſur les lieux par Iean de/ Lery natif de la Margelle, terre/ de ſainɛ̂t Sene au Duché de/ Bourgongne./ Seigneur, ie te celebreray entre les peu-/ples & te diray Pſeaumes entre les na-/ tions. Pseav. CVIII. [*A la Rochelle.*] Pour Antoine Chuppin. M.D.LXXVIII./ *First Edition.* 24 *prel. leaves, and* 424 *pp*. *Table* 12 *pp*. *Errata* 1 *page.* *Vellum.* 8vo. (2l. 2s. 1682)

LERY (JEAN DE). Histoire/ d'vn Voyage/ faict en la terre dv/ Breſil, avtrement/ dite Amerique./ Contenant la navigation,/ & choſes remarquables, veuës ſur mer par l'auɛ̂teur: Le com-/portement de Villegagnon en ce pays-/la. Les mœurs & façons/ de viure eſtranges des Sauuages Ameriquains: auec vn collo-/que de leur langage. Enſemble la deſcription de pluſieurs A-/nimaux, Arbres, Herbes, & autres choſes ſingulieres, & du/ tout incōnues par deçà: dont on verra les ſommaires des cha-/pitres au commencement du liure./ Reveve corrigee, et bien/ augmentee en ceſte ſeconde Edition, tant de fi-/gures, qu'autres chſoes notables ſur le/ ſuiet de l'auteur. Le tout recueilli ſur les lieux par Iean de/ Lery, natif de la Margelle, terre/ de ſainɛ̂t Sene, au Duché de/ Bourgongne./

[*A la Rochelle*] Pour Antoine Chuppin./ M.D.LXXX./ 22 prel. leaves, and 382 pp. Table 10 pp. Errata 1 page. Vellum. 8vo. (1l. 5s. 1683)

LERY (JEAN DE). Historia/ Navigationis/ in Brasiliam,/ quæ et America/ dicitvr./ Qva describitvr avtoris/ nauigatio, quæque in mari vidit memoriæ pro-/denda: Villagagnonis in America gefta: Brafi-/lienfium victus & mores, à noftris admodum a-/lieni, cum eorum linguæ dialogo: animalia etiam,/ arbores, atque herbæ, reliquáque fingularia & no-/bis penitùs incognita./ A Ioanne Lerio Bvrgvndo/ Gallicè fcripta. Nunc verò primum Latinitate/ donata, & variis figuris illustrata./ Excvdebat/ Evstathivs Vignon./ Anno CIƆ IƆ LXXXVI./ [*Geneva*] 32 prel. leaves, the last blank; Text 342 pp. Index 16 pp. At page 178 is a woodcut 6¼ by 9 inches. Vellum. 8vo. (1l. 10s. 1684)

LERY (JEAN DE). Historia/ Navigationis/ in Brasiliam/ quæ et America/ dicitur./ Qva describitvr avthoris/ nauigatio, quæque in mari vidit memoriæ prodenda: Villa-/gagnonis in America gefta: Brafilienfium victus & mores, à/ noftris admodum alieni, cum eorum linguæ dialogo: ani-/malia etiam, arbores, atque herbæ, reliquáque fingularia &/ nobis penitus incognita./ A Joanne Lerio Bvrgundo/ Gallicè fcripta. Nunc verò primùm Latinitate/ donata, & varijs figuris illuftrata./ Secvnda Editio./ *Genevæ*./ Apud hæredes Euftathij Vignon./ CIƆ IƆ XCIIII. *Title, reverse blank;* 'Epistola,' *3 leaves;* Epigrams *2 leaves;* 'Totivs Historiæ Svmma Capita,' *2 leaves;* 'Praefatio,' *21 leaves; text* 340 pp. 'Index,' *8 leaves; with folding woodcut to face p.* 178. *Fine copy. Old calf*. 8vo. (1l. 10s. 1685)

LE SAGE (M.) The Adventures of Robert Chevalier, call'd De Beauchene, Captain of a Privateer in New-France. By Monfieur Le Sage, Author of Gil-Blas. In Two Volumes. *London*: T. Gardner, M,DCC,XLV. *Two Volumes.* Vol I. 4 prel. leaves, and 307 pp. Vol. II. 4 prel. leaves, and 287 pp. 12mo. (10s. 6d. 1686)

LESLIE (CHARLES). A New and Exact Account of Jamaica, wherein The Antient and Prefent State of that Colony, its Importance to Great Britain,

Laws, Trade, Manners and Religion, together with the moſt remarkable and curious Animals, Plants, Trees, &c. are deſcribed: With a particular Account of the Sacrifices, Libations, &c. at this Day in Uſe among the Negroes. The Third Edition. To which is added, An Appendix, containing an Account of Admiral Vernon's Success at Porto Bello and Chagre. *Edinburgh:* R. Fleming, MDCCXL. 4 *prel. leaves, and* 376 *pp. Calf.* 8*vo.* (10*s.* 6*d.* 1687)

LESSEPS (M. DE). Travels in Kamtschatka, during the years 1787 and 1788. Translated from the French of M. De Lesseps, Consul of France, and Interpreter to the Count de la Perouse, now engaged in a Voyage round the World, by Command of his most Christian Majesty. In Two Volumes. *London:* J. Johnson, 1790. *Two Volumes.* Vol. I. *xvi and* 283 *pp. Map.* Vol. II. *viii and* 408 *pp. Calf.* 8*vo.* (10*s.* 6*d.* 1688)

LETERA de la nobil cipta: nouamente ritrouata alle Indie con li coſtumi & modi del ſuo Re & ſoi populi: Li modi del ſuo adorate con la bella vſanza de le donne loro: & de le dua perſone ermafrodite donate da quel Re al Capitano de larmata. [*at the end*] Data in Peru adi. xxv. de Nouembre. Del MDXXXIIII. [*Reprint, Milan,* 1830?] 8 *pp. boards.* 4*to.* (1*l.* 1*s.* 1689)

LETRAS Anvas/ de la Compania/ de Iesvs/ de la Provincia/ del Nvevo Reyno/ de Granada./ Desde el Ano de Mil y Seys cientos/ y treinta y ocho,/ hasta el Ano de Mil y Seys cientos/ y quaranta y tres./ En Zaragoza Año de 1645./ Impreſas con liceucia delos Superiores./ 239 *pp. Old calf.* 4*to.* (1*l.* 11*s.* 6*d.* 1690)

LETTER (A) from a Merchant at Jamaica to a Member of Parliament in London, Touching the African Trade. To which is added, A Speech made by a Black of Gardaloupe, at the Funeral of a Fellow-Negro, *London,* A. Baldwin. MDCCIX. 31 *pp. Uncut. Half mor. Small* 8*vo.* (4*s.* 6*d.* 1691)

LETTER (A) from South Carolina; giving an Account of the Soil, Air, Product, Trade, Government, Laws, Religion, People, Military Strength, &c., of that Province; Together with the manner

and neceffary Charges of Settling a Plantation there, and the Annual Profit it will produce. Written by a Swifs Gentleman, to his friend at Bern. *London*, A. Baldwin, 1710. 63 *pp. Half morocco.*
8vo. (10s. 6d. 1692)

LETTER (A) To the Right Honourable The Lords Commiffioners of Trade & Plantations: Or, A fhort Essay on the Principal Branches of the Trade of New-England, with the Difficulties they labour under; and Some Methods of Improvement. *London:* 1715. *2 prel. leaves; viz. Title and Dedication, Signed* 'T. B.' *Text* 19 *pp. Half morocco.*
8vo. (12s. 6d. 1693)

LETTER (A) To the Right Reverend the Lord Bifhop of London, from An Inhabitant of his Majesty's Leeward-Caribbee-Iflands. Containing fome Considerations on His Lordfhip's Two Letters of May 19, 1727. The first To the Masters and Mistresses of Families in the Englifh Plantations abroad; The second To the Missionaries there. In which is Inferted, A Short Essay concerning the Conversion of the Negro-Slaves in our Sugar-Colonies; Written in the Month of June, 1727, by the fame Inhabitant. *London:* J. Wilford, 1730. *Half-title, title, and text* 103 *pp. Half morocco.*
8vo. (7s. 6d. 1694)

LETTER (A Second) From a Minifter of the Church of England To his Diffenting Parifhioners, In Anfwer to Some Remarks made on the former, by one J. G. *Boston:* Printed in the Year 1734. *Half-title, title and* 113 *pp. Errata* 1 *page, half mor.*
8vo. (7s. 6d. 1695)

LETTER (A) To a certain Eminent British Sailor. Occafion'd by his Specimen of Naked Truth. From a zealous Affertor of his Merit, and fincere Wellwifher to his Person. *London:* M. Moore, M.DCCXLVI. 32 *pp. half mor.* 8vo. (6s. 1696)

LETTER (A) to Mrs. P------- S. In which fome Facts in her laft Number are refcued from the falfe Light fhe has put them in, and fome others which fhe has omitted, are fupply'd. *London:* H. Carpenter, M.DCC.XLIX. *Title and* 21 *pp. half mor.*
8vo. (7s. 6d. 1697)

LETTER (A) to the People of England, on the Prefent Situation and Conduct of National Affairs. Letter I. The Third Edition. *London:* Printed in the Year, 1756. 56 *pages. Half morocco.* 8vo. (4s. 6d. 1698)

LETTER (A Second) to the People of England on Foreign Subsidies, Subsidiary Armies, and Their Confequences to this Nation. The Third Edition. *London:* J. Scott, MDCCLVI. 56 *pp. Half morocco.* 8vo. (4s. 6d. 1699)

LETTER (A Third) to the People of England, on Liberty, Taxes, And the Application of Publick Money. The Third Edition. *London:* Printed in the Year, 1756. *Title and pp. 5-54. half morocco.* 8vo. (4s. 6d. 1700)

LETTER (A Fourth) to the People of England. On the conduct of the M———rs in Alliances, Fleets, and Armies, fince the firft Differences on the Ohio, to the taking of Minorca by the French. *London:* M. Collier, 1756. *Half-title, title, and* 111 *pp. half mor.* 8vo. (4s. 6d. 1701)

LETTER (A) to a Clergyman, in the Colony of Connecticut, from his Friend. In which, the true Notion of Orthodoxy is enquired into; and fome Thoughts are fuggefted concerning publick Tefts of Orthodoxy, and the mifchievous Effects of fetting up falfe Tefts thereof. *New-Haven:* Printed by James Parker, and Company. MDCCLVII. 24 *pp. signed* 'Catholicus.' 8vo. (4s. 6d. 1702)

LETTER (A) to the Right Honourable William Pitt, Esq; from an Officer at Fort Frontenac. *London:* J. Fleming, MDCCLIX. *Half-title, title, and* 38 *pp.* 8vo. (7s. 6d. 1703)

LETTER (A) to the Glergy of the Colony of Connecticut, from an Aged Layman of faid Colony. [*New-Haven ?*] Printed in the Year 1760. 22 *pp.* 8vo. (4s. 6d. 1704)

LETTER (A) Addressed to Two Great Men, on the Prospect of Peace; And on the Terms neceffary to be infifted upon in the Negociation. *London:* A. Millar, MDCCLX. *Title and* 56 *pp. Half morocco.* 8vo. (5s. 6d. 1705)

LETTER (A) Addressed to Two Great Men, on the Prospect of Peace; And on the Terms neceſſary to be infifted upon in the Negociation. The Second Edition, correčted. *London*: A Millar, MDCCLX. *Half-title, title, and text 56 pp. Half morocco.* 8vo. (5s. 6d. 1706)

LETTER (A) To an Honourable Brigadier General, Commander in Chief of his Majefty's Forces in Canada. *London*, J. Burd, 1760. *Title and 32 pp. half mor.* 8vo. (5s. 6d. 1707)
<small>Now generally acknowledged to be by Junius. It has been reprinted by Mr. Simons of the British Museum.</small>

LETTER (A) to the People of England, on the Necessity of putting an Immediate End to the War; and The Means of obtaining an Advantageous Peace. *London*: R. Griffiths, MDCCLX. *Title and 52 pp. half mor.* 8vo. (4s. 6d. 1708)

LETTER (A) to a Great M----------R, on the Proſpect of a Peace; Wherein the Demolition of the Fortifications of Louisbourg Is ſhewn to be abſurd; The Importance of Canada fully refuted; The proper Barrier pointed out in North America; and the Reaſonableneſs and Neceffity of retaining the French Sugar Islands. Containing Remarks on ſome preceding Pamphlets that have treated of the Subject, and a fuccinct View of the whole Terms that ought to be infifted on from France at a future Negociation. By an unprejudiced Observer. *London*: G. Kearsly, MDCCLXI. *Title and 148 pp. half mor.* (7s. 6d. 1709)

LETTER (A) to G. G. *Stiff in Opinions, always in the wrong. London*: J. Williams, MDCCLXVII. *Half-title, title, and text 96 pp. Half morocco.* 8vo. (7s. 6d. 1710)
<small>This letter is signed L, at the end, and is dated "Richmond, Jan. 18, 1767." It was addressed to George Grenville, the Minister, and relates entirely to American Affairs.</small>

LETTER, (A) concerning an American Bishop, &c. To Dr. Bradbury Chandler, Ruler of St. John's Church, in Elizabeth-Town. In Anſwer to the Appendix Of His Appeal to the Public, &c. Printed, A.D. 1768. *19 pp. Half morocco.* 8vo. (7s. 6d. 1711)

LETTER (A) To the Right Honourable The Earl of H---- B-----H, His M——y's S——y of

S—te for the C—l——s, on the Present Situation of Affairs in the Island of Gr—n—da. *London:* J. Wilkie, M.DCC.LXIX. 54 *pp. Half morocco.* 8*vo.* (4*s.* 6*d.* 1712)

LETTER (A) to Samuel Johnson, L.L.D. [in answer to the False Alarm,] J. Almon, 1770. *Title, and pp.* 5-54. *half mor.* 8*vo.* (3*s.* 6*d.* 1713)

LETTER (A) from a Virginian to the Members of the Congrefs to be held at Philadelphia, on The Firft of September, 1774. Boston, printed: *London,* reprinted; J. Wilkie 1774. *Title,* 4 *and* 60 *pp. half mor.* 8*vo.* (5*s.* 6*d.* 1713*)

LETTER (A) to Doctor Tucker on his proposal of a Separation between Great Britain and her American Colonies. *London.* J. Becket, MDCCLXXIV. *Title and* 36 *pp. half mor.* 8*vo.* (5*s.* 6*d.* 1714)

LETTER (A) to a Member of Parliament on the Present Unhappy Dispute between Great-Britain and her Colonies. Wherein the Supremacy of the Former is Afferted and Proved; and the Necessity of Compelling the Latter to pay due Obedience to the Sovereign State, is Enforced, upon Principles of Sound Policy, Reason, and Justice. *London:* J. Walter, MDCCLXXIV. *Title and* 47 *pp. half mor.* 8*vo.* (5*s.* 6*d.* 1715)

LETTER (A) to [William Pitt] the Earl of Chatham, on the Quebec Bill. *London:* T. Cadell, MDCCLXXIV. *Title and* 36 *pp. Half morocco.* 8*vo.* (4*s.* 6*d.* 1716)

LETTER (A) to the People of Great-Britain, in Answer to that published by the American Congress. *London:* F. Newbery, MDCCLXXV. 59 *pp. half mor.* 8*vo.* (5*s.* 6*d.* 1717)

LETTER (A) to the Right Honourable Lord Camden, on the Bill for restraining the Trade and Fishery of the Four Provinces of New England. *London:* T. Cadell, MDCCLXXV. *Title and* 44 *pp. half mor.* 8*vo.* (7*s.* 6*d.* 1718)

LETTER (A) to Doctor Mather. Occafioned by his difingenuous Reflexions upon a certain Pamphlet, entitled, Salvation for all Men. By One who wifhes well to Him in common with Mankind.

[*Rev. John Clark, of Boston.*] Boston: Printed and fold by T. and J. Fleet at the Bible and Heart in Cornhill, 1782. *Title, and text 9 pp. Unbound.* 8vo. (2s. 6d. 1719)

LETTERS (Two) of the Lord Bifhop of London: The First, To the Mafters and Miftreffes of Families in the Englifh Plantations abroad; Exhorting them to Encourage and Promote the Inftruction of their Negroes in the Chriftian Faith. The Second, To the Missionaries there; Directing them to diftribute the faid Letter, and Exhorting them to give their Affiftance towards the Inftruction of the Negroes within their feveral Parifhes. London: Joseph Downing, M.DCC.XXVII. 20 *pp. Half mor.* 4to. (7s. 6d. 1720)

LETTERS from a Farmer in Pennfylvania, To the Inhabitants of the British Colonies. *Boston:* Printed by Mein and Fleeming, and to be sold by John Mein, at the London Book-Store, North-Side of King-Street. MDCCLXVIII. *Title and pp.* 5-146. 'To the ingenious Author,' *etc. 2 pp. Half morocco.* 8vo. (5s. 6d. 1721)

LETTERS and other Papers relating to the Proceedings of his Majefty's Commiffioners. By the Earl of Carlisle, Sir Henry Clinton, William Eden, Esquire, and George Johnstone, Esquire, Commiffioners appointed by his Majefty in Purfuance of an Act of Parliament, to treat, confult, and agree upon the Means of quieting the Diforders now subfifting in certain of the Colonies, Plantations, and Provinces of North-America. 55 *pp.* Propofed Appendix to the feveral Publications relating to the Proceedings of His Majesty's Commissioners. By a Well Wifher to the Profperity both of Great-Britain and North-America. [Rivington, New-York, 1778] 10 *leaves. Privately printed. Half mor.* 8vo. (10s. 6d. 1722)

LETTERS of Papinian: In which The Conduct, prefent State, and Profpects of the American Congress are Examined. New-York, Printed: London: Reprinted for J. Wilkie, MDCCLXXIX. *3 prel. leaves, and text 86 pp. uncut. Half morocco.* 8vo. (5s. 6d. 1723)

LETTERS to a Nobleman, on the Conduct of the War in the Middle Colonies. *London:* J. Wilkie, MDCCLXXIX. 3 *prel. leaves, and* 101 *pp. With a Plan.* 8*vo.* (5*s.* 6*d.* 1724)

LETTERS to a Nobleman, on the Conduct of the War in the Middle Colonies. The Fourth Edition. *London:* G. Wilkie, MDCCLXXX. 3 *prel. leaves, and* 101 *pp. With the Plan.* 8*vo.* (5*s.* 6*d.* 1725)

LETTERS and Dissertations, by the Author of the Letter Analysis A. P. On the Disputes between Great Britain and America. *London:* Printed for the Author. M.DCC.LXXXII. 130 *pp. half mor.* 12*mo.* (7*s.* 6*d.* 1726)

LETTERS and Papers on Agriculture: Extracted from the Correspondence of a Society instituted at Halifax, for Promoting Agriculture in the Province of Nova-Scotia. To which is added a selection of Papers on various branches of Husbandry, from some of the best publications on the subject in Europe and America. Vol. I. [*all published?*] *Halifax:* Printed by John Howe, in Barrington-Street. M.DCC.XCI. 139 *pp. Contents* 2 *pp. Old green morocco extra.* 8*vo.* (7*s.* 6*d.* 1727)

With the Autograph of John Inglis, Bishop of Nova Scotia, on the title-page.

LETTRES/ à un Amériquain/ sur l'histoire naturelle, générale et par-/ticuliere de monsieur de Buffon./ troisiéme partie./ à *Hamburg*/ 1.7.5.1./ *Title,* 31, 96, *and* 69 *pp. Small* 8*vo.* (10*s.* 6*d.* 1728)

LEWIS (MERRIWETHER.) The Travels of Capts. Lewis & Clarke, from St. Louis, by way of the Missouri and Columbia Rivers, to the Pacific Ocean; performed in the years 1804, 1805, & 1806, by Order of the Government of the United States. Containing delineations of the Manners, Customs, Religion, &c. Of the Indians, compiled from Various Authentic Sources, and Original Documents, and a Summary of the Statistical View of the Indian Nations, from the Official communications of Merriwether Lewis. Illustrated with a Map of the Country, inhabited by the Western Tribes of Indians. *London:* Longman, 1809. *ix and* 309 *pp. Map.* 8*vo.* (7*s.* 6*d.* 1729)

LEWIS (MERRIWEATHER.) Travels to the Source of the Missouri River and across the American Continent to the Pacific Ocean. Performed by Order of the Government of the United States, in the Years 1804, 1805, and 1806. By Captains Lewis and Clarke. Published from the Official Report and Illustrated by a Map of the Route, and other Maps. *London:* Longman, 1814. *xxiv and 663 pp. Large map and 2 small maps at page 379. Calf.* 4to. (15s. 1730)

LEYES y ordenanzas nuevamente hechas/ por su Magestad, para la gobernacion de las/ Indias y buen tratamiento y conservacion de los/ Indios; que se han da guardar en el consejo y au-/diencias reales que en ellas residen: y por todos/ los otros gobernadores, juezes y personas particu-/lares de ellas./ Con privilegio imperial./ [*Colophon*] Las presentes leyes, y nuevas/ ordenanzas y declaracion dellas/ para la governacion de las In-/dias, y buen tratamiento de los/ naturales dellas. Fueron im-/ presas por mandado de/ los señores: presidente, y/ del consejo de las In-/dias: en la villa/ de *Alcala/ de/ Henares:* en casa de Joan/ de Brocar á ocho dias del/ mes de Julio del año/ de nro salvador/ Jesu cris-/to./ M.D.XLIII./ *Black letter. Folio.* (7l. 7s. 1731)

This copy is MS. except folios 2 to 9, which are original.

LIBERTY (THE) and Property of British Subjects Asserted: In a Letter from An Assembly-Man in Carolina, To his Friend in London. *London:* Printed for J. Roberts in Warwick-lane, M.DCC. XXVI. 39 pp. *Signed* 'J---- N----.' *unbound.* 8vo. (4s. 6d. 1732)

LIGON (RICHARD). A True & Exact/ History/ Of the Iſland of/ Barbadoes./ Illuſtrated with a Map of the Iſland, as alſo the/ Principal Trees and Plants there, ſet forth in/ their due Proportions and Shapes, drawn out by their ſeveral and re-ſpective Scales./ Together with the Ingenio that makes the Sugar, with/ the Plots of the ſeveral Houſes, Rooms, and other places, that/ are uſed in the whole proceſs of Sugar-making; viz. the Grinding-/room, the Boyling-room, the Filling-room, the Curing-/houſe, Still-houſe, and Furnaces;/ All cut in Copper./ By Richard Ligon,

Gent./ *London,/* Printed and are to be fold by Peter Parker, at his Shop at the Leg and Star/ over againſt the Royal Exchange, and Thomas Guy at the corner/ Shop of Little Lumbard-ſtreet and Cornhill, 1673./ *Title reverse blank, and 122 pp. Contents 2 pp. An Index, etc. after folio 84, 1 page. With* 'A topographicall Description and/ Admeasurement of the Yland of/ Barbados in the Weſt Indyaes/ With the M^{rs}. Names of the Severall plantacons/' *6 copperplates at pp.* 70, 76, 78, 80, 82, 84, *and 3 Engraved Plans. Half russia. Folio.* (1*l*. 10s. 1733)

LIMA. A True and Particular Relation Of the Dreadful Earthquake Which happen'd At Lima, the Capital of Peru, and the neighbouring Port of Callao, On the 28th of October, 1746. With an Account likewife of every Thing material that paſſed there afterwards to the End of November following. Publiſhed at Lima by Command of the Viceroy, And tranſlated from the Original Spaniſh, By a Gentleman who reſided many Years in thoſe Countries. To which is added, A Defcription of Callao and Lima before their Deſtruction; and of the Kingdom of Peru in General, with its Inhabitants; ſetting forth their Manners, Cuſtoms, Religion, Government, Commerce, &c. Interſperſed with Paſſages of Natural Hiſtory and phyſiological Difquifitions; particularly an Enquiry into the Cause of Earth-quakes. The whole illuſtrated with A Map of the Country about Lima; Plans of the Road and Town of Callao, another of Lima; and feveral Cuts of the Natives drawn on the Spot by the Tranſlator. The Second Edition. *London:* T. Osborne, MDCCXLVIII. *xxiii and* 341 pp. *Copperplates numbered* I-IX. *Calf.* 8*vo.* (8s. 6d. 1734)

LINSCHOTEN (JAN HUYGEN VAN). Semper Eadem/ Iohn/ Hvighen Van/ Linschoten./ his Difcours of Voyages/ into ye East & West/ Indies/ Diuided into foure Bookes/ Printed at *London* by/ Iohn Wolfe/ Printer to y^c Honorable Cittie of/ London/ [1598] Willms Rogers/ ciuis Londi-/ nenfis Inuentor/ et ſculptor./ I W/ 5 *prel. leaves; viz. Engraved title, the reverse blank.* 'To the Right VVorshipfull/ Ivlivs Caesar Doctor of the Lawes,/ Iudge of the High Court of Admiralty,/ Maſter

of Requests to the Queenes/ Maiesty, and Master of
Saint Katherines./ 3 *pp. signed* ' Iohn VVolfe.'
'To the Reader.' 4 pp. Text 197 pp. 'The Second
Booke, etc. 1598.' *Title, reverse blank, and Text*
pp. 197-259. ' The Thirde Booke, etc. 1598.' *Title,
reverse blank, and Text* pp. 307-447. 'The Fovrth
Booke, etc, 1598.' *Title, reverse blank, and Text*
pp. 451-462. *Fine copy. Folio.* (7l. 7s. 1735)
With Twelve Copperplate Maps. viz.—
 I. Typvs Orbis Terrarvm. *at p.* 1.
 II. The description of the Islandes and Castle of Mozambique, etc. Grauen by William Rogers. *at p.* 8.
 III. The description or Caerd of the Coastes, *etc.* called Terrado Natal, *etc.* Robertus Beckit. *at p.* 12.
 IV. The description of the Coast of Abex, The Streaights of Meca, *etc.* Grauen by Robert Beckit. *at p.* 12.
 V. The trew description of all the Coasts of China, *etc.* Grauen by Robert Beckit. *at p.* 32.
 VI. The Island of Sct Helena, *etc.* Grauen by Raygnald Elstrake. *at p.* 172.
 VII. The true description and scituation of the Island St Helena on the East, North, and West sydes, *etc.* Grauen by Raygnald Elstrak. *at p.* 172.
 VIII. The Trve Description of the Island of Ascention, *etc.* Grauen by William Rogers. *at p.* 174.
 IX. A discripsion of Ægipt from Cair downeward, *etc.* Grauen by William Rogers. *at p.* 197.
 X. The description of the Coast of Guinea, Manicongo, and Angola, *etc.* R. E. sculpsit. *at p.* 197.
 XI. The description of the whole coast lying in the South seas of America called Peru, *etc.* Grauen by Robert Becket. *at p.* 216.
 XII. Insvlae Molvccae, *etc.* Grauen by Robert Beckit. *at p.* 328.

LINSCHOTEN (JAN HUYGEN VAN). Navigatio/
ac Itinerarivm/ Iohannis Hvgonis Lin-/scotani in
Orientalem sive Lvsitano-/rvm Indiam. Descriptiones eivsdem Terræ ac Tractvm/ Littoralium.
Præcipuorum Portuum, Fluminum, Capitum, Locorumque, Lusita-/norum hactenus navigationibus
detectorum, signa & notæ. Imagines habi-/tus
gestusque Indorum ac Lusitanorum per Indiam
viventium, Tem-/plorum, Idolorum, Ædium, Arborum, Fructuum, Herbarum,/ Aromatum, &c.
Mores genitum circa sacrificia, Poli-/tiam ac rem
familiarē. Enarratio Mercature, quo-/modo &
vbi ea exerceatur. Memorabilia/ gesta suo tempore
iis in partibus./ Collecta omnia ac descripta per
eundem Belgicè; Nunc vero Latinè reddita, in
vsum/ commodum ac voluptatem studiosi Lectoris
novarum memoriáque/ dignarum rerum, diligenti
studio ac operà./ *Hagæ-Comitis*/ Ex officinâ Alberti
Henrici. Impensis Authoris & Cornelii Nicolai,/
prostantque apud Ægidium Elsevirum. Anno 1599./
4 *prel. leaves; viz. Title, on the reverse* 'Ad Illvs-

trissimvm' *etc. Engraved Coat of Arms* 1 *leaf.*
'Illvstrissimo atqve Serenissimo Principi ac Domino
D. Mavritio Lantgravio Hessiæ, Comiti in Cat-
zenelnbogen, Dietz, Zigenhain, Nidda, &c.' 2 *pp.*
' Praefatio ad Lectorem.' 1 *page, on the reverse Portrait of Linschoten. Text* 124 *pp.* ' Descriptio Totivs
Gvineae Trac-/tvs, Congi, Angolae,' *etc.* 45 *pp.*
'Index' 3 *pp. With* 37 *Maps and Plates. Unbound.*
Folio. (2*l.* 2*s.* 1736)

LINSCHOTEN (JAN HUYGEN VAN). Histoire/ de
la Navi-/gation de Iean Hv-/gves de Linscot Hollandois et de/ fon voyagees Indes Orientales ; contenante diuerfes defcriptions des/ Pays, Coftes,
Haures, Riuieres, Caps, & autres lieux iufques à
prefent/ defcouuerts par les Portugais : Obferuations des couftumes des na-/tions de delà quant à
la Religion, Eftat Politic & Domeftic, de leurs/
Commerces, des Arbes, Fruicts, Herbes, Efpiceries,
& autres/ fingularitez qui s'y trouuent : Et narrations des chofes/ memorables qui y font aduenues
de/ fon temps./ Avec Annotations de Bernard
Palv-/danus Docteur en Medecine, fpecialement
fur la matiere des plantes &/ efpiceries : & diuerfes
figures en taille douce, pour illu-/ftration de
l'œuure./ A Qvoy sont adiovstees qvelqves av-/
tres defcription tant du pays de Guinee, & autres
coftes d'Ethiopie,/ que des nauigations des Hollandois vers le Nord au Vay-/gat & en la nouuelle
Zembla./ Le Tovt recveilli et descript par le
mesme/ de Linfcot en bas Alleman, & nouuellement traduict/ en François./ A *Amstelredam,*/ De
l'Imprimerie de Theodore Pierre./ M DC. X./ 2
prel. leaves; viz. Title, reverse blank, ' Preface av
Lectevr.' 1 *page; Text* 275 *pp. With* 8 *copperplate
Maps and numerous Engravings with the text.*
Folio. (2*l.* 12*s.* 6*d.* 1737)

LINSCHOTEN (JAN HUYGEN VAN). Itinerario./
Voyage ofte Schipvaert, van Jan/ Huygen van
Linfchoten naer Ooft ofte Portugaels Jn=/dien, inhoudende een corte befchryvinghe der felver Landen ende Zee-cuften, met aen=/wyfinge van alle de
voornaemde principale Havens, Revieren, hoecken
ende plaetfen, tot noch/ toe vande Portugefen
ontdeckt ende bekent : Waer by ghevoecht zijn,
met alleen die Conter=/feytfels vande habyten,

drachten ende wefen, fo vande Portugefen aldaer, refiderende, als van=/de ingeboornen Indianen, ende huere Tempels, Afgoden, Huyfinge, met die voornaemfte/ Boomen, Vruchten, Kruyden, Speceryen, ende diergelijcke materialen, als oot die/ manieren des felkden Volckes, fo in hunnen Godtsdienften, als in Politie/ eñ Huijf-hondinghe : maer ooc een corte verhalinge van de Coophan=/ delingen, hoe eñ waer die ghedreven eñ ghevonden worden,/ met die ghedenck weerdichfte gefchiedeniffen,/ voorghevallen den tijt zijnder/ refidentie aldaer./   Alles befchreven ende by een vergadert, door den felfden, feer nut, oorbaer,/ ende oock vermakelijcken voor alle curieufe ende Lief-/hebbers van vreemdigheden./ t'*Amstelredam*./ By Cornelis Claefz. op't VVater, in't Schrijf-boeck, by de oude Brugghe./   Anno cɪɔ. ɪɔ. xcvɪ./ *First Edition. Three Parts*. Part I. 4 *prel. leaves*; *viz. Title, on the reverse* 'Extract uyt't Regifter' *etc.* 'Aende Hooghende VVelghe borene,' *etc.* 2 *pp.* 'Prohemio ofte voorreden totten leser.' 1 *page.* 'Sonnet.' 1 *page.* 'Ode.' 1 *page, on the reverse Portrait of Linschoten. Text* 16ɔ *pp.* Part II. Reysgheschrift *etc.* M. D. XCV. 134 *pp.* 'Een feker Extract ende *etc.* cɪɔ. ɪɔ. xcvɪ.' *Title reverse blank,* 'Aende VVelgheborene,' *etc.* 1 *page on the reverse* 'Ad Io. Hvg. Linscotvm' *etc. Text pp.* 135-147. Part III. 'Befchryvinghe *etc.* M.D.XCVI.' 82 *pp. followed by 5 leaves containing lists of Plates and Maps, Register etc.* 42 *maps and plates. Fine copy.* Folio.   (3*l.* 3*s.*   1738)

LIST (A) of Copies of Charters, from the Commiffioners for Trade and Plantations, Prefented to the Honourable the Houfe of Commons, in Purfuance of their Address to His Majesty, of the 25th of April 1740. viz. Maryland Charter, granted by King Charles I. in the 8th Year of His Reign. Connecticut Charter granted by King Charles II. in the 14th Year of His Reign. Rhode-Island Charter, granted by King Charles II. in the 15th Year of His Reign.   Pensylvania Charter, granted by King Charles II. in the 33d Year of His Reign. Massachusets Bay Charter, granted by King William and Queen Mary, in the 3d Year of Their Reign.   Georgia Charter, granted by His Majesty, in the 5th Year of His Reign.   *London:*

Printed in the Year M.DCC.XLI. *Title:* 12, 10, 14, 12, 21, *and* 18 *pp. half mor.* 4to. (7s. 6d. 1739)

LITERARY AND HISTORICAL SOCIETY. Transactions of the Literary and Historical Society of Quebec: founded, January 6, 1824. Volume I. *Quebec:* Printed for the Literary and Historical Society; by François Le Maitre, Star office. 1829. 3 *prel. leaves,* xxxvi *and* 261 *pp;* Errata 1 *page.* 'Catalogue of the Mineralogical Collection belonging to the Literary and Historical Society of Quebec.' 72 *pp.* 'Solar Spots.' 1 *page.* With 12 *plates.* 8vo. (10s. 6d. 1740)

LITTLE (OTIS). State of Trade in the Northern Colonies considered; with An Account of their Produce, And a Particular Description of Nova Scotia. *London:* G. Woodfall M.DCC.XLVIII. *viii and* 84 *pp. half mor.* 8vo. (7s. 6d. 1741)

LITTLE (OTIS). The State of Trade in the Northern Colonies considered; with An Account of their Produce, And a particular Description of Nova Scotia. London Printed, 1748. *Boston* Re-printed and fold by Thomas Fleet, at the Heart and Crown in Cornhill. 1749. 43 *pp.* 8vo. (7s. 6d. 1742)

LITURGY. A/ Liturgy,/ collected principally from the/ Book of Common Prayer,/ for the use of the/ First Episcopal Church/ in/ Boston ;/ together with the/ Psalter, or Psalms/ of/ David./ *Boston,/* Printed by Peter Edes, in State-Street./ MDCC LXXXV. 4 *prel. leaves and signatures,* A to B bb *in fours. Fine clean copy uncut.* 8vo. (12s. 6d. 1743)

LITURGY. The Book of Common Prayer, And Administration of the Sacraments, and other Rites and Ceremonies of the Church, according to the use of the Church of England: Together with a Collection of Occasional Prayers, and divers Sentences of Holy Scripture, Neceffary for Knowledge and Practice. Formerly collected, and tranflated into the Mohawk Language under the direction of the Miffionaries of the Society for the Propagation of the Gofpel in Foreign Parts, to the Mohawk Indians. A New Edition: To which is added The Gofpel according to St. Mark, Tranflated into the Mohawk Language, By Capt[n]. Joseph Brant, An

Indian of the Mohawk Nation. *London*: C. Buckton 1787. Ne Yakawea Yondereanayendaghkwa Oghseragwegouh, neoni yakawea ne orighwa dogeaghty Yondatnekosseraghs neoni Tekarighwagehhadont, oya oni Adereanayent, ne teas nikariwake Raditsihuhstatsygowa Ronaderighwissoh Goraghgowa a-onea Rodanhaouh. Oni, watkanissaaghtoh Oddyake Adereanayent, neoni tsiniyoghthare ne Kaghyadoghseradogeaghty, Newahòeny Akoyendarake neoni Ahhondatterihhonny. A-onea wadiròroghkwe, neoni Tekaweanadènnyoh Kanyenkehàga Tſikaweanondaghko, ne neane Raditſihuhſtatſy ne Radirighwawakoughkgòwa ronadanhà-outh, Kanyenke waondye tſi-radinakeronnyo Ongwe-oewe. Keagaye ase yondereanayendaghkwa. Oni tahoghsonderoh St. Mark Raorighwadogeaghty, Tekaweanadennyoh Kanyenkehàga Rakowànea T'Hayen danegea, Roewayats. *London*: C. Buckton, 1787. *Two Titles, iii and* 506 *pp*; 18 *copperplates, old calf.* 8*vo.* (15*s.* 1744)

LOCKE (John). A Collection of several Pieces of Mr. John Locke, Never before printed, or not extant in his Works. Publiſh'd by the Author of the Life of the ever-memorable Mr. John Hales, &c. *London*: J. Bettenham for R. Francklin, M.DCC.XX. 31 *prel. leaves and* 362 *pp. Index and Errata* 19 *pp. Calf.* 8*vo.* (5*s.* 6*d.* 1745)

The Fundamental Constitution of Carolina, drawn up by Locke, fills pages 1 to 53 of this volume.

LOCKMAN (John). Travels of the Jesuits, into Various Parts of the World: Particularly China and the East-Indies. Intermix'd with an Account of the Manners, Government, Civil and Religious Ceremonies, Natural History, and Curiosities, of the ſeveral Nations viſited by thoſe Fathers. Translated from the celebrated *Lettres edifiantes & curieuses, ecrites des Missions etrangeres, par les Missionaires de la Compagnie de Jesus.* A Work ſo entertaining and curious, that it has already been tranſlated into moſt of the European Languages. This Work is illuſtrated with Maps and Sculptures, engraved by the beſt Maſters. To which is now prefixed, An Account of the Spanish Settlements in America, with a general Index to the whole Work. By Mr. Lockman. Second Edition, cor-

rected. T. Piety, [*London*] 1762. *Two Volumes.*
Vol. I. 16 *prel. leaves, and* 488 *pp.* Vol. II. 5 *prel.
leaves, and* 508 *pp. General Index* 19 *pp.* ' A Concise
Account of the Spanish Dominions in America.'
24 *pp.* 8*vo.* (18*s.* 1746)

LONG (J.) Voyages and Travels of an Indian Interpreter and Trader, describing The Manners and Customs of the North American Indians; with an Account of the Posts situated on the River Saint Laurence, Lake Ontario, &c. To which is added a Vocabulary of The Chippeway Language. Names of Furs and Skins, in English and French. A List of Words in the Iroquis, Mohegan, Shawanee, and Esquimeaux Tongues, and a Table, shewing The Analogy between the Algonkin and Chippeway Languages. By J. Long. *London:* Printed for the Author; M,DCC,XCI. 7 *prel leaves, and* 295 *pp. With Sketch of the Western Countries of Canada.* 4*to.* (15*s.* 1747)

LONGACRE (JAMES B.) The National Portrait Gallery of Distinguished Americans. Conducted by James B. Longacre, Philadelphia; and James Herring, New York: Under the Superintendence of the American Academy of the Fine Arts. *Philadelphia,* Henry Perkins, 1834. *Four Volumes.*
Vol. I. 5 *prel. leaves, the contents stating the number of pages to each Portrait.* 36 *Portraits.* Vol. II. 1835. 5 *prel. leaves, the contents stating the number of pages to each Portrait.* 36 *Portraits.* Vol. III. 1836. 5 *prel. leaves, the contents stating the number of pages to each Portrait.* 36 *Portraits.* Vol. IV. James B. Longacre, 1839. 5 *prel. leaves, the contents stating the number of pages to each Portrait.* 39 *Portraits. Large paper copy. Half morocco extra.*
4*to.* (6*l.* 6*s.* 1748)

LOOKING-GLASS (A) for Presbyterians. Or, A brief Examination of their Loyalty, Merit, and other Qualifications for Government. With fome Animadverfions on the Quaker unmask'd. Humbly Addrefs'd to the Confideration of the Royal Freemen of Pennsylvania. *Philadelphia.* Printed in the Year M,DCC,LXIV. 18 *pp. Signed* ' Philo-Libertatis.' *Uncut.* 8*vo.* (7*s.* 6*d.* 1749)

This piece is marked " Numb. 1 " at the top of the title.

LOPEZ DE ESCOBAR (Diego). Relacion/ de los Particvlares/ feruicios que ha hecho a V. Mageftad Don/ Diego Lopez de Efcobar Gouernador y Ca-/ pitan general de la Isla de la Trinidad, y de las/ Prouincias del Dorado, hijo del Capitan/ Diego Lopez de la Fuente, en/ el año de 1636./ Con Licencia/ En Madrid. Por la vuida de Iuan Gonçalez./ Año M.DC.XXXVII./ *Title reverse blank, and* 8 *pp. half morocco. Folio.* (18s. 1750)

LORD (Joseph). Reafon Why, not Anabaptift Plunging but Infants-Believer's Baptism Ought to be approved, Is becaufe the Lord Jesus Christ, and His Apoftles, Preached it and Practiced it. In Anfwer to the Anabaptift Reafon Why. With Remarks pointing at the Notable Fallacies that are every where to be found, in the Notes on the Forty one Texts of Scripture; The Arguments and Anfwers to Objections, and other things contained in that Book, Together with fundry Evidences of the Churchmemberfhip of Infants of Believers, and regularity of Sprinking, In Old Testament Scriptures attefted to in the New-Teftament. Old-Testament Prophecies relating to New-Teftament Times, and New-Testament Testimonies. By Joseph Lord. *Boston:* Printed by S. Kneeland, for Samuel Gerrifh, at his Shop in Cornhill, 1719. *Title, viii and* 170 *pp. Old calf.* 12*mo.* (16s. 1751)

LORENZANA (Francisco Antonio). Concilios Provinciales Primero, y Segundo, celebrados en la muy Noble, y muy leal Ciudad de México, Presidiendo en Illmo. y Rmo. Señor D. Fa. Alonso de Montufar, En los años de 1555, y 1565. Dalos a luz El Ill.mo S.r D. Francisco Antonio Lorenzana, Arzobifpo de efta Santa Metropolitana Iglefia. Con las Licencias Necesarias En México, en la Imprenta de el Superior Gobierno, de el Br. D. Jofeph Antonio de Hogal, en la Calle de Tiburcio, Año de 1769, 5 *prel. leaves,* 184 *pp.* 'CIƆIƆLXV. Años. Concilio Provincial,' *etc.* 1 *page; pp.* 185-396. 'Indice de los Capitulos.' 12 *pp.* 'Concilium Mexicanum Provinciale III. Celebratum Mexici anno MDLXXXV. Præside D. D. Petro Moya, et Contreras Archiepiscopo ejusdem urbis. Confirmatum Romæ die XXVII. Octobris Anno MDLXXXIX. Poftea Juffu Regio editum Mexici

Anno MDCXXII. fumptibus D. D. Joannis Perez de
la Serna Archiepiscopi. Demum typis mandatum
cura, & expenfis D. D. Francisci Antonij A Lorenzana Archipræsulis. Mexici Anno MDCCLXX. Superiorum Permissu. Ex Typographia Bac. Jofephi Antonij de Hogal. 6 *prel. leaves and* 328 *pp.* ' Index ' 4 *pp.* 'Statuta Ordinata a Sancto Concilio Provinciali Mexicano III. Anno Domini MDLXXXV. Ex Præscripto Sacrosancti Concilij Tridentini Decreto Seff. 24. Cap. 12. de Reform. verbo Cetera. Revisa a Catholica Majestate, et a Sacrosancta sede Apostolica Confirmata Anno Domini milleffimo quingentiffimo octuageffimo nono. *Title and* 141 *pp. Index* 3 *pp. Two Volumes. Vellum.*
Folio. (2*l.* 12*s.* 6*d.* 1752)

LORENZO DE SAN MILIAN (FRANCISCO). Por/ D. Francisco Lorenzo/ de San Milian,/ Iuez oficial de la Cafa de/ la Contratacion de la Ciudad de Seuilla,/ y Contador de la Vifita del Tribunal de/ Quentas de la Ciudad de Mexico, y/ de las caxas Reales della, y de las de-/mas del Reyno de Nueua/ Efpaña./ En la Cavsa/ qve en virtvd de cedvla de sv/ Mageftad fe ha actuado, contra el dicho Don Fran-/cifco, fobre fus procedimientos en el juizio de vi-/fita de las caxas, y Minas de la Ciudad/ da Zacatecas./ [1672?] 19 *folioed leaves.* half mor. Folio. (1*l.* 1*s.* 1753)

LORING (ISRAEL). Juftification not by Works, but by Faith in Jesus Christ. A Practical Difcourfe Exhibited on Gal. II. 16. By Ifrael Loring, M.A. And Paftor of the Weft Church in Sudbury. *Boston* : Printed & Sold by Kneeland and Green, in Queen-Street, 1749. *Title and* 93 *pp. Uncut.*
12*mo.* (10*s.* 6*d.* 1754)

LORT (MICHAEL). Account of an antient Infcription in North America. By the Rev. Michael Lort, D.D. V.P.A.S. [With Col. Vallancey's Observations] 17 *pp; and* 2 *plates. Half morocco.*
4*to.* (4*s.* 6*d.* 1755)

LOSA (FRANCISCO). La Vie/ de/ Gregoire/ Lopez/ dans la Novvelle/ Espagne,/ composee en Espagnol/ par François Losa Preftre,/ Licentié, & iadis Curé de l'Eglife/ Cathedrale de Mexico./ Et traduite nouuellement en François, par vn Pere de la Compagnie de/ Iesvs./ Seconde Edition./ A *Paris,*/ Chez Iean Henavlt, Libraire Iuré,/ ruë S. Iacques, à l'Ange Gardien/ & fainct Raphaël./ M.DC.LVI./ Auec Priuilege dv Roy./ *12 prel. leaves and text 260 pp. Table des Chapitres 3 pp. Old calf. 12mo.* (10s. 6d. 1756)

LOSKIEL (GEORGE HENRY). History of the Miſsion of the United Brethren among the Indians in North America. In Three Parts. By George Henry Loskiel. Translated from the German. By Christian Ignatius La Trobe. *London*: Printed for the Brethren's Society for the furtherance of the Gospel: 1794. *xii pp. Map. Part I.* 159 *pp. Part II.* 234 *pp. Part III.* 233 *pp. Index* 21 *pp. Uncut.* 8vo. (12s. 6d. 1757)

LOTTERY MAGAZINE (THE); Or, Compleat Fund of Literary, Political and Commercial Knowledge. For August and September, 1776. *London*: Johnson and Co. [1776] 8vo. (2s. 6d. 1758)
The Number for August contains the Declaration of Independence, probably the earliest publication of it in England. The September Number has a description of the City of New York, with a plan.

LOUISBOURG. An Authentic Account of the Reduction of Louisbourg, In June and July 1758. By a Spectator. *London*: W. Owen, 1758. 60 *pp. half mor.* 8vo. (10s. 6d. 1759)

LOUISIANA. Voyage a la Louisiane, et sur le Continent de L'Amérique Septentrionale, fait dans les années 1794 à 1798; Contenant un Tableau historique de la Louisiane, des observations sur son climat, ses riches productions, le caractère et le nom des Sauvages; des remarques importantes sur la navigation; des principes d'administration, de législation et de gouvernement propres à cette Colonie, etc. etc. Par B*** D***. [Baudry les Lozieres] Orné d'une belle carte. *Paris*, Dentu, An XI-1802. *3 prel. leaves, and* 382 *pp. Map. mor.* 8vo. (10s. 6d. 1760)

LÖW (CONRAD). Meer oder Seehanen Buch,/ Darinn/ Verzeichnet feind, die Wun=/derbare, Gedenckwürdige Reife vnd Schiffarhten, fo/ recht vnd billich geheiſſen Meer vnd Seebanen, der Königen von Hi=/fpania, Portugal, Engellandt vnd Franckreich, inwendig den letſt vergangnen hun=/dert

Jahren, gethan. Auff vnd durch welche Schiffarten, ein Newe Welt gegen/ Nidergang, vnd groſſe Königreichen, Landtſchafften vnd Inſulen,/ gegen Auffgang gelegen, erfunden vnd/ entdeckt ſeind./ Hierzu ſeind noch geſetzt zwey ſeltzame vnd gedenckwürdige Stück./ Das eine iſt,/ Die Erzehlung der Schiffart, ſo im Jahr 1594. gethan ſiben Schiff,/ welche die Vnierte Niderländiſche Ständ geſchickt gegen Mitternacht, vmb von/ dannen jren lauff nach China zu nemen. Dieſelbige Schiff ſeind gefahren, durch die Enge oder/ Strafz zwiſchen den Landtſchafften des Grofzfürſten von der Moſcow, vnd der Inſel Waigatz,/ bey Noua Zemla gelegen, bifz ins groſſe Tartariſche Meer, Welches auff Latein Oceanus/ Scythicus oder Mare Tabin genennet wirt, vnd haben entdeckt den Flufz/ Giliſſy nur 13. Meil vom groſſen Flufz/ Obij gelegen./ Das ander ſtück iſt./ Ein Warhaffter, klarer, eigentlicher Bericht, von der weiten vn̄ wun=/derbaren Reiſe oder Schifffahrt, ſo drey Schiff vnd ein Pinafz, aufz Holland, bifz in/ Indien gegen Auffgang gethan. Dieſelbe Schiff ſeind von Texel in Hollandt abgefaoren am an-/dern tag Aprilis, im Jar 1595. Haben vmbgeſägelt das Vorhaupt Bonæ Spei, vnd ſeind ahn der/ groſſen Inſel Madagaſcar jetzt S. Laurentz Inſel geheiſſen, angefahren. Von dannen ſeind ſie/ geſagelt gen Samatra, vorzeïten Taprobana, vnd fehrner gen Bantam, ein groſſe Gewerbſtatt/ in der Inſel Iaua Maior, weiter gen Sidaya, vnd der Inſel Bally. Von dannen ſeind ſie am 26./ Februarij 1597. wider nach Hollandt gefahren, vnd ohn jrgendts ahnzuländen, am 10. tag/ Augſtmonats deſſelben Jars mit freuden zu Haufz amkomen. Haben mitbracht/ Pfeffer, Nägelein, Muscat Nüsz vnd Blumen. Neben dem einen/ wunderbarlichen Vogel, der Fewrkolen verſchlucket./ Gantz luſtig zuleſen./ Diſe Reiſen vnd Schiffahrten ſeind zuſamen, aufz an=/dern Spraachen ins Teutſch gebracht,/ Durch/ Conrad Löw der Hiſtorien Liebhaber./ Getruckt zu Cölln, auff der Burgmauren, Bey/ Bertram Buchholtz, Im Jahr/ 1598. *Title reverse blank, and text* 110 pp. *With Map. Vellum.* (Book of the Ocean or sea-cocks In which are related the wonderful memorable travels and voyages which the rightly and justly called Ocean or Sea-cocks of

the Kings of Spain, Portugal, England, and France
have made within the last past hundred years. In
and by means of which voyages a New World
situated towards the West and great Kingdoms,
countries, and islands towards the east have been
found and discovered. Hereto are yet added two
curious & remarkable pieces. One is the relation
of the voyage which seven ships, which the United
States of the Netherlands sent to the North in order
to take thence their course to China, performed in
the year 1594. The said ships proceeded through
the pass or straits between the territories of the
Great Prince of Moscow and the Island Waigatz
situated near Nova Zembla, into the great Tartaric
Sea, which is called in Latin Oceanus Scythicus or
Mare Tabin; and have discovered the River Gilissy
situated only 13 miles from the great River Obij.
The other piece is a true, clear, and accurate account of the distant and wonderful voyage which
three ships and a pinnace made from Holland to
India towards the East. These ships proceeded
from Texel in Holland on the second day of April
in the year 1595. They sailed round the Cape of Good
Hope and proceeded to the great Island Madagas
car, now called St. Lawrence Island. Hence they
sailed to Sumatra, formerly Taprobana and further
to Bantam a great trading city in the Island of
Java Major, further to Sidaya and the island Bally.
Thence they proceeded on the 26th of February
1597 again towards Holland, and arrived at home
with joy on the 10th day of August in the same
year without landing any where. They have
brought with them pepper, cloves, nutmeg, nuts,
and flowers, together with a wonderful bird which
swallows red-hot Coals. Very pleasant to read.
These travels and voyages have been collected in
German, out of other languages, by Conrad Low,
a lover of histories. Printed at Cologne on the
Castle-walls by Bertram Buchholz. In the year
1598.) *Folio.* (5*l*. 15*s*. 6*d*. 1761)

LUSSAN (Raveneau de). Journal/ du Voyage/
fait a la mer de Sud,/ avec les Flibustiers/ De
L'Amerique en 1684./ & années fuivantes./ Seconde Edition./ Par le Sieur Raveneau De Lussan./ A *Paris,*/ Jean Bapt. Coignard,/ et/ Jean
Baptiste Coignard, Fils,/ MDCLXXXXIII. Avec pri-

vilege de sa Majeste./ 8 *prel. leaves, and* 448 pp.
Privilege and Colophon 2 *leaves. Old calf.*
12mo. (10s. 6d. 1762)

LYNE (CHARLES). A Letter to the Right Honourable Lord Castlereagh, &c. &c. &c. on the North American Export Trade During the War, and during any time the Import and use of our Manufactures are interdicted in the United States. To which is added, the resolutions of the Manufacturers, Exporters of Goods, and Merchants, of the City of Glasgow. By Charles Lyne. *London:* J. M. Richardson, 1813. *Title and* 46 pp. *unbound.*
8vo. (3s. 6d. 1763)

LYTTELTON (THOMAS, *Lord*). A Letter from Thomas Lord Lyttelton to William Pitt, Earl of Chatham, on the Quebec Bill. *Boston:* Printed by Mills and Hicks, for Cox and Berry, in King-Street. M,DCC,LXXIV. 17 pp. *Half morocco.*
8vo. (5s. 6d. 1764)

LYTTELTON (THOMAS, *Lord*). A Letter from Thomas Lord Lyttelton, to William Pitt, Earl of Chatham, on the Quebec Bill. *New-York:* Reprinted by James Rivington. M,DCC,LXXIV. 20 pp. *half mor.* 8vo. (4s. 6d. 1765)

ABLY (ABBE DE). Remarks concerning the Government and the Laws of the United States of America: In Four Letters, addressed to Mr. Adams; Minister Plenipotentiary from the United States of America to those of Holland; and one of the Negociators for the purpose of concluding a general Peace, from the French of the Abbé de Mably: With Notes, by the Translator. *London:* J. Debrett, M,DCC,LXXXIV. *Half-title, title, and 280 pp. 8vo.* (4s. 6d. 1766)

MABLY (ABBE DE). Remarks concerning the Government and the Laws of the United States of America: In four Letters, addressed to Mr. Adams, Minister Plenipotentiary from the United States of America to those of Holland; and one of the Negociators for the purpose of concluding a general peace, from the French of the Abbé de Mably: With Notes, by the Translator. *Dublin:* Moncrieffe, *etc.* MDCCLXXXV. *Half-title, title, and 280 pp. Old calf. 8vo.* (4s. 6d. 1767)

MACAULAY (CATHARINE). Observations on a Pamphlet, entitled, Thoughts on the Cause of the Present Discontents. By Catharine Macaulay. The Third Edition, Corrected. *London:* Edward and Charles Dilly. MDCCLXX. *31 pp. Half mor. 8vo.* (4s. 6d. 1768)

MACAULAY (CATHARINE). An Address to the People of England, Scotland, and Ireland, on the present Important Crisis of Affairs. By Catharine Macaulay. R. Cruttwel, *Bath,* MDCCLXXV. *29 pp. Half mor. 8vo.* (4s. 6d. 1769)

MAC CLURE (DAVID). Memoirs of the Rev.

Eleazar Wheelock, D.D. Founder and President of Dartmouth College and Moor's Charity School; with a summary history of the College and School. To which are added, copious Extracts from Dr. Wheelock's Correspondence. By david M'Clure, D.D., S.H.S. Pastor of a Church in East Windsor, Con. and Elijah Parish, D.D. Pastor of the Church in Byfield, Mass. *Newburyport:* Edward Little & Co. 1811. 336 *pp. Portrait of Eleazar Wheelock. Calf.* 8*vo.* (7*s.* 6*d.* 1770)

MAC DONALD (JOHN). Emigration to Canada. Narrative of a Voyage to Quebec, and Journey from thence to New Lanark, in Upper Canada. Detailing the hardships and difficulties which an Emigrant has to encounter, before and after his settlement; With an Account of the Country, as it regards its climate, soil, and the actual condition of its inhabitants. By John M'Donald. Eighth Edition. *London:* H. Arliss. 1826. 36 *pp. half mor.* 8*vo.* (3*s.* 6*d.* 1771)

MACER (JOHN). Les trois liures de/ l'Histoire des/ Indes, acomplie/ de plufieurs chofes memorables, autant fidelement que fommaire-/ment compofez en Latin, & depuis/ nagueres faictz en Françoys./ Par Maiftre Iehan Macer,/ licencié en droict./ Avec Privilege./ A *Paris./* Chez Guillaume Guillard en la rue/ Sainct Iacques à l'enfeigne/ Saincte Barbe./ 1555./ 96 *folioed leaves. Vellum.* 16*mo.* (1*l.* 10*s.* 1772)

MAC GREGOR (JAMES). Letter from the Reverend Mr. James M'Gregor, Minister, at Pictou, Nova, Scotia, to the General Associate Synod, April 30th, 1793. Published by order of Synod. *Paisley:* Printed by John Neilson. M.DCC.XCIII. 16 *pp.* 8*vo.* (4*s.* 6*d.* 1773)

MAC KENNEY (THOMAS L.) Sketches of a Tour to the Lakes, of the character and customs of the Chippeway Indians, and of incidents connected with the Treaty of Fond du Lac. By Thomas L. Mc Kenney, of the Indian Department, And joint Commissioner with his Excellency Gov. Cass, in negotiating the Treaty. Also, a Vocabulary of the Algic, or Chippeway Language, formed in part, and as far as it goes, upon the basis of one furnished

by the Hon. Albert Gallatin. Ornamented with
twenty-nine Engravings, of Lake Superior, and
other Scenery, Indian Likenesses, Costumes, &c.
Baltimore: Fielding Lucas, Jun'r. 1827. 294 pp.
29 plates. 8vo. (7s. 6d. 1774)

MACKENZIE (ALEXANDER). Voyages from Montreal, on the River St. Lawrence, through the Continent of North America, to the Frozen and Pacific Oceans; In the Years 1789 and 1793. With a preliminary account of the Rise, Progress, and Present State of the Fur Trade of that Country. Illustrated with Maps. By Alexander Mackenzie, Esq. *London:* T. Cadell, Jun. M.DCCC.I. *Half-title, title, viii and cxxxii pp : Text* 412 *pp. Errata* 2 *pp. With Portrait of the Author, and* 3 *Copperplate Maps.*
4to. (10s. 6d. 1775)

MAC KINNEN (DANIEL). A Tour through the British West Indies, in the Years 1802 and 1803, giving a particular Account of the Bahama Islands. By Daniel McKinnen, Esq. *London:* J. White. 1804. *Half-title, title, viii and* 272 *pp. With Map.*
8vo. (5s. 6d. 1776)

MAC LANE (DAVID). The Trial of David M'Lane for High Treason, before a Special Court of Oyer and Terminer at Quebec, on the 7th July 1797. *Quebec:* Printed and Sold by J. Neilson, 1797. 21 *pp. half mor.* 8vo. (5s. 6d. 1777)

MAC MAHON (JOHN V. L.) An Historical View of the Government of Maryland, from its Colonization to the present day. By John V. L. McMahon. *Baltimore:* F. Lucas, Jr. 1831. Vol. I. *xvi and* 539 *pp.* (12s. 6d. 1778)

MAC NEILL (HECTOR). Observations on the Treatment of the Negroes, in the Island of Jamaica, including some Account of their Temper and Character, with Remarks on the Importation of Slaves from the Coast of Africa. In a Letter to a Physician in England, from Hector M'Neill. *London:* G. G. and J. Robinson, *vi and* 46 *pp. half morocco.*
8vo. (3s. 6d. 1779)

MACQUEEN (JAMES). The Colonial Controversy containing a Refutation of the Calumnies of the Anticolonists: the State of Hayti, Sierra Leone,

India, China, Cochin China, Java, &c. &c.; the Production of Sugar, &c. and the state of the Free and Slave Labourers in those Countries; fully considered in a Series of Letters, addressed to The Earl of Liverpool; with a supplementary Letter to Mr. Macaulay. By James Macqueen. *Glasgow:* Khull, Blackie, & Co. 1825. 223 *pp. half mor.* 8vo. (4s. 6d. 1780)

MADRE DE DEOS (GASPAR DA). Memorias para a Historia da Capitania de S. Vicente, hoje chamada de S. Paulo, do estado do Brazil publicadas de Ordem da Academia R. das Sciencias por Fr. Gaspar da Madre de Deos, Monge Benedictino, e correspondente da mesma Academia. *Lisboa:* Na Typografia da Academia. 1797. 4 *prel. leaves, and text* 242 *pp.* 'Catalogo' *etc.* 2 *pp. Half calf.* 4to. (7s. 6d. 1781)

MAFFEIUS (JOANNES PETRUS). Ioan. Petri/ Maffeii,/ Bergomatis,/ e Societate Iesv,/ Historiarvm/ Indicarvm/ Libri XVI./ Selectarvm, item, ex India/ Epistolarum, eodem interprete, Libri IV./ Accessit Ignatii Loiolæ vita./ Omnia ab Auctore recognita, & nunc primùm in Germania excusa./ Item, in singula opera copiosus Index./ His nunc recèns adiecta est charta geographica, x renitidissimè expressa, qua Lectori vtriusq;/ Indiæ situs, & longinqua ad eas nauigatio, accuratè ob oculos spectanda pro-/ponitur, non minus adspectu, quàm historia ipsa lectu iucunda./ *Coloniæ Agrippinæ,*/ In Officina Birckmannica, sumptibus/ Arnoldi Mylij./ Anno M. D.XCIII./ Cum Gratia & Priuilegio S. Cæsarea Maiestatis./ 2 *prel. leaves; viz. Title, reverse blank,* 'Philippo Re=/gi Catho=/ lico.' 2 *pp; Text* 541 *pp.* 'Compendiosvs Index,' *etc.* 35 *pp. Pigskin. Folio.* (15s. 1782)

MAFFEIUS (JOANNES PETRUS). Ioan. Petri/ Maffeii,/ Bergomatis,/ e Societate/ Iesv,/ Historiarvm/ Indicarvm/ Libri XVI./ Selectarvm, Item, ex In-/dia Epistolarvm Libri IV./ Accessit liber recentiorum Epistolarvm, a Ioanne Hayo Dalgattiensi/ Scoto ex eadem Societate nunc primùm excusus, cum/ Indice accurato./ Dvobvs Tomis Distribvti./ Omnia ab Auctore recognita & emendata./ In singula copiosus Index./ *Antverpiæ,* Ex Officina

Martini Nutij, ad infigne dua-/rum Ciconiarum, Anno M. DC. V./ 36 prel. leaves; Text 'Liber Primvs' 478 pp; 1 blank leaf. 'Selectarvm Epistolarvm ex India Libri Qvatvor,' etc. 402 pp. Index 6 pp. Pigskin. 8vo. (15s. 1783)

MAGELLANS. Appendice a la Relacion del Viage al Magallanes de la Fragata de Guerra Santa María de la Cabeza, que contiene el de los Paquebotes Santa Casilda y Santa Eulalia para completar el Reconocimiento del estrecho en los Años de 1788 y 1789. Trabajado de Orden Superior. *Madrid* MDCCLXXXXIII. En la Imprenta de la Viuda de D. Joaquin Ibarra. *2 prel. leaves and* 128 *pp. Carta Estrecho de Magullanes,* 1786, *y* 1789. 4to. (10s. 6d. 1783*)

MALOUET (V. P.) Examen de cette question : Quel sera pour les Colonies de l'Amérique le Résultat de la Révolution Françoise, de la Guerre qui en est la Suite, & de la Paix qui doit la terminer ? Par M. Malouet, Député de la Colonie de St. Domingue. *A Londres:* Baylis, 1797. 29 *pp. half mor.* 8vo. (3s. 6d. 1784)

MALOUET (V. P.) Lettre à M.S.D., Membre du Parlement, sur l'Intérêt de l'Europe, au Salut des Colonies de l'Amérique. Par M. Malouet, Député de la Colonie de St. Domingue. *Londres:* Baylis, 1797. *Half-title, title, and* 36 *pp. Uncut.* 8vo. (3s. 6d. 1785)

MALOUET (V. P.) Collection de Mémoires et Correspondances Officielles sur l'Administration des Colonies, Et notamment sur la Guiane française et hollandaise, par V. P. Malouet, ancien administrateur des Colonies et de la Marine. *Paris,* Baudouin, An X. [1802] *Four Volumes.* Tome Premier. *Half-title, title, and* 484 *pp.* Tome II. *Half-title, title, and* 379 *pp.* Tome III. *Half-title, title, and* 388 *pp.* Tome IV. *Half-title, title, and* 378 *pp. half calf.* 8vo. (10s. 6d. 1786)

MANSIE (ALEXANDER). Dedicated by permission to his Excellency the Governor. The Apprenticed Labourer's Manual: Or An Essay on the Apprenticeship System, and the Duties of the Apprenticed Labourers, Including several of the Personal and Relative Duties binding on Mankind in general.

By Alexander Mansie, Wesleyan Minister. *British Guiana:* Published by the Society for the Instruction of the Labouring Classes. 1837. *xiv and 217 pp.* 'A Catechism of certain Moral, Social, and Civil Duties; adapted to existing circumstances. By the Wesleyan Missionaries of Antigua. Originally printed by Order of the Legislature of that Colony.' 13 pp. 8vo. (5s. 1787)

MASON (J. M.) An Oration commemorative of the late Major-General Alex^r. Hamilton; pronounced before the New-York State Society of the Cincinnati, on Tuesday, July 31, 1804. By J. M. Mason, D.D. Pastor of the first Associate Reformed Church in the City of New York. With an Appendix, containing the Particulars of the Duel between General Hamilton and Colonel Burr, a Copy of the Paper left by the General, and The Rev. Dr. Mason's Letter to the Editor of the Commercial Advertiser, Giving an Account of the General's last Moments. *London:* R. Edwards, 1804. 38 pp. *Uncut.* 8vo. (2s. 6d. 1788)

MARBAN (PEDRO). Arte/ de la Lengva/ Moxa,/ consu Vocabulario, y Cathecismo./ Compuesto/ por el M. R. P. Pedro Marban/ de la Compañia de Jesvs, Superior, que fue,/ de las Mifsiones de Infieles, que tiene la Com=/pañia de efta Provincia de el Perù en las/ dilatadas Regiones de los Indios/ Moxos, y Chiquitos./ Dirigido./ Al Exc.^{mo} Sor D. Melchor/ Portocarrero Laffo, de la Vega. Conde/ de la Monclova, Comendador de la/ Zarza, del Ordẽ de Alcantara, del Con-/fejo de Guerra, y Junta de Guerra de Indias, Virrey, Governando, y Capitan/ General, que fue del Reyno de la Nueva/ Efpaña, y actual, q es de eftos Rey=/nos, y Provincias del Peru./ [*Lima* 1701] Con Licencia de los Svperiores. En la Imprenta Real de Jofeph de Contreras. 8 *prel. leaves, and* 664 *pp;* 'Cathecismo Meno' *etc.* 202 *pp;* 'Indice' 1 *page. Vellum. Small* 8vo. (3l. 13s. 6d. 1789)

MARKHAM (WILLIAM). A Sermon Preached before the Incorporated Society for the Propagation of the Gofpel in Foreign Parts; at their Anniversary Meeting in the Parifh Church of St. Mary-le-Bow, On Friday February 21. 1777. By the Moft

Reverend Father in God, William Lord Archbifhop of York. *London:* T. Harrison and S. Brooke, MDCCLXXVII. 104 *pp.* ' The Form of a Legacy to this Society.' 1 *page. half mor.* 8*vo.* (3*s.* 6*d.* 1790)

MARQUETTE (Le P.) Voyage et découverte de quelques Pays et Nations de l'Amérique Septentrionale par Le P. Marquette et Sr. Joliet. A Paris, Chez Estienne Michallet ruë S. Jaques à l'Image S. Paul. M.DC.LXXXI. Avec privilege du Roy. *Paris.* Maulde et Renou, 1845. *Half-title, title; and* 43 *pp. Map. Morocco extra. A reprint for Mr. O. Rich. Small* 8*vo.* (12*s.* 6*d.* 1791)

MARRANT (John). A Narrative of the Lord's wonderful Dealings with John Marrant, a Black, (Now going to Preach the Gospel in Nova-Scotia) Born in New-York, in North-America. Taken down from his own Relation, Arranged, Corrected, and Published By the Rev. Mr. Aldridge. The Second Edition. *London:* Gilbert and Plummer. 1785; 38 *pp.* 8*vo.* (4*s.* 6*d.* 1792)

MARSHALL (Humphry). Arbustrum Americanum: The American Grove, or, an Alphabetical Catalogue of Forest Trees and Shrubs, natives of the American United States, arranged according to the Linnæan System. Containing, The particular diftinguifhing Chara&ers of each Genus, with plain, fimple and familiar Defcriptions of the Manner of Growth, Appearance, &c. of their feveral Species and Varieties. Also some hints of their uses in Medicine, Dyes, and Domestic Oeconomy. Compiled from actual knowledge and observation, and the assistance of Botanical Authors, By Humphry Marshall. *Philadelphia:* Printed by Joseph Crukshank, in Market-Street, between Second and Third-Streets. MDCCLXXXV. *xx and* 174 *pp. unbound.* 8*vo.* (7*s.* 6*d.* 1793)

MARSTON (Edward). To The Moft Noble Prince Henry Duke of Beaufort, Marquifs and Earl of Worcefter, Baron Herbert, Lord of Ragland, Chepftow and Gower. Palatine of the Province of South Carolina in America. [*London,* 1712.] 12 *pp. half mor.* 4*to.* (18*s.* 1794)

MARTENS (Friderich). Friderich Martens/ von Hamburg/ Spitzbergifche oder Groenlandifche/

Reife Befchreibung/ gethan im Jahr 1671./ Aus/ eigner Erfahrunge befchrieben, die dazu erforderte/ Figuren nach dem Leben felbft abgeriffen, (fo hierbey in/ Kupfferzufehen) und jetzo durch den/ Druck mitgetheilet./ Hamburg,/ Auff Gottfried, Schultzens Koften, gedruckt, Im Jahr 1675./ *4 prel. leaves and 132 pp.* 'Regifter' *2 pp.* 'Errata.' *1 page. 15 Copperplates. 4to.* (1*l.* 5*s.* 1795)

MARTENS (FREDERICH). [*Engraved title*] Vojagie naar/ Groenland of Spitsbergen/ mits gaders een net verhaal der/ Walvis vanghst/ en der zelve behandeling./ Met veel Avontuurlyke voorvallen door F. Martens./ Te Dordrecht,/ Gedrukt by Hendrik Walpot, boekverkooper overt Stadhuys./ [*Printed title*] Fredrik Martens/ Naukeurige Beschryvinge/ van/ Groenland/ of/ Spitsbergen,/ Waer in de Walvifch-Vangft, gelogentheyd van/ 't Ys, en haer wonderlyke kragt en Figuren duydelyk worden/ aengewefen :/ Nevens/ Den Aard van't Land, Gewaffen, Ys-Bergen, Gevogelte,/ Viervoetige Dieren, en Viffchen defer Contryen./ Ook hoe de Walviffchen gevangen, gekapt en gefneden worden :/ Benevens verfcheyde Avontuurlyke voorvallen in Groenland./ Met een Verhael van de gevange Walvifch by St. Anne-Land./ Als mede een Gevegt en fpringen van twee Schepen, een Frans en een En-/gels: Nevens alle de Gevaaren haar overgekomen./ Met Kopere Platen Verçiert./ Te *Dordrecht,/* Gedrukt by Hendrik Walpot, Boekdrukker en Boekverkooper/ over 't Stadthuys./ [1710?] *5 prel. leaves, and 88 pp. Copperplates at pp. 46, 58, 68. 4to.* (1*l.* 11*s.* 6*d.* 1796)

MARTINI (FRANCIS). Argo-Navta/ Batavvs,/ Sive expeditionis Navalis, quam alter nofter/ Jason, & Heros fortiffimus, Petrvs/ Heinivs, fub aufpicijs Illuftriffimorum &/ potentiffimorum DD. Ordd: &/ Illuftriffimi Principis Auraici, In-/clytæq; Societatis Indiæ Occi-/dentalis duc̈tu nuper/ fufcepit:/ Et Victoriæ in finu Matanzæ divinitus/ reportatæ/ Historia/ Carmine heroico defcripta, & publicé recitata,/ à/ Francisco Martini/ Scholæ Campenfis Difcipulo./ *Campis.*/ Ex officina Petri Henrici Wyringani,/ fub figno Typographiæ./ CIƆIƆCXXIX/ *Title and 28 pp. 4to.* (2*l.* 2*s.* 1797)

MARTINIERE (Sieur de la). A New/ Voyage/ into the/ Northern Countries/ Being a Difcription of the Manners,/ Cuftoms, Superftition, Buildings,/ and Habits of the Norwegians, La-/ponians, Kilops, Borandians, Sib-/erians, Samojedes, Zemblans and Iflanders./ With Reflexions upon an Error in/ our Geographers about the fcitua-/tion and Extent of Greenland and/ Nova Zembla./ London/ Printed for John Starkey, at the Miter/ in Fleetftreet near Temple-/Bar. 1674./ 5 prel. leaves and 153 pp. Old calf. 12mo. (1l. 1s. 1798)

MARTINIERE (Sieur de la). [Engraved title] Voyage/ Des Païs/ Septentrionavx/ Par le S^r. D. L M./ A Paris/ Chez Louis Vandosme proche/ Monfeig^r. le Premier Prefident./ G. Ladame [Printed title] Voyage/ des Pays/ Septentrionavx./ Dans lequel fe void les mœurs, maniere de vivre, & fuperfti-/tions des Norweguiens, Lap-/pons, Kiloppes, Borandiens,/ Syberiens, Samojedes, Zem-/bliens, Iflandois./ Par le fieur de la Martiniere,/ Seconde Edition, reveuë & augmentée/ de nouveau./ A Paris,/ Chez Louis Vendosme, Libraire/ au Palais dans la Salle Royalle,/ au Sacrifice d'Abraham 1676./ Avec Privilege dv Roy./ 6 prel. leaves, and 322 pp. 'Extraict du Privilege du Roy.' 2 pp. Old calf. 12mo. (15s. 1799)

MARTYN (Benjamin). Reasons For Establishing the Colony of Georgia, With Regard to the Trade of Great Britain, the Increafe of our People, and the Employment and Support it will afford to great Numbers of our own Poor, as well as foreign perfecuted Protestants. With fome Account of the Country and the Defign of the Trustees. By Benjamin Martyn Efq. The Second Edition. London: W. Meadows, Mdccxxxiii. 48 pp. Frontispiece & Map, both engraved on copper. Half morocco. 4to. (15s. 1800)

MARTYR (Peter). De orbe nouo Decades. [tres. Colophon] Cura & diligentia uiri celebris Magiftri Antonii Ne=/briffenfis historici regii fuerunt hæ tres protono/tarii Petri martyris decades Impreffæ in/ contubernio Arnaldi Guillelmi in/ Illustri oppido carpetanæ puī-/ciæ cōpluto quod uulgari/ter diciter Alcala pfe/ctū eft nonis No/uēbris An./ 1516./ Without pagination or catchwords. On the *reverse of the Title* "Clarissimo Principi Carolo Regi Catholico:" *The Preface occupies the next page* a ii, *on the reverse of which begins the text which ends on the reverse of* i. iii; 'Ad Lectorem de qvibusdam locis leviter depravatis" *2 pages followed by one blank leaf*: " Vocabula Barbara," *5 pages ending with the Colophon, reverse blank; Signatures* a *to* i *in eights, except* a *and* h, *which have only six leaves each.* "Incipitur Legatio Babylonica " *16 leaves, signatures* A *and* B. *Splendid copy with rough leaves in red morocco extra by Bedford. Folio.* (10l. 10s. 1801)

MARTYR (Peter). De Nvper/ svb D. Carolo Reper-/tis Infulis, fimulque incolarum/ moribus, R. Petri Marty-/ris, Enchiridion, Domi-/næ Margaritæ, Diui/ Max. Cæf. filiæ/ dicatum./ *Basileæ,* Anno/ M.D.XXI. 43 *pp.* 4*to.* (2l. 2s. 1802)

MARTYR (Peter). Petri Martyris/ ab Angleria Mediolanen. Oratoris/ clariffimi, Fernandi & Helifabeth Hifpaniarum quondam regum/ à confilijs, de rebus Oceanicis & Orbe nouo decades tres: quibus/ quicquid de inuentis nuper terris traditum, nouarum rerum cupi=/dum lectorem retinere poffit, copiofe, fideliter, eruditeque docetur./ Eivsdem praeterea/ Legationis Babylonicae li/bri tres: vbi praeter oratorii mvneris pulcherrimum exemplum, etiam quicquid in uariarum gentium mori=/bus & inftitutis infigniter præclarum uidit, quæque terra marique acciderunt,/ omnia lectu mirè iucunda, genere dicendi politiffimo traduntur. *Basileae,*/ apud Ioannem Bebelium./ M.D.XXXIII. *12 prel. leaves and 92 folioed leaves. Fine copy in Spanish morocco by Leighton. Folio.* (1l. 11s. 6d. 1803)

MARTYR (Peter). Relationi/ del S. Pietro Martire/ Milanese./ Dell cofe notabili della prouincia dell' E-/gitto fcritte in lingua Latina alli Serenifs,/ di felice memoria Re Catolici D. Fernando,/ e D. Ifabella, & hora recate nella Italiana./ Da Carlo Passi./ Con Privilegio./ In *Venetia* appreffo Giorgio de' Caualli 1564. *7 prel. leaves; viz. Title reverse blank,* 'All' Illustriss. et Eccellentiss. Signora Givlia Sforza Pallavicina,' *etc.* 5 *pp;* 'Discorso di Carlo Passi,' *etc.* 6 *pp. Text* 71 *folioed leaves,* ' Tavola,' *etc.* 12 *pp;* ' Errori fatti nello ftamparfi,' *etc.* 3 *pp. calf. Small* 8*vo.* (1l. 1s. 1804)

MARTYR (Peter). De Rebus/ Oceanicis/ et Novo Orbe, de-/cades tres, Petri Mar-/tyris ab Angleria/ Mediolanensis./ Item eivsdem,/ de Babylonica/ Legatione, Libri III./ et item/ de Rebvs Aethiopicis,/ Indicis Lufitanicis & Hifpanicis, opufcula quædā/ Hiftorica doctiffima, quæ hodiè non facilè/ alibì reperiuntur, Damiani/ A Goes Equitis/ Lufitani./ Quæ omnia fequens pagina lattùs demonftrat./ Cum duplici locupletiffimo Indice./ *Coloniæ*, Apud Geruinum Calenium & hæredes/ Quentelios. M.D. LXXIIII./ Cum gratia & Privilegio Cæsareo./ 24 *prel. leaves and* 655 *pp.* 'Index,' 28 *pp. Fine copy, Vellum. Small* 8vo. (1*l.* 10s. 6d. 1805)

MARTYR (Peter). De Novo Orbe,/ or/ the Historie of/ the weft Indies, Contaying the actes/ and aduentures of the Spanyardes, which haue/ conquered and peopled thofe Countries,/ inriched with varietie of pleafant re-/lation of the Manners, Ceremonies,/ Lawes, Gouernments, and/ Warres of the Indians./ Comprifed in eight Decades./ Written by Peter Martyr a Millanoife of Algeria, Cheife/ Secretary to the Emperour Charles the fift,/ and of his Priuie Councell./ Whereof three, haue beene formerly tranflated in-/to Englifh, by R. Eden, whereunto the other/ fiue, are newly added by the Induftrie, and/ painefull Trauaile of M. Lok Gent./ *London*/ Printed for Thomas Adams./ 1612./ 5 *prel. leaves; viz. Title, reverse blank* 'Epistola Dedicatoria' 4 *pp. Signed* 'Michael Lok.' *To the Reader* ' 4 *pp. Signed* 'M. Lok.' *Text* 318 *folioed leaves. Wanting leaf folioed* 158. 4*to.* (2*l.* 12s. 6d. 1806)

MARTYR (Peter). The/ famovs/ Historie of/ the Indies:/ Declaring the aduentures of/ the Spaniards, which haue conque-/red thefe Countries, with varietie of Relations/ of the Religions, Lawes, Gouernments, Manners,/ Ceremonies, Cuftomes, Rites, Warres,/ and Funerals of the People./ Comprifed into fundry Decads./ Set forth firft by M[r] Hackluyt, and now pub-/lifhed by L. M. Gent./ The fecond Edition./ *London:* Printed for Michael Sparke dwelling at the figne/ of the blue Bible in Green-Arbor. 1628./ 3 *prel. leaves; viz. Title the reverse blank;* 'To the Reader' *Signed* 'M. Lok.' 4 *pp. Text* 318 *folioed leaves. Calf extra by Bedford.* 4*to.* (4*l.* 14s. 6d. 1807)

MARTYR; OVIEDO & XERES. Libro Primo/ della Histo/ria de l'In/die Oc/ciden/tali ❧/ [verso] Svmmario de la Generale/ Historia de l'Indie Oc‑/ci=/dentali cavato da li=/bri scritti dal si=/gnor don Pietro/ Martyre del consi/glio delle Indie/ della Maesta/ de l'Imperadore,/ et da molte/ altre par=/ ticvla=/ri rela=/tioni./ *79 folioed leaves, the 80th blank.* Libro Secon/do delle In/die Oc/ciden/tali/ ✣ MDXXXIIII./ Con gratia & priuilegio./ [verso] Svmmario de la/ Naturale et General Histo/ria de l'Indie occidentali, compofta da Gonzalo ferdi=/ nando del Ouiedo altrimenti di valde, natio de/ la terra di Madril : habitatore & rettore de/ la citta di ſanta Maria antica del Darien,/ in terra ferma del' indie : ilqual fu riue/duto & corretto per ordine de la/ Maefta del Imperadore, pel ſuo/ real config‑ lio, de la dette In/die. & tradotto di lingua/ caftig‑ liana in Italia=/na. Cõ priuilegio/ de la Illuftriff./ Signoria di/ Vinegia,/ per āni xx. *64 folioed leaves, the 65th containing the Table and the 66th the expla‑ nation of the maps.* Libro vltimo del svmma/rio delle/ Indie Oc/ciden/tali/ MDXXXIIII. [*Colophon*] ❡ In *Venegia,* Del meſe d'Ottobre./ MDXXXIIII./ *16 leaves, the 16th being blank. The three Parts complete, a very large copy, with the Map of* ' Isola Spagnvola' *and* 'La carta uniuersale della terra firme,' *both of which are here inserted in facsimile.*
4to. (2l. 12s. 6d. 1808)

MARYLAND. A/ Relation/ of/ Maryland ;/ Toge‑ ther,/ With [A Map of the Countrey,/ The Condi‑ tions of Plantation,/ His Majefties Charter to the/ Lord Baltemore, tranflated/ into Englifh./ Thefe Bookes are to bee had, at Mafter William/ Peafley Efq ; his houfe ; on the back-fide of Dru-/ry-Lane, neere the Cock-pit Playhoufe ; or in/ his abfence ; at Mafter Iohn Morgans houfe in/ high Holbourn, over againft the Dolphin, *London.*/ September the 8. Anno Dom. 1635./ *Title reverse blank, and 56 pp.* 'The Charter of Maryland.' *25 pp. Blue morocco extra by Hayday. Map* 15⅜ *by* 11¾ *inch. wanting.*
4to. (3l. 3s. 1809)

MARYLAND. The/ Declaration/ of the/ Reasons and Motives/ For the Present/ Appearing in Arms/ of/ Their Majesties/ Protestant Subjects/ In the Province of/ Maryland./ Licens'd, November

28th 1689. J. F./ [*Colophon*] Maryland, Printed by William Nuthead at the City of St./ Maries./ Re-printed in London, and Sold by Randal Tay-/lor near Stationers Hall, 1689./ 8 *pp. unbound.*
Folio. (1*l.* 11*s.* 6*d.* 1810)

MARYLAND. The Charter/ of/ Maryland./ [*London*] 23 *pp.* 8*vo.* (10*s.* 6*d.* 1811)

MASSACHUSETTENSIS. *Letters numbered* I *to* XVII. [*Boston*, 1775.] 118 *pp. First Edition. half mor.* 8*vo.* (10*s.* 6*d.* 1812)

MASSACHUSETTENSIS: Or a Series of Letters, containing a faithful state of many important and striking facts, which laid the foundation of the present Troubles in the Province of the Maffachufetts-Bay; interspersed with Animadversions and Reflections, originally Addreffed to the People of that Province, and worthy the confideration of the True Patriots of this Country. By a Person of Honor upon the Spot. The Third Edition. Boston printed. *London* reprinted for J. Mathews, MDCCLXXVI. *viii and* 118 *pp. half mor.* 8*vo.* (7*s.* 6*d.* 1812*)

MASSACHUSETTENSIS: Or a Series of Letters, containing a faithful state of many important and striking facts, which laid the foundation of the present Troubles in the Province of the Maffachufetts-Bay; interspersed with Animadversions and Reflections, originally Addreffed to the People of that Province, and worthy the Confideration of the True Patriots of this Country. By a Person of Honor upon the Spot. The Fourth Edition. Boston printed: *London* reprinted for J. Mathews, MDCCLXXVI. *viii and* 118 *pp. Half morocco.*
8*vo.* (7*s.* 6*d.* 1813)

MASSACHUSETTS. An Account of the Massachusetts State Prison. Containing a description and Plan of the Edifice; the Law, Regulations, Rules and Orders: With a view of the present State of the Institution. By the Board of Visitors. *Charlestown*: Printed by Samuel Etheridge. 1806. 48 *pp. With 2 folded plates.* 8*vo.* (2*s.* 6*d.* 1814)

MASSACHUSETTS-BAY. A/ Collection/ Of the Proceedings of the/ Great and General Court or Affembly/ Of His Majesty's Province of the/ Maffachufetts-Bay,/ in/ New-England;/ Containing several Inſtructions from the Crown, to the/ Council and Aſſembly of that Province, for fixing a/ Salary on the Governour, and their Determinations/ thereon./ As also,/ The Methods taken by the Court for Supporting the ſeveral/ Governours, ſince the Arrival of the preſent Charter./ Printed by Order of the House of Repreſentatives./ *Boston:* Printed by T. Fleet, in Pudding-Lane./ 1729./ 112 pp. *half calf*. 4to. (1*l*. 1s. 1815)

MASSACHUSETTS BAY. A Brief State of the Services and Expences of the Province of the Massachusett's Bay, In the Common Cause. *London:* J. Wilkie, MDCCLXV. 24 pp. *Half morocco*. 8vo. (7s. 6d. 1816)

MASSACHUSETTS BAY. The Proceedings of the Council, and the House of Representatives Of the Province of the Maſsachusetts-Bay, relative to the Convening, holding and keeping The General Aſsembly At Harvard-College in Cambridge: And The ſeveral Meſſages which paſsed between His Honor the Lieutenant Governor and The Two Houſes, Upon the Subject. Publiſhed by Order of the Houſe of Representatives. *Boston:* Printed by Edes and Gill, Printers to the Honorable Houſe of Representatives, 1770. *Title, and pp. 5-83. half mor.* 8vo. (7s. 6d. 1817)

MASSIE (J.) Calculations and Observations relating to an Additional Duty upon Sugar. *Dated Westminster,* 20th January 1759. *2 pp. single sheet. Folio.* (4s. 6d. 1818)

MASSIE (J.) A State of the British Sugar-Colony Trade; shewing, That an Additional Duty of Twelve Shillings per 112 Pounds Weight may be laid upon Brown or Muscovado Sugar (and proportionably higher Duties upon Sugar refined before imported) without making Sugar dearer in this Kingdom than it hath been of late Years, and without Diſtreſſing the Britiſh Sugar-Planters ; for their Profits will then be Twice as much Money per acre of Land, as the Landholders of England receive for their Eſtates. All which Matters are plainly made appear, and the vaſt loſſes which this Kingdom hath suffered by the Sugar-Colony Trade, written Thirty Years laſt paſt, are particularly pointed out. Moſt humbly ſubmitted to the conſideration of the Honourable House of Commons. By J. Maſſie. *London*, T. Payne, MDCCLIX. *Title and 40 pp. half calf. 4to.*   (5s. 6d. 1818*)

MATHER (COTTON). Late/ Memorable Providences/ Relating to/ Witchcrafts and Poſſeſſions,/ Clearly Manifeſting,/ Not only that there are Witches, but that Good Men (as well as others) may poſſibly have their Lives ſhortned/ by ſuch evil Inſtruments of Satan./ Written by Cotton Mather Miniſter of the/ Goſpel at Boſton in New-England./ The Second Impreſſion./ Recommended by the Reverend Mr. Richard/ Baxter in London, and by the Miniſters of/ Boſton and Charleſtown in New-England./ *London*, Printed for Tho. Parkhurſt at the Bible and/ Three Crowns in Cheapſide near Mercers-/Chapel. 1691./ 11 *prel. leaves, viz. Title reverse blank*, ' To the Honourable Wait Winthrop Eſq ;' 2 *pp*. 'To the Reader.' 4 *pp.* ' The Preface.' 9 *pp.* 'A Catalogue of Books' etc. 3 *pp.* ' The Introduction.' 2 *pp. Text* 144 *pp. Small 8vo.*   (2l. 2s. 1819)

MATHER (COTTON). The/ Life and Death/ Of The Renown'd/ Mr. John Eliot,/ Who was the/ Firſt Preacher/ of the/ Goſpel/ to the/ Indians in America./ With an Account of the Wonderful Suc-/ceſs which the Goſpel has had amongſt the Hea-/then in that part of the World: And of the/ many ſtrange Cuſtomes of the Pagan Indians,/ In New-England./ Written by Cotton Mather./ The Second Edition carefully corrected./ *London* :/ Printed for John Dunton, at the Raven/ in the Poultrey. MDCXCI./ 3 *prel. leaves, and* 138 *pp. calf. Small 8vo.*   (1l. 5s. 1820)

MATHER (COTTON). A/ True Account/ of the Tryals, Examinations,/ Confeſſions, Condemnations,/ and Executions of divers/ Witches,/ At Salem, in New-England,/ for/ Their Bewitching of ſundry People and Cattel/ to Death, and doing other great Miſchiefs,/ to the Ruine of many People about them./ With/ The Strange Circumſtances that attended/ their Enchantments :/ And/ Their Converſation with Devils, and other/ Infernal Spirits./ In a Letter to a Friend in London./

Licenſed according to Order./ *London*, Printed for J. Conyers, in Holbourn./ 8 *pp*. 'Salem, 8th. Month, 1692. Signed C. M.' 4*to*. (2*l*. 2*s*. 1821)

MATHER (COTTON). The Wonders of the In-viſible World :/ Being an Account of the/ Tryals/ of Several Witches,/ Lately Executed in/ New-England :/ And of several remarkable Curioſities therein Occurring./ Together with,/ I. Obſervations upon the Nature, the Number, and the Operations of the Devils./ II. A ſhort Narrative of a late outrage committed by a knot of Witches in/ Swede-Land, very much reſembling, and ſo far explaining, that under which/ New-England has laboured./ III. Some Councels directing a due Improvement of the Terrible things lately/ done by the unuſual and amazing Range of Evil-Spirits in New-England./ IV. A brief Diſcourſe upon thoſe Temptations which are the more ordinary Devi-/ces of Satan./ By Cotton Mather./ Publiſhed by the Special command of his Excellency the Governour of/ the Province of the Maſſachuſetts-Bay in New-England./ Printed firſt, at Boſton in New-England; and Reprinted at *Lon-/don*, for John Dunton, at the Raven in the Poultry. 1693./ First Edition. Title, and 98 *pp. unbound.* 4*to*. (2*l*. 2*s*. 1822)

MATHER (COTTON). The Wonders of the In-viſible World :/ Being an Account of the/ Tryals/ of/ Several Witches/ Lately Executed in/ New-England :/ And of ſeveral Remarkable Curioſities therein Occurring./ By Cotton Mather./ Publiſhed by the Special Command of his Excellency the/ Governour of the Province of the Maſſachuſetts-Bay in New-/England./ The Second Edition./ Printed firſt, at Boſton in New-England, and reprinted at *London*, for/ John Dunton, at the Raven in the Poultrey. 1693./ 3 *prel. leaves, and pp.* 9-62. *half mor.* 4*to*. (2*l*. 2*s*. 1823)

MATHER (COTTON). The Wonders of the Inviſible World :/ Being an Account of the/ Tryals/ of/ Several Witches/ Lately Executed in/ New-England :/ And of ſeveral Remarkable Curioſities/ therein Occurring./ By Cotton Mather./ Publiſhed by the Special Command of his Excellency/

the Governour of the Province of the Maffachufetts-Bay in/ New-England./ The Third Edition./
Printed firft at Bofton in New-England, and reprinted at *London*,/ for John Duneon, at the Raven
in the Poultrey. 1693./ 4 *prel. leaves, and pp.* 9-64.
half mor. 4*to.* (2*l.* 2*s.* 1824)

MATHER (COTTON). The Order of the Churches
in New-England. Vindicated. [*Boston* 1700 ?]
pp. 13-144. *Wanting the title and prel. leaves.*
12*mo.* (7*s.* 6*d.* 1825)

MATHER (COTTON). Magnalia Chrifti Americana:
Or, the Ecclefiaftical Hiftory of New-England,
from Its Firft Planting in the Year 1620. unto the
Year of our Lord, 1698. In Seven Books. I. An-
tiquities: In Seven Chapters. With an Appendix.
II. Containing the Lives of the Governours, and
Names of the Magiftrates of New-England: In
Thirteen Chapters. With an Appendix. III. The
Lives of Sixty Famous Divines, by whofe Miniftry
the Churches of New-England have been Planted
and Continued. IV. An Account of the Univer-
fity of Cambridge in New-England; in Two Parts.
The Firft contains the Laws, the Benefactors, and
Viciffitudes of Harvard College; with Remarks
upon it. The Second Part contains the Lives of
fome Eminent Perfons Educated in it. V. Acts
and Monuments of the Faith and Order in the
Churches of New-England, paffed in their Synods;
with Hiftorical Remarks upon thofe Venerable
Affemblies; and a great Variety of Church-Cafes
occurring, and refolved by the Synods of thofe
Churches: In Four Parts. VI. A Faithful Re-
cord of many Illuftrious, Wonderful Providences,
both of Mercies and Judgments, on divers Perfons
in New-England: In Eight Chapters. VII. The
Wars of the Lord. Being an Hiftory of the Manifold Afflictions and Difturbances of the Churches
in New-England, from their Various Adverfaries,
and the Wonderful Methods and Mercies of God
in their Deliverance: In Six Chapters: To which
is fubjoined, An Appendix of Remarkable Occurrences which New-England had in the Wars with
the Indian Salvages, from the Year 1688, to the
Year 1698. By the Reverend and Learned Cotton
Mather, M.A. And Paftor of the North Church in

Bofton, New-England. *London*: Printed for Thomas Parkhurft, at the Bible and Three Crowns in Cheapfide. MDCCII. 14 *prel. leaves; viz. Title, Attestation, Poems, General Introduction, and Contents.* 'Antiquities. The First Book.' *Title and* 38 *pp.* 'Ecclefiarum Clypei. The Second Book.' *Title and* 75 *pp.* ' Polybius. The Third Book.' *Title and* 238 *pp.* ' Sal Gentium. The Fourth Book.' *Title and pp.* 125-222. ' Acts and Monuments. The Fifth Book.' *Title and pp.* 3-100. 'Thaumaturgus. The Sixth Book.' *Title and* 88 *pp. blank leaf.* ' Ecclesiarum Prœlia: The Seventh Book.' *Title and pp.* 3-118. ' Books,' *etc.* 2 *pp. With map. Old calf. Folio.* (3*l*. 3*s*. 1826)

MATHER (COTTON). The Curbed Sinner. A DiscourseUpon the Gracious and Wondrous Reftraints Laid by the Providence Of the Glorious God, On the Sinful Children of Men, to Withold them from Sinning againft Him. Occafioned by a Sentence of Death, paffed on a poor Young Man, for the Murder of his Companion. With fome Hiftorical Paffages referring to that Unhappy Spectacle. By Cotton Mather, D.D. *Boston*, N.E. Printed by John Allen, for Nicholas Boone, at the Sign of the Bible in Cornhil. 1713. *Title, xiv and* 64 *pp. Vellum.* 12*mo.* (10*s*. 6*d*. 1827)

MATHER (COTTON). A Prefent of Summer Fruit. A very brief Essay To Offer Some Instructions of Piety, Which the Summer-Season more Particularly and Emphatically Leads us to; But fuch alfo as are never out of Seafon. Being The fhort Entertainment of an Auditory in Bofton, on a Day diftinguifhed with the Heat of the Summer; 5d. 5m. 1713. By Cotton Mather, D.D. *Boston:* Printed and Sold by B. Green, in Newbury Street. 1713. *Title, and text* 29 *pp. Vellum.* 12*mo.* (10*s*. 6*d*. 1828)

MATHER (COTTON). The Grand Point of Solicitude. A very brief Essay upon Divine Defertions; the Symptoms of them, and The Methods of Preventing them. A Sermon Publifhed for the Service of Others, by One of the Hearers, more particularly affected in the Hearing of it. *Boston:* Printed by B. Green. 1715. *Blank leaf, Title, and* 31 *pp.* 12*mo.* (7*s*. 6*d*. 1829)

MATHER (Cotton). Fair Dealing between Debtor and Creditor. A very brief Essay upon The Caution to be ufed, about coming in to Debt, And getting out of it. Offered at Boston-Lecture; 5. d. xi. m. 17$\frac{13}{16}$. By Cotton Mather, D.D. & F.R.S. *Boston:* Printed by B. Green, for Samuel Gerrifh, at his Shop over againft the North fide of the Town-Houfe. 1716. *Title and 30 pp. unbound.* 16mo. (15s. 1830)

MATHER (Cotton). Desiderius. Or, A Defireable Man Defcrib'd; In the Characters of One Worthy to be, a Man Greatly Beloved. And An Example of One, who Lived very much Defired, and has Dyed as much Lamented; Given in fome Commemoration of the very Valuable and Memorable Mr. James Keith, Late Minifter of the Gospel in Bridgwater; Who Expired, on 23. d. V. m. 1719. In the Seventy Sixth Year of his Age. By Cotton Mather, D.D. & F.R.S. *Boston:* Printed by S. Kneeland, 1719. *Title, and text 34 pp. Vellum.* 12mo. (10s. 6d. 1831)

MATHER (Cotton). A Year and a Life Well Concluded. A brief Essay, On the Good Things Wherein The Last Works Of a Christian, may be, and fhould be, His Best Works. A Sermon Preached on the Last Day of the Year, 1719. *Boston:* Printed by S. Kneeland, for B. Gray, at the Corner Shop on the North fide of the Town-Houfe, 1719-20. 24 pp. 12mo. (10s. 6d. 1832)

MATHER (Cotton). Coheleth. A Soul upon Recollection; Coming into Inconteftible Sentiments of Religion; Such as all the Sons of Wisdom, will and muft forever Justify. Written by a Fellow of the Royal Society. Offering the Advice of a Father going out of the World, unto a Son coming into it. *Boston:* Printed by S. Kneeland, for S. Gerrish, and Sold at his Shop. 1720. *Title and 46 pp.* 12mo. (10s. 6d. 1833)

MATHER (Cotton). India Chriftiana. A difcourfe, Delivered unto the Commiffioners, for the Propagation of the Gospel among the American Indians which is Accompanied with feveral Instruments relating to the Glorious Design of Propagating our Holy Religion, in the Eastern as well as the Western, Indies. An Entertainment which they that are Waiting for the Kingdom of God will receive as Good News from a far Country. By Cotton Mather, D.D. and F.R.S. *Boston* in New-England: Printed by B. Green. 1721. *Title, Dedication ii pp. Text 94 pp.* 'Corrigenda,' 1 *page. Old calf. Small 8vo.* (1*l*. 1*s*. 1834)

MATHER (Cotton). A Paftoral Letter, to Families Vifited with Sicknefs. From feveral Ministers of Boston, At a time of Epidemical Sicknefs Diftreffing of the Town. The Third Impreffion. [*Colophon*] *Boston:* Printed by R. Green, for S. Gerrifh, at his Shop near the Brick Meeting-Houfe in Cornhill. 1721. *Half-title, and 24 pp. half morocco.* 12*mo*. (7*s*. 6*d*. 1835)

MATHER (Cotton). Silentiarius. A brief Essay on the Holy Silence and Godly Patience, that Sad Things are to be Entertained withal. A Sermon at Bofton-Lecture, On the Death of Mrs. Abigail Willard, And the Day before her Interment; who Expired Septemb. 26. 1721. By her Father. Whereto there is added, A Sermon on, The Refuge of the Diftreffed, which was Preached on the Lord's-Day preceeding. *Boston:* Printed by S. Kneeland, 1721. *On the reverse of the Title,* Introduction,' signed 'Cotton Mather.' 'The Silent Sufferer,' 34 *pp*. 'The Refuge of the Diftreffed.' 28 *pp. unbound.* 12*mo*. (15*s*. 1836)

MATHER (Cotton). Bethiah. The Glory Which Adorns the Daughters of God. And the Piety, Wherewith Zion wifhes to fee her Daughters Glorious. *Boston:* Printed by J. Franklin, for S. Gerrifh, at his Shop in Cornhill. 1722. 60 *pp*. 12*mo*. (10*s*. 6*d*. 1837)

MATHER (Cotton). Columbanus. Or, The Doves Flying to the Windows of their Saviour. A Sermon to a Religious Society of Young People. June 4th. 1722. *Boston:* Printed by S. Kneeland, for J. Edwards, Sold at his Shop. 1722. *Title and 22 pp.* 12*mo*. (10*s*. 6*d*. 1838)

MATHER (Cotton). Honefta Parfimonia: Or, Time Spent as it fhould be. Proposals, To prevent that Great Folly and Mischief, The Lofs of Time;

And Employ the Talent of Time So Watchfully and Fruitfully that a Good Account may at Laſt be given of it. *Boston:* Printed by S. Kneeland, for J. Edwards, and Sold at his Shop. 172[2?] *Half-title, Title, and* 23 *pp.* 12*mo.* (10s. 6d. 1839)

MATHER (Cotton). The Minister. A Sermon, Offer'd unto the Anniverſary Convention of Ministers, From ſeveral Parts of New-England, Met at Boston, 31 d. III m. 1722. By One of their Number. And publiſhed at the Requeſt of them that heard it. *Boston:* Printed in the Year 1722. *Half-title* ' Dr. Cotton Mather's Sermon, at the Anniversary Convention of Ministers, May 31ſt. 1722.' *and* 45 *pp.* 8*vo.* (10s. 6d. 1840)

MATHER (Cotton). Pia Diſideria. Or, The Smoaking Flax, raiſed into a Sacred Flame; In a Short and Plain Essay upon thoſe Pious Deſires, Which are the Introduction and Inchoation of all Vital Piety, Delivered unto a Religious Society of Young People; On the Lord's-Day-Evening, Aug. 5. 1722. *Boston:* Printed by S. Kneeland for S. Gerriſh, at his Shop in Cornhill. 1722. *Title and* 22 *pp.* 12*mo.* (10s. 6d. 1841)

MATHER (Increase). The/ Mystery/ of/ Iſrael's Salvation,/ Explained and Applyed :/ Or,/ A Discourse/ Concerning the General Converſion of the/ Israelitish Nation./ Wherein is Shewed,/ 1. That the twelve Tribes ſhall be ſaved./ 2. When this is to be expected./ 3. Why this muſt be./ 4. What kind of Salvation the Tribes of Israel/ ſhall partake of. (viz.) A Glorious, Wonder-/ful, Spiritual, Temporal Salvation./ Being the Subſtance of ſeveral Ser-/mons Preached./ By Increase Mather, M.A./ Teacher of a Church in Boſton in New-England./ *London*, Printed for John Allen in Wentworth-ſtreet, near/ Bell-Lane, 1669. 23 *prel. leaves; viz. Title reverse blank,* ' An Epistle to the Reader.' *signed* ' John Davenporte.' 11 *pp.* ' To the Reader.' *signed* ' W. G.' 4 *pp.* ' To the Reader.' *signed* ' W. H.' 14 *pp.* ' The Authors Preface To The Reader.' *signed* 'J. M.' 14 *pp: Text* 181 *pp.* ' The Names of Writers,' *etc. being* ' The Table.' 5 *pp.* ' Places of Scripture opened,' *etc.* 4 *pp. Calf extra by Bedford. Small* 8*vo.* (1*l.* 16s. 6d. 1842)

MATHER (INCREASE). The/ First Principles/ of/ New-England,/ Concerning/ The Subject of Baptifme/ &/ Communion of Churches./ Collected partly out of the Printed Books, but chiefly/ out of the Original Manufcripts of the Firft and chiefe/ Fathers in the New-Englifh Churches ; With the Judg-/ment of Sundry Learned Divines of the Congregational/ Way in England, Concerning the faid Queftions./ Publifhed for the Benefit of thofe who are of the Rifing Gene-/ration in New-England./ By Increase Mather, Teacher of a Church/ in Bofton in New-England/ Cambridge/ Printed by Samuel Green, 1675./ 4 prel. leaves; viz. Title in a narrow metal type border, the reverse blank, ' To the Reader.' signed ' Increase Mather.' 6 pp; Text 40 pp. 'Postscript' signed 'Iohn Allin.' 1 page. 'A Letter concerning the Subject of Baptifme,' etc. signed 'Jonathan Mitchel.' pp. 2-7. Calf extra by Bedford. 4to. (4l. 4s. 1843)
With the Autograph of White Kennett on the Title.

MATHER (INCREASE). The/ Divine Right/ of/ Infant-Baptifme,' ..ferted and Proved from/ Scripture/ And/ Antiquity. By Increase Mather,/ Teacher of a Church of Chrift in Bofton in New-England./ Boston,/ Printed by John Fofter, in the Year 1680./ 4 prel. leaves; viz. Title the reverse blank; ' Christian Reader.' 5 pp. Signed 'Urian Oakes.' Text 27 pp. Calf extra, gilt by Bedford. 4to. (4l. 4s. 1844)

MATHER (INCREASE). Returning unto God the great concernment/ of a Covenant People./ Or/ A Sermon/ Preached to the fecond Church in Boston in/ New-England, March 17. 16$\frac{79}{80}$. when/ that Church did folemnly and explicitly/ Renew their Covenant with/ God, and one with another./ By Increase Mather Teacher of that Church./ Boston, Printed by John Fofter. 1680./ 3 prel. leaves; viz. Title, reverse blank; ' To the fecond Church of Chrift' in Boston in New-England.' 4 pp. Text 21 pp. Fine copy in morocco by Bedford. 4to. (3l. 3s. 1845)

MATHER (INCREASE). Diatriba/ de signo/ Filii Hominis/ et de/ Secundo Messiæ Adventu ;/ Ubi de modo futuræ Judæorum Converfionis :/ Nec non de fignis Novifsimi diei, differitur./ Authore/ Cres-

centio Mathero/ V.D.M. apud Boftonienfis in Novâ
Angliâ. *Amstelodami*,/ Apud Mercy Browning
Juxta Burfam. 1682./ 4 *prel. leaves and* 98 *pp.
Index* 5 *pp. Corrigenda*, 1 *page. Calf extra by Bed-
ford.* 8*vo.* (1*l.* 11*s.* 6*d.* 1846)

MATHER (INCREASE). KOMHTOΓPAΦIA./ Or
a/ Difcourfe Concerning/ Comets ;/ Wherein the
Nature of Blazing Stars/ is Enquired into :/ With
an Hiftorical Account of all the Comets/ which
have appeared from the Beginning of the/ World
unto this prefent Year, M.DC.LXXXIII./ Expreffing/
The Place in the Heavens, where they were seen,/
Their Motion, Forms, Duration; and the Re-/
markable Events which have followed/ in the
World, fo far as they have been/ by Learned Men
Obferved./ As alfo two Sermons,/ Occafioned by
the late Blazing Stars./ By Increase Mather,
Teacher of a Church/ at Bofton in New-England./
Boston In New-England./ Printed by S. G. for
S. S. And fold by J. Browning/ At the corner of
the Prifon Lane next the Town-/Houfe. 1683./ 6
prel. leaves; *viz. Title*. ' To the Reader' 4 *pp. signed*
'John Sherman.' ' To the Reader,' 3 *pp.* 'The
Contents' 2 *pp. Text* 143 *pp. Errata* 1 *page.* Heaven's/ Alarm/ to the/ World./ Or/ A Sermon,
wherein is shewed,/ That Fearful/ Sights/ And
Signs in Heaven, are the Presa-/ges of great Calamities at hand./ Preached at the Lecture of Bofton
in New-England ;/ January, 20. 1680./ By Mr.
Increase Mather./ The Second Impression./ *Boston*
in New-England,/ Printed for Samuel Sewall.
And are to be fold by/ Jofeph Browning at the
Corner of the Prifon-Lane/, Next the Town-Houfe.
1682./ 4 *prel. leaves*; *viz. Title*, ' To the Reader.'
6 *pp; Text* 38 *pp.* ' The Latter/ Sign/ Difcourfed
of,/ in a Sermon/ Preached at the Lecture of Bofton in/ New-England ;/ August, 31.1682./ Wherein is fhewed, that the Voice of/ God in Signal Providences, efpecially/ when repeated and Iterated,
ought to be/ Hearkned unto/ By Increase Mather./
Title and 32 *pp. small* 8*vo.* (2*l.* 2*s.* 1847)

MATHER (INCREASE). The/ Mystery/ of/ Christ/
opened and applyed./ In several Sermons, Concerning the/ Perfon, Office, and Glory of Jefus
Chrift./ By Increase Mather,/ Teacher of a Church

at Bofton in N. England./ [*Boston*] Printed in the year MDCLXXXVI. *Title 6 and* 212 *pp. The Contents* 1 *page. Books printed, etc. Calf extra by Bedford.* 12*mo.* (1*l.* 11*s.* 6*d.* 1848)

MATHER (INCREASE). De/ Succeffu Evangelij/ Apud Indos/ in/ Novâ-Angliâ/ Epistola./ Ad Cl. Virum/ D. Johannem Leufdenum,/ Linguæ Sanctæ in Ultra-/jectinâ Academiâ Pro-/fefforem, Scripta./ A Crefcentio Mathero/ Apud Boftonienfes V.D.M. nec non/ Collegij Harvardini quod eft Canta-/ brigiæ ov-Anglorum, Rectore./ *Londini*, Typis J. G. 1688./ *Title and* 13 *pp. Green morocco.* 12*mo.* (1*l.* 1*s.* 1849)

MATHER (INCREASE). De/ Succeffu Evangelii/ Apud/ Indos/ occidentales,/ In Novâ-Angliâ;/ Epistola./ Ad Cl. Virum/ D. Johannem Leusdenum/ Linguæ Sanctæ in Ultrajectinâ Acade-/ miâ Profefforem, Scripta,/ A Crefcentio Mathero./ Apud Boftonienfes V. D. M. nec non Collegii/ Harvardini quod eft Cantabrigia Nov-An-/glorum, Rectore./ Londini, Typis J. G. 1688,/ Jam recufua, & fuccefsu Evangelii apud In-/dos Orientales aucta./ *Ultrajecti,* /Apud Wilhelmum Broedeleth,/ Anno 1699./ 16 *pp.* 8*vo.* (12*s.* 6*d.* 1850.)

MATHER (INCREASE). A Further/ Account/ of the/ Tryals/ of the/ New-England Witches./ With the Obfervations/ Of a Perfon who was upon the Place feveral/ Days when the fufpected Witches were/ firft taken into Examination./ To which is added,/ Cafes of Confcience/ Concerning Witchcrafts and Evil Spirits Per-/fonating men./ Written at the Requeft of the Minifters of New-England./ By Increafe Mather, Prefident of Harvard Colledge./ Licenfed and Entred according to Order./ *London:* Printed for J. Dunton, at the Raven in the Poultrey/ 1693. Of whom may be had the Third Edition of Mr. Cotton/ Mather's Firft Account of the Tryals of the New-England/ Witches, Printed on the fame fize with this Laft Account,/ that they may bind up together./ *Title and* 10 *pp*: "Cases of Confcience" *etc. Title; and* 'Chriftian Reader' 2 *pp*: *Text* 40 *pp.* 'Postscript' 4 *pp. half mor.* 4*to.* (2*l.* 2*s.* 1851)

MATHER (INCREASE). Angelographia,/ or/ A Dif-courſe/ Concerning the Nature and Power of the/ Holy Angels, and the Great Benefit/ which the True Fearers of God Receive/ by their Miniſtry :/ Delivered in ſeveral/ Sermons :/ To which is added, A Sermon concerning the Sin and/ Miſery of the Fallen Angels :/ Alſo a Diſquiſition concerning/ Angelical Apparitions./ By Increase Mather, Pre-ſident of Harvard/ Colledge, in Cambridge, and Preacher of the/ Goſpel at Boſton in New-England./ *Boston* in N. E. Printed by B. Green & J. Allen,/ for Samuel Phillips at the Brick Shop. 1696./ 8 *prel. leaves; viz. Title,* ' The Epiſtle Dedicatory,' 2 *pp.* ' To the Reader,' 12 *pp: Text* 132 *pp.* ' A Diſquiſition' *etc.* 44 *pp. Portrait of Increase Mather. Calf extra by Bedford. Small* 8*vo.* (2*l.* 2*s.* 1852)

MATHER (INCREASE). Two Plain and Practical/ Discourſes/ Concerning/ I. Hardneſs of Heart./ Shewing,/ That ſome, who live under the Goſpel,/ are by a Judicial Diſpenſation, given/ up to that Judgment; and the Signs/ thereof./ II./ The Sin and Danger/ of/ Diſobedience to the Goſpel./ By Increaſe Mather, Preſident of Harvard-/College in Cambridge, and Preacher of/ the Goſpel at Boſton in New-England./ *London.* Printed for J. Ro-binſon, and are to/ be Sold by Samuel Phillips, Bookſeller in Boſton,/ in New-England. 1699./ 187 *pp. Books lately Printed, etc.* 5 *pp. Calf extra by Bedford.* 12*mo.* (18*s.* 1853)

MATHER (INCREASE). Meditations on the Glory of the Lord Jeſus Chriſt: Delivered in ſeveral Ser-mons. By Increaſe Mather. Boston in New-England. Printed by Bartholomew Green, for Benj. Eliot, at his Shop under the Weſt-End of the Town-houſe, 1705. *viii. and* 162 *pp.* (*wanting all after page* 162). 16*mo.* (7*s.* 6*d.* 1854)

MATHER (INCREASE). The Doctrine of Singular Obedience, As the Duty and Property of the True Chriſtian: Opened & Applied. In a Sermon, Preached by I. Mather, D.D. *Boston* in New-England, Printed & Sold by Timothy Green, at the North End of the Town, 1707. 29 *pp; Adver-tisement,* 1 *page. Vellum.* 12*mo.* (1*l.* 1*s.* 1855)
A presentation copy " To Mr. Samuel Mather."

MATHER (INCREASE). A Discourse Concerning

the Maintenance, Due to thofe that Preach the Gofpel: In which The Question, Whether Tithes Are by the Divine Law, the Minifters Due? is considered: and the Negative Prov'd. By J. Mather, D.D. Bofton, N. E. Printed 1706, and Reprinted at *London*, 1709. *2 prel. leaves; and 32 pp. Small 8vo.* (12s. 6d. 1856)

MATHER (INCREASE). Practical Truths, Plainly Delivered. Wherein is Shewed, I. That true Believers on Jefus Chrift, fhall as certainly enjoy Everlasting Life in Heaven, as if they were there already. II. That there is a bleffed Marriage between Jefus Chrift the Son of God, and the true Believer. III. That Men are Infinitely concerned, not only to hear the Voice of Chrift, but that they do it, To Day. IV. The Work of the Miniftry, defcribed, in an Ordination Sermon. By Increafe Mather, D.D. *Boston*, N. E. Printed by B. Green, for Daniel Henchman, and Sold at his Shop, 1718. *2 prel. leaves, and 134 pp. (Wanting all after page 134.) 16mo.* (16s. 1857)

MATHER (INCREASE). Memoirs of the Life Of the late Reverend Increafe Mather, D.D. Who died Auguft 23, 1723. With a Preface by the Reverend Edmund Calamy, D.D. *London*: John Clark and Richard Hett, MDCCXXV. *4 prel. leaves, and 88 pp. 8vo.* (16s. 1858)

MATHER (NATHANAEL). Twenty-Three Select Sermons Preached at the Merchants-Lecture, at Pinners-Hall, and in Lime-ftreet. Wherein several Cafes of Confcience, and Other Weighty Matters, are propounded, and handled. By the Judicious and Learned Mr. Nathanael Mather. *London*: N. Hiller, 1701. *4 prel. leaves, and 480 pp. calf. 8vo.* (10s. 6d. 1859)

MATHER (RICHARD). A/ Modeft & Brotherly/ Answer/ To Mr. Charles Herle his Book,/ againft the Independency of Churches./ Wherein his foure Arguments for the Govern-/ment of Synods over particular Congregati-/ons, are friendly Examined, and/ clearly Anfwered./ Together, with Chriftian and Loving Ani-/madverfions upon fundry other obfervable paffa-/ges in the faid Booke./ All tending to declare the true ufe of Synods, and the/

power of Congregationall Churches in the points of/ electing and ordaining their owne Officers,/ and cenfuring their Offendors./ By Richard Mather Teacher of the Church at Dorchefter; And William Tompson Paftor of the Church at/ Braintree in New-England./ Sent from thence after the Affembly of Elders were diffolved that/ laft met at Cambridg to debate matters about Church-government./ *London*, Printed for Henry Overton in Popes-head alley, 1644./ *2 prel. leaves, and 58 pp. 4to.* (15s. 1860)

MATHER (RICHARD). A/ Reply/ to/ Mr. Rutherfurd,/ or,/ A defence of the Anfwer to Re-/verend Mr. Herles Booke againft the/ Independency of Churches./ Wherein fuch Objections and/ Anfwers, as are returned to fundry paffages/ in the faid Anfwer by Mr. Samuel Rutherfurd,/ a godly and learned Brother of the Church of Scotland, in his Booke Entituled The Due/ Right of Presbyters, are examined and removed, and the Anfwer juftified/ and cleared./ By Richard Macher Teacher to/ the Church at Dorchefter in New/ England. 1646./ *London*,/ Printed for J. Rothwell, and H. Allen at the Sun/ and Fountaine in Pauls Churchyard, and/ the Crown in Popes-head Alley, 1647,/ *4 prel. leaves, and 109 pp. 4to.* (15s. 1861)

MATHER (SAMUEL). Early Piety,/ exemplified/ in the/ Life and Death/ of Mr. Nathanael Mather,/ who/ Having become at the Age of/ Nineteen, an Inftance of more/ than common/ Learning and Virtue,/ Changed Earth for Heaven, Oct. 17. 1688./ Whereto are added/ Some Difcourfes on the true Nat /the great Reward, and the /Seafon of fuch/ A Walk With Go /as he left a Pattern of./ *London*,/ Printed by J. Aftwood for J. Dun [*date cut off*]/ *5 prel. leaves, and 60 pp.* 'Several Sermons/ Concerning,/ Walking/ with/ God,/ and that/ In the Dayes of Youth:/ Preached/ At Bofton in New-England./ By Cotton Mather, Paftor of a Church there./ *London*, Printed by J. Aftwood for J. Dunton, at the Black/ Raven in the Poultrey, over againft the Compter. 1689.'/ *Title and 86 pp. Old calf. Small 8vo.* (15s. 1861*)

MATHER (SAMUEL). The/ Figures/ or/ Types/

of the/ Old Teftament,/ by which/ Christ and the Heavenly Things of the/ Gofpel were Preached and Shadowed to the/ People of God of Old./ Explain'd and Improv'd in fundry/ Sermons./ By Samuel Mather, fometime Paftor/ of a Church in Dublin./ The Second Edition, To which is annex'd, (more than/ was in the former Edition) a Scheme and Table of the whole,/ whereby the Reader may readily turn to any Subject treated/ of in this Book./ *London*,/ Printed for Nath. Hillier, at the Prince's Arms in Leaden-/hall-ftreet, over againft St. Mary Axe, 1705./ *6 prel. leaves; viz. Title, and To the Reader, vii pp. Signed* 'Nathanael Mather.' *Books &c. 1 page, Scheme 4 pp. Text 540 pp. Table 11 pp. Errata 1 page. Old calf. 4to.* (1*l*. 5*s*. 1862)

MATHER (SAMUEL). An Apology For the Liberties of the Churches in New England: To which is prefix'd, A Difcourfe concerning Congregational Churches. By Samuel Mather, M.A. Paftor of a Church in Bofton, New England. *Boston:* Printed by T. Fleet, for Daniel Henchman, over againft the Brick Meeting Houfe in Cornhill. 1738. *4 prel. leaves, ix pp. Errata 1 page, and text 116 pp. Old calf.* 8*vo*. (12*s*. 6*d*. 1863)

MAUDUIT (ISRAEL). A Short View of the History of the Colony of Massachusett's Bay, With Refpect to their Original Charter and Constitution. *London:* J. Wilkie, 1769. *Title and 71 pp. half morocco.* 8*vo*. (7*s*. 6*d*. 1864)

MAUDUIT (ISRAEL). A Short View of the History of the Colony of Maffachufetts Bay, With Refpect to their Charters and Constitution. By Israel Mauduit. The Third Edition, To which is now added the Original Charter granted to that Province in the 4th of Charles I. and never before printed in England. *London:* J. Wilkie, MDCCLXXIV. *Title, and pp. 5-93. half mor.* 8*vo*. (7*s*. 6*d*. 1865)

MAUDUIT (ISRAEL). A Short View of the History of the New England Colonies, With Refpect to their Charters and Constitution. By Israel Mauduit. The Fourth Edition, To which is now added, An Account of a Conference between the late Mr. Grenville and the feveral Colony Agents, in the Year 1764, previous to the paffing the Stamp Act.

Alfo the Original Charter granted in the 4th of
Charles I. and never before printed in England.
London: J. Wilkie, MDCCLXXVI. *Title, and pp.* 5-100.
half mor. 8vo. (7s. 6d. 1866)

MAW (HENRY LISTER). Journal of a Passage from
the Pacific to the Atlantic, crossing the Andes in
the Northern Provinces of Peru, and descending
the River Marañon, or Amazon. By Henry Lister
Maw, Lieut. R. N. *London:* John Murray,
MDCCCXXIX. *xv and* 486 *pp. With Map. Unbound.*
8vo. (5s. 6d. 1867)

MAXIMILIANUS (TRANSYLVANUS). De Molvccis
in/ fulis, itemq; alijs pluribus mirãdis, quæ/ nouiffima Caftellanorum nauigatio Se-/renifs. Imperatoris Caroli. V. aufpicio/ fufcepta, nuper inuenit:
Maximiliani/ Tranfyluani ad Reuerendifs. Car-
dina-/lem Saltzburgenfem epiftola lectu per-/quam
iucunda./ [*Colophon*] *Coloniæ* in ædibus Eucharij
Ceruicorni. Anno uir-/ginei partus. M. D. XXIII.
menfe/ Ianuario.·./ 15 *unfolioed leaves; Signature*
A. *in eight,* B. *in seven leaves. Red morocco extra
by Bedford. Small* 8vo. (4l. 14s. 6d. 1868)

MAYHEW (EXPERIENCE). Grace Defended, in a
Modeft Plea for an Important Truth; Namely,
That the Offer of Salvation made to Sinners in the
Gofpel, comprifes in it an Offer of the Grace given
in Regeneration. And Shewing the Confiftency
of this Truth with the Free and Sovereign Grace
of God, in the whole Work of Man's Salvation.
In Which The Doctrine of Original Sin and Humane Impotence, the Object and Extent of Redemption, the Nature of Regeneration, the Difference between Common and Special Grace, the
Nature of juftifying Faith, and other Important
Points, are confidered and cleared. By Experience
Mayhew. *Boston:* Printed by B. Green, and Company, for D. Henchman, in Cornhil. 1744. *Title,
vi and* 208 *pp.* 8vo. (10s. 6d. 1869)

MAYHEW (JONATHAN). Seven Sermons Upon
the following Subjects; viz. I. The Difference
betwixt Truth and Falfhood, Right and Wrong.
II. The natural Abilities of Men for discerning
thefe Differences. III. The Right and Duty of
private Judgment. IV. Objections confidered.

V. The Love of God. VI. The Love of our Neighbour. VII. The firſt and great Commandment, &c. Preached at a Lecture in the Weſt Meeting-Houſe in Boston, Begun the firſt Thurſday in June, and ended the laſt Thurſday in Auguſt, 1748. By Jonathan Mayhew, D.D. Paſtor of the Weſt Church in Boſton. Firſt Printed at Boston in New-England. *London* Reprinted, John Noon, MDCCL. 3 *prel. leaves and text* 132 *pp. Unbound.* 8*vo.* (4*s.* 6*d.* 1870)

MAYHEW (JONATHAN). A Discourse Occaſioned by the Death of The Honourable Stephen Sewall, Eſq; Chief-Tustice of the Superiour Court of Judicature, Court of Aſſize, and General-Goal-Delivery; as alſo A Member of His Majesty's Council for the Province of the Massachusetts-Bay in New-England: Who departed this Life On Wedneſday-Night, September 10. 1760. Ætatis 58. Delivered the Lord's-Day after his Deceaſe. By Jonathan Mayhew, D.D. Paſtor of the Weſt-Church in Boston. *Boston:* Printed by Richard Draper, in Newbury-Street: Edes and Gill, in Queen-Street: And Thomas and John Fleet, in Cornhill. MDCCLX. *Title, and pp.* 5-66. *half mor.* 8*vo.* (5*s.* 6*d.* 1871)

MAYHEW (JONATHAN). Observations on the Charter and Conduct of the Society for the Propagation of the Gospel in Foreign Parts; designed to shew Their Non-conformity to each other. With Remarks on the Mistakes of East Apthorp, M.A. Miſſionary at Cambridge, in Quoting and Repreſenting the Senſe of ſaid Charter, &c. As also Various incidental Reflections relative to the Church of England, and the State of Religion in North-America, particularly in New-England. By Jonathan Mayhew, D.D. Paſtor of the Weſt-Church in Boston, To which is subjoined Apthorp's Considerations. Boston, in New-England, printed: *London,* reprinted for W. Nicoll, MDCCLXIII. 164 *pp. half mor.* 8*vo.* (5*s.* 6*d.* 1872)

MAYHEW (JONATHAN). An Answer to Dr. Mayhew's Obſervations on the Charter and Conduct of the Society for the Propagation of the Gospel in Foreign Parts. *London,* John Rivington, M.DCC. LXIV. 68 *pp. half mor.* 8*vo.* (4*s.* 6*d.* 1873)

MAYHEW (Jonathan). The Claims of the Church of England feriously examined: In a letter to the Author of an Answer to Dr. Mayhew's observations on the Charter and Conduct of the Society for Propagating the Gofpel in Foreign Parts. By a Protestant Diffenter of Old England. *London*: W. Nicholl, 1764. 28 *pages. Half morocco.* 8vo. (4s. 6d. 1874)

MAYHEW (Jonathan). A Defence Of the Observations on the Charter and Conduct of the Society for the Propagation of the Gofpel in Foreign Parts, against An anonymous Pamphlet falfly intitled, a Candid Examination Of Dr. Mayhew's Obfervations, &c. And also against The Letter to a Friend annexed thereto, faid to contain a short Vindication of faid Society. By one of its Members. By Jonathan Mayhew, D.D. Paftor of the West Church in Bofton. Boston printed: *London*: reprinted for W. Nicoll, M.DCC.LXIV. 120 *pp. half mor.* 8vo. (5s. 6d. 1875)

MAYHEW (Jonathan). Remarks on an Anonymous Tract, entitled An Answer to Dr. Mayhew's Observations On the Charter and Conduct of the Society for the Propagation of the Gofpel in Foreign Parts. Being a Second Defence of the faid Observations. By Jonathan Mayhew, D.D. Paftor of the West Church in Bofton. *Boston*: Printed and Sold by R. and S. Draper, in Newbury Street; Edes and Gill, in Queen-Street; and T. & J. Fleet, in Cornhill. 1764. 86 *pp.* 'Advertifement.' 1 *page Signed* 'J. Mayhew.' *Soliciting contributions in Europe, for the loss of the Library of Harvard College by Fire. Half mor.* 8vo. (5s. 6d. 1876).

MAYHEW (Jonathan). Sermons to Young Men. In Two Volumes. By Jonathan Mayhew, D.D. *London*, T. Becket MDCCLXVII. *Two Volumes.* Volume the First. *xx and* 275 *pp.* Volume the Second. *Title, iv and text* 304 *pp. Old calf.* 12mo. (8s. 6d. 1877)

MAYNAS. Copia de dos Cartas Escritas de vn/ Mifsionero, y del Superior de las Mifsiones de los Maynas,/ en el Rio Marañon, jurifdiccion de la Real Audiencia de Qui-/to, avifando al Padre Vice-Provincial de la Compañia de/ Iesvs, del Nuevo

Reyno de Granada; el vno, el eſtado del/ Pueblo en que aſsiſte; y el otro, el que tiene parte de aquella/ glorioſa Miſsion, que avia viſitado el año paſſado de 1681./ Primera Carta./ 4 *unfolioed pp. Folio.* (1*l*. 11*s*. 6*d*. 1878)

MEAD (Joseph). An Essay on Currents at Sea; By which it appears, There is Reaſon to apprehend, that the Sea is not a Fluid in a State of Rest, except thoſe Motions which are cauſed by the Impulse of Winds, and that known by the Name of Tides: And consequently, That this Earth is not of a uniform Denſity, according to the Suppoſition of Sir Isaac Newton; but that the Currents of the Gulph of Florida, alſo on the Coaſt of Braſil, and the Northern In-draught on this Weſtern Coaſt, are Currents of Circulation, kept up by different Denſities in this Earth, and its Motion round its Axis. By Joseph Mead. *London:* J. Marshall, M,DCC,LVII. *Title having on the reverse* 'Errata.' 5 *lines, Text* 48 *pp. half mor.* 8*vo.* (7*s*. 6*d*. 1879)

MEAD (Matthew). The Almoſt Chriſtian Discovered or, the Falſe Profeſſor Tryed and Cast. Being the Subſtance of Seven Sermons, Firſt Preached at Sepulchers, London, 1661 And now at the Importunity of Friends made Publick. The Fourteenth Edition. By Matthew Mead. *Boston*: Printed for Joſeph Edwards at the corner Shop on the North ſide of the Town-Houſe, & Hopeſtill Foſter in Cornhill. 1730. 4 *prel. leaves and* 194 *pp.* 12*mo.* (10*s*. 6*d*. 1880)

MEDINA (Antonio de). Sermon/ predicado en/ el Castillo de San Felipe/ del Puerto del Callao, a ſu Dedicacion y benedi-/cion; eſtando deſcubierto el Santiſsimo Sacra-/mento, y en preſencia de todo el/ Preſidio./ Por el P. F. Antonio de Medina del Orden/ de Predicadores, Letor de Teologia del Conuento del Cuzco, à onze/ de Mayo de 1625. años./ ¶ A Don Fernando de Castro Cavallero/ del Abito de Santiago, y Teniente de Capitan General, por el/ Excellentiſsimo Señor Marques de Guadalcaçar./ Virrey deſtos Reynos del Pirù./ Con licencia./ Impreſſo en *Lima;* por Geronymo de Contreras./ Año de 1625./ 18 *folioed leaves, half mor.* 4*to.* (10*s*. 6*d*. 1881)

MEDRANO (SEBASTIAN FERNANDEZ DE). Breve/ descripcion del/ Mundo/ o Guia Geographica/ de Medrano./ Lo mas principal de ella en Verſo., Dirigida/ A la Catholica Mageſtad del Rey Nueſtro Señor/ Don Carlos Segundo,/ Monarcha de las Eſpañas./ Debajo/ De la protecion del Excelentiſſimo Señor/ Marques de Jodar./ En *Brusselas,*/ En caſa de Lamberto Marchant,/ Mercader de Libros/ M.DC.LXXXVIII./ 108 *pp. Old calf*. 12*mo.* (10s. 6d. 1882)

MEMOIRES/ tovchant/ l'Etabliſſement/ d'vne/ Mission Chreſtienne/ dans/ le Troisieme Mónde,/ Autrement appellé,/ La Terre Auſtrale, Meridionale,/ Antartique, & Inconnuë./ Dediez à Noſtre S. Pere le Pape/ Alexandre VII./ Par vn Eccleſiaſtique Originaire de cette/ meſme Terre. [Juan Paulymer]/ A *Paris,*/ Chez Clavde Cramoisy, ruë Saint/ Victor, proche la place Maubert,/ au Sacrifice d'Abel./ M.DC.LXIII./ Avec privilege dv Roy./ 18 *prel. leaves and* 216 *pp. With copperplate map of the World. Old calf*. 8*vo.* (1*l.* 11*s.* 6*d.* 1883)

MEMOIRES des Commissaires du Roi et de ceux de sa Majesté Britannique, Sur les poſſeſſions & les droits reſpectifs des deux Couronnes en Amérique; Avec les Actes publics & Piéces juſtificatives. Contenant les Mémoires ſur l'Acadie & ſur l'iſle de Sainte-Lucie. A *Paris,* de l'Imprimerie Royale. M.DCCLV. *Four Volumes.* Tome Premier. *viii; lxxv; and* 181 *pp.* ' Premier Memoire' *etc.* 61 *pp.* ' Memoire de Messieurs les Commissaires Anglois,' *etc. cvii pp.* 'Second Memoire,' *etc.* 120 *pp. Map.* Tome Second. *xiii and* 646 *pp.* Tome Troisième. *xvi and* 319 *pp.* Tome Quatrième, M.DCCLVII. 3 *prel. leaves; xxv and* 654 *pp. Map. Fine copy. Calf extra.* 4*to.* (3*l.* 13*s.* 6*d.* 1884)

MEMOIRS of an Unfortunate Young Nobleman, Return'd from a Thirteen Years Slavery in America, Where he had been ſent by the Wicked Contrivances of his Cruel Uncle. A Story founded on Truth, and addreſs'd equally to the Head and Heart. *London:* J. Freeman, MDCCXLIII. *Halftitle, title, and* 277 *pp. Old calf.* 12*mo.* (8*s.* 6*d.* 1885)

MEMOIRS of the Principal Tranſactions of the Last War between the English and French in North

America. From the Commencement of it in 1744, to the Conclufion of the Treaty at Aix la Chapelle. Containing in Particular An Account of the Importance of Nova Scotia or Acadie and Ifland of Cape Breton to both Nations. [By William Shirley.] *London:* R. and J. Dodsley, M.DCC.LVII. *viii and* 102 *pp. half mor. 8vo.* (7s. 6d. 1886)

MEMOIRS of the Principal Tranfactions of the Last War between the Englifh and French in North-America. From the Commencement of it in 1744, to the Conclufion of the Treaty at Aix la Chapelle. Containing in Particular An Account of the Importance of Nova Scotia or Acadie, and the Ifland of Cape Breton to both Nations. The Third Edition. London, Printed. *Boston,* New-England; Re-printed and Sold by Green and Russell, at their Printing-Office in Queen-ftreet. MDCCLVIII. *iv and* pp. 9-80. *8vo.* (7s. 6d. 1888)

MEMORIAL/ (✠)/ de lo Svcedido en/ la ciudad de Mexico, defde el dia pri/mero de Nouiembre, de 1623. haf/ta quienze de Enero de/ 1624./ 28 *folioed leaves. Folio.* (1l. 1s. 1889)

MEMORIAL (A) Relating to the Tobacco-Trade. Offer'd to The Confideration of the Planters of Virginia and Maryland. *Williamsburgh:* Printed by William Parks, M,DCC,XXXVII. 25 *pp.* Signed ' Daniel Mac Kercher.' *half mor. 8vo.* (10s. 6d. 1890)

MEMORIALS (The) of the Englifh and French Commissaries concerning St. Lucia. *London;* Printed in the Year MDCCLV. *Title and* 550 *pp. Fine copy. Old calf. 4to.* (1l. 1s. 1891)

MEMORIALS (The) of the Englifh and French Commissaries Concerning the Limits of Nova Scotia or Acadia. *London:* Printed in the Year MDCCLV. 2 *prel. leaves, and* 771 *pp. Map. Fine copy. Old calf. 4to.* (1l. 10s. 1892)

MENDOCA (Juan Gonçales de). Historia/ de las Cosas/ mas Notables,/ Ritos y Costvmbres,/ Del gran Reyno dela China, fabidas affi por los libros/ delos mefmos Chinas, como por relacion de Religio-/fos y otras perfonas que an eftado en el dicho Reyno./ Hecha y ordenada por el mvy R. P. Maestro Fr. Ioan Gonçalez de Mendoça dela Orden de S. Auguſtin, y peniten-/ciatio Appoſtolico a quien la Mageſtad Catholica embio con ſu real/ carta y otras coſas para el Rey de aquel Reyno el año. 1580./ Al Illvstrissimo S. Fernando/ de Vega y Fonſeca del conſejo de ſu Mageſtad y ſu/ preſidente en el Real delas Indias./ Con vn Itinerario del nueuo Mundo./ Con Priuilegio y Licencia de ſu Sanctidad./ En *Roma*, a coſta de Bartholome Graſſi. 1585/ en la Stampa de Vincentio Accolti./ 16 *prel. leaves, the* 16*th blank; and* 440 *pp. Vellum.* 8*vo.* (15*s.* 1893)

MENDOCA (JUAN GONÇALES DE). Dell' Historia/ della China,/ Deſcritta nella lingua Spagnuola, dal P. Maeſtro/ Giouanni Gonzalez di Mendozza,/ dell' Ord. di S. Agoſtino./ Et tradotta nell' Italiana, dal Magn. M. Franceſco/ Auanzo, cittadino originario di Venetia./ Parti dve,/ Diuiſe in tre libri, & in tre viaggi, fatti in quei paeſi,/ da i Padri Agoſtiniani & Franciſcani./ Doue ſi deſcriue il ſito, & lo ſtato di quel gran Regno,/ & ſi tratta della religione, de i coſtumi, & della/ diſpoſition de ſuoi popoli, & d'altri luochi/ più conoſciuti del mondo nuouo./ Con due Tauole, l'vna de' Capitoli, & l'altra delle coſe notabili./ In *Venetia*, MDLXXXVI./ Appreſſo Andrea Muſchio./ 16 *prel. leaves, the* 16*th blank, and* 462 *pp*; 1 *blank leaf, and* ' Tavola,' *etc.* 40 *pp. Vellum.* 8*vo.* (15*s.* 1894)

MENDOCA (JUAN GONÇALES DE). L'Historia/ del gran Regno/ della China,/ Compoſta primieramente in iſpagnuolo da/ maeſtro Giouanni Gonzalez di Men-/dozza, monaco dell' ordine di/ S. Agoſtino:/ Et poi fatta vulgare da Franceſco Auanzi/ cittadino Vinetiano./ Stampata la terza volta, & molto più dell' al-/tre emendata./ Con due tauole l'una dé Capitoli, & l'altra delle/ coſe più notabili./ In *Vinegia*. 1587./ Per Andrea Muſchio./ 508 *pp.* ' Lo ſtampatore,' *etc.* 1 *page;* 'Tavola,' *etc.* 77 *pp.* ' Errori' *etc.* 1 *page. Old calf.* 12*mo.* (15*s.* 1895)

MENDOCA (JUAN GONÇALES DE). Histoire/ dv Grand/ Royavme de la/Chine, sitvé avx/ Indes orientales, diuiſée/ en deux parties./ Contenant en la Premiere, la ſituation, antiquité, fertilité,/ religion, ceremonies, ſacrifices, rois magiſtrats, mœurs,/

vs, loix, & autres chofes memorables dudit royaume./ Et en la Seconde, trois voyages faits vers iceluy en l'an/ 1577, 1579 & 1581. auec les fingularitez plus remarqua-/bles y veües & entendües: enfemble vn Itinerarie/ du nouueau monde, & le defcouurement du/ nouueau Mexique en l'an 1583./ Faite en efpagnol par R. P. Ivan Gonçales de Men-/doce, de l'ordre de S. Auguftin : & mife en François auec/ des additions en marge, & deux Indices./ Par Lvc de la Porte, Parifien,/ docteur és droits./ A/ Monseignevr le Chancelier./ A *Paris*, Chez Ieremie Perier, ruë S. Iean de/ Beuuais, au franc Meurier./ 1589./ Avec privilege dv Roy./ 12 *prel. leaves, and* 323 *folioed leaves;* ' Indice des choses Notables,' *etc.* 48 *pp.* ' Tautes,' *etc.* 1 *page. Old calf.* 8vo. (1l. 1s. 1896)

MENDOZA (DIEGO DE). Chronica/ de la Provincia de S. Antonio/ de los Charcas/ del orden de Nr̃o. Seraphico P./ S. Francisco/ En la Indias Occidentales Reyno del Peru/ Escrita/ por el R. P. Predicador F. Diego de Mendoza/ Chronifta y l'adre de la mesma Prouincia./ Dedicala/ Al Illmo. Yr^{mo}. S. D. F. Gabriel/ de Guillestegui del Confejo de fu Mag^d./ y Obifpo del Paraguay./ P'a Villafranca fculptor Regius, fculpfit *Matriti*, 1664./ *Engraved title*, 14 *prel. leaves, and* 601 *pp.* 'Protesta de el Autor.' 1 *page;* ' Indice de los Capitvlos,' *etc.* 6 *pp. Vellum. Folio.* (2l. 2s. 1897)

MERCATOR (GERARDUS). Gerardi Mercatoris/ Atlas/ sive/ Cosmographicæ/ Meditationes/ de/ fabrici Mundi et/ fabricati Figvra./ Iam tandem ad finem perductus, quamplurimus æneis ta=/bulis Hispaniæ, Africæ, Afiæ & Americæ auctus ac/ illuftratus à Iudoco Hondio. Quibus etiam additæ (præter Mercatoris) dilucidæ & accuratæ omnium tabu=/larum defcriptiones novæ, ftudio et opera Pet. Montani./ Excufum in ædibus Iudoci Hondij *Amsterodami*. 1606. 10 *prel. leaves, and* 354 *pp. Index etc.* 18 *leaves. Maps with the text. Fine copy. Old calf. Large Folio.* (1l. 11s. 6d. 1898)

MERCATOR (GERARDUS). Atlas/ Minor/ Gerardi Mercatoris/ à I. Hondio plurimis æneis tabulis/ auctus atque illuftratus./ *Amsterodami*/ Excusum in ædibus Iudoci Hondij./ veneunt etiam apud

Corneliũ Nicolai./ item apud Ioannem Ianſoniũ Arnhemi./ [*Colophon*] *Dordrechti*/ Excudebat Adrianus Bottius/ Anno cɪɔ ɪɔ cx./   4 *prel. leaves, and* 684 *pp.   Vellum.   Oblong* 4*to*.   (15*s*.   1899)

MERCATOR (GERARDUS). [*Engraved title*] Historia lvx ævi/ Geographia Mvndi./ Historia Mvndi/ or Mercators Atlas. Containing his Cosmographicall Descriptions/ of the Fabricke and Figure of the world./ Latelij rectified in diuers places, as alſo beutified/ and enlarged with new Mapps and Tables/ by the Studious industrie of Iodocvs Hondy/ Englished by W. S. Generosus & Regin: Oxoniæ./   London/ Printed for/ Michaell/ Sparke, and are to be ſowld in/ greene Arbowre/ 1637/ Second Edytion/ [*Printed title*] Historia Mvndi¨:/ Or/ Mercator's/ Atlas./ Containing his Cosmographicall/ Deſcription of the Fabricke and/ Figure of the World./ Lately reƈtified in divers places, as alſo beautified/ and enlarged with new Mappes and Tables ;/ By the Studious induſtry,/ Of/ Ivdocvs Hondy./ Englished/ By/ W. S./ Generoſus, & Coll. Regin. Oxoniæ./   *London*/ Printed by T. Cotes, for Michael Sparke and/ Samuel Cartwright. 1635./   12 *prel. leaves; 56 pp; The Preface upon Atlas* 2 *pp. and* 930 *pp.   Tables etc.* 32 *pp.   Old calf. Folio.*   (1*l*. 1*s*.   1900)

MESSAGES (THREE) from the President of the United States, to the Congress, in November 1811, Together with Documents accompanying the same. Washington; Printed 1811: *London:* Reprinted for J. Hatchard, 1812. 260 *pp.* 8*vo.* (4*s*. 6*d*.   1901)

MEXICO. Album Méjicano Tributo de gratitud al Civismo nacional Retratos de los Personages iluſtres de la primera y segunda época de la Independencia Mejicana y notabilidades de la présente. *Méjico* C. L. Prudhomme Editor 2ª Calle de los Plateros Nº. 12. 1843. *Title, Advertencia, and* 21 *plates, each with* 4 *portraits.* 4*to.* (10*s*. 6*d*.   1902)

M'FINGAL: A Modern Epic Poem, in Four Cantos. By John Trumbull. The Fifth Edition, With Explanatory Notes. *London:* J. S. Jordan, M,DCCXCII. *xv and* 142 *pp.* 8*vo.*   (7*s*. 6*d*.   1903)

MICHAUX (F. A.). Travels to the Westward of

the Allegany Mountains, in the States of the Ohio, Kentucky, and Tennessee, and return to Charlestown, through the Upper Carolinas; containing details on the present State of Agriculture and the Natural Productions of these Countries; as well as information relative to the commercial connections of these States with those situated to the Eastward of the Mountains and with Lower Louisiana. Undertaken in the year X, 1832, under the auspices of His Excellency M. Chaptal, Minister of the Interior. With a very correct Map of the States in the Centre, West and South of the United States. By F. A. Michaux, M.D. Member of the Society of Natural History of Paris, and Correspondent of the Society of Agriculture of the Department of the Seine and Oise. Faithfully Translated from the Original French, by B. Lambert. *London:* J. Mawman, 1805. *xvi and* 350 *pp. Map, boards.* 8*vo.* (7*s.* 6*d.* 1904)

MICHAUX (F. A.). Travels to the West of the Alleghany Mountains, in the States of Ohio, Kentucky, and Tennessea, and back to Charleston, by the Upper Carolines; comprising The most interesting Details on the present State of Agriculture, and the Natural produce of those Countries: Together with Particulars relative to the Commerce that exists between the above-mentioned States, and those situated East of the Mountains and Low Louisiana, Undertaken, in the Year 1802, under the auspices of His Excellancy M. Chaptal, Minister of the Interior, By F. A. Michaux, Member of the Society of Natural History at Paris; Correspondent of the Agricultural Society in the Department of the Seine and Oise. Second Edition. *London:* B. Crosby & Co. 1805. *xii and* 294 *pp. Calf.* 8*vo.* (7*s.* 6*d.* 1905)

MIDDLETON (CHRISTOPHER). A Vindication of the Conduct of Captain Chriftopher Middleton, in a Late Voyage on Board His Majefty's Ship the Furnace, for Difcovering a North-weft Paffage to the Weftern American Ocean. In Answer To certain Objections and Afperfions of Arthur Dobbs, Efq; with an Appendix: Containing The Captain's Inftructions; Councils held; Reports of the Inferior Officers; Letters between Mr. Dobbs, Capt.

Middleton, &c. Affidavits and other Vouchers refer'd to in the Captain's Anſwers, &c. With as much of the Log-Journal as relates to the Discovery. The Whole as lately deliver'd to the Lords Commiſſioners of the Admiralty. To which is annex'd, An Account of the Extraordinary Degrees and Surprizing Effects of Cold in Hudſon's-Bay, North America, read before the Royal Society. By Christopher Middleton, Late Commander of the Furnace, and F.R.S. *London:* Jacob Robinſon, 1743. 2 *prel. leaves, and* 206 *pp.* 'Several Abbreviations,' *etc.* 1 *page. Log-Journal* 48 *pp. Old calf.* 8*vo.* (7*s.* 6*d.* 1906)

MIDDLETON (CHRISTOPHER). A Vindication of the Conduct of Captain Chriſtopher Middleton, in a Late Voyage on Board His Majesty's Ship the Furnace. For Diſcovering a North-Weſt Paſſage to the Weſtern American Ocean. In Answer To certain Objections and Aſperſions of Arthur Dobbs, Eſq; with an Appendix: Containing The Captain's Inſtructions; Councils held; Reports of the Inferior Officers, Letters between Mr. Dobbs, Capt. Middleton, &c. Affidavits and other Vouchers refer'd to in the Captain's Anſwers, &c. With as much of the Log-Journal as relates to the Discovery. The Whole as lately deliver'd to the Lords Commiſſioners of the Admiralty. To which is Annex'd, An Account of the Extraordinary Degrees and Surprizing Effects of Cold in Hudſon's-Bay, North-America, read before the Royal Society. By Christopher Middleton, Late Commander of the Furnace, and F.R.S. *Dublin:* J. Jackson, M,DCC, XLIV. 168 *and* 48 *pp. half mor.* 8*vo.* (7*s.* 6*d.* 1907)

MIDDLETON (CHRISTOPHER). A Reply to the Remarks of Arthur Dobbs, Eſq; on Capt. Middleton's Vindication of his Conduct on board his Majesty's Ship the Furnace, when Sent in Search of a North-weſt Passage, by Hudson's-Bay, to the Weſtern American Ocean. Humbly Inſcribed to the Right Honorable the Lords Commissioners for executing the Office of Lord High Admiral of Great-Britain and Ireland, &c. By Christopher Middleton, Eſq; *London:* George Brett, MDCCXLIV. *x and* 192 *pp.* 'Appendix' 94 *pp. Errata and Index,* 8 *pp.* 8*vo.* (7*s.* 6*d.* 1908)

MIDDLETON (CHRISTOPHER). Forgery Detected. By which is evinced how groundless are All the Calumnies caſt upon the Editor, in a Pamphlet publiſhed under the Name of Arthur Dobbs, Esq ; By Capt. Christopher Middleton, late Commander of his Majeſty's Ship, Furnace, when ſent upon the Search of a North-Weſt Paſſage to the Weſtern American Ocean. *London:* M. Cooper, M.DCC.XLV. *Title, v and 35 pp. half mor. 8vo.* (10s. 6d. 1909)

MILIUS (ABRAHAM). De Origine/ Animalium,/ et Migratione/ Populorum,/ Scriptum Abrahami Milii./ Ubi inquiritur, quomodo quaque via Homines cætera-/que Animalia Terreſtria provenerint; & poſt De-/luvium in omnes Orbis terrarum partes & regiones :/ Aſiam, Europam, Africam, utramque Americam,/ & Terram Auſtralem, ſive Magellanicam pervene-/rint./ *Genevæ :/* Apud Petrum Columesium. M.DC.LXVII./ 68 pp. *Calf extra by Bedford. 12mo.* (15s. 1910)

MILLS (HENRY JAMES). Mills's Trinidad Almanac and Pocket Register for the Year of our Lord 1840, Being Bissextile or Leap Year. Calculated to the Meridian of Port of Spain. Port of Spain is situated in Latitude 10 deg. 39 m. N. Longitude 61 deg, 34 m. W. *Port of Spain.* Henry James Mills, [1840] 62 pp. *With Plan.* 'Trinidad imports etc. 1839.' *folded sheet at page 60. 12mo.* (2s. 6d. 1911)

MILLS (SAMUEL J.) Report of a Missionary Tour through that part of the United States which lies West of the Allegany Mountains ; performed under the direction of the Massachusetts Missionary Society. By Samuel J. Mills and Daniel Smith. *Andover:* Flagg and Gould. 1815. 64 pp. *Uncut. 8vo.* (2s. 6d. 1912)

MILTON (CHARLES WILLIAM). Narrative of the Gracious dealings of God in the Conversion of W. Mooney Fitzgerald and John Clark, two malefactors, Who were Executed on Friday, Dec. 18, 1789, At St. John's New Brunſwick, Nova Scotia, for Burglary; in a Letter from The Reverend Mr. Milton to the Right Honourable the Countess Dowager of Huntingdon. *London:* Printed in the year 1790. 22 pp. *12mo.* (4s. 6d. 1913)

MINISTERIAL (A) Catechise, Suitable to be Learned by all Modern Provincial Governors, Penfioners, Placemen, &c. Dedicated to T - - - - - - H - - - - - - - - -, Efq. *Boston*: Printed and Sold by Isaiah Thomas, near the Mill-Bridge. MDCCLXXI. 8 *pp. half mor.* 8*vo*. (10s. 6d. 1914)

MINOT (GEORGE RICHARDS). The History of the Insurrections, in Massachusetts, In the Year MDCCLXXXVI, and the Rebellion consequent thereon. By George Richards Minot, A.M. Printed at Worcester, Massachusetts, by Isaiah Thomas. MDCCLXXXVIII. 192 *pp*. 8*vo*. (7s. 6d. 1915)

MISSA Gothica seù Mozarabica, et Officium itidèm Gothicum diligentèr ac dilucidè explanata ad Usum Percelebris Mozárabum Sacelli Toleti á Munificentissimo Cardinali Ximenio erecti; et in Obsequium Ill^{mi}. Perindè ac Venerab. D. Decani et Capituli Sanctae Ecclesiae Toletanae, Hispaniarum et Indiarum Primátis. *Angelopoli*: Typis Seminarii Palafoxiani Anno Domini M.DCC.LXX. 4 *prel. leaves*; 137 *and* 198 *pp*. *2 Copperplates*. *Old red morocco*. *Folio*. (3*l*. 13*s*. 6*d*. 1916)

MITCHIL (JONATHAN). A/ Discourse/ of the/ Glory/ To which God hath called/ Believers/ By Jesus Christ./ Delivered in fome Sermons out/ of the I Pet. 5 Chap. 10 Ver./ Together with an annexed Letter./ Both, by that Eminent and Worthy Mi/nifter of the Gofpel, Mr. Jonathan/ Mitchil, late Paftor to the Church/ at Cambridge in New-England. *London*: Printed for Nathaniel Ponder at the/ Peacock in the Poultry, Anno Dom. 1677./ 8 *prel. leaves; viz. Title*, 'To the Reader.' 11 *pp.* signed 'John Collins.' *Text* 263 *pp*. 'A Letter,' *etc*. 20 *pp*. *Small* 8*vo*. (15*s*. 1917)

MOCQUET (JAN). Wunderbare/ Jedoch/ Gründlich=und warhaffte Gefchichte/ und/ Reife Begebniffe/ In Africa, Afia, Oft=und/ West=Indien/ von/ Jan Mocquet aus Frankreich,/ Ihrer Königlichen Majeftät Heinrichs des Groffen oder IV./ und Ludwigs des XIII. dafelbft gewefnen geheimen Hof= und Cammer=/Apotheckers, wie auch wolbeftellten Verwefers, derer dafelbft befindlichen frem=den,/ ausländifchen, und in unfern Landen unbekannten Früchten, Gewächfen, Kräutern/ und Blumen, in dero Königlichen Refidenz=Stadt zu Paris,/ in der Tuillerie./ Nebft eigent=licher Befchreibung derer Städte, Königreiche, Infeln und/ Provinzen, wie felbige itziger Zeit annoch zu befinden, und Er zu verfchiednen/ malen mit langwirigen Sorgen, Mühe und Befchwerniffen zu Waffer und Lande, in Hitz und/ Froft, Hunger und Durft, Armuth und Mangel, nach unzehlich erdultetem Elend und/ Ungemach, in höchfter Lebens=Gefahr, Krankheit und Gefängniffen, auch endlich erlittnen/ Schiffbruch, ganzer zwanzig Jahr, durch Gottes Gnade, durchzureifen/ über fich genommen, ausgeftanden und geendiget./ Allen Liebhabern verwun=derfamer Begebniffen und Reife=Gefchichten/ zu angenehmer Ergötzlichkeit in unterfchiednen Büchern aus dem Franzöfichen/ in Hochteutfche Sprache überfetzet und entdecket/ durch/ Johann Georg Schoeben. *Lüneburg,/* [1688.] In Verlegung Johann Georg Lippers./ *30 prel. leaves; Engraved Frontispiece; and Text 632 pp. Copperplates numbered 1 to X, and plan of* 'Ierusalem.' *4to.* (1*l.* 1*s.* 1918)

MODEST (A) Proof of the Order and Government Settled by Chrift and his Apoftles in the Church. By Shewing I. What Sacred Offices were inftituted by them. II. How thofe Offices were Diftinguifhed. III. That they were to be Perpetual Standing in the Church. And, IV. Who Succeed in them, and rightly Execute them to this Day. *Boston:* Reprinted by Tho. Fleet, and are to be Sold by Benjamin Eliot in Bofton, Daniel Aurault in Newport, Gabriel Bernon in Providence, Mr. Gallop in Briftol, Mr. Jean in Stratford, and in moft other Towns within the Colonies of Connecticut and Rhode-Ifland. 1723. *Title, v pp. and text 63 pp. Unbound.* 16*mo.* (1*l.* 1*s.* 1919)

MOLINA (Alonso de). Vocabvlario/ en lengva Castellana y Mexicana, [y Mexicana y Castellana] com-/puefto por el muy Reuerendo Padre Fray Alonfo de Molina, dela/ Orden del bienauenturado nueftro Padre fant Francifco./ Dirigido al mvy Excelente Senor/ Don Martin Enriquez, Viforrey deftanueua Efpaña./ En *Mexico,/* En Cafa de Antonio de Spinofa./ 1571./ [*Colophon.*] ¶ Soli Deo honor et Gloria./ ¶ Aqvi hazen fin los dos vocabvlarios, en lengva Caste/ llana y nahual o Mexicana que hizo y recopilo el muy Reuerendo padre, fray Alonſo de Mo-/lina : de la orden de ſeñor ſan Franciſco. Imprimieronſe enla muy inſigne y gran ciudad/ de Mexico : en caſa de Antonio de Spinoſa. enel Año de nueſtra redēpcion. de. 1571./ ¶ Nicantzon qvi ça yn ontetl vocabvlario Sy-/pan Caſtillan tlatolli yuan nauatlatolli, y oquimotlalili cenca mauiztililoni, to/ tatzin fray Alonſo de Molina, teupixqui Sant Franciſco. Omicuilo/ nican ypan vey altepetl ciudad Mexico : ychā/ Antonio de Spinoſo. Ypan xiuitl./ 1571. Años./ *Two Parts.* Part I. *4 prel. leaves; viz. Title, on the reverse,* ' Licencias.' ' *Epistola Nvncvpatoria.*' *2 pp;* '¶ Prologo al Lector.' *2 pp*; ' Avisos.' *2 pp; Text 121 folioed leaves,* ' Dirigatvr Oratiomea,' *etc. with woodcut figure 1 page, on the reverse woodcut device.* Part II. *Title, with woodcut of Saint Francis; on the reverse,* ' ¶ Prologo al Lector,' *and* ' Avisos.' *2 pp; Text 162 folioed leaves; the last leaf containing the colophon as above, and on the reverse a large woodcut device. Old calf.* *Folio.* (21*l*. 1920)

MOLINA (JUAN IGNATIUS). Essai sur l'Histoire Naturelle du Chili, Par M. l'Abbé Molina; Traduit de l'Italien, & enrichi de notes, Par M. Gruvel, D. M. *A Paris,* Née de la Rochelle, M.DCC. LXXXIX. *xvi pp. and text 352 pp. Old calf, gilt back.* 8*vo.* (7*s*. 6*d*. 1921)

MOLINA (JUAN IGNATIUS). The Geographical Natural, and Civil History of Chili. Translated from the original Italian of the Abbe Don J. Ignatius Molina. To which are added, Notes from the Spanish and French Versions, and two Appendixes, by the English Editor ; the first, an Account of the Archipelago of Chiloe, from the Descripcion Historial of P. F. Pedro Gonzalez de Agueros; the second, an Account of the Native Tribes who inhabit the Southern extremity of South America, extracted chiefly from Falkner's description of Patagonia. In Two Volumes. Longman, 1809. *Two Volumes.* Vol. I. *xx and* 321 *pp. Map.* Vol. II. *xii and* 385 *pp.* 8*vo.* (8*s*. 6*d*. 1922)

MONARDES (NICOLO). Primera y/ Segvnda y Tercera/ Partes de la Historia/ Medicinal de las cosas/ que ſe traen de nueſtras Indias Occi-/dentales que firuen en/ Medicina./ Tratado de la Piedra/ Bezaar, y dela yerua Efcuerconera./ Dialogo de las Gran-/dezas del Hierro, y de fus virtudes/ Medicinales/ Tratado de la Nieve y del beuer frio./ Hechos por el Do-/ɛtor Monardes Medico/ de Seuilla./ Van en esta impression/ la Tercera parte y el Dialogo del Hierro nueua-/mente hechos, que no han fido impreffos/ hafta agora. Do ay cofas grandes/ y dignas de faber./ ¶ Con licencia y Preuilegio de fu Mageftad./ En *Sevilla*/ En cafa de Alonfo Efcriuano./ 1574./ 6 prel. *leaves; viz. Title reverse blank;* 'Licencia y Previlegio.' *2 pp;* 'Elogio hecho,' *etc. 4 pp.* 'Sanctis D. N. Gregorio XIII. Pont. Opt. Max. Doct. Nicolaus Monardus Medicus Hifpalenfis. S.P.D.' *3 pp; Text 206 folioed leaves; Woodcut and Colophon on the reverse of folio* 206, 'In Lavdem Dotiffimi Nicolai Monardis Medici Hifpalensis.' 1 *page.* 'Erratas.' 1 *page. Vellum.* 4*to.* (2*l.* 2*s.* 1923)

MONARDES (NICOLO). ¶ Ioyfvll/ Nevves ovt of/ the newe founde worlde, wherein is/ declared the rare and fingular vertues of diuerfe/ and fundrie Hearbes, Trees, Oyles, Plantes, and Stones, with their aplications, af well for Phificke as Chirurgerie, the faied be/yng well applied bryngeth fuche prefent remedie for/ all defeafes, as maie feme altogether incredible:/ notwithftandyny by practize founde out,/ to bee true: Alfo the portrature of the faied Hearbes, very apt=/ly difcribed: Engli=/fhed by Jhon/ Framp=/ton/ Marchaunt./ ¶ Imprinted at *London* in/ Poules Churche-yarde, by/ Willyam Norton./ Anno Domini./ 1577./ 3 *prel. leaves; viz. Title, reverse blank,* '¶ To the right worfhipfull Maifter/ Edvvarde Dier Efquire, Jhon Framp-/ton wifheth muche healthe, with profpe-/rous and perfite felicitie./ 3 *pp. in Italics. Text in* 109 *folioed leaves;* 'The Table of the/ thinges that thefe three Bookes/ doe containe./' 2 *pp. Black Letter. First Edition.* 4*to.* (3*l.* 13*s.* 6*d.* 1924)

MONARDES (NICOLO). Delle cose,/ che vengono/ portate dall' Indie/ Occidentali pertinenti all' vfo/ della Medicina./ Raccolte, & trattate dal Dottor Nicolò/ Monardes, Medico in Siuiglia,/ Parte Prima./ Nouamente recata dalla Spagnola nella nostra/ lingua Italiana./ Doue ancho tratta de Veneni,

& della lor cura./ Aggiuntiui doi Indici; vno de' Capi principali; l'altro delle cofe piu ri-/leuanti, che fi ritrouano in tutta l'opera./ Con privilegio./ In Venetia, Appreſſo Giordan Ziletti. 1582./ 8 *prel. leaves*; *viz. Title the reverse blank*, ' Al Clarisſimo mio Sig. osservand. Il Sig. Andrea Contarini, fu del Clarifs. M. Dionigi.' 6 *pp.* 'Giordan Ziletti a' Lettori.' *3 pp. the reverse blank*; 'Capi del primo libro.' *1 page; and one blank leaf. Text* 249 *pp.* 'Tavola.' 13 *pp.* 'Dve Libri/ dell' Historia/ de i Semplici, Aromati,/ et altre cose; che venegono/ portate dall' Indie Orientali pertinenti/ all' vſo dell Medicina./ Di. Don Garzia dall' Horto,/ Medico Portugheſe; con alcune breui Annotationi/ di Carlo Clvsio./ Et dve Altri Libri/ Parimente di quelle che ſi portano dall' Indie Occidentali,/ Di Nicolò Monardes, Medico di Siuiglia./ Hora tutti tradotti dalle loro lingue nella noſtra Italiana da M./ Annibale Briganti, Marrucino da Ciuità di Chieti, Dottore & Medico excellentiſſimo./ Con Privilegio./ In *Venetia*, Appreſſo Francefco Ziletti. 1582./ *12 prel. leaves; viz. Title the reverse blank*, ' All' lllvstriss. Signore il Signor Don Ferrante de Alarcon, e di Mendoza, Marchefe della Valle.' 9 *pp. the reverse blank*; 'Tavola' 12 *pp*; *Text* 347 *pp. Vellum.* 8*vo.* (1*l.* 11*s.* 6*d.* 1925)

MONARDES (Nicolo). Ioyfvll Newes/ Out of the New-found/ VVorlde./ Wherein are declared, the rare and/ finguler vertues of diuers Herbs, Trees,/ Plantes, Oyles & Stones, with their ap-/plications, aſ well to the vſe of Phiſicke, as of/ Chirurgery: which being well applyed, bring/ ſuch prefent remedie for all difeafes, as may/ feeme altogether incredible: notwith-/ſtanding by practice found out/ to be true./ Alſo the portrature of the faid Hearbs,/ verie aptly defcribed:/ Engliſhed by John Frampton Marchant./ Newly corrected as by conference with/ the olde copies may appeare. Wher=/vnto are added three other bookes/ treating of the Bezaar ſtone, the herb/ Eſcuerconera, the properties of Iron/ and Steele in Medicine, and the be=/nefit of Snow./ *London*,/ Printed by E. Allde. by the afsigne of/ Bonham Norton./ 1596./ *3 prel. leaves; viz. Title in a broad type metal border, the reverse blank*, '¶ To the right worfhipful Mayſter/ Edwarde Dier Eſquier, Iohn Frampton wi-/ſheth

much health, with prosperous and/ perfect felicitie./
Signed ' John Frampton.' 3 *pp. in roman type;
Text in* 187 *folioed leaves. Black Letter. Green
Morocco extra. Fine copy.* 4to. (2*l.* 12*s.* 6*d.* 1926)

MONARDES (Nicolo). Histoire des/ Simples
Medica-/mens Apportés de l'A-meriqve, defqvels/
on fe fert en la Medicine./ Efcrite premierement en
Efpangnol, par M. Nicolas/ Monard, Medecin de
Siuille./ Du defpuis mife en Latin, & illuftrée de
plufieurs Annota-/tions, par Charles l'Eclufe d'
Arras./ Et nouuellement traduicte en François
par Anthoine Colin/ Maiftre Apoticaire Iuré de la
ville de Lyon./ Edition feconde augmentée de
plufieurs fi-/gures & Annotations./ *A Lyon,*/ Aux
defpens de Iean Pillehotte,/ à l'enfeigne du nom
de Iesvs./ M.DC.XIX./ Auec Priuilege du Roy./
262 *pp. Table, etc.* 6 *pp.* 8*vo.* (10*s.* 6*d.* 1927)

MONROE (James). A View of the Conduct of the
Executive in the Foreign Affairs of the United
States, as connected with the Mission to the French
Republic, during the years 1794, 5, and 6. By
James Monroe, late Minister Plenipotentiary to
the said Republic. Illustrated by his Instructions
and Correspondence, and other Authentic Documents. The Second Edition. Philadelphia, Printed.
London: Reprinted for James Ridgway, 1798.
viii and 117 *pp.* 8*vo.* (2*s.* 6*d.* 1928)

MONTANO (Benito Arias). Relacion Cierta y
Verdadera,/ del famofo fuceffo y vitoria que tuvo
el Capitan/ Benito Arias Montano, fobrino del
doctifsimo Arias Montano, natural de Eftremadura,
Gover-/nador y Capitan general de la Provincia de
la nue/va Andaluzia, y ciudad de Cumana, y Alcayde de/ la fuerea de Araya, por el Rey nueftro
feñor, con/tra los enemigos Oladefes, q eftavan fortificados/ en una falina que eftá riberas del rio Vñare,
que es/ en efta governacion, veynte y quatro leguas
de la/ ciudad de Cumana, efte año de 1633./ [*Colophon*] Con licencia, impreffo en Sevilla por Francifco de Lyra,/ Año de 1634./ 4 *pp. half morocco.
Folio.* (1*l.* 11*s.* 6*d.* 1929)

MONTANUS (Arnold). [*Engraved title*] America/
T'Amsterdam/ By Jacob van Meurs, Plaetfnyder

en Boeckverkooper op de Keyfers graft in de Stadt Meurs. 1671./ [Printed title] De Nieuwe en Onbekende/ Weereld :/ Of/ Beschryving/ van/ America/ in 't Zuid-Land,/ Vervaetende/ d'Oorfprong der Americaenen en Zuid-/landers, gedenkwaerdige togten derwaerds,/ Gelegendheid/ Der vafte Kuften, Eilanden, Steden, Sterkten, Dorpen, Tempels,/ Bergen, Fonteinen, Stroomen, Huifen, de natuur van Beeften, Boomen, Planten en vreemde Gewaffchen, Gods-dienft en Zeden, Wonderlijke/ Voorvallen, Vereeuwde en Nieuwe Oorloogen :/ Verciert met Af-beeldfels na 't leven in America gemaekt, en befchreeven/ Door/ Arnoldus Montanus./ t'*Amsterdam*,/ By Jacob Meurs Boek-verkooper en Plaet-fnyder, op de Kaifars-graft,/ fchuin over der Wefter-markt, in de ftad Meurs. Anno 1671. Met Privilegie./ 4 *prel. leaves and* 585 *pp*: 'Blad-Wyzer,' *etc.* 25 *pp*; ' Naemen der Schryvers,' *etc.* 1 *page*; ' Aenwyzing Voor der Boekbinders' *etc.* 1 *page*. Portrait of ' Ioan Maurits, Prius van Nassouw.' *and* 54 *Maps and Plates.*
Folio. (1*l*. 1*s*. 1930)

MONTCALM (Marquis de). Lettres de Monsieur Le Marquis de Montcalm, Gouverneur-General en Canada; a Messieurs de Berryer & de la Molé, Ecrites dans les Années 1757, 1758, & 1759. Avec une Verfion Angloife. A *Londres*: J. Almon, m.dcc.lxxvii. Letters from the Marquis de Montcalm, Governor-General of Canada; to Meffrs. De Berryer & de la Molé, In the Years 1757, 1758, and 1759. With an Englifh Tranflation. *London*: J. Almon, m.dcc.lxxvii. *Title, and* 28 *pp. doubly numerated. French and English. Half morocco.*
8*vo*. (7*s*. 6*d*. 1931)

MONTESINOS (Fernando de). Avto/ de la Fe/ celebrado en/ Lima a 23. de Enero/ de 1639./ Al Tribvnal del Santo Ofi-/cio de la Inquificion, de los Reynos del Perù,/ Chili, Paraguay, y Tucuman./ Por el licenciado D. Fer-/nando de Montefinos Presbitero, natural de Offuna./ Con Licencia/ de sv Excelencia, del Ordi-/nario, y del fanto Oficio. Impreffo en *Lima*,/ por Pedro de Cabrera; Año de 1639./ Vendenfe en la tienda de Simon Chirinos, Mercader de Libros./ 4 *prel. leaves, and Text, signatures A to G in fours.* 4*to*. (1*l*. 1*s*. 1932)

MOODY (James). Lieut. James Moody's Narrative of his Exertions and Sufferings in the Cause of Government, Since the Year 1776; Authenticated by proper Certificates. The Second Edition. *London*: Richardson and Urquhart, MDCCLXXXIII. Title and 57 pp. 'Appendix' 7 pp. *half morocco.* 8vo. (7s. 6d. 1933)

MOORE (Daniel). A Representation of Facts, Relative to the Conduct of Daniel Moore Efquire, Collector of His Majeftys Cuftoms at Charles-Town, In South Carolina. From the Time of his Arrival in March, 1767, to the Time of his Departure in September following. Transmitted By the Merchants of Charles-Town, to Charles Garth, Efquire, in London, Agent for the Province of South-Carolina; and, Recommended in a Letter from the Honourable The Committee of Correfpondence. *Charlestown, South Carolina*: Printed by Charles Crouch, at his Printing-Office in Elliott-ftreet. 1767. *viii and pp.* 3-43. *Folio.* (2l. 2s. 1934)

MOORE (Francis). A Voyage to Georgia. Begun in the Year 1735. Containing An Account of the Settling the Town of Frederica, in the Southern Part of the Province; and a Defcription of the Soil, Air, Birds, Beasts, Trees, Rivers, Islands, &c. With The Rules and Orders made by the Honourable the Trustees for that Settlement; including the Allowances of Provifions, Cloathing, and other Neceffaries to the Families and Servants which went thither. Also a Defcription of the Town and County of Savannah, in the Northern Part of the Province; the manner of dividing and granting the Lands, and the Improvements there: With an Account of the Air, Soil, Rivers, and Islands in that Part. By Francis Moore, Author of Travels into the Inland Parts of Africa. *London*: Jacob Robinson, 1744. 108 pp. & 1 *leaf at end with Author's advertisement of voyage to Georgia in 1738, etc. half mor.* 8vo. (7s. 6d. 1935)

MOORE (JAMES L.) The Columbiad: An Epic Poem on the Discovery of America and the West Indies by Columbus. In Twelve Books. By the Rev. James L. Moore, Master of the Free Grammar School, in Hertford, Herts. *London*: F. and

C. Rivington, 1798. *Title and 455 pp. Russia extra.*
8vo. (10s. 6d. 1936)

MOORE (Sir THOMAS). Mangora, King of the Timbusians. Or the Faithful Couple. A Tragedy. By Sir Thomas Moore. *London:* W. Harvey, 1718. 4 *prel. leaves and text 54 pp. Half morocco.*
4to. (10s. 6d. 1937)

MORETON (J. B.) West India Customs and Manners, containing strictures on the soil, cultivation, produce, trade, officers, and inhabitants; with the method of establishing and conducting a Sugar Plantation. To which is added, the Practice of training new Slaves. By J. B. Moreton, Esq. A new edition. *London:* J. Parsons, 1793. 192 *pp. half mor.* 8vo. (4s. 6d. 1938)

MORGAN (JOHN). A Discourse Upon the Institution of Medical Schools In America; Delivered at a Public Anniversary Commencement, held in the College of Philadelphia May 30 and 31, 1765. With a Preface Containing, amongſt other things, The Author's Apology For attempting to introduce the regular mode of praƈtifing Physic in Philadelphia: By John Morgan, M.D. Fellow of the Royal Society at London; Correſpondent of the Royal Academy of Surgery at Paris; Member of the Arcadian Belles Lettres Society at Rome; Licentiate of the Royal Colleges of Phyſicians in London and in Edinburgh; and Profeſſor of the Theory and Praƈtice of Medicine in the College of Philadelphia. *Philadelphia:* Printed and ſold by William Bradford, at the Corner of Market and Front-Streets, MDCC,LXV. 18 *prel. leaves and* 63 *pp. calf.*
8vo. (1l. 1s. 1939)

MORNING (THE) and Evening Prayer. The Litany, and Church Catechiſm. Ne Orhoengene neoni Yogaraskhagh Yondereanayendaghkwa, Ne Ene Niyoh Raodeweyena, neoni Onoghſadogeaghtige Yondadderighwanondoenthia. *Boston,* New-England: Printed by Richard and Samuel Draper. 1763. *Title and* 24 *pp.* 'The Church Catechiſm.' 18 *pp. half mor.* 4to. (3l. 3s. 1940)

MORRIS (VALENTINE). A Narrative Of the Official Conduct of Valentine Morris, Eſq. late Captain General, Governor in Chief, &c. &c. of the Island of St. Vincent and its Dependencies. Written by himself. Supported by his Official Correspondence with the Secretary of State, Lords of the Treafury, and other of his Majefty's Servants, Admirals, Governors, &c. The Originals to be found in the refpective Offices, and the Duplicates now in his Poffeffion. Alfo by other Documents equally Authentic. *London:* Printed at the Logographic Prefs, by J. Walter, Printing-House-Square, Black-Friars, MDCCLXXXVII. *Half-title, title, xvii, 3, and 467 pp.* (6s. 6d. 1941)

MORSE (JEDIDIAH). The American Geography; or, A View of the Present Situation of the United States of America. Containing Aftronomical Geography. Geographical Definitions. Difcovery, and General Defcription of America. Summary account of the Difcoveries and Settlements of North America; General View of the United States; Of their Boundaries; Lakes; Bays and Rivers; Mountains; Productions; Population; Government; Agriculture; Commerce; Manufactures; Hiftory; Concife Account of the War, and of the important Events which have fucceeded. Biographical Sketches of feveral illuftrious Heroes. General account of New England; Of its Boundaries; Extent; Divifions; Mountains; Rivers; Natural History; Productions; Population; Character; Trade; Hiftory. Particular Defcriptions of the Thirteen United States, and of Kentucky, The Weftern Territory and Vermont.—Of their Extent; Civil Divifions; Chief Towns; Climates: Rivers; Mountains; Soils; Productions; Trade; Manufactures; Agriculture; Population; Character; Conftitutions; Courts of Juftice; Colleges; Academies and Schools; Religion; Iflands; Indians; Literary and Humane Societies; Societies; Springs; Curiofities; Hiftories. Illuftrated with two Sheet Maps —One of the Southern, the other of the Northern States, neatly and elegantly engraved, and more correct than any that have hitherto been publifhed. To which is added, a concife Abridgment of the Geography of the Britifh, Spanifh, French and Dutch Dominions in America, and the Weft-Indies —Of Europe, Afia, and Africa. By Jedidiah

Morse. *Elizabeth Town:* Printed by Shepard Kollock, for the Author. M,DCC,LXXXIX. *xii and* 534 *pp.* 'The Reader' *etc.* 1 *page. Without the maps. Calf.* 8vo. (12s. 6d. 1942)

MORSE (JEDIDIAH). A Sermon, exhibiting the present dangers, and consequent duties of the Citizens of the United States of America. Delivered at Charlestown, April 25, 1799. The day of the National Fast, By Jedidiah Morse, D.D. Paftor of the Church in Charleftown. Published at the request of the hearers. *Charlestown:* Printed and sold by Samuel Etheridge, next door to Warren-Tavern./ 1799. 50 *pp.* 8vo. (2s. 6d. 1943)

MORSE (JEDIDIAH). A Sermon, delivered before the Ancient & Honourable Artillery Company, In Boston, June 6, 1803, being the Anniversary of their Election of Officers. By Jedidiah Morse, D.D. Minister of the Congregational Church in Charlestown. *Charlestown:* Samuel Etheridge, 1803. 32 *pp.* 8vo. (2s. 6d. 1944)

MORSE (JEDIDIAH). A Compendious History of New England, exhibiting an interesting view of the first settlers of that Country, their Character, their Sufferings, and their Ultimate Prosperity. Collected and arranged, from authentic sources of information, By Jedidiah Morse, D.D. and Rev. Elijah Parish, A. M. of Boston, New England. *London:* William Burton, 1808. 6 *prel. leaves, and* 207 *pp. Calf.* 8vo. (5s. 1945)

MORSE (JEDIDIAH). A Report to the Secretary of War of the United States, on Indian Affairs, comprising a Narrative of a Tour performed in the Summer of 1820, under a Commission from the President of the United States, for the purpose of ascertaining for the use of the Government, the actual state of the Indian Tribes in our Country: Illustrated by a Map of the United States; ornamented by a correct Portrait of a Pawnee Indian. By the Rev. Jedidiah Morse, D.D. Late Minister of the First Congregational Church in Charlestown, near Boston, now resident in New Haven. *New-Haven:* 1822. 400 *pp. Errata* 1 *page. Colored Map; and Portrait. Uncut.* 8vo. (6s. 6d. 1946)

MORTON (Thomas). New English Canaan/ or/ New Canaan./ Containing an Abſtract of New England,/ Compoſed in three Bookes./ The firſt Booke ſetting forth the originall of the Natives, their/ Manners and Cuſtomes, together with their tractable Nature and/ Love towards the Engliſh./ The ſecond Booke ſetting forth the naturall Indowments of the/ Country, and what ſtaple Commodities it/ yealdeth./ The third Booke ſetting forth, what people are planted there,/ their proſperity, what remarkable accidents have happened ſince the firſt/ planting of it, together with their Tenents and practiſe/ of their Church./ Written by Thomas Morton, of Cliffords Inne gent, upon tenne/ yeares knowledge and experiment of the/ Country./ Printed at *Amsterdam*,/ By Jacob Frederick Stam./ In the yeare 1637./ 188 *pp*. 'A Table' etc. 3 *pp*. 4to. (4*l*. 4*s*. 1947)

MOST (A/) Exact and Accurate/ Map/ of the/ Whole World:/ Or the/ Orb Terreſtrial deſcribed in Four plain Maps,/ (viz.)/ Asia, Evrope, Africa, America./ Containing all the known and moſt Remarkable/ Capes, Ports, Bayes and Iſles, Rocks, Rivers, Towns,/ and Cities; together with their Scituation, Commodities,/ Hiſtory, Cuſtomes, Government; and a new and exact Geography,/ eſpecially their Longitudes and Latitudes, in Alphabetical Order, and fitted/ to all Capacities./ A Work, as well uſeful as delightful, for all Schollars,/ Merchants, Mariners, and all ſuch as deſire to know Forreign/ parts, and is very helpful for the ready finding out any place mentioned in/ large Maps./ D. L. M.A./ *London*, Printed for John Garrett, at his Shop as you go/ up the Stairs of the Royal Exchange in Cornhil: where is Printed,/ Coloured and Sold, a Map of the World in four Sheets with Engliſh de-/ſcriptions: And where you may have alſo choice of all ſorts of Maps,/ and Pictures for Houſes, Studies, or Cloſets. 4 *prel. leaves,* and 192 *pp. Poor copy, wanting several leaves.* 4to. (5*s*. 1948)

MOULTRIE (John). Dissertatio Medica Inauguralis, de Febre maligna bilioſa Americæ; quam. Annuente deo ter opt. max. Ex auctoritate reverendi admodum Viri. D. Gulielmi Wishart

S. T. D. Academiae Edinburgenæ præfecti, nec non Amplissimi Senatus Academici consensu, et nobilissimae Facultatis Medicinae decreto; pro gradu doctoratus, summisque in Medicina honoribus ac priviligüs rite et legitime consequendis, Eruditorum Examini Subjicit Joannes Moultrie ex Meridionali Carolinæ provincia, A et R. Ex officina Roberti Flaminii. M.DCCXLIX. *2 prel. leaves, and 24 pp;* 'Ephemerides Meteorologicae,' *etc. 8 pp. 4to.* (4s. 6d. 1949)

MOUNTGOMERY (Sir ROBERT). A Discourse Concerning the defign'd Establishment of a New Colony to the South of Carolina, in the Moft delightful Country of the Univerfe. By Sir Robert Mountgomery Baronet. *London:* Printed in the Year. 1717. *Title and 30 pp. Large Copperplate Plan at page 11. half mor. 8vo.* (10s. 6d. 1950)

MUHLENBERG (HENRY). Descriptio Uberior Graminum et Plantarum Calamariarum Americæ Septentrionalis indigenarum et cicurum. Auctore D. Henrico Muhlenberg, Societ. Physic. Gotting. —Berolini Imperalis Naturæ Curiosorum-Phytogr. Gotting.—Physiogr. Lund.—Americ. Philosoph. etc. Membro. *Philadelphiæ:* Solomon W. Conrad, 1817. *Title, ii and 295 pp. 8vo.* (7s. 6d. 1951)

MUNOZ (JUAN BAUTISTA). Historia del Nuevo-Mundo escribíala D. Juan Baut. Muñoz. Tomo I. en *Madrid* por la Viuda de Ibarra MDCCXCIII. *3 prel. leaves, xxx and 364 pp. Portrait and Map. Large Paper. half calf. 8vo.* (15s. 1952)
No second Volume was ever published.

MUNOZ (JUAN BAPTISTA). The History of the New World, by Don Juan Baptista Munoz. Translated from the Spanish, with Notes by the Translator, an Engraved Portrait of Columbus, and a Map of Espanola. *London:* G. G. and J. Robinson, 1797. Vol. I. *xv and 552 pp. Map & Portrait. 8vo.* (8s. 6d. 1953)

MUNSTER (SEBASTIAN). Cosmographia./ Bfchreibūg/ aller Lender Dürch/ Sebaftianum Munfterum/ in welcher begriffen,/ Aller völcker, Herrfchafften,/ Stetten, vnd namhafftiger flecken herkomen:/ Sitten gebreüch, ordnung, glauben, fecten, vnd hautie-/rung, durch die gantze welt,

vnd fürnem̄/lich Teütſcher nation./ Was auch
beſunders in iedem landt gefunden,/ vnnd darin
beſchenſey./ Alles mit figuren vnd ſchönen landt
taflen erklert,/ vnd für augen geſtelt./ Getruckt
zü *Basel* durch Henrichum/ Petri. Anno M. D.
xLiiij./ *6 prel. leaves; 24 woodcut Maps of 2 leaves
each, and Text* dclix *pp. Woodcut maps at pp.* 546,
554. *and 2 plates at pp.* 630, & 631. *Pigskin.*
Folio. (2*l.* 12*s.* 6*d.* 1954)

MURRAY (James). An Impartial History of the
present War in America; Containing An Account
of its Rise and Progress, The Political Springs
thereof, with its various Successes and Disapoint-
ments on both sides. By the Rev. James Murray,
of Newcastle. *London:* R. Baldwin, [1778.]
Two Volumes. Vol. I. 373 *pp.* Vol. II. 376 *pp. 22
Copperplate Portraits, and Plan of the Town of Boston. Calf.* 8*vo.* (1*l.* 10*s.* 1955)

MURRAY (William, *Earl of Mansfield*). Lord
Mansfield's Speech In giving the Judgment of the
Court of King's-Bench, On Monday, November
28, 1774, In the Cause of Campbell againſt Hall,
respecting the King's Letters Patent, of the 20th
of July, 1764; for raising a Duty of Four and an
Half per Cent. On all the Exports from the Island
of Granada. Accurately taken by a Barrister. A
New Edition Corrected. *London:* G. Kearsly.
m.dcc.lxxv. *Title, and text* 23 *pp. Half morocco.*
8*vo.* (3*s.* 6*d.* 1956)

MYSTERY (The) Reveal'd; or, Truth brought to
Light. Being a Diſcovery of ſome Faċts, in Relation to the Conduċt of the late M———y, which how-
ever extraordinary they may appear, are yet ſup-
ported by ſuch Teſtimonies of authentick Papers
and Memoirs as neither Confidence, can, out-brave;
nor Cunning invalidate. By a Patriot. *London:*
W. Cater, 1759. *Title and* 319 *pp. Half morocco.*
8*vo.* (4*s.* 6*d.* 1957)

ARBOROUGH (Sir JOHN and Others). An/ Account/ Of Several Late/ Voyages & Difcoveries/ To the Sovth and North./ Towards The Streights of Magellan, the South Seas, the vaſt/ Tracts of Land beyond Hollandia Nova &c./ Also/ Towards Nova Zembla, Greenland or Spitsberg,/ Groynland or Engrondland, &c./ By Sir John Narborough, Captain Jasmen/ Tasman, Captain John Wood, and/ Frederick Marten of Hamburgh./ To which are Annexed a Large/ Introduction and Supplement,/ giving/ An Account of other Navigations/ to thoſe Regions of the Globe./ The Whole Illuſtrated with/ Charts and Figures./ *London*: Printed for Sam Smith and Benj. Walford, Printers to the/ Royal Society, at the Prince's Arms in S. Paul's Churchyards, 1694./ 18 *prel. leaves, Map of the Streights of Magellan, and* 196 *pp. Map of the North East, etc. at page* 143. 'The First Part of the Voyage into Spitzbergen,' *etc.* 207 *pp. Table at page* 1; *and Plates lettered A to S,* 2 *of the letter P. Fine copy. Old calf.* 8vo. (12s. 6d. 1958)

NARRATIVE (A) of Occurrences in the Indian Countries of North America, since the Connexion of the Right Hon. The Earl of Selkirk with the Hudson's Bay Company, and his attempt to Establish a Colony on the Red River; with a detailed account of his Lordship's Military Expedition to, and subsequent proceedings at Fort William, in Upper Canada. *London:* B. McMillan, 1817. *xiv and* 152 *pp.* 'Appendix.' 2 *prel. leaves and* 87 *pp.* 8vo. (6s. 6d. 1959)

NEAL (DANIEL). The History of New-England, Containing an Impartial Account of the Civil and

Ecclefiaftical Affairs Of the Country, To the Year of our Lord, 1700. To which is added, The Present State of New-England. With a New and Accurate Map of the Country. And an Appendix Containing their Prefent Charter, their Ecclefiaftical Difcipline, and their Municipal-Laws. In Two Volumes. The Second Edition. With many Additions by the Author. By Daniel Neal, A.M. *London:* A. Ward, MDCCXLVII. *Two Volumes.* Vol. I. 8 *prel. leaves and* 392 *pp. Map.* Vol. II. 2 *prel. leaves and text* 380 *pp. Index.* 15 *pp. Old calf.* 8*vo.* (18*s.* 1960)

NECK (JACOB CORNELIUS). The/ Iovrnall, or Day-/ly Regifter,/ Contayning a Trve/ manifeftation, and Hiftoricall declaration of the/ voyage, accomplifhed by eight fhippes of Amfterdam, vnder/ the conduct of Iacob Cornelifzen Neck Admirall, & Wybrandt/ van Warwick Vice-Admirall, which fayled from Amfter-/dam the firft day of March,/ 1598./ Shewing the covrse they/ kept, and what other notable matters happened/ unto them in the fayd voyage./ Imprinted at *London* for Cuthbert Burby & Iohn Flafket:/ And are to be fold at the Royall Exchange, & at the figne/ of the blacke beare in Paules Church-yard./ 1601./ *Title, with Woodcut of Ship in full sail, the reverse blank.* 'To the Right Worship-/fvll, Master Thomas Smith,/ Sheriffe of the honorable Citie of London, and/ Gouernor of the famous companie of the Englifh Marchants/ trading to the Eaft Jndies, Sumatra, Iava, the Ifles of the Malucos,/ Banda, and the Rich and Mightie Kingdome of Chyna: and to the/ right VVorfhipfull the Aldermen, and the reft of the Commit-/ties and focietie of the faid corporation. William/ Walker vvifheth all profperitie and/ happie fucceffe./ 2 *pp. signed* 'William Walker.' *Text in* 58 *folioed leaves.* 'Some words of the Malifh fpeech, which/ language is vfed throughout the Eaft Indies, as/ French is in our Countrie, wherewith a man may trauell/ ouer all the Land. The Portugals fpeech is apt and pro-/fitable in thefe Iflands, for there are many Inter-/preters which fpeake Portugall./ 9 *pp.* 4*to.* (2*l.* 2*s.* 1961)
This copy is imperfect, wanting several leaves.

NECESSITY (THE) of Repealing the American

Stamp-Act demonstrated: Or, a Proof that Great-Britain muft be injured by that Act. In a Letter to a Member of the British House of Commons. *London*: J. Almon, MDCCLXVI. 46 *pp. half mor.* 8vo. (4s. 6d. 1962)

NEILSON (JOHN). Second Series of The Present and Future Prospects of Jamaica considered, Pointing out the Advantages which may be derived from the Extinction of Slavery, and Shewing the causes which oppose themselves to the successful Working of the Apprenticeship system, in accelerating that object, and proposing a remedy, Suggesting the means for establishing a Bank, on a solid basis, by John Neilson. *Kingston-Jamaica*: Printed at the office of the Commercial Advertiser. 1834. 20 *pp.* 8vo. (2s. 6d. 1963)

NEUE NACHRICHTEN von denen neuentdekten Infuln in der See zwifchen Afien und Amerika; aus mitgetheilten Urkunden und Auszügen verfaffet von J. L. S. ** *Hamburg* und *Leipzig*, bey Friedrich Lugo Ludwig Gleditfch. 1776. *Title and* 173 *pp.* 8vo. (4s. 6d. 1964)

NEU=EROFFNETES Amphitheatrvm, Worinnen Nach dem uns bekanten gantzen Welt=Greifz, Alle Nationen Nach ihrem Habit, infaubern Figuren repräfentiret. Anbey Die Länder nach ihrer Situation, Climate, Fruchtbarkeit, Inclination und Befchaffenheit der Einwohner, Religion, vornehmften Städten, Ertz=Bifthümern, Univerfitäten, Häfen, Veftungen, Commercien, Macht, Staats=Intereffe, Regierungs=Form, Raritäten, Müntzen, Prætensionibus, vornehmften Ritter=Orden und Mappen aufgeführet find, Und welches, mit Zuziehung der Land=Charten, zu vieler Beluftigung, vornehmlich aber der ftudierenden Jugend, als ein fehr nützliches und anmuthiges Compendium Geographicum, Genealogicum, Heraldicum, Curiofum, Numifmaticum, kangebrauchet werden. *Frfurth*, Gedruckt und verlegt von Johann Michael Funcken, 1723. *Five Parts. General Title, Vorrede*, 2 *pp.* 'I. Aus dem gantzen Europa, *etc.* 1722.' 66 *leaves.* 'II. Aus dem gantzen Africa, *etc.* 1723.' 2 *prel. leaves, and* 96 *pp.* 'III. Aus dem gantzen America, *etc.* 1723.' 2 *prel. leaves and* 124 *pp.* 'Aus dem Südlichen Asia, *etc.* 1728.' *Title and* 142 *pp.* 'Turcicum, *etc.* 1724.' *172 pp. Register* 4 *pp. Woodcuts with the text. Folio.* (1*l.* 10*s.* 1965)

NEVE, Y MOLINA (LUIS DE). Reglas de Orthographia, Diccionario, y Arte del Idioma Othomi breve instruccion para los principiantes, qve dictó el L. D. Lvis de Neve, y Molina, Cathedratico Proprietario de dicho Idioma en el Real, y Pontificio Colegio Seminario, Examinador Synodal, é Interprete de el Tribunal de Fé en el Proviforato de Indios de efte Arzobifpado, y Capellan del Hofpital Real de efta Corte. Dedicalo al Gloriosissimo Señor San Joseph, Padre Putativo del Verbo Eterno, y bajo fu Proteccion lo faca a luz. Impreffas en *Mexico*, con las licencias neceffarias, en la Imprenta de la Bibliotheca Mexicana, en el Puente del Efpiritu Santo. Año de 1767. 12 *prel. leaves and* 160 *pp. at page* 12 *Engraved leaf* 'Antes de leer el Diccionario, &c,' *etc.* 1 *page. Old calf. Small 8vo.* (3*l.* 3*s.* 1966)

NEVIS AND ST. CHRISTOPHERS. To the Honourable the Knights, Citizens, and Burgeffes in Parliament Affembled. The humble Petition of feveral Proprietors of Plantations in the Iflands of Nevis and St. Chriftophers in America, and Merchants Trading to the fame; on behalf of themfelves and other Inhabitants and Traders to the aforefaid Iflands. [*London*] *A single sheet. Folio.* (2*s.* 6*d.* 1967)

NEW (A) Essay [By the Pennfylvanian Farmer] on the Constitutional Power of Great-Britain over the Colonies in America; with the Resolves of the Committee for the Province of Pennsylvania, and their Instructions To their Representatives in Assembly. Philadelphia Printed, and *London* Reprinted for J. Almon, 1774. *viii and* 126 *pp. half mor. 8vo.* (5*s.* 6*d.* 1968)

NEW BRUNSWICK. Hand Book for Emigrants to the Province of New Brunswick, Containing the average price of Land, Provisions, Clothing, Farm Stock, Building and other Materials, &c., and the rate of Wages to Mechanics, Labourers, &c. With other necessary information for persons with Capital, as well as for Mechanics, Farm Servants, Labourers, &c. intending to settle in the Province. Compiled From Returns in the Office of the Provincial Secretary. *Fredericton:* John Simpson, Printer to the Queen's Most Excellent Majesty. 1841. 15 pp. 8vo. (2s. 6d. 1969)

NEWE/ vnbekanthe/landte/ Und/ein/newe/ Weldte/ in/ kurtz/ verganger/ zeythe/ erfunden/ [*Colophon*] ¶ Alſo hat ein endte dieſes Büchlein, wel=/ches aufz welliſcher ſprach, in die dewtſchen/ gebrachte vnd gemachte iſt worden, durch/den wirdigē vnd hochgelarthen herrē Job-/ſten Ruchamer der freyen künſte, vnd artz-/enncien Doctorē ᴛc. Vnd durch mich Geor=/gen Stüchſzen zu *Nüreinberghk,* Gedrückte/ vnd volendte nach Chriſti vnſers lieben her/ren geburdte. M.cccc.viij. Jare, am Mit-/ woch ſanctii Mathei, des heiligen apoſtols/ abenthe, der do was der zweigntzigiſte tage/ des Monadts Septembris./ *68 leaves, in double columns without catchwords or pagination, but with signatures* a *to* k *in sixes, and* l *in four leaves, with 4 leaves of register.* Vellum. Folio. (5l. 5s. 1970)

NEW-ENGLAND. An/ Abstract/ of the/ Lawes/ of/ New England,/ As they are now eſtabliſhed./ *London,/* Printed for F. Coules, and W. Ley at Paules Chain,/ 1641./ *Title reverse blank, and* 15 *pp.* ' The Table of the Chapters.' 2 *pp. Unbound.* 4to. (2l. 2s. 1971)

NEVV/ ENGLANDS/ First Fruits ;/ in reſpect,/
Firſt of the { Converſion of ſome, Conviction of divers, Preparation of ſundry } of the Indians.
2. Of the progreſſe of Learning, in the Colledge at/ Cambridge in Maſſachuſetts Bay./ With/ Divers other ſpeciall Matters concerning that Countrey./ Publiſhed by the inſtant requeſt of ſundry Friends, who deſire/ to be ſatisfied in theſe points by many New-England Men/ who are here preſent, and were eye or eare-/witneſſes of the ſame./ *London*, Printed by R. O. and G. D. for Henry Overton, and are to be/ ſold at his Shop in Popes-head Alley. 1643./ *Title reverse blank, and 26 pp. Calf extra, by Bedford.* 4to. (2l. 2s. 1972)

NEW-ENGLAND. A Brief/ Narration/ of the/ Practices/ of the/ Churches in New-England./ Written in private to one that deſired/ information therein; by an Inhabitant there,/ a Friend to Truth and Peace./ Publifhed according to Order./ *London,*/ Printed by Matth. Simmons for John Rothwell, and/ are to be fold at his Shop, at the figne of the Sunne/ in Pauls Churchyard, 1645./ Title and 18 *pp.* (1*l.* 11*s.* 6*d.* 1973)

NEW-ENGLAND. A Brief/ Narration/ of the/ Practices/ of the/ Churches in New-England, in/ their folemne Worfhip of God./ Written to one that defired infor-/mation therein; by an Inhabitant there;/ a Friend to Truth and Peace./ Publifhed according to Order./ *London;* Printed by Matthew Simmons, and are to be fold by/ John Pounfet at the lower end of Budge-Row/ neere Canning-streete. 1647./ *Title and Text in* 18 *pp.* 4*to.* (1*l.* 11*s.* 6*d.* 1974)

This differs from the preceding only in the title.

NEW-ENGLAND. The/ Day-Breaking,/ if not/ The Sun-Rifing/ of the/ Gospell/ With the/ Indians in New-England./ *London,*/ Printed by Rich. Cotes, for Fulk Clifton, and are to bee/ fold at his fhop under Saint Margarets Church on/ New-fifh-ftreet Hill, 1647./ *Title in a narrow type metal border, on the reverse* ' To the Reader. *signed* ' Nathan. Warde.' *Text* 25 *pp. Calf extra by Bedford.* 4*to.* (2*l.* 2*s.* 1795)

NEW-ENGLAND. An Act/ For the promoting and propagating the/ Gospel/ of/ Jefus Chrift/ in/ New-England./ *London,* Printed for Edward Hufband, Printer to the Parliament of England, and are to be fold at his Shop in Fleetftreet, at the Sign of the Golden-/Dragon, near the Inner-Temple, 1649./ *Title and pp.* 407-412. *Black Letter, half mor. Folio.* (15*s.* 1976)

NEW-ENGLAND. The Light appearing more and more to-/wards the perfect Day./ Or,/ A farther Difcovery of the prefent ftate/ of the Indians/ in/ New-England,/ Concerning the Progreffe of the Gofpel/ amongft them./ Manifefted by Letters from fuch as preacht/ to them there./ Publifhed by H. Whitfield, late Paftor to the Chuch/ of Chrift at Gilford in New-England, who came/ late thence./ *London,* Printed by T. R. & E. M. for John Bartlet, and are to be/ fold at the Gilt Cup, near St. Auſtins gate in Pauls/ Church-yard. 1651./ 4 prel. leaves; viz. ' The Lord, who is wonderful in Councel,' etc. signed ' Joſeph Caryl.' on the reverse of the first leaf; Title in a type metal border, the reverse blank. ' To the Right Honorable the Parliament of England and the Councel of State.' Signed ' Henry Whitfeld.' 4 pp : Text 46 pp. Calf extra by Bedford. 4to. (2l. 2s. 1977)

NEW-ENGLAND. Strength/ ovt of/ Weakneſſe; Or a Glorious/ Manifeſtation/ Of the further Progreſſe of/ the Goſpel among the Indians/ in Nevv-England./ Held forth in Sundry Letters/ from divers Miniſters and others to the/ Corporation eſtabliſhed by Parliament for/ promoting the Goſpel among the Hea-/then in New-England; and to particular/ Members thereof ſince the laſt Trea-/tiſe to that effect, Publiſhed by/ Mr. Henry Whitfield late Paſtor/ of Gilford in New-England./ London ;/ Printed by M. Simmons for John Blague and/ Samuel Howes, and are to be ſold at their/ ſhop in Popes-Head-Alley. 1652./ 8 prel. leaves; viz. Title in a type metal border, the reverse blank; ' To the Supreame Authoritie of this Nation, The Parliament of the Common-Wealth of England.' Signed by ' John Owen' and 11 others, 4 pp ; ' To the Reader. Signed ' W. Gouge.' and 13 others, 5 pp. ' To the Chriſtian Reader.' 3 pp. Text 40 pp. 4to. (1l. 11s. 6d. 1978)

NEW-ENGLAND. Strength out of Weakneſs./ Or a Glorious/ Manifeſtation/ Of the further Progreſſe of the/ Goſpel/ amongſt/ the Indians/ in/ New-England./ Held forth in ſundry Letters/ from divers Miniſters and others to the/ Corporation eſtabliſhed by Parliament for/ promoting the Goſpel among the Hea-/then in New-England; and to particular/ Members thereof ſince the laſt Trea-/tiſe to that effect, formerly ſet/ forth by Mr Henry Whitfield/ late Paſtor of Gilford in/ New-England./ Publiſhed by the aforeſaid Corporation./ London,/ Printed by M. Simmons for John Blague/ and Samuel Howes, and are to be ſold at their/ Shop in Popes Head Alley. 1652./ 8 prel. leaves ; viz. Title in a type metal border, the reverse blank, ' To the Supreame Authoritie of this Nation, The Parliament of the Common-Wealth of England.' Signed

'William Steele, Prefident.' 4 *pp*; 'To the Reader.' *signed* 'William Gouge.' *and* 17 *others*, 5 *pp*. 'To the Chriftian Reader.' 3 *pp*: *Text* 40 *pp. Calf extra by Bedford*. 4*to*. (2*l*. 2*s*. 1979)

NEW-ENGLAND. Strength/ ovt of/ Weaknesse;/ Or a Glorious/ Manifestation/ Of the further Progreſſe of/ the Goſpel among the Indians/ in Nevv-England./ Held forth in Sundry Letters/ from divers Minifters and others to the/ Corporation eftablifhed by Parliament for/ Promoting the Goſpel among the Hea-/then in New-England; and to particular/ Members thereof fince the laſt Trea-/tife to that effect, formerly fet forth by Mr Henry Whitfield/ late Paftor of Gilford in New-England./ Publifhed by the aforefaid Corporation./ *London*; Printed by M. Simmons for John Blague and/ Samuel Howes, and are to be fold at their/ Shop in Popes-Head-Alley. 1652./ 8 *prel. leaves; viz. Title in a metal type border, the reverse blank;* 'To the fupreame Authoritie of this Nation, The Parliament of the Common-Wealth of England.' *signed* 'William Steele, Prefident.' 4 *pp*; 'To the Reader.' *signed* 'William Gouge' *and* 13 *others*, 5 *pp*. Strength ovt of Weaknesse; Or a Glorious Manifestation Of the further Progreſſe of the Goſpel among the Indians in New-England.' 4 *pp*: Text 40 *pp. Fine copy in calf extra by Bedford.* 4*to*. (2*l*. 2*s*. 1980)

NEW-ENGLAND. A/ History/ of/ New-England./ From the Englifh planting in the Yeere/ 1628. untill the Yeere 1652./ Declaring the form of their Government,/ Civill, Military, and Ecclefiaſtique. Their Wars with/ the Indians, their Troubles with the Gortonifts,/ and other Heretiques. Their manner of gathering/ of Churches, the commodities of the Country,/ and defcription of the principall Towns/ and Havens, with the great encou-/ragements to increaſe Trade/ betwixt them and Old/ England. With the names of all their Governours, Magiſtrates,/ and eminent Minifters./ *London*,/ Printed for Nath: Brooke at the Angel/ in Corn-hill. 1654./ 2 *prel. leaves; viz. Title, and* 'To the Reader.' *signed* 'T. H.' 2 *pp*: *Text* 236 *pp.* 'Brooke's Catalogue' 4 *pp*. 4*to*. (4*l*. 14*s*. 6*d*. 1981)

NEW-ENGLAND. The/ Secret Workes/ Of a Cruel/ People/ Made manifest;/ Whofe little finger is become he-/vier then their persecutors the bishops Loyns, who have/ fet up an Image amongst them in New-England, which/ all that will not bow down unto, and worship, must un-/dergo all fuch Sufferings as can be invented and/ inflicted by the hearts and hands of such/ men whofe tender mercies are cruel./ Which may be feen in this fhort relation of their cruelty,/ which was prefented to Parliament, and now recom-/mended to the consideration of all fober people, that/ they may fee how these profeffors of New-England have/ loft their former tenderneff, who fled from persecution,/ and now are become the chiefeft of Persecutors./ Whereunto is annexed a Copy of a Letter which came/ from one who had been a Magistrate among them,/ to a friend of his in London, wherein he gives an/ account of the cruel fufferings of the/ people of God in those parts under the/ Rulers of New-England and their un-/righteous Laws./ *London,* Printed in the Year 1659./ *Title, reverse blank, and 26 pp: at page 18 signed* 'John Rous.' 4to. (2l. 2s. 1982)
The title is in manuscript.

NEW-ENGLAND. The Humble/ Petition/ and/ Address/ Of the General Court fitting at/ Bofton in New-England,/ unto/ The High and Mighty/ Prince/ Charles/ the Second./ And prefented unto His Moft-Gracious/ Majefty Feb. 11. 1660./ [*London*] Printed in the Year 1660./ *8 pp. signed* 'John Endecot Gov\.r/ In the Name, and with the con-/ fent of the General Court.' *Calf extra by Bedford.* 4to. (2l. 2s. 1983)

NEW ENGLAND. The Necessity/ of/ Reformation/ With the Expedients fubfervient/ thereunto, afferted ;/ in Anfwer to two/ Qvestions/ I. What are the Evils that have provoked the Lord to bring his Judg-/ments on New-England ?/ II. What is to be done that fo thofe Evils may be Reformed ?/ Agreed upon by the/ Elders and Messengers/ Of the Churches affembled in the/ Synod/ At Bofton in New-England,/ Sept. 10. 1679./ *Boston;/* Printed by John Fofter. In the Year 1679./ *4 prel. leaves; viz.* 1st, 'At a General Court held at Bofton in New-England, 15th. of October 1679.' signed 'By the Court Edward Rawfon Secr.' 2nd, Title the reverse blank. 3rd, and 4th, 'The Epiftle Dedicatory.' Text 15 pp. Fine copy in morocco by Bedford. 4to. (4l. 4s. 1984)

NEW-ENGLAND'S Faction Discovered;/ Or,/ A Brief and True Account of their Perfecution of the Church/ of England; the Beginning and Progrefs of the War/ with the Indians; and other Late Proceedings there, in/ a Letter from a Gentleman of that Country, to a Perfon/ of Quality./ Being, an Anfwer to a moft falfe and fcandalous Pamphlet late-/ly Publifhed; Intituled, News from New-England, &c./ [Colophon] London,/ Printed for J. Hindmarfh, at the Sign of the Golden Ball, over againft/ the Royal Exchange in Cornhill. 1690./ 8 pp. signed 'C. D.' Poor copy closely cut. Unbound. 4to. (1l. 1s. 1985)

NEW-ENGLAND. The/ Humble Addrefs/ of the/ Publicans/ of/ New-England,/ To which King you pleafe./ With some Remarks/ Upon it./ London: Printed in the Year, 1691./ 35 pp. Fine copy. calf extra by Bedford. 4to. (2l. 2s. 1986)

NEW-ENGLAND. A brief Review of the Rise and Progress, Services and Sufferings, of New England, especially the Province of Massachuset's-Bay. Humbly fubmitted to the Confideration of both Houfes of Parliament. London: J. Buckland, MDCCLXXIV. 32 pp. half mor. 8vo. (7s. 6d. 1987)

NEW-ENGLAND, and her Institutions: By One of her Sons. [Jacob Abbot.] R. B. Seeley and W. Burnside: London. MDCCCXXXV. 4 prel. leaves and 393 pp. 8vo. (4s. 6d. 1988)

NEW-JERSEY An/ Abstract,/ or/ Abbreviation/ Of fome Few of the/ Many (Later and Former) Testimonys/ from the/ Inhabitants of/ New-Jersey,/ And Other/ Eminent Perfons,/ Who have Wrote particularly concerning/ That Place./ London, Printed by Thomas Milbourn, in the Year, 1681./ 32 pp. 4to. (3l. 13s. 6d. 1989)

NEW-JERSEY. The Acts Of the General Assembly Of the Province of New-Jersey, From the Time of the Surrender of the Government of the faid Province, to the Fourth Year of the Reign of King George the Second. Collected and Published by Order of the faid Assembly. With a Table of the Principal Matters therein contained. *Philadelphia:* Printed and Sold by William and Andrew Bradford, Printers to the King's Moft Excellent Majefty, for the Province of New-Jerfey, MDCC XXXII. *7 prel leaves and wanting all after p.* 332. *Old calf. Folio.* (15s. 1990)

NEW-JERSEY. The Acts of the General Assembly of the Province of New-Jersey, From the Year 1753, being the Twenty-fixth of the Reign of King George the Second, where the Firft Volume ends, to the Year 1761, being the Firft of King George the Third. With proper Tables; and an alphabetical Index; containing all the principal Matters in the Body of the Book: Together with an Appendix; containing the feveral Acts of Parliament now in Force in America, relating to his Majefty's Forces, and the Articles of War. Collected and publifhed by Order of the General Assembly of the faid Province. By Samuel Nevill, Efq; Second Juftice of the Supreme Court of Judicature of the faid Province. Volume the Second. *Woodbridge,* in New-Jersey: Printed by James Parker, Printer to the King's Moft Excellent Majefty, for the Province. M.DCC.LXI. *xvi and* 401 *pp. Index* 56 *pp*; *Appendix* 59 *pp*; *Index to the Appendix pp.* 61-64. *Old calf. Folio.* (1*l*. 10s. 1991)

NEW-YORK. Laws, Statutes, Ordinances and Constitutions, Ordained, made and Established, by the Mayor, Alderman, and Commonalty, of the City of New-York, Convened in Common-Council, for The good Rule and Government of the Inhabitants and Refidents of the faid City. Published the Ninth Day of November, in the third Year of the Reign of our Sovereign Lord, George the Third, by the Grace of God, of Great Britain, France and Ireland, King, Defender of the Faith, &c. Annoque Domini 1762. And in the Mayoralty of John Cruger, Efq; To which is added, An Appendix, containing Extracts of fundry Acts of the General Affembly, of the Colony of New-York, immediately relating to the good government of the faid City and Corporation. [*New-York*] Printed and Sold, by John Holt, at the Printing Office, at the lower End of Broad Street, oppofite the Exchange, 1763. 2 prel. leaves and pp. 3-108. Table 2 pp. Folio. (1l. 11s. 6d. 1992)

NEW-YORK. The Charter of the City of New-York; Printed by Order of the Mayor, Recorder, Aldermen and Commonalty of the City aforefaid. To which is annexed, The Act of the General Affembly confirming the fame. New York, Printed by W. Weyman, in Broad-Street, 1765. 50 pp. Folio. (1l. 11s. 6d. 1993)

NEW-YORK. Authentic Account of the Proceedings of the Congress held at New-York, In MDCCLXV, On the Subject of the American Stamp Act. MDCCLXVII. Title and 37 pp. Half morocco. 8vo. (7s. 6d. 1993*)

NEW-YORK. The Constitution of the State of New-York. Philadelphia: Printed and Sold by Styner and Cist, in Second-ftreet, fix Doors above Arch-ftreet. MDCCLXXVII. 32 pp. Half calf. 8vo. (7s. 6d. 1994)

NEW-YORK. The Charter of the City of New-York. Printed by Order of the Mayor, Recorder, Aldermen and Commonalty Of the City aforefaid. To which is annexed, The Act of the General Affembly confirming the fame. New-York: Printed by Samuel and John Loudon, Printers to the State. M,DCC,LXXXVI. Title and pp. 3-44. Folio. (1l. 10s. 1995)

NEW-YORK. Laws and Ordinances, Ordained and Established by the Mayor, Aldermen and Commonalty of the City of New-York, In Common Council convened; For the good Rule and Government of the Inhabitants and Residents of the faid City. Published the Twenty-Ninth Day of March, 1786, in the Tenth Year of our Independence, And in the Mayoralty of James Duane, Efq. New-York: Printed by Samuel and John Loudon, Printers to the State. M,DCC, LXXXVI. 29 pp. Folio. (1l. 10s. 1996)

NICHOLSON (FRANCIS). A Modeft Answer To a Malicious Libel Againft his Excellency Francis Nicholfon, Efq; &c. Or An Examination of that Part of Mr. Blair's Affidavit, relating to the

School-Boys of the Grammar-School, in her Majefty's Royal College of William and Mary in Virginia. Written in Virginia, in the Year 1704. [*London.* 1706.] *Privately printed, beginning with page* 1, *without separate title.* 55 *pp. Calf extra by Bedford.* 8*vo.* (1*l.* 1*s.* 1997)

NICHOLSON (FRANCIS). An Apology or Vindication of Francis Nicholfon, Efq; His Majesty's Governor of South-Carolina, From the Unjuft Afperfions caft on Him by fome of the Members of the Bahama-Company. *London,* Printed in the Year 1724. 62 *pp. Calf extra by Francis Bedford.* 8*vo.* (1*l.* 1*s.* 1998)

NICHOLSON (FRANCIS). Papers Relating to An Affidavit Made by His Reverence James Blair, Clerk, pretended Prefident of William and Mary College, and fuppofed Commiffary to the Bifhop of London in Virginia, against Francis Nicholfon, Efq; Governour of the faid Province. Wherein His Reverence's great Refpect to Government, and obedience to the Ninth Commandment, *Thou shalt not bear false Witness,* &c. will plainly appear; as will alfo his Gratitude to the faid Governour, from whom he had received fo many Favours, and to whom he was himfelf fo highly obliged, in feveral original Letters under his own Hand, fome whereof are here publifhed, and more (God willing) fhall hereafter. [*London.*] Printed in the Year 1727. 2 *prel. leaves and* 104 *pp. Calf extra by Bedford.* 8*vo.* (1*l.* 1*s.* 1999)

NISBET (CHARLES). Monody to the Memory of the Rev. Dr. Charles Nisbet, many years first Minister of Montrose, and late President of the College of Carlisle in Pennsylvania. *Edinburgh:* James Ballantyne, 1805. 23 *pp. Half morocco.* 8*vo.* (3*s.* 6*d.* 2000)

NODAL (BARTOLOME GARCIA DE, *and* GONÇALO DE). Relacion/ del Viaje qve por/ orden de sv Mag.^{d}/ y acverdo del Real Consejo/ de Indias Hezieron los Capitanes/ Bartolome Garcia de Nodal, y Gonçalo/ de Nodal hermanos, naturales de Ponte/ Vedra, al defcubrimiento del Estrecho/ nuebo de S. Vicente y reconofinj°:/ del de Magallanes./ A Don Fernando Carrillo/ Cauallero del abito de

Santiago Prefidente/ en el mifmo Confejo./ Con Privilegio/ En *Madrid.* Por Fernando Correa-/ de Montenegro. Año. 1621./ N. S. de Atocha N. S. del becen Suceffo./ I de Courbes Sculpfit./ *12 prel. leaves; viz. Engraved title with Portraits of the two brothers Nodal, the reverse blank;* ' Fee de aprouacion.' *3 pp;* ' Suma del priuilegio.' *1 page;* ' Tassa.' *1 page;* ' Erratas.' *1 page;* ' A Don Fernando Carrillo, Cauallero del Abito de Sätiago, Prefidente del Real Confejo de Indias.' *3 pp;* ' Al Lector.' *5 pp;* ' Advertencias.' *3 pp;* ' Variacion de la aguja' *3 pp;* Reglas para faber la variacion de la aguja al nacer y pouer del Sol.' *2 pp; Text 65 folioed leaves:* ' Tabla Para Saler Las horas ' *etc.* 1 *leaf:* ' Relacion svmaria de los Servicios de los Capitanes Bartolome Garcia de Nodal, y Gonçalo de Nodal hermanos.' *folioed leaves 2-15. At fol. 35 is a copperplate Map entitled* ' Reconocimiento de los Estrechos de Magallanes ' *etc.* ' I de Courbes fculpfit.' 13½ by 15½ *inches. Fine copy in morocco by Bedford. 4to.* (10*l.* 10*s.* 2001)

NOMENCLATURA Brevis Anglo=Latino in usum Scholarum. Together with Examples of the Five Declenfions of Nouns: With the Words in Propria quæ Maribus and Quæ Genus reduced to each Declenfion. Per F. G. *Boston,* in New-England: Printed by J. Draper, for J. Edwards and H. Fofter in Cornhil. 1735. *2 prel. leaves and 88 pp. Calf. 12mo.* (10*s.* 6*d.* 2002)

NOOTKA SOUND. An Authentic Statement of all the Facts relative to Nootka Sound; its discovery, history, settlement, trade, and the probable advantages to be derived from it; in an Address to the King. *London:* J. Debrett, MDCCXC. *Title and 26 pp: signed* ' Argonaut.' 8*vo.* (4*s.* 6*d.* 2003)

NORGATE (E.) Mr. John Dunn Hunter defended: Or, some Remarks on an Article in the North American Review, in which that Gentleman is branded as an impostor. By E. Norgate. *London:* John Miller, 1826. 38 *pp.* 8*vo.* (2*s.* 6*d.* 2004)

NORTH-AMERICAN (THE) and the West-Indian Gazetteer. Containing An Authentic Defcription of the Colonies and Islands in that part of the Globe, Shewing their Situation, Climate, Soil, Produce, and Trade: With their Former and Prefent Condition. Also an exact Account of the Cities, Towns, Harbours, Ports, Bays, Rivers, Lakes, Mountains, Number of Inhabitants, &c. Illustrated with maps. *London,* G. Robinson, MDCCLXXVI. 3 *prel. leaves; Introduction* xxiv *pp; Text, signatures B. to T, in sixes & U.* 1. *Addenda* 2 *pp.* 2 *maps. Old calf.* 12*mo.* (4s. 6d. 2005)

NORTH-AMERICAN (THE) and the West-Indian Gazetteer. Containing An Authentic Defcription of the Colonies and Islands in that part of the Globe, shewing their Situation, Climate, Soil, Produce, and Trade; With their Former and Prefent Condition. Also An exact Account of the Cities, Towns, Harbours, Ports, Bays, Rivers, Lakes, Mountains, Number of Inhabitants, &c. Illustrated with Maps. The Second Edition. *London:* G. Robinson, MDCCLXXVIII. 3 *prel. leaves. Introduction* xxiv *pp. Text, signatures B. to T. in sixes & U.* 1. 2 *Maps.* 12*mo.* (4s. 6d. 2006)

NORTHERN TOUR (A): Being A Guide to Saratoga, Lake George, Niagara, Canada, Boston, &c. &c. Through the States of Pennsylvania, New Jersey, New York, Vermont, New Hampshire, Massachusetts, Rhode Island, and Connecticut; embracing an account of the Canals, Colleges, Public Institutions, Natural Curiosities, and interesting objects therein. *Philadelphia:* H. C. Carey & I. Lea. 1825. 4 *prel. leaves and* 279 *pp. Half calf.* 12*mo.* (5s. 2007)

NORTON (JOHN). A/ Discussion/ of that Great Point in/ Divinity,/ the/ Sufferings of Christ;/ And the Questions about his/ Righteoufneffe Active, Paffive:/ and the Imputation thereof./ Being an Answer to a Dialogue/ Intituled/ The Meritorious Price of our Redemption,/ Juftification, &c./ By John Norton Teacher of the Church/ at Ipfwich in New-England./ Who was appointed to draw up this Anfwer by the Generall Court./ *London,* Printed by A. M. for Geo. Calvert at the Sign of the half/ Moon, and Jofeph Nevill at the Sign of the Plough in the/ new Buildings in Pauls Churchyard. 1653./ 8 *prel. leaves and* 270 *pp. Mottoes* 1 *page.* 'The Copy of a Letter,' *etc.* 3 *pp. Unbound.* 8*vo.* (10s. 6d. 2008)

NORTON (John). The/ Orthodox Evangelift./ Or a/ Treatife/ Wherein many Great/ Evangelical Truths/ (Not a few whereof are much oppofed and Eclipfed/ in this perillous hour of the Paffion of the Gofpel)/ Are briefly Difcuffed, cleared, and con-/firmed: As a further help, for the Begeting, and Eftablifhing of the Faith which is in Jefus./ As also the State of the Bleffed, Where;/ Of the condition of their Souls from the/ inftant of their Diffolution: and of their/ Perfons after their Re- furrection./ By John Norton, Teacher of the Church/ at Ipfwich in New England./ *London,*/ Printed by John Macock, for Henry Cripps, and Lodowick Lloyd,/ and are to be fold at their fhop in Popes head Alley,/ neer Lombard ftreet. 1654./ 8 *prel. leaves and* 356 *pp*. 'An Alphabetical Table,' *etc.* 14 *pp*. 4*to*. (18*s*. 2009)

NORTON (John). Abel being Dead yet fpeaketh;/ or, the/ Life & Death/ Of that defervedly Famous Man of God,/ M*r* John Cotton,/ Late Teacher of the Church of/ Christ, at Boston in/ New-Eng- land./ By John Norton, Teacher/ of the fame Church./ *London,*/ Printed by Tho. Newcomb for Lodowick Lloyd, and/ are to be fold at his Shop next the Caftle-/Tavern in Cornhill. 1658./ 51 *pp*. 'A Catalogue of fome Books *etc.*' 5 *pp*. *Calf extra, by Bedford*. 4*to*. (2*l*. 2*s*. 2010)

NORTON (John). The/ Heart of New England/ Rent at the/ Blasphemies/ of the prefent Genera- tion./ Or a brief/ Tractate,/ Concerning the/ Doc- trine of the Quakers,/ Demonftrating the deftruc- tive nature/ thereof, to Religion, the Churches, and/ the State; with confideration of the Re-/medy againft it./ Occafional Satisfaction to Objections, and Confirmation of the contrary Truth./ By John Norton, Teacher of the Church of/ Chrift at Bof- ton./ Who was appointed thereunto by the Order of the/ General Court./ *London*, Printed by J. H. for John Allen at the Rifing-/Sunne in St. Pauls Church-yard. 1660./ *Title and* 83 *pp*. *Unbound.* 16*mo*. (3*l*. 3*s*. 2011)

NOVA SCOTIA. A Genuine Account of Nova Scotia: Containing a Defcription of its Situation, Air, Climate, Soil and its Produce; alfo Rivers,

Bays, Harbours, and Fifh, with which they abound in very great Plenty. To which is Added His Majefty's Proposals, as an Encouragement to thofe who are willing to fettle there. London Printed: And *Dublin*, Re-printed for Philip Bowes, MDCCL. 16 pp. *half mor.* 8vo. (5s. 6d. 2012)

NOVA SCOTIA. The Conduct of the French, With Regard to Nova Scotia, From its firft Settlement to the prefent Time. In which are expofed the Falfehood and Abfurdity of their Arguments made ufe of to elude the Force of the Treaty of Utrecht, and ' fupport their unjuft Proceedings. In a Letter to a Member of Parliament. *London*: T. Jefferys. MDCCLIV. *Title, and text* 77 *pp. Half morocco.* 8vo. (7s. 6d. 2013)

NOVA SCOTIA. A fair Representation of His Majefty's Right to Nova Scotia or Acadie. Briefly ftated from the Memorials of the English Commiffaries; with an Answer to the Objections Contained In the French Memorials, and In a Treatise, Entitled, Difcuffion Sommaire fur les anciennes Limites de l'Acadie. *London:* Edward Owen, MDCCLVI. 64 *pp. half mor.* 8vo. (7s. 6d. 2014)

NOVA SCOTIA. An Account of the Present State of Nova Scotia. *Edinburgh:* William Creech; M,DCC,LXXXVI. *viii and text* 157 *pp. Uncut.* 8vo. (7s. 6d. 2015)

NOVVS ORBIS Regio-/nvm ac Insvlarvm veteribvs incognitarvm,/ unà cum tabula cofmographica, & aliquot alijs confimilis/ argumenti libellis, quorum omnium catalogus/ fequenti patebit pagina./ His acceffit copiofus rerum memorabilium index./ *Busileae* apvd Io. Hervagivm, mense Martio, Anno M.D.XXXII./ 24 *prel. leaves; viz. Title, on the reverse,* ' Catalogvs eorvm qvae hoc' *etc.* 'Excellenti viro Georgio Collimitio Danstettero Artis Medicae et disciplinarū Mathematicarū omnium facile principi, Simon Grynaevs S.' 3 *pp.* 'Index rervm' *etc.* 18 *pp.* 'Index e Brocardo,' *etc.* 13 *pp.* 'Typi Cosmographici et declaratio et ufus Sebaftianum Munfterum.' 12 *pp. Text* 584 *pp. and Colophon leaf. Fine copy. Old stamped calf. Folio.* (1*l.* 10s. 2016)

NOVVS ORBIS Re-/gionvm ac Insvlarvm ve-/teribus incognitarum, unà cum tabula cofmographica,

&/ aliquot aliis confimilis argumenti libellis, quorum/ omnium catalogus fequenti patebit pagina./ His acceffit copiofus rerum memorabilium index./ *Parisiis* apvd Galeotvm à/ Prato, in aula maiore regii Palatii ad primam columnam/ [*Colophon*] Impreffum Parifiis apud Antonium Augerellum, impenfis Ioannis/ Parui & Galeoti à Prato. Anno M. D. XXXII. VII./ Calen. Nouembris./ 26 *prel. leaves; viz. Title, vn the reverse,* 'Catalogvs' *etc.* 'Excellenti viro Georgio' *etc.* 3 *pp.* 'Index rervm' *etc.* 37 *pp.* 'Typi Cosmographici et Declaratio,' *etc.* 10 *pp. Text* 507 *pp.* [*for* 514] *colophon leaf as above. Vellum. Folio.* (1*l.* 10*s.* 2017)

NOVVS ORBIS. Die New/Welt, der landfchaf=/ ten vnnd Infulen, fo/bis hie her allen Altweltbefchrybern vnbekant,/ Jungft aber von den Portugalefern vnnd Hifpaniern jm/ Nider=/genglichen Meer herfunden. Sambt den fitten vnnd gebreuchen der Inwonenden/ völcker. Auch was Gütter oder Waren man bey jnen funden, vnd jnn/ vnfere Landtbracht hab. Do bey findt man auch hie den vrfprung vnd/ altherkummen Fürnembften Gwaltigften Völcker der Alt=/bekanten Welt, als do feind die Tartern, Mofcouiten,/ Reuffen, Preuffen, Hungern, Sfchlafen. etc./ nach anzeygung vnd jnnhalt difs vmb=/gewenten blats./ Gedruckt zü *Straszburg* durch Georgen Vlricher,/ von Andla, am viertzehenden tag des Mertzens./ An. M.D.XXXIIII. 6 *prel. leaves; viz. Title, on the reverse,* 'Anzeygung vnd Iñhalt diffes Büchs der Newen Welt.' 'Dem Wolgebornen Herrn Herrn Reynharten Graffen zü Hanaw, Herrn zü Lichtenberg, des Hohen Stiffts zü Strafzburg Thümcufter feinem Gnedigen Herrn. etc." 10 *pp. Text* 242 [*for* 252] *folioed leaves. Folio.* (1*l.* 10*s.* 2018)

NOVVS ORBIS Regio-/nvm ac Insvlarvm veteribvs incognitarvm/ una cum tabula cofmographica, & aliquot alijs confimilis/ argumenti libellis, quorum omnium catalogus/ fequenti patebit pagina./ His acceffit copiofus rerum memorabilium index./ Adiecta est hvic postremae Editioni/ Nauigatio Caroli Cæfaris aufpicio in comi-/tijs Auguftanis inftituta./ *Basileae* apvd Io. Hervagivm mense/ Martio Anno M.D.XXXVII. 24 *prel. leaves; viz. Title, on the reverse,* 'Catalogus' *etc.* 'Excellenti viro Georgio,' *etc.* 3 *pp.* 'Index rervm' *etc.* 18 *pp.* 'Index e Brocardo,' *etc.* 13 *pp.* 'Typi Cosmographici' *etc.* 12 *pp. Text* 600 *pp ; and blank leaf with woodcut on verso. Old stamped calf. Folio.* (1*l.* 10*s.* 2019)

NOVVS ORBIS Re-/gionvm ac Insvlarvm vete=/ribvs incognitarvm vna cvm Tabvla Cos-/mographica, & aliquot alijs confimilis argumenti libellis, nunc no-/nis navigationibvs auctus, quorum omnium catalogus/ fequenti patebit pagina./ His accefsit copiofus rerum memorabilium index./ Adiecta est hvic postremae Editioni/ Nauigatio Caroli Caesaris aufpicio in comi-/tijs Auguftanis inftituta./ *Basileæ* apvd Io. Hervagivm, Anno M.D.LV./ 26 *prel. leaves; viz. Title, on the reverse,* 'Catalogvs' *etc.* 'Excellenti viro Georgio,' *etc.* 3 *pp.* 'Index rerum' *etc.* 33 *pp. Errata on the last page; blank leaf;* 'Typi cosmographici' *etc.* 12 *pp. Text* 677 *pp; blank leaf with woodcut on the reverse. With Map. Fine copy. Best Edition. Folio.* (1*l.* 10*s.* 2020)

NOVUS ORBIS./ id eft,/ Navigationes/ Primæ in Americam:/ quibus adjunximus/ Casparis Varrerii discvrsvm/ fuper Ophyra Regione./ Elenchum Autorem versa pagina/ Lector inveniet./ *Roterodami,*/ Apud Iohannem Leonardi Berewout/ Anno cIɔ. Iɔ. cxvi./ 8 *prel. leaves; viz. Title, on the reverse* 'Elenchvs Avtorvm.' 'Ornatisfimis, Prudentifimisque viris in Collegio Thalassiarchico vrbis Roterod. Dominis fuis.' 13 *pp: Text* 570 *pp; and* 1 *blank leaf.*/ 'Casparis/ Varrerii Lvsitani/ Commentarius/ de Ophyra/ Regione,/ In facris litteris Lib. III. Regum/ & II. Paralipomenon./ Roterodami,/ Apud Ioannem Leonardi Berevvout,/ Anno 1616./ *Title, and* 82 *unnumbered pages. Fine copy. Small* 8*vo.* (2*l.* 12*s.* 6*d.* 2021)

NUEVA ESPANA. Continente/ Americano,/ Argonauta/ de las Costas/ de/ Nueva-España,/ y/ Tierra-Firme,/ Islas, y Baxos/ de esta Navegacion,/ Longitud,/ y Altura de Polo,/ de sus Puertos,/ y Noticias de estas Habitaciones. [*Cadiz* 1728?] 3 *prel. leaves and* 161 *pp. Old red morocco.* 8*vo.* (12*s.* 6*d.* 2022)

NUNEZ CABECA DE VACA (Alvar). ¶ La relacion y comentarios del gouerna/ dor Aluar nuñez cabeça de vaça, de lo acaefcido en las/ dos jor-

nadas quebizo a las Indias./ Con priuilegio./
¶ Efta taffada por los feñores del confejo en Ochēta
y cinco mr̃s./ [*Colophon*] ⁊ Impreffo en *Valladolid*, por Francifco fer-⁊/nandez de Cordoua. Año
de mil y quinien-/nientos y cinquenta y cinco años./
146 *leaves; viz. Title with engraved coat of Arms;
on the reverse* ' El Rey.' *signed* ' Francifco de Le-
defma.' *and* fol. ij. *to* fol. lvj. *the reverse blank.*⁊
Commenta⁊/rios de Alvar Nvnez Cabe/ça de
vaca, adelantado y gouernador dela pro/uinca del
Rio de la Plata./ Scriptos por Pero hernandez
fcriuano y fecre-/tario dela prouincia. Y dirigidos
al fereniff./ muy alto y muy poderofo feñor/ el In-
fante don Carlos. N. S./ 1 *page.* ' Prohemio.' 5 *pp;
the 4th page of the Prohemis is* ' Fol. lvij.' *and* fol.
lviij. *to* fol. clxiiii. [*for* cxliiii.] fol. xxv. [*for* xv.]
fol. lxi. [*for* lxii.] fol. lxxxiii. [*for* lxxxv.] *Black
letter. Fine large copy in blue mor. by Bedford.*
4to. (10*l*. 10*s*. 2023)

NUNEZ CASTAÑO (DIEGO). Breve compendivm/
Hostivm Haere-/ticorvm Olandensivm/ aduentum
in Valdiuian, explorato/rem miffum, & narrationem
eius,/ fugam illorum cum pacto redeun-/di : proui-
das difpofitiones Prorregis :/ Claffim expeditam ad
conditum e-/ius cum rebus neceffarijs,/ & alia continens./ Gvbernante Exc. D.D./ Petro à Toleto &
Ley va Prorrege./ Regnante Philippo IIII./ Hifpaniarum Rege./ Stvdio, et Labore/ Didaci Nuñes
Caftaño Prefbyteri./ *Limæ*, Anno 1645./ *Title, on
the reverse* ' Ad Oblationem Libri.' *and folioed leaves*
2-36. 16*mo*. (2*l*. 12*s*. 6*d*. 2024)

NUNEZ DE HARO (ALONSO). Nos el D^r. D. Alonso Nuñez de Haro, y Peralta, por la Gracia de Dios,
y de la Santa Sede Apóstolica, Arzobispo de Mé-
gico, del Consejo de su Magestad, &.. [*Mexico*]. *a
Broadside in 2 Sheets. Folio.* (7*s*. 6*d*. 2025)

BJECTIONS (The) to the Taxation of our American Colonies, by the Legislature of Great Britain, Briefly Confider'd. *London*: J. Wilkie, 1765. *Title, and pp.* 3-20. 4to. (7s. 6d. 2026)

OBSERVATIONS on American Independency. 24 pp. *signed* 'T. T. B.' 8vo. (4s. 6d. 2027)

OBSERVATIONS on the Conduct of Great Britain, with Regard to the Negociations and other Transactions Abroad. *London*, J. Roberts. 1729. 61 pp. 8vo. (5s. 6d. 2028)

OBSERVATIONS on the Case of the Northern Colonies. *London*: J. Roberts, 1731. 31 pp. *half mor.* 8vo. (7s. 6d. 2029)

OBSERVATIONS Occafion'd by reading a Pamphlet, intitled a Discourse concerning The Currencies of the Britifh Plantations in America. In a Letter to * * * * *. *London*: T. Cooper, 1741. 23 pp. *half mor.* 8vo. (4s. 6d. 2030)

OBSERVATIONS On the Inflaving, importing and purchafing of Negroes; With fome Advice thereon, extracted from the Epiftle of the Yearly-Meeting of the People called Quakers held at London in the Year 1748. Second Edition. *Germantown*: Printed by Christopher Sower. 1760. 16 pp. 8vo. (7s. 6d. 2031)

OBSERVATIONS on a late State of the Nation. *London*: J. Dodsley, mddclxix. *Title and* 97 pp. 4to. (4s. 6d. 2032)

OBSERVATIONS on a Late State of the Nation. The Fourth Edition. *London*, J. Dodsley, mdcc

LXIX. *Half-title, title, & 155 pp. Half morocco.*
8vo. (4s. 6d. 2033)

OBSERVATIONS on Several Acts of Parliament, passed In the Fourth, Sixth and Seventh Years of His Present Majesty's Reign. Publiſhed by the Merchants of Boston. Boston: Printed by Edes and Gill. *London:* Reprinted for G. Kearsly, M.DCC.LXX. *Title and text 37 pp. half morocco.*
8vo. (5s. 6d. 2034)

OBSERVATIONS: On the Reconciliation of Great-Btitain, and the Colonies; In which are exhibited Arguments for, and againſt, that Measure. By a Friend of American Liberty. *Philadelphia;* Printed, by Robert Bell, in Third-Street. MDCCLXXVI. *32 pp.* 'The Plan of an American Compact, with Great-Britain. Firſt Publiſhed at New-York.' *pp 33–40. half mor.* 8vo. (5s. 6d. 2035)

OBSERVATIONS on the Dutch Manifesto, addressed to the Earl of Shelburn. *London:* G. Kearsly, [1781]. *iv und 27 pp.* 8vo. (4s. 6d. 2036)

OBSERVATIONS on the Commerce of the American States. With an Appendix; containing An Account of all Rice, Indigo, Cochineal, Tobacco, Sugar, Molaſſes, and Rum imported into and exported from Great Britain the laſt ten Years. Of the Value of all Merchandize imported into and exported from England. Of the Imports and Exports of Philadelphia, New-York, &c. Alſo an Account of the Shipping employed in America previous to the War. The Second Edition. *London:* J. Debrett, MDCCLXXXIII. *2 prel. leaves and 122 pp.* 'The Tables' etc. *1 page,* 'Contents of the Appendix' *iv pp.* 'Appendix.' No. I to XVIII. Tables. *Half mor.* 8vo. (5s. 6d. 2037)

OBSERVATIONS on the Fift Article of the Treaty with America: And on The Neceſſity of appointing a Judicial Enquiry into the Merits and Losses of the American Loyalists. Printed by Order of their Agents. *London:* G. Wilkie, MDCCLXXXIII. *19 pp. half mor.* 8vo. (4s. 6d. 2038)

OBSERVATIONS on a Pamphlet, entitled A State of the Present Form of Government of the Province of Quebec; circulated in London, during the last summer. With an Appendix, containing information on the subject. By a Citizen of Quebec. *London:* J. Stockdale, MDCCXC. *Title & 78 pp. Half mor. 8vo.* (4s. 6d. 2039)

OBSERVATIONS on the Present War, the Projected Invasion, and a Decree of the National Convention, for the Emancipation of the Slaves in the French Colonies. [By the Rev. John Hampson]. *Sunderland:* [1793]. *Half-title, title, and pp.* 3-61. *half mor. 8vo.* (3s. 6d. 2040)

OBSERVATIONS on the System by which Estates have been and are still Managed in Jamaica; and on the Apprenticeship introduced by the recent Abolition Act. By a Proprietor. *Edinburgh:* Maclachlan and Stewart. MDCCCXXXVI. *27 pp.* *8vo.* (2s. 6d. 2041)

O'CALLAGHAN (E. B.) Jesuit Relations of discoveries and other occurrences in Canada and the Northern and Western States of the Union. 1632-1672. By E. B. O'Callaghan, M.D. Corresponding Member of the New York Historical Society, and Honorary Member of the Historical Society of Connecticut. From the Proceedings of the New York Historical Society, Nov. 1847. *New York:* Press of the Historical Society. MDCCXLVII. *22 pp. calf. 8vo.* (7s. 6d. 2042)

OCCASIONAL Reflections on the Importance of the War in America, And the Reasonableness and Justice of Supporting the King of Prussia, &c. In Defence of the Common Cause. Founded on a general View of the State and Connections of this Country; the General Syftem of Europe; and the ambitious Defigns of French Policy for overturning the Ballance of Power and Liberties of Europe. In a Letter to a Member of Parliament. *London:* J. Whiston and B. White. M.DCC.LVIII. *Half-title, title, and* 139 *pp. half mor. 8vo.* (7s. 6d. 2043)

OCCOM (SAMPSON). A Sermon at the Execution of Moses Paul, an Indian; Who had been guilty of Murder, Preached at New Haven in America. By Samson Occom, A native Indian, and Miffionary to the Indians, who was in England in 1776 [1766] and 1777, [1767] collecting for the

Indian Charity Schools. To which is added a short Account of the Late Spread of the Gospel, among the Indians. Also Observations on the Language of the Muhhekaneew Indians; communicated to the Connecticut Society of Arts and Sciences, by Jonathan Edwards, D.D. New Haven, Connecticut: Printed 1788. *London*: Reprinted, 1788, 24 pp. 'Observations,' etc. 16 pp. 8vo. (5s. 6d. 2044)

OCKANICKON. A True/ Account/ of the/ Dying Words/ of/ Ockanickon,/ an Indian/King./ Spoken to/ Jahkursoe,/ His Brother's Son, whom he appointed/ King/ after him./ [*London*] Printed in the Year 1683. 6 pp. *On the reverse of the title*, 'A Letter' *etc. dated* 'Burlington the 12th, of the 5th. Month, 1682.' *signed* 'John Cripps.' 4to. (1l. 11s. 6d. 2045)

O'DONOJU (Juan). Correspondencia entre el General D. Juan O-Donoju, y el Brigadier D. Francisco Lemaur, Y las últimas cartas de aquel al general Dávila, con las respuestas de éste. [*Colophon*] Habana. 1821. Diaz de Castro. 25 pp. half mor. 8vo. (3s. 6d. 2046)

O'DONOJU (Juan). Refutacion, con notas interesantantes, al parte que dirigio a Superior Gobierno el Teniente General Don Juan O-Donoju sobre el Tratado que Firmó en Córdoba. *Habana.*—1822. Pedro Nolásce Boloña, Title and 15 pp. half mor. 8vo. (3s. 6d. 2047)

OEXMELIN (Alexandre Olivier). Histoire/ des/ Avanturiers/ qui se sont signalez dans les Indes,/ contenant/ ce qu'ils ont fait de plus remarquable/ depuis vingt Anne'es./ Avec/ La Vie, les Mœurs, les Coûtumes des Habitans de Saint Do-/mingue & de la Tortuë, & une defcription exacte de ces/ lieux ;/ Où l'on voit/ L'etabliffement d'une Chambre des Comptes dans les Indes,/ & un Etat, tiré de cette Chambre, des Offices tant Eccle-/fiaftiques que Seculiers, où le Roy d'Efpagne pourvoit, les/ Revenus qu'il tire de l'Amerique, & ce que les plus grands/ Princes de l'Europe y poffedent./ Le tout enrichi de Cartes Geographiques & de Figures/ en Taille-douce./ Par Alexandre Olivier Oexmelin./ *A Paris*,/ Jacques le Febure,/ m.dc.lxxxviii./ Avec

Privilege du Roy./ *Two Volumes.* Tome Prémier.
12 *prel. leaves including Engraved title, and* 448 *pp.*
[*for* 248] *Table* 16 *pp. Maps at pp.* 1, 179. Tome
Second. 3 *prel. leaves and* 285 *pp. Table* 16 *pp.* ' Extrait du Privilege.' 1 *page. Map at page* 133. Old
calf. 12*mo.* (8*s.* 6d 2048)

OGDEN (UZAL). The Theological Preceptor; or
Youth's Religious lnstructor. Containing a Summary of the Principles, Rise, and Progreſs of Religion, from the Creation of the World, to the Confumation thereof;—together with moral Reflections, &c. and a Sketch of the Arguments in Favour
of Chriſtianity. In a Series of Dialogues. By
Uzal Ogden Jun. a Candidate for Holy Orders.
New York: Printed by John Holt, M,DCC,LXXII.
xii and 259 *pp.* 12*mo.* (10*s.* 6*d.* 2049)

OGLE (*Sir* CHALONER). The Tryal of Sir Chaloner
Ogle, Kt. Rear-Admiral of the Blue, before the
Chief Juſtice of Jamaica, For an Aſſault on the
Perſon of his Excellency Mr. Trelawney the Governor, committed in his own Houſe in Spaniſh
Town on the 22d Day of July laſt. With Authentic
Copies of the ſeveral Letters that paſſed on that
Occaſion, between Mr. Concanen, now Attorney-General of the Iſland, Sir Chaloner Ogle, the Governor, and A—l V—. [Admiral Vernon.] London Printed: *Dublin* Reprinted MDCCXLII. 16 *pp.*
Half morocco. 8*vo.* (7*s.* 6*d.* 2050)

OGLE (*Sir* CHALONER). The Tryal of Sir Chaloner
Ogle, Kt. Rear Admiral of the Blue. Before the
Chief Justice of Jamaica, For an Aſſault on the
Perſon of his Excellency Mr. Trelawney the Governor, committed in his own Houſe in Spaniſh
Town, on the 22d Day of July laſt. With Authentic Copies of the ſeveral Letters that paſſed on that
Occaſion, between Mr. Concanen, now Attorney
General of the lſland, Sir Chaloner Ogle, the Governor, and A—l V—. *London:* W. Webb,
M,DCCXLIII. 32 *pp. half mor.* 8*vo.* (7*s.* 6*d.* 2051)

OGLETHORPE (GENERAL). An Impartial Account Of the late Expedition Against St. Augustine
Under General Oglethorpe. Occaſioned by The
Suppreſſion of the Report, made by a Committee
of the General Aſſembly in South-Carolina, tranſ-

mitted, under the Great Seal of that Province, to their Agent in England, in order to be printed. With an Exact Plan of the Town, Caftle and Harbour of St. Auguftine, and the adjacent Coaft of Florida; fhewing the Difpofition of our Forces on that Enterprize. *London*: J. Huggonson, 1742. 68 pp. *With Plan of St. Augustine. Half mor.* 8vo. (10s. 6d. 2052)

OLD ENGLAND for Ever, or, Spanifh Cruelty difplay'd. [*London*, 1741?] pp. 7-320. *Title and prel. leaves wanting. Old calf.* 8vo. (7s. 6d. 2053)

ONA (PEDRO DE). Aravco/ domado./ Compvesto por el/ Licenciado Pedro de Oña, natural de los/ Infantes de Engol en Chile, Colegial del/ Real Colegio Mayor de San Felipe, y/ San Marcos fundado en la Ciu-/dad de Lima./ Dirigido a Don Hvrtado/ de Mendoça, Primogenito de don Garcia Hur-/tado de Mendoça, Marques de/ Cañete, &c./ Año, 1605./ Con privilegio;/ En Madrid, por Ivan de la Cuefta./ Vendefe en cafa de Francifco Lopez./ 16 prel. leaves; Text 342 folioed leaves. 'Tabla' 3 pp. *Old calf.* 8vo. (3l. 13s. 6d. 2054)

OPPORTUNITY (THE), or Reasons for an Immediate Alliance with St. Domingo. By the Author of "The Crisis of the Sugar Colonies." *London*: J. Hatchard, 1804. *viii and text* 156 pp. *Unbound.* 8vo. (3s. 6d. 2055)

ORDERS in Council; or, an Examination of the Justice, Legality, and Policy of the New System of Commercial Regulations. With an Appendix of State Papers, Statutes, and Authorities. The Second Edition. *London*: Longman, 1808. *Halftitle, title, and* 120 pp. 8vo. (3s. 6d. 2056)

ORFORD (ROBERT, *Earl of*). A Further Report from the Committee of Secrecy, Appointed to Enquire into the Conduct of Robert, Earl of Orford; During the laft Ten Years of his being Firft Commissioner of the Treasury, and Chancellor and Under-Treafurer of his Majesty's Exchequer. Delivered the 30th of June 1742. *London*: T. Leech, 1742. 132 pp. '*No. 13' a folded sheet between pp. 128 & 129. half mor.* 8vo. (4s. 6d. 2057)

ORIGIN (THE) of the Whale bone-petticoat. A

Satyr. *Boston*, Auguft 2d. 1714. 8 *pp. in Verse.*
8*vo.* (10*s.* 6*d.* 2058)

OSORIO (Hieronymo). De Rebvs,/ Emmanvelis Regis Lv-/sitaniæ Invictissimi Virtvte/ et Avspicio gestis libri/ dvodecim./ Auctore Hieronymo Oforio/ Episcopo Sylvensi./ *Olysippone.*/ Apud Antonium Gondifaluū Typographum./ Anno Domini m.d. lxxj./ Cvm Privilegio Regio./ 480 *pp. including the title. Privilege and Errata* 2 *pp. Fine copy, Old calf. Folio.* (1*l.* 1*s.* 2059)

OTHER (The) Side of the Queftion : Or a Defence of the Liberties of North-America. In Answer to a late Friendly Address to All Reafonable Americans, on The Subject of Our Political Confusions. By a Citizen. *New York:* Printed by James Rivington, fronting Hanover-Square. m,dcc,lxxiv. 30 *pp. half mor.* 8*vo.* (7*s.* 6*d.* 2060)

OTIS (James). The Rights of the Britifh Colonies Afferted and proved. By James Otis Efq, *Boston:* Printed and Sold by Edes and Gill, in Queen-Street. m,dcc,lxiv. 80 *pp. Half morocco.*
8*vo.* (5*s.* 6*d.* 2061)

OTIS (James). The Rights of the Britifh Colonies Afferted and proved. By James Otis, Efq ; The Second Edition. Boston, New England, Printed; *London* Reprinted for J. Almon, [1765?] 120 *pp. half mor.* 8*vo.* (5*s.* 6*d.* 2062)

OTIS (James). The Rights of the Britifh Colonies Afferted and proved. By James Otis, Efq ; The Third Edition, corrected. Boston, New-England, Printed: *London* Reprinted, for J. Williams, 1766. 120 *pp. half mor.* 8*vo.* (5*s.* 6*d.* 2063)

OTIS (James). A Vindication of the Britifh Colonies. By James Otis, Efq ; Of Boston. Boston, printed: *London,* reprinted for J. Almon, 1769. 2 *prel. leaves and text* 48 *pp. Half morocco.*
8*vo.* (6*s.* 6*d.* 2064)

OUSELEY (William Gore). Remarks on the Statistics and Political Institutions of the United States, with some Observations on the Ecclesiastical System of America, her Sources of Revenue, &c. To which are added Statistical Tables, &c. By William Gore Ouseley, Esq. Attaché to his Majesty's Legation at Washington. *London:* J. Rodwell, 1832. *iv and* 208 *pp.* 8vo. (3s. 6d. 2065)

OVALLE (ALONSO DE). Historica/ Relacion/ Del Reyno de Chile,/ Y delas miſſiones, y miniſterios que exercita en el/ la Compañia de Iesvs./ A Nvestro Senor/ Iesv Christo/ Dios Hombre,/ Y ala Santiſsima Virgen, y Madre/ Maria/ Señora del Cielo, y delaTierra,/ y alos Santos/ Ioseph, Ioachin, Ana/ ſus Padres, y Aguelos./ Alonso de Ovalle/ Dela Compañia de Iesvs Natural de Santia-/go de Chile, y ſu Procurador à Roma. En *Roma,* por Franciſco Cauallo. M.DC.XLVI./ Con licencia delos Superiores./ 5 *prel. leaves; viz.* [*Advertisement*] Varias, y Cvriosas Noticias del Reino de Chile,' *etc,* 1 *page the reverse blank; Title on the reverse* 'Qveſta Relatione del Chile,'*etc.* ' Prologo al letor.' 3 *pp.* 'Aduertencia para no errar en poner las Imagenes,'*etc.* 2 *pp:* ' Protesta del Avtor.' 1 *page. Text* 456 *pp. With Map of Chile, and* 37 *Copperplates at pp.* 51, 58, 88, 90, 91, 92, 104, 107, 186 (3), 288, 302, 322 (23), 393. *With* 18 *woodcuts at the end. Vellum. Folio.* (3*l.* 3*s.* 2066)

OVIEDO (HERNANDEZ DE). La hiſtoria general/ delas Indias./☙ Con priuilegio imperial ☙/ [*Colophon*] De *Seuilla* a treynta/ dias del mes de Setiembre: de M. d. τ treynta τ cinco años [1535]. *Title in black and red, having on the reverse* 11 *lines giving a fuller description of the book; Preface* 'Libro primero' 6 *pp; Text in* cxciij *folioed leaves. Very fine copy in Black Letter. Folio.* (10*l.* 10*s.* 2067)
At the end of the book is the autograph of the author.

OVIEDO Y VALDES (GONÇALO FERNANDEZ DE). ¶ Libro. xx. De la ſegunda parte de la general/ hiſtoría de las Indías. Eſcrípta por el Capítan/ Gonçalo Fernandez de Ouíedo, y Valdes. Alᷓ/cayde de la fortaleza y puerto de Sácto Domín/go, d'la iſla Eſpañola. Croniſta d' ſu Mageſtad./ Que trata del eſtrecho de Magallans./ ¶ En *Valladolid.* Por Franciſco Fernandez de Cordoua,/ Impreſſor de su Mageſtad. Año de M.D.LVII./ [*Colophon*] ¶ Impreſſo en Valladolid, por frāᷓ/cisco fernandez de Cordoua./ En eſte año de M.D.LVII./ 64 *folioed leaves including title. Black letter. Fine copy. Folio.* (4*l.* 14*s.* 6*d.* 2068)

AINE (ROBERT TREAT). The Works, in Verse and Prose, of the late Robert Treat Paine, Jun. Esq. With Notes. To which are prefixed, Sketches of his Life, Character, and Writings. *Boston:* J. Belcher. 1812. *xc and* 464 *pp. Errata* 1 *page. With Portrait of Paine.* Green morocco extra gilt. 8vo. (10s. 6d. 2069)

PAINE (THOMAS). The American Crisis, and a Letter to Sir Guy Carleton, on the murder of Captain Huddy, and the intended retaliation on Captain Asgill, of the Guards. By Thomas Paine, Author of Common Sense—Rights of Man—Age of Reason—and the Decline and Fall of the English System of Finance. *London:* Daniel Isaac Eaton, *Title and* 293 *pp.* 8vo. (7s. 6d. 2070)

PAINE (THOMAS). Observations on Paine's Rights of Man, in a Series of Letters, By Publicola, [John Adams]. *Newcastle:* Hall and Elliot. 36 *pp.* 12mo. (3s. 6d. 2071)

PAINE (THOMAS). A Letter addressed to the Abbe Raynal of the Affairs of North-America. In which The Miftakes in the Abbe's Account of the Revolution of America are corrected and cleared up. By Thomas Paine, M.A. Of the University of Pennsylvania, and Author of a Tract, entitled " Common Sense." Philadelphia, printed: *London,* reprinted, C. Dilly, M.DCC.LXXXII. *viii and* 76 *pp. half mor.* 8vo. (3s. 6d. 2072)

PAINE (THOMAS). Common Sense: Addreffed to the Inhabitants of America, On the following Interesting Subjects. I. Of the Origin and Defign of Government in general, with concife Remarks on the Englifh Conftitution. II. Of Monarchy and Hereditary Succession. III. Thoughts on the prefent State of American Affairs. IV. Of the prefent State of America, with fome Mifcellaneous Reflections. A New Edition. With feveral Additions in the Body of the Work. To which is added, an Appendix; together with an Addrefs to the People called Quakers. The New Edition here given increafes the Work upwards of One Third. By Thomas Paine. Secretary to the Committee for Foreign Affairs to Congrefs during the American War, and Author of the Rights of Man, and a Letter to the Abbé Raynal. *London:* Printed and sold by all the Booksellers. M.DCC.XCII. 58 *pp.* 12*mo.* (3*s.* 6*d.* 2073)

PAINE (THOMAS). Common Sense; addressed to the Inhabitants of America, On the following interefting Subjects: 1. Of the Origin and Defign of Government in general, with concife Remarks on the Englifh Conftitution. II. Of Monarchy and Hereditary Succeffion. III. Thoughts on the Prefent State of American Affairs. IV. Of the prefent Ability of America, with fome mifcellaneous Reflections. A New Edition with feveral Additions in the Body of the Work. To which is added, an Appendix; together with an Addrefs to the People called Quakers. N. B. The New Edition here given increafes the Work upwards of One-Third. By Thomas Paine, Secretary to the Committee for Foreign Affairs to Congrefs, during the American War, and Author of the Rights of Man, and a Letter to the Abbe Raynal. *London:* H. D. Symonds, 1792. 36 *pp. With Portrait of Thomas Paine.* 12*mo.* (4*s.* 6*d.* 2074)

PAINE (THOMAS). A Letter addressed to the Abbe Raynal, on the affairs of North-America. In which the mistakes in the Abbe's Account of the Revolution of America are corrected and cleared up. By Thomas Paine, Secretary for Foreign Affairs to Congress during the American War, and Author of Common Sense, and the Rights of Man. *London:* J. Ridgway, M,DCC,XCII. 46 *pp. Unbound.* 12*mo.* (4*s.* 6*d.* 2075)

PAINE (THOMAS). Letter addressed to the Addressers, of the late Proclamation. By Thomas Paine, Secretary for Foreign Affairs to Congress in the American War, and Author of the Works intitled "Common Sense," "Rights of Man, Two Parts," &c. *London:* II. D. Symonds, 1792. 40 *pp.* 12*mo.* (3*s.* 6*d.* 2076)

PAINE (THOMAS). Miscellaneous Articles, by Thomas Paine. Consisting of A Letter to the Marquis of Lansdowne. A Letter to the Authors of the Republican. A Letter to the Abbe Syeyes. Thoughts on the Peace, and the Probable Advantages thereof. First Letter to Mr. Secretary Dundas. Letter to Lord Onslow. Second Letter to Mr. Dundas. And A Letter to the People of France. *London:* J. Ridgway, M.DCCXCII. 36 *pp.* 12*mo.* (3*s.* 6*d.* 2077)

PAINE (THOMAS). Rights of Man: Being an Answer to Mr. Burke's Attack on the French Revolution. By Thomas Paine, Secretary for Foreign Affairs to Congress in the American War, and Author of the Works intitled "Common Sense," and "A Letter to the Abbe Raynal." Part I. *London:* H. D. Symonds, M,DCC,XCII. *iv and* 78 *pp. and* 1 *p.* 12*mo.* (4*s.* 6*d.* 2078)

PAINE (THOMAS). Rights of Man; part the Second. Combining Principle and Practice. By Thomas Paine, Secretary for Foreign Affairs to Congress in the American War, and Author of the Works entitled "Common Sense," and the "First Part of the Rights of Man." *London:* H. D. Symonds, 1792. 94 *pp. and* 1 *p.* 12*mo.* (4*s.* 6*d.* 2079)

PAINE (THOMAS). Rights of Man: Part the Second combining Principle and Practice. By Thomas Paine, Secretary for Foreign Affairs to Congress in the American War, and Author of the Works intitled "Common Sense," And the "First Part of the Rights of Man." *London:* Printed for the Booksellers. M,DCC,XCII. 82 *pp. Unbound.* 12*mo.* (3*s.* 6*d.* 2080)

PAINE (THOMAS). Mr. Paine's Principles and Schemes of Government examined, and his errors detected. *Edinburgh:* J. & J. Fairbairn, 1792. 2 *prel. leaves and* 60 *pp.* 8*vo.* (3*s.* 6*d.* 2081)

PAINE (THOMAS). Paine's Political and Moral Maxims; selected from the Fifth Edition of Rights of Man, Part I. and II. With Explanatory Notes and Elucidations; additional interefting Obfervations on the prefent State of Public Affairs; and important information for the benefit, not of the Houfe of Commons at Weftminfter but of the whole Commons of Great Britain and Ireland. And an Intro-ductory Letter to Mr. Paine. By a Free-Born Englishman. *London : Printed for the Booksellers. 1792. 47 pp. 8vo.* (3s. 6d. 2082)

PALAFOX (JUAN DE, *El Obispo de la Puebla de los Angeles*). Al/ Rey Nvestro Señor./ Satisfacion/ al Memorial de los/ Religiosos de la Compañia/ del nombre de Iesvs de la/ Nveva-España./ Por/ La Dignidad Epifcopal de la Puebla de los Angeles./ Sobre la Execvcion, y Obediencia/ del Breue Apoftolico de N. Santifsimo Padre/ Innocencio X./ Expedido en sv favor a XIIII./ de Mayo de M.DC.XLVIII./ Y/ Paffado repetidamente, y mandado executar por el/ Supremo Confejo de las Indias./ En el qual determinò fu Santidad veinte y feis Decretos/ Sacramentales, y Iurifdiccionales, importantes/ al bien de las almas./ Año de M.DC.LII./ *Title, reverse blank; 3 leaves and folioed leaves 4 to 157. Fiue copy. Vellum. Folio.* (1l. 1s. 2083)

PALAFOX (JUAN DE, *El Obispo de la Puebla de los Angeles*). [Memorial del Dr. Palafox al Rey Sobre el Tratamiento de los Indios] *Running title*, Virtudes/ del Indio./ [*Puebla*, 1634?] *Vellum.* 4to. (10l. 10s. 2084)

This Memorial, respecting the Virtues of the Indians, was probably privately printed for the use of the King and the Council of the Indies, as it is without date, place of printing, name of Printer, title or any of the usual '*Privileges*.' It fills 93 pages, and is divided into 21 Chapters preceded by an Introductory Address to the King. The work is a panegyric of the Indians, as will appear by the heading of the Chapters; viz.

Cap. I. Quam dignos fon los Indios del amparo Real | de V. Mageftad, por la fu auidad con que re- | cibieron la Ley de Chrifto Señor Nueftro | con el calor de fus Catolicas | vanderas. |

Cap. II. De lo que merecen los Indios el amparo Real | de V. Mageftad, por el fauor grande con que | fe exercitan en la Religion Chrif- | tiana. |

Cap. III. De lo que merecen el amparo Real de V. M. | los Indios, por la fu auidad con que han en- | trado en fu Real Corona, y fu fide- | lidad conftantif- | fima. |

Cap. IV. Del valor, y esfuerço de los Indios, y que fu | lealtad, y rendimiento a la Corona de V. | Mageftad, no procedo de bajez a de | animo, fino de vir- | tud. |

Cap. V. Quandignos fon los Indios de la proteccion | Real, por las vtilidades que han caufsedo | a la Corona de Ef- | paña. |
Cap. VI. De la innocencia de los Indios, y que fe hallan | comumente eſſentos de los vicios de foberuia, | ambicion, codicia, auaricia, Ira è embidia, | juegos, blasfemias, jur amentos, y mur- | muraciones. |
Cap. VII. De otros tres vicios de Senfualidad, Gule, | y Perez a, en que fuelen incurrir los | Indios. |
Cap. VIII. De la pobreza del Indio. |
Cap. IX. De la paciencia del Indio. |
Cap. X. De la Liberalidad del Indio. |
Cap. XI. De la honeſtidad del Indio. |
Cap. XII. De la parſimonia del Indio en fu comida. |
Cap. XIII. De la obediencia del Indio. |
Cap. XIIII. De la difcrecion, y elegancia del Indio. |
Cap. XV. De la agudez, y promptitud del Indio. |
Cap. XVI. De la induftria del Indio, feñaladamente en | las Artes mecanicas. |
Cap. XVII. De la juſticia del Indio. |
Cap. XVIII. De la valentia del Indio. |
Cap. XIX. De la Humildad, Cortefia Silencio, y Maña | del Indio. |
Cap. XX. De la Limpieça del Indio, y de fu Paz. |
Cap. XXI. Refpondefe à algunas objeciones que fe pueden | oponer. |

PALAFOX (JUAN DE, *El Obispo de la Puebla de los Angeles*). Carta Pastoral/ del Illvst.^{mo} y R.^{mo} Señor Obispo/ de la Pvebla de los Angeles,/ que oy es de osma./ A las Religiosas/ de aqvel Obispado,/ sir viendo aqvella Santa Iglesia/ Año de 1641./ Es muy vtil para el conocimiento de las obligacio-/nes de las Efpofas de Jefu Chrifto bien nueſtro,/ alteza de fu Dignidad, y atencion que/ deuen tener a fer-/uirle./ Imprimefe por orden de fu Eminencia, y concede cien/ dias de Indulgencia à quien leyere, ò oyere esta/ Carta Pastoral, tan docta, y efpiritual, En *To-/ledo* ù 25. de Março de 1659. años./ *Title reverse blank, and folioed leaves 2-10. 4to.* (1*l*. 1*s*. 2085)

PALOU (FRANCISCO). Relacion Historica de la vida y Apostolicas Tareas del venerable Padre Fray Junipero Serra, Y de las Misiones que fundó en la California Septentrional, y nuevos establecimientos de Monterey. Escrita Por el R. P. L. Fr. Francisco Palou, Guardian actual del Colegio Apostólico de S. Fernando de México, y Discipulo del Venerable Fundador: Dirigida a su Santa Provincia de la Regular observancia de Nrô. S. P. S. Francisco de la Isla de Mallorca. A Expensas de Don Miguel Gonzalez Calderon Sindico de dicho Apostolico Colegio. Impresa en *Mexico*, en la Imprenta de Don Felipe de Zúñiga y Ontiveros, calle del Espiritu Santo, año de 1787. 14 *prel. leaves,* and 344 pp. plate at p. 1 & Map of California engraved on Copper by Diego Froncoso in Mexico 1787. Fine copy. Vellum. 4to. (2l. 2s. 2086)

PANAMA. Original Papers Relating to the Expedition to Panama. London: M. Cooper, M.DCC. XLIV. Title and 224 pp. Wanting pp. 207-8. half mor. 8vo. (7s. 6d. 2087)

PAPERS and Letters on Agriculture, Recommended to the Attention of the Canadian Farmers, By the Agricultural Society in Canada. Quebec: Printed by Samuel Neilson, N°. 3 Mountain-street. M.DCC.XC. In English and French on opposite pages 5 prel. leaves and 34 doubly numbered pp. Thick paper: old green morocco extra, tooled sides. With the Autograph of Bishop Inglis of Nova Scotia on the title page. 8vo. (7s. 6d. 2088)

PARISH (ELIJAH). A Sermon preached at Boston, November 3, 1814, before the Society for Propagating the Gospel among the Indians and others in North-America. By Elijah Parish, D.D. S.A.S. Boston: Nathaniel Willis, 1814. 44 pp. Unbound. 8vo. (2s. 6d. 2089)

PARKER (THOMAS). The/ Visions and Prophecies/ of/ Daniel expounded :/ Wherein the Miftakes of former/ Interpreters are modeftly difcovered, and the true/ meaning of the Text made plain by/ the Words and Circumftances of it./ The fame alfo illuftrated by clear inftances taken/ out of Histories, which relate the Events/ of time, myftically foretold by the Holy Prophet./ Amongft other things of Note, touching/ The Two Witneffes, the New Jerufalem, the Thoufand/ yeers, etc. Here is propounded a new Way for the finding out of the/ determinate time fignified by Daniel in his Seventy Weeks:/ When it did begin, and when we are to expect the end thereof,/ Very confiderable, in refpect of the great ftirs and tumults/ of this prefent Age wherein we live./ By Thomas Parker of Newbery in Berkfhire, and now Paftor to the/ Church at Newbery in New-England./ London, Printed by Ruth Raworth and John Field, for Edmund Paxton, dwelling/ at Pauls chain neer Doctors Commons. 1646./ 2 prel. leaves and 156 pp. Old calf. 4to. (2l. 2s. 2090)

PARKINSON (SYDNEY). A Journal of a Voyage to the South Seas, in his Majefty's Ship, The Endeavour. Faithfully tranfcribed from the Papers of the late Sydney Parkinson, Draughtfman to Joseph Banks, Efq. on his late Expedition, with Dr. Solander, round the World. Embellished with Views and Defigns, delineated by the Author, and engraved by capital Artifts. *London:* Stanfield Parkinson, M.DCC.LXXIII. *xviii and 212 pp. Errata 2 pp. Portrait and 27 Plates. Large Paper. Calf.* 4to. (10s. 6d. 2091)

PARSONS (JONATHAN). Good News From a Far Country. In Seven Discourses From 1 Tim I. 15. Delivered at the Presbyterian Church in Newbury: And now publifhed at the Defire of many of the Hearers and Others. By Jonathan Parsons, A.M. And Minifter of the Gofpel there. *Portsmouth,* in New-Hampshire: Printed and Sold by Daniel Fowle. 1756. *viii and 168 pp. 8vo.* (7s. 6d. 2092)

PARSONS (JONATHAN). To live is Christ, to die is Gain. A Funeral Sermon On the Death of the Rev. Mr. George Whitefield, Chaplain to the Countefs of Huntington, Who died fuddenly of a fit of the Afthma, at New-bury Port, at Six of the Clock Lord's Day Morning, Sept. 30th, 1770. The Sermon preached the fame Day, Afternoon. By Jonathan Parsons, A.M. And Minifter of the Prefbyterian Church there. To which are added, An Account of his Interment; The Speech over his Grave, By the Rev. Mr. Jewet; And fome Verses to his Memory, By the Rev. Tho. Gibbons, D.D. Portsmouth, New-Hampshire, Printed, *London* Reprinted, For James Buckland, 1771. *2 prel. leaves and 36 pp. 8vo.* (4s. 6d. 2093)

PARSONS (MOSES). A Sermon preached at Cambridge, Before his Excellency Thomas Hutchinson, Esq; Governor: His Honor Andrew Oliver, Esq; Lieutenant-Governor, The Honorable his Majesty's Council, and the honorable House of Representatives, Of the Province of the Massachusetts-Bay in New-England, May 27th 1772. Being the Anniverfary for the Election of His Majesty's Council for faid Province. By Moses Parsons, A.M. Paftor of the Church at Newbury Falls,

Boston: Printed by Edes and Gill, Printers to the Honorable House of Representatives. M,DCC,LXXII. 43 pp. *half mor.* 8vo. (3s. 6d. 2094)

PARTICULAR (A) Account of the Commencement and Progress of the Insurrection of the Negroes in St. Domingo, which began in August, 1791: Being a Translation of the Speech made to the National Assembly, The 3d of November, 1791, by the Deputies from the General Assembly of the French Part of St. Domingo. The Second Edition, With Notes and an Appendix, containing Extracts from authentic Papers. *London:* J. Sewell, M.DCC. XCII. *iv and* 47 pp. 8vo. (4s. 6d. 2095)

PASCHOUD (Mr.) Historico-Political Geography: Or, A Particular Description Of the Several Countries in the World; in their Situation, Extent, Air, Soil, Divifions, Provinces, Rivers, Commodities, Rarities, Capital Cities, Chief Towns, Inhabitants, Manners, Languages, Populoufnefs, &c. The Genealogy, Pretenfions, Government, Titles, Revenues, Refidence, &c. of their Kings and Princes. Their refpective States, Courts of Juftice, Laws, Nobility, Orders of Knighthood, Clergy, Archbifhopricks, Bifhopricks, Universities, and Religion. The Second Edition, with Additions. *London:* William France, 1729. *Title xiv and* 395 pp; *Index* 5 pp. *Old calf.* 8vo. (7s. 6d. 2096)

PATRIOT (The). Addreffed to the Electors of Great Britain. *London:* MDCCLXXIV. *Title and* 33 pp. *half mor.* 8vo. (4s. 6d. 2097)

PATRIOTS (The) of North-America: A Sketch [*in verse*]. With Explanatory Notes. *New-York:* Printed in the Year M,DCC,LXXV. *iv and* 48 pp. *half mor.* 8vo. (10s. 6d. 2098)

PATTERSON (Walter). Some Facts stated, relative to the conduct of Walter Patterson, Efq; Late Governor and Lieutenant-Governor of the Ifland St. John. Of Edmund Fanning, Efq; The prefent Lieutenant-Governor; and of Peter Stewart, Efq; Chief Justice of the faid Ifland; Occafioned by fome Notes, contained in a Pamphlet, entitled The Criminating Complaint, &c. &c. *Title and* 40 pp. *half mor.* 8vo. (4s. 6d. 2099)

PAULLI (Simon). Simonis Paulli, D./ Medici Regii, ac Prælati Aarhufienfis/ Commentarius/ De/ Abusu Tabaci/ Americanorum Veteri,/ et/ Herbæ Thee/ Asiasticorum in Europa Novo,/ Quæ ipfiffima eft Chamæleagnos Dodonæi,/ Editio Secunda priori auctior & correctior./ *Argentorati/* Sumptibus B. Authoris Filii Simonis Paulli Bibliop./ Anno Salutis M.DC.LXXXI./ *30 prel. leaves including Portrait & Arms, &c. of Author, and 88 pp.* 'Syllabus Auctorum.' *4 pp.* 'Index Rerum.' *7 pp. 2 folding plates at pp. 76 & 77.* 4to. (10s. 6d. 2100)

PAUW (Mr. DE). Recherches Philosophiques sur les Americains, ou Mémoires intéreffants pour servir à l'Hiftoire de l'Efpece Humaine. Par Mr. de P***. Avec une Differtation fur l'Amérique & les Américains, par Don Pernety. Et la Défenfe de l'Auteur des Recherches contre cette Differtation. A Berlin, M.DCC.LXX. *Three Volumes.* Tome I. *xxiv and 326 pp. Table 25 pp.* Tome II. *Title and 366 pp. Table 31 pp.* Tome III. *136 pp.* 'Defense,' etc. *256 pp. Old calf.* Small 8vo. (10s. 6d. 2101)

PAUW (Mr. DE). Recherches Philosophiques sur les Americains, ou Mémoires intéreffants pour fervir à l'Hiftoire de l'Efpece Humaine. Par M. de P***. Avec une Differtation fur l'Amérique & les Américains, par Dom Peruety. A Londres. M.D.CC.LXXI. *Three Volumes.* Tome Premier. *xx and 276 pp. Table 26 pp. The 2nd and 3rd are of the edition above.* 12mo. (10s. 6d. 2102)

PAUW (Mr. DE). Selections from les Recherches Philosophiques sur les Americains of M. Pauw. By Mr. W***. [Webb.] *Bath,* Printed by R. Cruttwell. MDCCLXXXIX. *2 prel. leaves and 211 pp.* 8vo. (15s. 2103)
Fifty copies only of this work were printed, and given to the Author's friends.

PAYNE (JOHN HOWARD). Memoirs of John Howard Payne, the American Roscius: With Criticisms on his Acting, in the various Theatres of America, England and Ireland. Compiled from Authentic Documents. *London:* John Miller, 1815. *2 prel. leaves and 131 pp. With Portrait of Payne.* 8vo. (4s. 6d. 2104)

PEALE (REMBRANDT). Account of the Skeleton of The Mammoth, a non-descript Carnivorous

Animal of Immense Size, Found in America. By Rembrandt Peale, the Proprietor. *London:* E. Lawrence, 1802. 46 *pp.* 8*vo.* (4*s.* 6*d.* 2105)

PECKARD (P.) Memoirs of the Life of Mr. Nicholas Ferrar. By P. Peckard, D.D. Master of Magdalen College, Cambridge. *Cambridge,* J. Archdeacon, MDCCXC. *xvi and* 316 *pp. With Portrait and Pedigree of Nicholas Ferrar.* 8*vo.* (12*s,* 6*d.* 2106)

PEMBERTON (EBENEZER). Sermons and Discourses on Several Occafions. By the late Reverend and Learned Ebenezer Pemberton, A.M. Paftor of the South Church in Bofton, and Fellow of Harvard College in Cambridge, New-England. To which is added, A Sermon after his Funeral preached by the Reverend Mr. Colman, Paftor of a Church in Bofton: Containing fome Account of Mr. Pemberton's Life and Character. Now firft Collected into One Volume. *London:* J. Batley, MDCCXXVII. 4 *prel. leaves and* 310 *pp. Old calf.* 8*vo.* (7*s.* 6*d.* 2107)

PEMBERTON (EBENEZER). Heaven the Refidence of the Saints. A Sermon Occafioned by the fudden and much lamented Death of the Rev. George Whitefield, A.M. Chaplain to the Right Honourable the Countefs of Huntington. Delivered at the Thurfday Lecture at Boston, in America, October 11, 1770. By Ebenezer Pemberton, D.D. Paftor of a Church in Bofton. To which is added, An Elegiac Poem on his Death, By Phillis, a Negro Girl, of Seventeen Years of Age, Belonging to Mr. J. Wheatley of Bofton. Bofton, Printed: *London,* Reprinted, For E. and C. Dilly. M.DCC. LXXI. 31 *pp. half mor.* 8*vo.* (4*s.* 6*d.* 2108)

PEMBERTON (JOHN). A Testimony of the Monthly Meeting of Friends, at Pyrmont in Westphalia, Germany, concerning John Pemberton, of Philadelphia in North America: With his Epistle to the Inhabitants of Amsterdam. Philadelphia printed: *London* reprinted James Phillips & Son, 1798. 36 *pp.* 12*mo.* (1*s.* 6*d.* 2109)

PEMBERTON (JOHN). A Testimony of the Monthly Meeting of Friends, at Pyrmont in Westphalia, Germany, concerning John Pemberton, of Philadelphia in North America: With his Epistle to the Inhabitants of Amsterdam. *Philadelphia:* Printed by Henry Tuckniss. 1798. *v and pp.* 7-36. 12mo. (4s. 6d. 2110)

PENA MONTENEGRO (ALONSO DE LA). Itinerario/ para/ Parochos/ de Indios,/ en que se tratan las materias/ mas particulares, tocantes à ellos, para fu/ buena Adminiftracion :/ Compuefto/ por El llustrissimo, y Reverendissimo/ Señor Doctor Don Alonso/ de la Peña Montenegro,/ Obispo del Obispado de San Francisco del Quito,/ del confejo de fu Mageftad, Colegial que fue del Colegio mayor/ de la Univerfidad de Santiago, &c./ Nueva Edicion Purgada de muchos Yerros./ En *Amberes./* Por Henrico y Cornelio Verdussen./ Año M.DC. XCVIII./ Con Licencia./ *28 prel. leaves: Text* 697 *pp. double columns, followed by Indice* 43 *leaves &* 1 *page. Old calf. 4to.* (1l. 1s. 2111)

PENHALLOW (SAMUEL). The History of the Wars of New-England, With the Eaftern Indians. Or, a Narrative Of their continued Perfidy and Cruelty, from the 10th of Auguft, 1703. To the Peace renewed 13th of July, 1713. And from the 25th of July, 1722. To their Submiffion 15th December, 1725. Which was Ratified Auguft 5th, 1726. By Samuel Penhallow, Esq. *Boston:* Printed by T. Fleet, for S. Gerrifh at the lower end of Cornhill, and D. Henchman over-againft the Brick Meeting-Houfe in Cornhill, 1726. 4 *prel. leaves and* 134 *pp.* 'Advertifement.' 1 *page. Red mor. by Bedford. Small 8vo.* (10l. 10s. 2112)

PENINGTON (ISAAC). An/ Examination/ of the/ Grounds or Caufes,/ Which are faid to induce the Court of/ Bofton in New=England to make that Order or Law/ of Banifhment upon pain of Death againft the Quakers ;/ As alfo of the Grounds and Confiderations by them pro-/duced to manifeft the warrantablenefs and juftnefs both of/ their making and executing the fame, which they now ftand/ deeply engaged to defend, having already thereupon put/ two of them to death./ As alfo of fome further Grounds for juftifying of/ the fame, in an Appendix to John Norton's Book (which/ was Printed after the Book it felf, yet as part thereof) whereto/ he is faid to be appointed by the

General Court./ And likewife of the Arguments briefly hinted in that which/ is called, A true Relation of the Proceedings againft the Quakers, &c./ Whereunto fomewhat is added about the Authority and Go-/vernment which Chrift excluded out of his Church, which occafi-/oneth fomewhat concerning the true Church-Government./ By Ifaac Penington, the Younger./ *London*, Printed for L. Lloyd, next to the Sign of/ the Caftle in Cornhill, 1660./ 2 *prel. leaves and* 99 *pp.* 4to. (3*l.* 3*s.* 2113)

PENINGTON (JOHN). An/ Apoftate/ Expofed:/ Or,/ George Keith/ Contradicting himfelf and his Brother Bradford. Wherein Their Teftimony to the Chriftian Faith of the People called Qua-/kers, is oppofed to G. K's late/ Pamphlet, Stiled, Grofs Error/ and Hypocrife detected./ By John Penington./ *London*, Printed and Sold by T. Sowle, near the Meeting-/Houfe in White-Hart-Court in Grace-Church-ftreet, 1695./ *Title and pp.* 3-29. 12*mo.* (2*l.* 2*s.* 2114)

PENN (WILLIAM). A/ Letter/ from/ William Penn/ Proprietary and Governour of/ Pennsylvania/ In America, to the Committee/ of the/ Free Society of Traders/ of that Province, refiding in London./ Containing/ A General Defcription of the faid Province, its Soil, Air, Water, Seafons and Produce,/ both Natural and Artificial, and the good Encreafe thereof./ Of the Natives or Aborigines, their Language, Cuftoms and Manners, Diet, Houfes or Wig-/wams, Liberality, eafie way of Living, Phyfick, Burial, Religion, Sacrifices and Cantico,/ Feftivals, Government, and their order in Council upon Treaties for/ Land, &c. their Juftice upon Evil Doers./ Of the firft Planters, the Dutch, &c. and the prefent Condition and Settlement of the faid Province,/ and Courts of Juftices, &c./ To which is added, An Account of the City of/ Philadelphia/ Newly laid out. Its Scituation between two Navigable Rivers, Delaware and Skulkill,/ with a/ Portraiture or Platform thereof,/ Wherein the Purchafers Lots are Diftinguifhed by certain Numbers inferted./ And the Profperous and Advantagious Settlements of the Society aforefaid, within/ the faid City and Country, &c./ Printed and Sold by Andrew

Sowle, at the Crooked-Billet in Holloway-Lane in/ Shoreditch, and at feveral Stationers in *London*, 1683./ 10 pp. *With the Portraiture of the City of Philadelphia. Folio.* (2l. 12s. 6d. 2115)

PENNSYLVANIA. A/ Further Account/ Of the Province of/ Pennsylvania/ and its/ Improvements./ For the Satisfaction of thofe that are Adventurers, and/ enclined to be so. [*London* 1685.] *At the end Dated* ' Worminghurft-Place, 12fth of the 10th Month 85.' *Signed* ' William Penn.' 20 pp. Half mor. 4to. (1l. 11s. 6d. 2116)

PENNSYLVANIA. Some/ Letters/ and an/ Abftract of Letters/ from Pennsylvania,/ Containing/ The State and Improvement of that/ Province./ Publifhed to prevent Mif-Reports./ [*London*] Printed and Sold by Andrew Sowe, at the Crooked-Billet in Hollo-/way-Lane, in Shoreditch, 1691./ 12 pp. Uncut. 4to. (2l. 2s. 2117)

PENNSYLVANIA. The Charters of the Province of Pennsylvania and City of Philadelphia. *Philadelphia:* Printed and Sold by B. Franklin. MDCC XLII. 30 pp. Folio. (1s. 11s. 6d. 2118)

PENNSYLVANIA. A Collection of all the Laws Of the Province of Pennsylvania: Now in Force. Publifhed by Order of Assembly. *Philadelphia:* Printed and Sold by B. Franklin. M,DCC,XLII. 562 pp. 'An Appendix ; containing a Summary of such Acts of Assembly As have been formerly in Force within this Province, For Regulating of Defcents, And Transfering the Property of Lands, &c. But fince expired, altered or repealed. *Philadelphia:* Printed by B. Franklin. M,DCC,XLII. *iv pp. and wanting all after p.* 16. *Folio.* (18s. 2119)

PENNSYLVANIA. A Brief State of the Province of Pennsylvania, in which The Conduct of their Assemblies for feveral Years paft is impartially examined, and the true Caufe of the continual Encroachments of the French difplayed, more efpecially the fecret Defign of their late unwarrantable Invafion and Settlement upon the River Ohio. To which is annexed, An eafy Plan for Reftoring Quiet in the Public Meafures of that Province, and defeating the ambitious Views of the French in time to come. In a Letter from a

Gentleman who has refided many Years in Pennfylvania to his Friend in London [Benjamin Franklin]. *London*: R. Griffiths. 1755. *Half-title, title, and text pp. 3-45. Half morocco.* 8vo. (10s. 6d. 2120)

PENNSYLVANIA. A brief State of the Province of Pennsylvania, in which The Conduct of their Assemblies for feveral Years paft is impartially examined, and the true Caufe of the continual Encroachments of The French difplayed, more efpecially the fecret Defign of their late unwarrantable Invafion and Settlement upon the River Ohio. To which is annexed, An eafy Plan for reftoring Quiet in the public Meafures of that Province, and defeating the ambitious Views of the French in time to come. In a Letter from a Gentleman who has refided many Years in Pennfylvania to his Friend in London. The Second Edition. *London:* R. Griffiths, 1755. *Half-title, title, and text pp.* 3-45. *Half mor.* 8vo. (10s. 6d. 2121)

PENNSYLVANIA. An Answer To an invidious Pamphlet, intituled, *A Brief State of the Province of Pensylvania.* Wherein are expofed The many falfe Affertions of the Author or Authors, of the faid Pamphlet, with a View to render the Quakers of Penfylvania and their Government obnoxious to the Britifh Parliament and Miniftry; and the Several Tranfactions, moft grofly mifreprefented therein, fet in their true light. *London;* S. Blandon, MDCCLV. *Title and 80 pp. Half morocco.* 8vo. (10s. 6d. 2122)

PENNSYLVANIA. A Brief View Of the Conduct of Pennsylvania, For the Year 1755; So far as it affected the General Service of the British Colonies, particularly the expedition under the late General Braddock. With an Account of the fhocking Inhumanities, committed by the Incurfions of the Indians upon the Province in October and November; which occafioned a Body of the Inhabitants to come down, while the Affembly were fitting, and to infift upon an immediate Sufpenfion of all Difputes, and the Paffing of a Law for the Defence of the Country. Interfpers'd with feveral interefting Anecdotes and original Papers, relating to the Politics and Principles of the People called Quakers: Being a Sequel to a late well known Pamphlet, Intitled, A Brief State of Pennsylvania. In a Second Letter to a Friend in London. *London*: R. Griffiths. 1756. 88 *pp.* *Half morocco.* 8*vo.* (10*s.* 6*d.* 2123)

PENNSYLVANIA. An Historical Review of the Constitution and Government of Pennsylvania From its Origin; So far as regards the feveral Points of Controverfy, which have, from Time to Time, arifen between The feveral Governors of that Province, and Their feveral Assemblies. Founded on authentic Documents. [By Dr. Franklin] *London:* R. Griffiths, MDCCLIX. *viii pp. Contents* 18 *pp; and Text* 444 *pp. Old calf.* 8*vo.* (7*s.* 6*d.* 2124)

PENNSYLVANIA. A New Essay [By the Pennfylvanian Farmer] On the Constitutional Power of Great-Britain over the Colonies in America; with the Resolves of the Committee for the Province of Pennsylvania, and their Instructions To their Representatives in Assembly. Philadelphia Printed; and *London* Re-printed for J. Almon, 1774. *viii and* 126 *pp. Half mor.* 8*vo.* (5*s.* 6*d.* 2125)

PENNSYLVANIA. The Acts of the General Affembly of the Commonwealth of Penfylvania, Carefully compared with the Originals. And an Appendix, Containing the Laws now in Force, paffed between the 30th Day of September, 1775, and the Revolution. Together with The Declaration of Independence; the Conftitution of the State of Pennsylvania; and the Articles of Confederation of the United States of America. Publifhed by order of the General Affembly. *Philadelphia:* Printed and Sold by Francis Bailey, in MarketStreet, M,DCC,LXXXII. *Two Volumes.* Vol. I. 2 *prel. leaves,* xxxii *and* 527 *pp. Index or Table viii pp.* Vol. II. Hall and Sellers, *Title and pp.* 3-704. *Tables at pp.* 82-3, 110, 254, 270, 369, 400, 588, 704. Volumes IV. V. *and* VI. 400 *pp. Tables at pp.* 8, 88, 180, 194, 314, 400. *Fine copy in Old calf.* Folio (1*l.* 11*s.* 6*d.* 2126)

PENNSYLVANIA. Proceedings and Debates of the General Assembly of Pennsylvania, As taken in short-hand by Thomas Lloyd. *Philadelphia:* Printed by Joseph James, in Chesnut-Street. M,DCC,LXXXVII. Volume the Second. *Title and* 189 pp. *Errata* 1 *page.* 8vo. (3s. 6d. 2127)

PENNSYLVANIA. Observations upon the present Government of Pennsylvania. In four letters to the People of Pennsylvania. *Philadelphia:* Printed and Sold by Styner and Cist, in Second-ſtreet, five doors above Arch-ſtreet. MDCCLXXVII. 24 *pp. Half mor.* 8vo. (5s. 2128)

PENNSYLVANIA. An Historical Review of the Constitution and Government of Pennsylvania, from its origin; so far as regards the several points of controversy which have from time to time arisen between the several Governors of Pennsylvania and their several Assemblies. Founded on Authentic Documents. [By Dr. Franklin] 1808, Reprinted at Philadelphia by Wm. Duane, from the London Edition of 1759. *Title and pp. xv-xxxvi. Text* 431 *pp.* 8vo. (7s. 6d. 2129)

PENNSYLVANIA HOSPITAL. Continuation of the Account of the Pennſylvania Hoſpital; From the Firſt of May 1754, to the Fifth of May 1761. With an alphabetical List of the Contributors, and of the Legacies which have been bequeathed, for Promotion and Support thereof, from its firſt Rise to that Time. *Philadelphia:* Printed by B. Franklin, and D. Hall. MDCCLXI. *Title and pp.* 41-77. 4*to.* (1*l.* 10s. 2130)

PENNSYLVANIA MAGAZINE (The): Or, American Monthly Museum. MDCCLXXV. Volume I. *Philadelphia:* Printed and sold by R. Aitken, Printer and Bookseller, opposite the London Coffee-House, Front-Street. 4 *prel. leaves and text pp.* 9-625. *Index* 5 *pp. With several copperplates. Old calf.* 8vo. (15s. 2131)

PEREZ (Francisco). Catecismo de la Doctrina Cristiana en lengua Otomi, traducida literalmente al Castellano por el Presbitero D. Francisco Perez, catedratico propietario de dicho idioma en la nacional y pontificia universidad de la Ciudad federal de los estados Mexicanos, examinador sinodal de dicho Idioma de este arzobispado.

Mexico: Imprenta de la Testamentaria de Valdés, a cargo de José Maria Gallegos. 1834. 5 *prel. leaves and* 17 *pp.* 'Manualito' *etc.* 46 *pp.* Half mor. 8*vo.* (1*l.* 1*s.* 2132)

PEREZ (MANUEL). Arte de el Idioma Mexicano. Por el P. Fr. Manuel Perez, del Orden de N. P. San Auguftin, hijo de la Santa Provincia del Santiffimo Nombre de Jesvs, actual Vifitador en ella. Cura Miniftro, por fu Mageftad, de la Parroquia de los Naturales del Real Collegio de San Pablo, y Cathedratico de dicho Idioma en la Real Vniverfidad de Mexico. Dedicalo a la dicha Santiffima Provincia. Con Licencia. En *Mexico,* por Francisco de Ribera Calderon, en la calle de San Auguftin. Año de 1713. 8 *prel. leaves and* 80 *pp.* 'Indice,' 3 *pp.* 4*to.* (4*l.* 14*s.* 6*d.* 2133)

PEREZ (MANUEL). Farol Indiano, y Gvia de Curas de Indios. Summa de los Cinco Sacramentos que adminiftran los Miniftros Evangelicos en efta America. Con todos los cafos morales que fuceden entre Indios. Deducidos de los mas claficos Authores, y amoldados à las coftumbres, y privilegios de los Naturales. Por el P. Fr. Manuel Perez, del Orden de N. P. S. Auguftin, hijo de efta Provincia del Santiffimo Nombre de Jesus. Vifitador actual de ella, Cura-Miniftro, por fu Mageftad, de la Parroquia de Naturales de S Pablo de Mexico, y Cathedratico de Lengua Mexicana en la Vniverfidad. Dedicala Al Santiffimo Efpofo de la Efpofa, y Madre de Dios, y Patron de Efta Nueva-Efpaña, Señor San Joseph. Con Licencia de los Svperiores. En *Mexico,* por Francifco de Rivera Calderon, en la calle de San Auguftin. Año de 1713. 24 *prel. leaves and* 192 *pp.* 'Indice de los Capitulos,' 3 *pp.* 4*to.* (2*l.* 2*s.* 2134)

PERNETTY (DOM). Histoire d'un Voyage aux Isles Malouines, Fait en 1763 & 1764; avec des Observations sur le Detroit de Magellan, et sur les Patagons, Par Dom Pernetty, Abbé de l'Abbaye de Burgel, Membre de l'Académie Royale des Sciences & Belles-Lettres de Pruffe; Affocié Correfpondant de calle de Florence, & Bibliothécaire de Sa Majefté le Roi de Pruffe. Nouvelle Edition. Refondue & augmentée d'un Difcours Préliminaire, de Remarques fur l'Histoire Natu-

relle, &c. A *Paris*, Saillant & Nyon, M.DCC.LXX.
Two Volumes. Tome Premier. *iv and* 385 *pp.*
Tome Second. *Title and* 334 *pp. Approbation and
Privilege* 2 *pp. With* 18 *folded plates at end. Old
calf.* 8*vo.* (8*s.* 6*d.* 2135)

PERU. Conquefte van Indien./ De wonderlijcke ende warach=/tighe Hiftorie vant Coninckrijck van Peru,/ ghelegen in Indien, inde welcke verhaelt wordt de gheleghenthept,/ coftuymen, manieren van leven, overuloedicheyt des Goudts ende Silvers,/ ende voorts alle de fonderlingfte dinghen van den felven lande./ Infghelijcks van den/ fteden, plaetfen ende inwoonders deffelfs Coninckrijcx, daer beneven, hoet ghevonden/ ende eerft by de Keyferlijcke Mayefteyt hoochloflijcker memorien gheconque=/fteert ende vercreghen is, met alle de Oorloghen, ende ftrijden, die ghe=/ buert zijn, foo teghens d' Indianen, als oock om tgoe=/vernement d'een teghens den anderen./ De Caerte van America./ [*Engraved on Copper on the title.*] *t'Amstelredam.*/ By Cornelis Claefz, woonende opt Water, by de Oude Brugghe,/ Int Schrijf Boeck. Anno. 1598./ *Title, on the reverse,* 'Tot den Lefer.' *Text in* 148 *leaves very irregularly folioed; copperplate engraving of* 'Cerro de Potosi' *on the reverse of sig.* E e ij. 'Tafel oft Regifter des boeckx' 20 *pp. Fine copy. Old calf.*
4*to.* (2*l.* 2*s.* 2136)

PERU. Constitucion. Politica de la Republica Peruana Jurada en Lima el 20 de Noviembre de 1823. *Lima:* 1825. Imprenta del estado por J. Gonzalez. *cxii and* 52 *pp. Indice* 2 *pp. Unbound.*
16*mo.* (5*s.* 2137)

PETERS (BERNHARD MICHAEL). Eine befonders merkwürdige Reife von Amfterdam nach Surinam, und von da zurück nach Bremen, in den Jahren 1783 und 1784. von Bernhard Michael Peters, einem Jeverländer. Wobei die Reifen und Lebensgefchichte John Thomfons eines Engländers, feines vertrauten Freundes und Reifegefährten auf der See. *Bremen,* 1788. *Two Volumes.* Erfter Theil. 4 *prel. leaves and* 214 *pp.* Zweyte und letzte Theil. 1790. 6 *prel. leaves and* 188 *pp. boards.*
8*vo.* (7*s.* 6*d.* 2138)

PETERS (HUGH). An Historical and Critical Account of Hugh Peters. After the Manner of Mr. Bayle. *London:* J. Noon. MDCCLI. 72 pp. Half mor. 8vo. (4s. 6d. 2139)

PETITIONS from the Old and New Subjects, Inhabitants of the Province of Quebec, to the Right Honourable the Lords Spiritual and Temporal. *London:* Printed in the Year 1791. *2 prel. leaves and* 55 pp. *Half mor.* 8vo. (4s. 6d. 2140)

PHILIPOT (THOMAS). The Original and Growth/ of/ The Spanifh/ Monarchy/ United with the House of/ Austria./ Extracted from thofe Chronicles,/ Annals, Regifters and Genealogies,/ that yeild any faithful Reprefentation/ how the Houfes of Caftile, Aragon and/ Burgundy became knit and combin'd/ into one Body./ To which are added feveral Difcourfes of thofe/ Acceffions and Improvements in Italy,/ Africk, with the Eaft and Weft-Indies,/ that are now annexed by Alliance or Con-/queft to the Diadem of Spain./ By Thomas Philipot, M.A./ Formerly of Clare-Hall in Cambridge./ *London*, Printed by W. G. for R. Taylor, in St. Martins le/ Grand neer St. Leonards Church yard. 1664./ *4 prel. leaves and text 264 pp. With portrait of Phillip the IV. of Spain. Small* 8vo. (18s. 2141)

PHILIPS (MILES). The Voyages and Adventures of Miles Philips, A Weft-Country Sailor. Containing A Relation of his various Fortune both by Sea and Land; the inhuman Ufage he met with from the Spaniards at Mexico, and the Salvage Indians of Canada and other barbarous Nations; and the Sufferings he and his Companions underwent by their Confinement and Sentence in the Spanifh Inquifition. Together with A Natural Defcription of the Countries he vifited, and particular Obfervations on the Religion, Cuftoms and Manners of their refpective Inhabitants. Written by Himself in the plain Stile of an Englifh Sailor. *London:* T. Payne, 1724. *6 prel. leaves and* 216 pp. *Wanting pages* 17, 18, 101, *to* 116, 203, *to* 206, *inclusive. Old calf.* 12mo. (14s. 6d. 2142)

PHILLIP (WILLIAM). The/ True and perfect De-/ fcription of three Voy-/ages fo ftrange and woonderfull,/ that the like hath neuer been/ heard of before :/ Done and performed three yeares, one after the other by the Ships of/ Holland and Zeland, on the North fides of Norway, Mufcouia and/ Tartaria, towards the Kingdomes of Cathaia and China; fhewing/ the dilcouerie of the Straights of Weigates Noua Zembla,/ and the Countrie lying vnder 80 degrees; which is/ thought to be Greenland; where neuer any man had/ bin before; with the cruell Beares, and other/ Monfters of the Sea, and the vnfup-/portable and extreame cold/ that is found to be in/ thofe places./ And how that in the laft Voyage, the Shippe was fo inclofed by the/ Ice, that it was left there, whereby the men were forced to build a/ houfe in the cold and defart Countrie of Noua Zembla wherin/ they continued 10 monthes togeather, and neuer faw nor/ heard of any man, in moft great cold and extreame/ miferie; and how after that, to faue their liues, they/ were conftrained to sayle aboue 350 Duch-/miles, which is above 1000 miles Englifh,/ in little open boates, along and ouer the/ maine Seas, in moft great dannger,/ and with extreame labour, vn-/fpeakable troubles, and/ great hunger./ Imprinted at London, for T. Pauier./ 1609./ 2 prel. leaves; viz. Title the reverse blank, 'To the Right Wor-/fhipfull, Sir Thomas Smith Knight, Gouer-/nour of the Mufcouy Company, &c.' Signed 'William Phillip.' 2 pp. Text in 97 unfolioed leaves. Signatures B. to V. in fours, and X. in 3 leaves. Morocco extra, by Riviere. 4to. (4l. 4s. 2143)

PHILOPONUS (HONORIUS). Nova Typis/ Transacta Na-/vigatio./ Novi Orbis Indiæ Occi-/dentalis/ Admodvm Re-/verendissimorvm P.P./ ac F.F. Reverendiffimi ac Illustriffimi Domini,/ Dn. Bvellii Cataloni Abbatis montis/ Serrati, & in vniverfam Americam, five Novum,/ Orbem Sacræ Sedis Apoftolicæ Romanæ à Latere/ Legati, Vicarij, ac Patriarchæ Sociorumq; Mo-/nachorum ex Ordine S. P. N. Benedicti ad fuprà/ dicti Novi Mundi barbaras gentes Chrifti S. Evan-/gelium prædicandi gratia delegatorum Sacerdo-/tum. Dimiffi per S. D. D. Papam Alexandrum/ VI. Anno Chrifti, 1492./ Nvnc Primvm/ E varijs Scriptoribus in vnum colle-/cta, & figuris ornata./ Avthore/ Venerando Fr. Don Honorio Philopono/ Ordinis

S. Benedicti Monacho. 1621./ 3 *prel. leaves including the engraved title, and* 101 *pp. with* 3 *seq. pp. There are* 18 *copperplate engravings. Vellum. Folio.* (2*l.* 12*s.* 6*d.* 2144)

PHILOSOPHIC SOLITUDE: Or, the choice of a rural life: A Poem. By a Gentleman educated at Yale College. The Third Edition. *New-York:* Printed by John Holt at the Exchange. [1769?] 40 *pp. Half mor.* 8*vo.* (10*s.* 6*d.* 2145)

PHILOTHEUS. A True and Particular History of Earthquakes. Containing A Relation of that dreadful Earthquake which happen'd at Lima and Callao, in Peru, October 28, 1746; publiſh'd at Lima by Command of the Vice-Roy, and now tranſlated from the Original Spaniſh; alſo of that which happen'd in Jamaica in 1692, and of others in different Parts of the World. Accurately deſcribing The dreadful Devaſtations that have been made by thoſe horrible Convulſions of the Earth; whereby Mountains have been thrown down, or remov'd to great Diſtances; Cities, with all their Inhabitants, ſwallow'd up in a Moment; whole Flocks and Herds, with their Keepers, ingulph'd in the termendous Chaſms and Openings of Valleys; large Foreſts ſunk, and for ever buried in an Inſtant. Extracted from Authors of the moſt unexceptionable Credit and Reputation. By Philotheus. *London:* for the Author, 1748. xvi and 176 *pp. Old calf.* 8*vo.* (7*s.* 6*d.* 2146)

PIECES Justificatives des Mémoires concernant les Limites de L'Acadie. *A Paris,* de L'Imprimerie Royale. M.DCCLIV. *Title and* 646 *pp. Old calf.* 4*to.* (1*l.* 5*s.* 2147)

PIGGOTT (S.) An Authentic Narrative of four years residence at Tongataboo, One of the Friendly Islands, by Geo. V—— Who together with 28 other Missionaries was sent thither by the London Society in the Ship Duff, under Captain Wilson in 1796, and survived them all; and lived as one of the Natives for two Years. With an Appendix by an Eminent Writer, By the Rev. S. Piggott, A.M. Domestic Chaplain to the Right Hon. Viscount Lord Galway, and perpetual Curate of St. James' Church, Latchford, Warrington. *London:* Long-

man & Co. 1815.   xv and 234 pp.   Errata 1 page.
With plate and chart.   8vo.   (5s. 6d.   2148)

PIKE (ZEBULON MONTGOMERY). Exploratory Travels through the Western Territories of North America: Comprising a Voyage from St. Louis, on the Mississipi, to the Source of that River, and a Journey through the Interior of Louisiana, and the North-Eastern Provinces of New Spain. Performed in the years 1805, 1806, 1807, by Order of the Government of the United States. By Zebulon Montgomery Pike, Major 6th Regt. United States Infantry. *London:* Longman, 1811. *xx pp. and text 436 pp. With 2 Maps. Half calf. 4to.* (10s. 6d. 2149)

PIMIENTA (FRANCISCO DIAZ). Relacion del Svcesso Qve/ Tvvo Francisco Diaz Pimienta, General de la Real/ Armada de las Indias, en la Isla de fanta Catalina. Dafe cuenta como la/ tomò a los enemigos que la poffeìan, echandolos della, y de la/ eftimacion de los defpojos, y numero de los/ prifioneros./ [*Colophon*] Con licencia. En Madrid, Por Iuan Sanchez. Año 1642./ *6 unnumbered pages. Half mor. Folio.* (1l. 11s. 6d. 2150)

PIMIENTA (FRANCISCO DIAZ). Relacion del svcesso qve tvvo Francisco/ Diaz Pimienta, General de la Real Armada de las Indias, en la If-/la de S. Catalina. Dafe cuenta de como la tomò a los enemigos que/ la poffeian, èchandolos della, y la eftimacion de los defpojos, y nu-/mero de prifioneros./ [*Colophon*] Con licencia del feñor don Miguel de Luna y Arellano, Cavallero del Abito de San-/tiago, del Confejo de fu Mageftad, y fu Oydor en la Real Audiencia de Sevi-/lla lo imprimio Francifco de Lyra, Año 1642./ *12 unnumbered puges. Half mor. 4to.* (1l. 11s. 6d. 2151)

PINES. The Isle of/ Pines,/ or,/ A late Discovery of a fourth Island in/ Terra Auftralis, Incognita./ Being/ A True Relation of certain Englifh perfons,/ Who in the dayes of Queen Elizabeth, making a/ Voyage to the Eaft India, were caft away, and wrack-/ed upon the Ifland near to the Coaft of Terra Auftra-/lis Incognita, and all drowned, except one Man and/ four Women, whereof one was a Negro. And now/ lately Anno Dom. 1667. a Dutch ship driven by foul/ weather there by chance have found their Pofterity/ (fpeaking good Englifh) to amount to ten or twelve/ thoufand perfons, as they fuppofe. The whole Rela-/tion follows, written, and left by the Man himfelf a/ little before his death, and declared to the Dutch by/ his Grandchild./ Licenfed June 27. 1668./ *London*,/ Printed by S. G. for Allen Banks and Charles Harper/ at the Flower-Deluice near Cripplegate Church,/ 1668./ *Title and 9 pp. half mor. 4to.* (1*l*. 1*s*. 2152)

PINTO (FERDINAND MENDEZ). Wunderliche und Merckwürdige/ Reisen/ Ferdinandi/ Mendez Pinto,/ Welche er iñerhalb ein und zwantzig Jah=/ren, durch Europa, Afia, und Africa, und deren Königreiche/ und Länder; als Abyffina, China, Japon, Tartarey, Siam, Calamin-/ham, Pegu, Martabane, Bengale, Brama, Ormus, Batas, Queda,/ Aru, Pan, Ainan, Calempluy, Cauchenchina,/ und andere Oerter verrichtet. Darinnen er befchreibet/ Die ihme zu Waffer und Land zugeftoffene groffe/ Noht und Gefahr; wie er nemlich fey dreyzehnmal gefangen genom=/men und fiebenzehnmal verkaufft worden; auch vielfältigen/ Schiffbruch erlitten habe:/ Dabey zugleich befindlich eine gar genaue Entwerffung der/ Wunder und Raritäten erwehnter Länder; der Gefetze, Sitten, und Gewon=/heiten derfelben Völker; und der groffe Macht und Heeres=Krafft/ der Einwohner./ Nun erft ins Hochteutfche überfetzet, und mit unter=/fchiedlichen Kupferftükken gezieret./ *Amsterdam,/* Bey Henrich und Dietrich Boom, Buchhändlern,/ Im Jahr Chrifti 1671./ *4 prel. leaves including Frontispiece title; and 393 pp. Maps & Plates at pp. 1, 13, 30, 98, 159, 217, 256, 267. Pagination very irregular, 4to.* (10*s.* 6*d.* 2153)

PINTO (J. DE). Reponse de M^r. J. de Pinto, aux observations d'un homme impartial, Sur fa Lettre à Mr. S. B., Docteur en Médecine à Kingfton dans la Jamaïque, au fujet des Troubles qui agitent actuellement toute l'Amérique Septentrionale. A *La Haye,* Pierre-Frederic Gosse, MDCCLXXVI. *60 pp. half mor. 8vo.* (4*s.* 6*d.* 2154)

PIRATAS/ de la/ America./ Y Luz à la defenfa de

las Coſtas/ de Indias Occidentales/ Dedicado/ Al muy Noble Señor Don/ Francisco Lopez Suazo./ Traducido/ De la lengua Flamenca en Eſpañola, por/ el D^{or}. de Buena-Maiſon Medico/ Practico en la opulentiſsima/ Ciudad de Amſterdam./ Segunda Impression./ En *Colonia Agrippina,*/ En caſa de Lorenço Struik-/Man Año de 1682./ *24 prel. leaves and* 490 *pp.* 'Tabla De los Capitulos' 8 *pp.* Vellum. 12mo. (1*l.* 1*s.* 2155)

PIRATAS (✤) de la/ America./ Y Luz à la defenſa de las Coſtas/ de Indias Occidentales/ Dedicado/ Al muy Noble Señor Don/ Ricardo de Whyte,/ Cavellero del Orden Militar/ de Calatrava &c^a./ Traducido/ De la lengua Flamenca en Eſpañola,/ por el D^{or}. de Bonne-Maiſon./ Impression Segunda./ En *Colonia Agrippina,*/ En caſa de Lorenco Struik-/Man, Año de 1682./ *28 prel. leaves and* 490 *pp.* 'Tabla De los Capitulos' 8 *pp.* Vellum. 12mo. (1*l.* 1*s.* 2156)

PISO (GULIELMUS). Gulielmi Pisonis/ Medici Amstelædamensis/ de/ Indiæ Utriusque/ re Naturali et Medica/ Libri Qvatvordecim/ Quorum contenta pagina ſequens/ exhibet./ [Gvlielmi Pisonis,/ Medici Amſtelædamenſis,/ I. De Aëribus, Aquis, & Locis./ II. De Natura & cura Morborum, Occidentali Indiæ, imprimis/ Braſiliæ, familiarium./ III. De Animalibus, aquatilibus, volatilibus, & terreſtibus, edulibus./ IV. De Arboribus, fructibus, & herbis medicis, atque alimentariis,/ naſcentibus in Braſilia & regionibus vicinis./ V. De Noxiis & venenatis, eorumque Antidotis. Quibus inſertæ ſunt/ Animalium quorundam vivæ ſectiones; Tum & aliquot Me-/tamorphoſes Inſectorim./ VI. Mantiſſa aromatica &c. Poſita poſt Bontii tractatus./ Georgii Margravii De Liepſtadt/ I. Tractatus Topographicus & Meteorologicus Braſiliæ, cum Ob-/ſervatione Ecliplis Solaris./ II. Commentarius de Braſilienſium & Chilenſium indole ac lingua &c./ Iacobi Bontii, Bataviæ in majore Java novæ Medici ordinarii,/ I. De Conſervanda valetudine./ II. Methodus medendi./ III. Obſervationes in cadaveribus./ IV. Notæ in Garciam ab Orta. V. Hiſtoria Animalium. VI. Hiſtoria Plantarum.] Quibus ſparſim inſeruit G. Piso Annotatio-/nes & Additiones quà icones atque res ne-/ceſſarias./]

Amsteladami,/ Apud Ludovicum et Danielem/ Elzevirios./ A°. cIↄ Iↄ CLVIII./ 13 *prel. leaves*; *viz.* *Engraved title,* 'Avtores et Titvli,' 1 *page*; 'Dedicatoria,' 4 *pp*; 'Præfatio,' 4 *pp*; *Verses, etc.* 12 *pp.* *Half-title*; *Text pp.* 3-327. 'Index' 5 *pp.* 'Georgii Marcgravii' *etc.* 39 *pp.* 'Jacobi Bontii,' *etc.* 326 *pp.* 'Index rervm' 2 *pp. Fine copy. Vellum. Folio.* (18s. 2157)

PITMAN (HENRY). A/ Relation/ of the/ Great Sufferings/ and/ Strange Adventures/ Of Henry Pitman,/ Chyrurgion to the late Duke of Monmouth, contain-/ing an Account;/ 1. Of the occafion of his being engaged in the Duke's Service. 2. Of/ his Tryal, Condemnation, and Tranfportation to Barbadoes, with/ the moft fevere and Unchriftian Acts made againft him and his Fellow-fufferers, by the/ Governour and General Affembly of that Ifland. 3. How he made his efcape in a fmall/ open Boat with fome of his fellow Captives, namely, Jo. Whicker, Peter Begwell, William/ Woodcock, Jo. Cooke, Jeremiah Atkins, &c. And how miraculoufly they were preferved/ on the Sea. 4. How they went afhore on a uninhabitable Ifland, where they met/ with fome Privateers that burnt their Boat, and left them on that defolate place to fhift/ for themfelves. 5. After what manner they lived there for about three Months until/ the faid Henry Pitman was taken aboard a Privateer, and at length arrived fafe in En-/gland. 6. How his Companions were received aboard another Privateer that was after-/wards taken by the Spaniards, and they all made Slaves; And how aftar fix Moneths/ Captivity they were delivered, and returned to England alfo./ Licenfed, June 13th, 1689. *London,* Printed by Andrew Sowle: And are to be Sold by John Taylor, at the Sign/ of the Ship in Paul's Church-Yard, 1689./ *Title and pp.* 3-38. *Advertisements* 1 *page. Calf extra by Bedford.* 4*to.* (1*l.* 11*s.* 6*d.* 2158)

PITMAN (ROBERT BIRKS). A Succinct View and Analysis of Authentic Information extant in Original Works, on the practicability of joining the Atlantic and Pacific Oceans, by a Ship Canal acrofs the Isthmus of America. By Robert Birks Pitman. *London*: J. M. Richardson, 1825. *viii and* 229 *pp.*

Errata 1 page. *Map of the Isthmus of America facing Title.* 8vo. (7s. 6d. 2159)

PLAIN TRUTH: Addressed to the Inhabitants of America. Containing Remarks on a late Pamphlet, intitled Common Sense: Wherein are fhewn, that the Scheme of Independence is ruinous, delufive, and impracticable; that were the Author's Affeverations, refpecting the Power of America, as real as nugatory, Reconciliation on liberal Principles with Great Britain would be exalted Policy; and that, circumftanced as we are, permanent Liberty and true Happinefs can only be obtained by Reconciliation with that Kingdom. Written by Candidus. Philadelphia, Printed. *London*, Reprinted for J. Almon, M.DCC.LXXVI. *2 prel. leaves and 47 pp. half mor.* 8vo. (4s. 6d. 2160)

PLAIN TRUTH: Or, a Letter to the Author of Dispassionate Thoughts on the American War. In which The Principles and Arguments of that Author are refuted, and the Neceffity of carrying on that War clearly demonftrated. By the Author of Letters to a Nobleman on the Conduct of the American War; and of Cool Thoughts on the Consequences of American Independence. *London:* G. Wilkie, MDCCLXXX. *vii and 76 pp. half morocco.* 8vo. (4s. 6d. 2161)

PLAIN TRUTH, in a Series of Numbers from the New-York Daily Advertiser. *New-York.* Daniel Fanshaw, 1821. *56 pp.* 12mo. (2s. 6d. 2162)

PLAN (A) of a Proposed Union between Great-Britain and The Colonies of New-Hampfhire, Maffachufetts-Bay, Rhode-Ifland, New-York, New-Jerfey, Pennfylvania, Maryland, Delaware Counties, Virginia, North Carolina, South Carolina, and Georgia.. Which was produced by one of the Delegates from Pennfylvania, in Congrefs, as mentioned in the preceeding Work. *4 pp. half mor.* 8vo. (2s. 6d. 2163)

PLAN (A) to reconcile Great Britain & her Colonies, and preserve the Dependency of America. *London:* J. Almon, MDDCLXXIV. [1774]. *xvi prel. pp.* Signed 'Cosmopolite.' *Text 40 pp. half mor.* 8vo. (5s. 6d. 2164)

PLAN (A) for conciliating the Jarring Political Interests of Great Britain and her North American Colonies, and For promoting a general Re-union throughout the Whole of the British Empire. *London:* J. Ridley, 1775. *xviii pp. Uncut and Unbound.* 8*vo.* (4*s.* 6*d.* 2165)

PLAN (A) for conciliating the Jarring Interests of Great Britain and her North American Colonies, and For promoting a general Re-union throughout the Whole of the British Empire. *London:* J. Ridley, 1775. *xviii pp.* 'Letters, &c.' [*Boston*, 1775.] *127 pp. half mor.* 8*vo.* (10*s.* 6*d.* 2166)

PLANTAGANET (BEAUCHAMP). A/ Description/ of the/ Province/ of/ New Albion./ And a Direction for Adventurers/ with fmall ftock to get two for one, and good land freely./ And for Gentlemen, and all Servants, Labourers,/ and Artificers, to live Plentifully./ And a former Defcription Reprinted of the healthieft, plea-/fanteft, and richeft Plantation of Nevv Albion in/ North Virginia, proved by thirteen Witneffes./ Together with/ A Letter from Mafter Robert Evelin, that lived/ there many yeers, fhewing the particularities, and ex-/cellency thereof./ With a Brief of the Charge of Victual, and Neceffaries, to tranf-/port and buy ftock for each Planter, or Labourer, there to get/ his Mafter fifty pounds per Annum, or more, in twelve Trades,/ and at ten pounds charges only a man./ *London,*/ Printed by James Moxon, in the Yeer MDCL./ *4 prel. leaves; viz. Title having on the reverse 3 woodcuts of the* ' Ploydens Armes. Albions Armes. The Order, Medall and Riban of the Albion Knights,' *etc.* 'This Epiftle and Preface fhews Cato's beft Rules for a Plantation.' *etc. at the end dated* 'Middleboro this 5 of Decemb. 1641.' *Signed* 'Beauchamp Plantagenet.' *6 pp : Text 32 pp. Fine large copy, with rough leaves; morocco by Bedford.* 4*to.* (21*l.* 2167)

PLANTATION WORK/ the/ Work/ of this/ Generation./ Written in True-Love/ To all fuch as are weightly inclined to Transplant themfelves and Fami-/lies to any of the Englifh Plantati-/ons in/ America./ The/ Moft material Doubts and Objections againft it/ being removed, they may more cheerfully pro-/ceed to the Glory and Renown of the God of/ the whole Earth, who in all Undertakings is to/ be looked unto, Praised and Feared for Ever./ *London*, Printed for Benjamin Clark in George-Yard in/ Lombard-ftreet, 1682./ Title and 18 pp. 4to. (1l. 11s. 6d. 2168)

PLANTERS/ PLEA/ (The)./ Or/ the Grovnds of Plan-/tations Examined,/ And vfuall Objections anfwered./ Together with a manifeftation of the caufes mooving/ fuch as have lately vndertaken a Plantation in/ Nevv-England :/ For the fatiffaction of thofe that queftion/ the lawfulneffe of the Action./ *London*,/ Printed by William Iones./ 1630./ *Title, reverse blank*; 'To the Reader.' 2 pp. Text 84 pp. *Fine copy.* 4to. (6l. 6s. 2169)

PLATFORM (A) of Church Discipline: Gathered out of the Word of God and agreed upon by the Elders and Messengers of the Churches Assembled in the Synod at Cambridge, in New-England : To be presented to the Churches and General Court, for their consideration and acceptance in the Lord, the eighth month, Anno 1648. *Boston*: Belcher and Armstrong, 1808. 118 pp. 'Confession of Faith' etc. 36 pp. *Calf.* 12mo. (4s. 6d. 2170)

POINTIS (Louis de). Relation/ de ce qui s'est fait a la prise/ de Cartagene,/ scitue'e aux/ Indes Espagnoles,/ par l'Escadre Commande'e/ par Mr. de Pointis./ A *Bruxelles*,/ Chez Jean Fricx, Imp./ & Marchand Libraire./ M.DC.XCVIII./ *Title and* 141 pp. *Old calf.* 12mo. (10s. 6d. 2171)

POINTIS (Louis de). Monfieur De Pointi's/ Expedition/ to/ Cartagena :/ Being/ A particular Relation,/ I. Of the Taking and Plundering of that/ City, by the French, in the/ Year 1697./ II. Of their Meeting with Admiral Nevil,/ in their Return, and the Courfe they/ fteer'd to get clear of him./ III. Of their Paffing by Commadore Norris,/ at Newfound-Land./ IV. Of their Encounter with Capt. Harlow,/ at their going into Brest./ Englifh'd from the Original publifh'd at Paris/ by Monfieur De Pointis himfelf. And/ Illuftrated with a large Draught of the City/ of Cartagena, its Harbour and Forts./ *London* :/ Sold by S. Crouch, at the

Corner of Pope's Head-Alley, in Cornhil ;/ Richard Mount at the Poftern, upon Tower-hill ;/ S. Buckley, againft St. Dunftan's Church, in Fleet-ftreet; and/ A. Feltham, at the foot of the Parliament Stairs, Weftminster, 1699./ 4 prel. leaves, including title and text 134 pp. Plan wanting. Old calf. 8vo. (1l. 1s. 2172)

POINTIS (LOUIS DE). A Genuine and Particular Account of the Taking of Carthagena by the French and Buccaniers, In the Year 1697. Containing an Exact Relation of that Expedition, from their firft fetting out, to their Return to Breft; wherein are defcrib'd their feveral Engagements with the Englifh, in their Paffage home. By the Sieur Pointis, Commander in Chief. With a Preface, giving an Account of the Original of Carthagena in 1532, to the prefent time: Alfo an Account of the Climate and Product of that Place, and the Country adjacent. *London*, Olive Payne, 1740. *viii and 86 pp. half mor.* 8vo. (10s. 6d. 2173)

POINTIS (LOUIS DE). An Authentick and Particular Account Of the Taking of Carthagena by the French In the Year 1697. Containing An exact Relation of that Expedition, (in all its Circumftances) from their firft Setting out, to their Return to Breft; wherein are defcrib'd their feveral Engagements with the Englifh Fleets, in their Paffage home. By the Sieur Pointis, Commander in Chief. With a Preface, giving an Account of the Original of Carthagena in 1532, to the prefent Time; alfo an Account of the Climate and Product of that Place, and the Country adjacent. The Second Edition. *London:* Olive Payne, 1740. *viii and 86 pp. With plan of Carthagena. Half morocco.* 8vo. (10s. 6d. 2174)

POLITICAL (A) Analysis of the War: The Principles of the prefent political Parties examined; and A juft, natural and perfect Coalition propos'd between Two Great Men, whofe Conduct is particularly confider'd. The Second Edition. With an Appendix, Enforcing the Coalition propos'd; and proving, from our late Acquifition of the Havanna, that we are now in the moft happy Situation for continuing the War, or concluding a Peace. *Lon-*

don: Tho. Payne, 1762. *Title and* 86 *pp. half mor.*
8*vo.* (7*s.* 6*d.* 2175)

POLITICAL DEBATES [on American Affairs]. A *Paris,* J. W. MDCCLXVI. *Title and* 18 *pp. half mor.* 8*vo.* (4*s.* 6*d.* 2176)

POLITICAL (THE) Detection; or the Treachery and Tyranny of Administration, both at Home and Abroad; displayed in a Series of Letters, signed Junius Americanus. *London:* J. and W. Oliver, MDCCLXX. *Title and text* 151 *pp. half morocco.* 8*vo.* (6*s.* 2177)

POLITICAL Electricity, or, An Historical & Prophetical Print in the Year 1770. Bute & Wilkes invenᵗ. Mercurius & Apelles fecᵗ. Publish'd according to Act of Parliament. [*London,* 1770.] *Large sheet, Folio.* (4*s.* 6*d.* 2178)

POLITICAL Reflections on the late Colonial Governments: In which Their original Constitutional Defects are pointed out, and fhown to have naturally produced the Rebellion, which has unfortunately terminated in the Difmemberment of the British Empire. By An American. *London:* G. Wilkie, MDCCLXXXIII. 3 *prel. leaves and* 259 *pp. Calf extra by Bedford.* 8*vo.* (15*s.* 2179)

PONCE DE LEON (FRANCISCO). Descripcion/ del Reyno de Chile,/ de fus Puertos, Caletas, y fitio de Val-/diuia, con algunos difcurfos para fu/ mayor defenfa, Conquifta,/ y duracion./ Consagrale al Rey Nvestro/ Señor, en fu Real Confejo de/ las Indias,/ El Maestro Fray Francisco/ Ponce de Leon, del Orden de nueftra Señora de la Mer-/ced, Procurador General del Reyno de Chile, y del/ Real Exercito que fu Mageftad tiene en el Conquif-/tador, y Defcubridor de las Prouincias del Rio Mara-/ñon, Fundador de la ciudad de fan Francifco de Borja,/ Prouifor, Gouernado, Vicario General, y Iuez Ecle-/fiaftico en los Obifpados, de Quito, Truxillo, y Chile, Vi-/cario Prouincial de la Prouincia de Lima, y fu Vifita-dor: y Reformador General de las de Chile,/ y Tucuman: Prouincial de la de Chile, Capellan/ Mayor de los Reynos del Peru, y Chile, y/ Comiflario del fanto Oficio./

[Madrid 1644]. *Title and* 15 *folioed leaves. Unbound.* 4to. (3l. 3s. 2180)

POOR SOLDIER (THE); an American Tale: Founded on a recent Fact. Inscribed to Mrs. Crespigny. The Second Edition. *London:* J. Walter, M.DCC.LXXXIX. *3 prel. leaves and* 43 *pp. half morocco.* 4to. (4s. 6d. 2181)

PORCACCHI (TOMASO). L'Isole/ piv Famose/ del Mondo,/ descritto da/ Tomaso Porcacchi/ da Castiglione Arretino,/ et intagliate/ da Girolamo Porro/ Padovano./ Di nuovo corrette, & illuſtrate con l'aggiunta dell' Iſtria, &/ altre Iſole, Scogli, e nuove curioſità. Eſſendovi una/ diſtinta deſcrittione della Città di Conſtantino-/poli, e della Peniſola di Morea./ Consecrate/ All' Illuſtriſſimo, & Eccelentiſſimo Sign. il Sign./ Pietro Gritti/ Q. Lvigi, Q. Raimondo,/ nobile Veneto./ In *Venetia,* M.DC. LXXXVI. Preſſo Pietr' Antonio Brigonci. Con Licenza de' Superiori, e Privilegio./ *2 prel. leaves and* 200 *pp. Small copperplate Maps at pp.* 1, 93, 95, 102, 104, 107, 108, 111, 112, 114, 115, 117, 119, 127, 128, 130, 143, 156, 160, 166, 169, 171, 174, 176, 179. 4to. (10s. 6d. 2182)

PORCEL (FRANCISCO MORENO). Retrato de Manuel de Faria y Sousa, Cavallero del Orden Militar de Chriſto, y de la Caſa Real. Contiene una Relacion de ſua Vida, un Catalogo de ſus Eſcritos, y un ſumario de ſus Elogios, recogidos de varios Autores, por D. Francisco Moreno Porcel; Aora nuevamenta acreſcentado con un Juiſio Hiſtorico, que compuzo el Excellentiſſimo Senhor Don Franciſco Xavier de Meneſes, Conde de la Erizeira. Ofrecido al Excellentissimo Senhor D. Luis de Meneses Quinto Conde de la Erizeira, del Concejo Su Mageſtad, Coronel, y Brigadero de Infanteria, Vi-Rey, y Capitan General que fue en los Eſtados de la India, &c. *Lisboa* Occidental, en la Officina Ferreiriana. M.DCC.XXXIII. Com todas las licencias neceſſarias. *8 prel. leaves, and* 103 *pp. Unbound. Folio.* (2l. 2s. 2183)

PORCUPINE (PETER). Observations on the Debates of the American Congress, or the Addresses presented to General Washington, on his resignation: With remarks on the Timidity of the

Language held towards France; The Seizures of American Veffels by Great Britain and France; and on the relative situations of those countries with America. By Peter Porcupine, Author of the Bone to gnaw for Democrats,—Letter to Tom Paine, &c. &c. To which is prefixed, General Washington's Address to Congress; and the answers of the Senate and House of Representatives. Philadelphia printed: *London* reprinted, David Ogilvy and Son, 1797. *Title and 38 pp. 8vo.* (2s. 6d. 2184)

PORCUPINE'S WORKS; containing various Writings and Selections, exhibiting a faithful Picture of the United States of America; of their Governments, Laws, Politics, and Rescources; of the characters of their Presidents, Governors, Legislators, Magistrates, and Military Men; and of the Customs, Manners, Morals, Religion, Virtues and Vices of the People: Comprising also a complete series of historical documents and remarks, from the end of the War, in 1783, to the Election of the President, in March, 1801. By William Cobbett. In Twelve Volumes. (*A Volume to be added annually.*) *London*: Cobbett and Morgan, May, 1801. *Twelve Volumes.* Vol. I. 400 pp. Vol. II. *2 prel. leaves and* 472 *pp.* Vol. III. *2 prel. leaves and* 440 *pp.* Vol. IV. *2 prel. leaves and* 444 *pp.* Vol. V. *2 prel. leaves and* 432 *pp.* Vol. VI. *2 prel. leaves and* 432 *pp.* Vol. VII. *2 prel. leaves and* 430 *pp.* Vol. VIII. *2 prel. leaves and* 480 *pp.* Vol. IX. *2 prel. leaves and* 412 *pp.* Vol. X. *2 prel. leaves and* 449 *pp.* ' Postscript.—To the Public.' 3 *pp.* Vol. XI. *2 prel. leaves and* 434 *pp.* Vol. XII. *2 prel. leaves and* 252 *pp.* ' Index' 81 *pp. Half calf. 8vo.* (2l. 2s. 2185)

PORTER (ELIPHALET). A Discourse before the Society for Propagating the Gospel among the Indians and others in North-America, delivered November 5th, 1807. By Eliphalet Porter, D.D. Pastor of the first Church in Roxbury. *Boston*: Munroe, Francis, & Parker, 1808. *24 pp. Uncut 8vo.* (2s. 6d. 2186)

PORTEUS (BEILBY). A Letter to the Governors, Legislatures, and Proprietors of Plantations, in the

British West-India Islands. By the Right Reverend Beilby Porteus, D.D. Bishop of London. *London*: T. Cadell and W. Davies, 1808. 48 *pp.* 8*vo.* (3*s.* 6*d.* 2187)

POTENT (The) Enemies of America laid open: Being Some account of the baneful effects attending the ufe of Distilled Spirituous Liquors, and the Slavery of the Negroes; To which is added, The happinefs attending life, when dedicated to the honour of God, and good of mankind, in the fentiments of fome perfons of eminence near the clofe of their lives, viz. the earl of Effex, count Oxciftern, H. Grotius, D. Brainard, John Lock, &c. *Philadelphia:* Printed by Joseph Crukshank in Market-Street, between Second and Third Streets. *A Collective title of the following:*—1*st.* 'The Mighty Destroyer displayed, In some Account of the Dreadful Havock made by the miftaken Use as well as Abuse of Distilled Spirituous Liquors. By a Lover of Mankind. *Philadelphia:* Printed by Joseph Crukshank, between Second and Third Streets, in Market-Street. M.DCC.LXXIV.' 48 *pp.* 2*nd.* 'Thoughts upon Slavery. By John Wesley, A. M. London Printed: Re-printed in *Philadelphia*, with notes and fold by Joseph Crukshank. MD,CC,LXXIV.' 83 *pp.* 3*rd.* 'To the foregoing teftimonies of the happinefs of a life fpent in the fervice of God, may be added that of a faithful fervant of Christ from amongft ourfelves, to wit, David Brainard,' etc. 16 *pp.* 4*th.* 'The Dreadful Visitation, in a short Account of the Progress and Effects of the Plague, The laft time it fpread in the city of London, in the year 1665, extracted from the memoirs of a perfon who refided there during the whole time of that infection. *Philadelphia:* Printed by Joseph Crukshank on the North fide of Market-Street, between Second and Third Streets. MDCC LXXIV.' 16 *pp.* Small 8*vo.* (15*s.* 2188)

POTHERIE (Bacqueville de la). Histoire de L'Amerique Septentrionale. Divifée en quatre Tomes. Tome Premier. Contenant le Voyage du Fort de Nelfon, dans la Baye d'Hudfon, a l'extrémité de l'Amerique. Le premier établiffement des François dans ce vafte païs, la prife dudit Fort de Nelſon, la Deſcription du Fleuve de ſaint Laurent, le gouvernement de Quebec, des trois Rivieres & de Montreal, depuis 1534. juſqu' à 1701. Par Mr. de Bacqueville de la Potherie, né à la Guadaloupe, dans l'Amerique Meridionale, Aide Major de la dite Iſle. Enrichie de Figures. *A Paris* Jean-Luc Nion et Francois Didot, M.DCC. XXII. Tome I. *7 prel. leaves including Engraved title, and 370 pp. Table 4 pp. Copperplates at pp. 16, 17, (2) 51, 56, 66, 67, 76, 80, 81, 100, 105, 132, 232, 311, 334, 351. Vol. I. only. Old calf.* 12mo. (4s. 6d. 2189)

POTTER (LYMAN). A Sermon preached before the General Aſſembly of the State of Vermont, On the Day of their Anniversary Election, October 11, 1787, at Newbury. By Lyman Potter, A.M. Pastor of the Church in Norwich. *Windsor* [*Vermont*] Printed by Hough & Spooner. M.DCC. LXXXVIII. *23 pp. 8vo.* (4s. 6d. 2190)

POWNALL (THOMAS). Principles of Polity, being the Grounds and Reasons of Civil Empire. In Three Parts. By Thomas Pownall, Eſq; *London:* Edward Owen, MDCCLII. *viii, and text 142 pp. With 1 leaf of errata. Half morocco.* 4to. (10s. 6d. 2191)

POWNALL (THOMAS). Speedily will be Publiſhed, [Sold by J. Almon, opposite Burlington-House, Piccadilly] A Map of the Middle Britiſh Colonies in North-America. First published by Mr. Lewis Evans, of Philadelphia, in 1755; and ſince corrected and improved, as alſo extended, with the Addition of New-England, &c. and bordering Parts of Canada; from actual Surveys now lying at the Board of Trade. By T. Pownall, M.P. Late Governor, &c. &c. of his Majesty's Provinces of Maſſachuſets-Bay and South-Carolina, and Lieutenant-Governor of New-Jersey. *4 pp. followed by* 'Books printed for J. Almon in Piccadilly,' *pp. 4-8. Half mor. 8vo.* (4s. 6d. 2192)

POWNALL (THOMAS). The Administration of the Colonies. By Thomas Pownall, Late Governor and Commander in Chief of his Majeſty's Provinces, Maſſachuſets-Bay and South-Carolina, and

Lieutenant-Governor of New-Jersey. The Second Edition, Revifed, Corrected, and Enlarged. London: J. Dodsley, MDCCLXV. 13 *prel. leaves and* 202 *pp.* 'Appendix. Section I. *and* II.' 60 *pp.* Half-mor. 8vo. (7s. 6d. 2192*)

POWNALL (THOMAS). The Administration of the Colonies. By Thomas Pownall, Late Governor and Commander in Chief of his Majefty's Provinces, Maffachufets-Bay, and South-Carolina, and Lieutenant-Governor of New-Jerfey. The Third Edition, Revifed, Corrected and Enlarged. To which is added, An Appendix, N°. III, containing, Confiderations on the Points lately brought into Queftion as to the Parliament's Right of taxing the Colonies, and of the Meafures neceffary to be taken at this Crifis. *London:* J. Dodsley, MDCCLXVI. 14 *prel. leaves and* 202 *pp.* 'Appendix. Section I. *and* II.' 60 *pp.* 'Appendix. Section III.' 52 *pp.* Calf. 8vo. (9s. 2193)

POWNALL (THOMAS). The Administration of the Colonies. (The Fourth Edition.) Wherein their Rights and Constitution Are difcuffed and ftated, By Thomas Pownall, Late Governor and Commander in Chief of his Majefty's Provinces, Maffachufetts-Bay and South-Carolina, and Lieutenant-Governor of New-Jerfey. *London:* J. Walter, MDCCLXVIII. *Title, v to xxxi and* 318 *pp.* 'Appendix' 73 *pp.* Calf. 8vo. (10s. 6d. 2194)

POWNALL (THOMAS). The Administration of the British Colonies. The Fifth Edition. Wherein their Rights and Constitution Are difcuffed and ftated. By, Thomas Pownall, Late Governor, Captain General, Commander in Chief, and Vice Admiral of His Majefty's Provinces, Maffachufetts-Bay, and South-Carolina; and Lieutenant-Governor of New-Jerfey. In Two Volumes. *London:* J. Walter, M.DCC.LXXIV. *Two Volumes.* Vol. I. *xi, and xv prel. pp. Text* 288 *pp.* Vol. II. *xi and* 171 *pp. followed by Half-title, errata, title, and* 308 *pp. Fine copy in Old calf. Best Edition.* 8vo. (15s. 2195)

POWNALL (THOMAS). A Topographical description of such Parts of North America as are contained in the (annexed) Map of the Middle British Colonies, &c. In North America. By T. Pownall, M.P. Late Governor, &c. &c. of his Majesty's Provinces of Massachusetts Bay and South Carolina, and Lieutenant Governor of New Jersey. *London:* J. Almon, MDCCLXXVI. *vi, 46 and Appendix* 16 *pp. With Map. Folio.* (1*l*. 1*s*. 2196)

POYNTZ (JOHN). The/ Prefent Profpect/ of the/ Famous and Fertile Island/ of/ Tobago,/ To the Southward of/ The Ifland of Barbadoes./ With/ A Defcription of the Scituation, Growth, Fertility/ and Manufacture of the faid Ifland: Setting forth/ how that 100*l*. Stock in feven Years may be improved to 5000*l*. per Annum./ To which is added/ Proposals for an Encouragement of all thofe that/ are minded to fettle there./ By Captain John Poyntz./ The Second Edition./ *London,/* Printed by John Attwood for the Author, and fold/ by William Starefmore at the Half Moon and Seven Stars in/ Cornhill, and at the Marine Coffee-houfe in Birchin-lane, 1695./ 3 *prel. leaves; viz. Title reverse blank.* ' To The Ever Honoured Sr Jofeph Herne.' 2 *pp.* ' To the Reader.' 2 *pp. Text* 50 *pp. Calf extra by Bedford.* 4*to.* (1*l*. 15*s*. 6*d*. 2197)
    With the Autograph of White Kennett on the title.

PRADT (M. DE). Des Colonies, et de la Révolution Actuelle de l'Amerique; par M. de Pradt, ancien Archev_ _e de Malines. *Paris,* F. Bechet, A. Egron, M.DCCC.XVII. *Two Volumes.* Tome Premier. *Half-title, title xxxii and* 403 *pp. Errata* 1 *page.* Tome Second. *Half-title, title, and* 394 *pp. Errata* 2 *pp. Calf extra.* 8*vo.* (8*s*. 6*d*. 2198)

PRECIOUS MORSELS. I. Features of Sundry great Personages; viz. His Majesty, George the Third; the late Earl of Bute, and present Lord Hawkesbury; King Midas marched from home; the Bamboozled Mynheers; his Serene Highness, John Bull, Pay Master General, &c. &c. II. A Tit-Bit for Billy Pitt, &c. &c. III. America fast A-Sleep. IV. The Wonders of the hatred of Liberty; a raree-show. [*London* 1794.] 4 *prel. leaves and* 44 *pp. Signed* ' Wm. Belcher.' *Unbound.* 8*vo.* (2*s*. 6*d*. 2199)

PRESENT (THE) Crisis, with respect to America,

considered. London: 1775. Title and 46 pp. half mor. 8vo. (4s. 6d. 2200)

PRESENT STATE (The) of the Britifh Sugar Colonies Consider'd: In a Letter From a Gentleman of Barbadoes to his Friend in London. London: Printed in the Year M.DCC.XXXI. 28 pp. half mor. 4to. (5s. 6d. 2201)

PRESENT STATE (The) of the Country and Inhabitants, Europeans and Indians, of Louisiana, On the North Continent of America. By an Officer at New Orleans to his Friend at Paris. Containing The Garrifons, Forts and Forces, Price of all Manner of Provifions and Liquors, &c. alfo an Account of their drunken lewd Lives, which lead them to Exceffes of Debauchery and Villany. To which are added, Letters from the Governor of that Province on the Trade of the French and Englifh with the Natives. Alfo Propofals to them to put an end to their Traffick with the Englifh. Annual Prefents to the Savages; a Lift of the Country goods, and thofe proper to be fent there, &c. Tranflated from the French Originals, taken in the Golden Lyon Prize, Rafteaux, Mafter, by the Hon. Capt. Aylmer, Commander of his Majefty's Ship the Portmahon, and by him sent to the Admiralty Office. London: J. Millan, 1744. 55 pp. half mor. 8vo. (£. s. 6d. 2202)

PRESENT STATE (The) of North America, &c. Part 1. The Second Edition, with Emendations. London: J. Dodsley. MDCCLV. 2 prel. leaves and 88 pp. Half mor. (7s. 6d. 2203)

PRESENT STATE (The) of Great Britain and North America, with regard to Agriculture, Population, Trade, and Manufactures, impartially confidered. Containing a particular Account of The dearth and fcarcity of the neceffaries of life in England; the want of staple commodities in the Colonies; the decline of their trade; increase of people; and neceffity of manufactures, as well as of a trade in them hereafter. In which The caufes and confequences of thefe growing evils, and methods of preventing them, are suggefted; The proper Regulations for the Colonies, and the taxes impofed upon them, are confidered, and compared

with their condition and circumstances. *London:*
T. Becket. MDCCLXVII. *12 prel. leaves & 364 pages.
Old calf. 8vo.* (7s. 6d. 2204)

PRESENT STATE (THE) of the Nation: Particularly with respect to its Trade, Finances, &c. &c. Addressed to The King and both Houfes of Parliament. *London:* J. Almon, MDCCLXIX. *Title, iv and pp. 9-107. half mor. 8vo.* (4s. 6d. 2205)

PRICE (RICHARD). Cursory Remarks on Dr. Price's Observations on the Nature of Civil Liberty. In a Letter to a Friend. By a Merchant. *London:* W. Nicoll, M,DCC,LXX,VI. *3 prel. leaves and 23 pp. half mor.* (3s. 6d. 2206)

PRICE (RICHARD). Observations on the Nature of Civil Liberty, the Principles of Government, and the Justice and Policy of the War with America, etc. London, Printed: *New-York,* Re-printed by S. Loudon, in Water-Street. 1776. *107 pp. half mor. 8vo.* (3s. 6d. 2207)

PRICE (RICHARD). Observations on the Nature of Civil Liberty, the Principles of Government, and the Justice and Policy of the War with America, etc. By Richard Price, D.D. F.R.S. The Third Edition. *London:* T. Cadell, M.DCC.LXXVI. *4 prel. leaves & 128 pp. half mor. 8vo.* (3s. 6d. 2208)

PRICE (RICHARD). Observations on the Nature of Civil Liberty, the Principles of Government, and the Justice and Policy of the War with America. To which is added An Appendix, Containing a State of the National Debt, an Eftimate of the Money drawn from the Public by the Taxes, and an Account of the National Income and Expenditure fince the laft War. By Richard Price, D.D. F.R.S. The Fourth Edition. *London:* T. Cadell, M.DCC.LXXVI. *4 prel. leaves and 128 pp. Unbound. 8vo.* (4s. 6d. 2209)

PRICE (RICHARD). Observations on the Nature of Civil Liberty, the Principles of Government, and the Justice and Policy of the War in America. To which are added an Appendix and Postscript, containing a State of the National Debt, an Eftimate of the Money drawn from the Public by the Taxes, and an Account of the National Income and Expenditure fince the laft War. By Richard Price, D. D. F. R. S. The Sixth Edition. *London:* T. Cadell, MDCC.LXXVI. 4 *prel. leaves and* 132 *pp. half mor.* 8*vo.* (4s. 6d. 2210)

PRICE (RICHARD). Observations on the Nature of Civil Liberty, the Principles of Government, and the Justice and Policy of the War with America, *etc.* By Richard Price, D.D. F.R.S. The Seventh Edition. With Corrections and Additions. *London:* T. Cadell, M.DCC.LXXVI. 4 *prel. leaves and* 134 *pp.* 8*vo.* (2s. 6d. 2211)

PRICE (RICHARD). Observations on the Nature of Civil Liberty, the Principles of Government, and the Justice and Policy of the War with America. To which are added, An Appendix and Postscript, Containing a State of the National Debt, an Eftimate of the Money drawn from the Public by the Taxes, and an Account of the National Income and Expenditure fince the laft War. By Richard Price, D.D. F.R.S. The Eighth Edition, newly correéted by the Author. *Edinburgh:* [By permiffion of the Author.] J. Wood and J. Dickson. M,DCC,LXXVI. 4 *prel. leaves and* 94 *pp.* 12*mo.* (3s. 6d. 2212)

PRICE (RICHARD). Observations on the Nature of Civil Liberty, the Principles of Government, and the Justice and Policy of the War with America. To which is added, An Appendix and Postscript, containing A State of the National Debt, An Estimate of the Money drawn from the Public by the Taxes, and An Account of the National Income and Expenditure fince the laft War. By Richard Price, D.D. F.R.S. The Ninth Edition. *London:* Edward and Charles Dilly, M.DCC.LXXVI. 48 *pp. half. mor.* 8*vo.* (3s. 6d. 2213)

PRICE (RICHARD). Observations on Dr. Price's Theory and Principles of Civil Liberty and Government, Preceded by a Letter to a Friend, on the Pretenfions of the American Colonies, In refpeét of Right and Equity. *York:* A. Ward, 1776. 4 *prel. leaves and* 147 *pp.* 8*vo.* (3s. 6d. 2214)

PRICE (RICHARD). Remarks on a Pamphlet lately published by Dr. Price, intitled, Observations on the Nature of Civil Liberty, the Principles of Government, and the Justice and Policy of the War with America, &c. In a Letter from a Gentleman in the Country to a Member of Parliament. *London:* T. Cadell, MDCCLXXVI. *Title and* 61 *pp. half mor.* 8*vo.* (4*s.* 6*d.* 2215)

PRICE (RICHARD). Remarks on Dr. Price's Observations on the Nature of Civil Liberty, &c. *London:* G. Kearsley, MDCCLXXVI. *2 prel. leaves and* 76 *pp. Half mor.* 8*vo.* (4*s.* 6*d.* 2216)

PRICE (RICHARD). Three Letters to Dr. Price, containing Remarks on his Observations on the Nature of Civil Liberty, the Principles of Government, and the Justice and Policy of the War with America. By a Member of Lincoln's Inn, F.R.S. F.S.A. *London,* T. Payne, MDCCLXXVI. *Half-title, title, xxii and* 163 *pp. Half mor.* 8*vo.* (4*s.* 6*d.* 2217)

PRICE (RICHARD). Additional Observations On the Nature and Value of Civil Liberty, and the War with America: Also Observations on Schemes for raifing Money by Public Loans; An Hiftorical Deduction and Analyfis of the National Debt; And a brief Account of the Debts and Resources of France. By Richard Price, D.D. F.R.S. *London:* T. Cadell, M.DCC.LXXVII. *xvi and* 176 *pp.* 8*vo.* (2*s.* 6*d.* 2218)

PRICE (RICHARD). Additional Observations On the Nature and Value of Civil Liberty, and the War with America: Also Observations on Schemes for raifing Money by Public Loans; An Hiftorical Deduction and Analyfis of the National Debt; And a brief Account of the Debts and Resources of France. By Richard Price, D.D. F.R.S. The Second Edition. *London:* T. Cadell, M.DCC.LXXVII. *xvi and* 176 *pp. half mor.* 8*vo.* (4*s.* 6*d.* 2219)

PRICE (RICHARD). Additional Observations On the Nature and Value of Civil Liberty, and the War with America: Also Observations on Schemes for raifing Money by Public Loans; An Hiftorical Deduction and Analyfis of the National Debt; And a brief Account of the Debts and Resources of France. By Richard Price, D.D. F.R.S. The Third Edition, with Additions. *London:* T. Cadell, M.DCCLXXVIII. *xxii and* 176 *pp.* 8*vo.* (4*s.* 6*d.* 2220)

PRICE (RICHARD). The General Introduction and

Supplement to The Two Tracts on Civil Liberty, the War with America, and the Finances of the Kingdom. By Richard Price, D.D. F.R.S. *London:* Printed for T. Cadell, in the Strand. MDCCLXXVIII. *Title, xxvi and pp.* 181-216. 'A Summary View' *etc. a folded sheet. 8vo.* (4s. 6d. 2221)

PRICE (RICHARD). A Sermon delivered to a Congregation of Protestant Dissenters, at Hackney, On the 10th of February laſt, Being the Day appointed for a General Fast. By Richard Price, D.D. F.R.S. The Third Edition. To which are added, Remarks on a Passage in the Bishop of London's Sermon on Ash-Wednesday, 1779. *London:* T. Cadell, M.DCC.LXXIX. *2 prel. leaves and 45 pp. Half mor. 8vo.* (2s. 6d. 2222)

PRICE (RICHARD). Three Letters to the Rev. Dr. Price: Containing Remarks upon his Fast-Sermon. By a Cobler. *London:* S. Bladon, MDCCLXXIX. *Half-title, title, and 35 pp.* (3s. 6d. 2223)

PRICE (RICHARD). Observations on the Importance of the American Revolution, and The Means of making it a Benefit to the World. To which is added, A Letter from M. Turgot, late Comptroller-General of the Finances of France: With An Appendix, containing a Tranſlation of the Will of M. Fortune Ricard, lately publiſhed in France. By Richard Price, D.D. L.L.D. And Fellow of the Royal Society of London, and of the Academy of Arts and Sciences in New-England. *London:* T. Cadell, M.DCC.LXXXV. *viii and* 156 *pp. Errata* 4 *lines. half mor. 8vo.* (4s. 6d. 2224)

PRiEST (WILLIAM). Travels in the United States of America; commencing in the year 1793, and ending in 1797. With the Author's Journals of his two Voyages across the Atlantic. By William Priest, Musician, late of the Theatres Philadelphia, Baltimore and Boston. *London:* J. Johnson, 1802. *x and* 214 *pp. Frontispiece. 8vo.* (5s. 2225)

PRIESTLEY (JOSEPH). Observations on the Emigration of Dr. Joseph Priestley, and on the several addresses delivered to him on his arrival at New-York. New Edition. Philadelphia, printed. *London:* Re-printed for John Stockdale, 1794. 63 *pp. 8vo.* (2s. 6d. 2226)

PRIMER,/ (A)/ for the Use of the/ Mohawk Children,/ To acquire the Spelling and Reading of their/ own, as well as to get acquainted with the/ English Tongue; which for that Purpose is put/ on the oppofite Page./ Waerighwaghsawe/ Iksaougvenwa/Tfiwaondad-derighhonny Kaghyadogh= fera; Nayon-/deweyeftaghk ayeweanaghnodonayeghyàdow Ka-/niyenkehàga Kaweanondaghkouh :' Dyorheaf-hàga/ oni tfinihadiweanotea./ London,/ Printed by C. Buckton, Great Pultney-Street/. 1786. *Frontispiece, and* 98 *pp. including Title. Old tree calf./* 24*mo.* (3*l.* 13*s.* 6*d.* 2227)

PRINCE (DEBORAH). Dying Exercises of Mrs. Deborah Prince: And Devout Meditations of Mrs. Sarah Gill, Daughters of the late Rev. Mr. Thomas Prince, Minifter of the South Church, Boston. *Edinburgh*: D. Paterson, MDCCLXXXV. 46 *pp.* 12*mo.* (7*s.* 6*d.* 2228)

PRINCE (THOMAS). A Sermon Delivered By Thomas Prince, M.A. On Wenfday October 1. 1718. At his Ordination to the Pastoral Charge Of the South Church in Bofton, N. E. In Conjunction with the Re-verend Mr. Joseph Sewall. Together with The Charge, By the Reverend Increase Mather, D.D. And a Copy of what was faid at giving the Right Hand of Fellowfhip: By the Reverend Cotton Mather, D.D. To which is added, A Discourse Of the Validity of Ordination by the Hands of Presbyters, Previous to Mr. Sewall's on September 16. 1713. By the Late Reverend and Learned Mr. Ebenezer Pemberton, Paftor of the fame Church. *Boston*: Printed by J. Franklin for S. Gerrish, and Sold at his Shop, near the Old Meeting-Houfe. 1718. 4 *prel. leaves and* 76 *pp.* ' A Discourse had By the late Reverend and Learned Mr. Ebenezer Pemberton, Previous to the Ordination Of the Reverend Mr. Jofeph Sewall, At Boston, September 16. 1713. Affirming and proving the Validity of Presbyterial Ordination. *Boston*: Printed by J. Franklin, for S. Gerrish, and Sold at his Shop near the Old Meeting Houfe. 1718.' 2 *prel. leaves and* 15 *pp. Small* 8*vo.* (1*l.* 11*s.* 6*d.* 2229)

PRINCE (THOMAS). The Departure of Elijah lamented A Sermon Occafioned By the Great & Publick Lofs In the Deceafe of the very Reverend & Learned Cotton Mather, D.D. F.R.S. And Senior Paftor of the North Church in Bofton: Who left this Life on Feb. 13th 1727, 8. The Morning after He finifhed the LXV Year of his Age. By Thomas Prince, M.A. And one of the Paftors of the South Church. *Boston* in New-England: Printed for D. Henchman, near the Brick Meeting Houfe in Cornhil. MDCCXXVIII. *Half-title, title, and* 26 *pp.* 8vo. (7s. 6d. 2230)

PRINCE (Thomas). A Chronological Hiftory of New-England In the Form of Annals: Being A fummary and exact Account of the moft material Tranfactions and Occurrences relating to This Country, in the Order of Time wherein they happened, from the Difcovery by Capt. Gosnold in 1602, to the Arrival of Governor Belcher, in 1730. With an Introduction, Containing A brief Epitome of the moft remarkable Tranfactions and Events Abroad, from the Creation: Including the connected Line of Time, the Succeffion of Patriarchs and Sovereigns of the moft famous Kingdoms and Empires, the gradual Difcoveries of America, and the Progress of the Reformation to the Difcovery of New England. By Thomas Prince, M.A. *Boston, N. E.* Printed by Kneeland & Green for S. Gerrish, MDCCXXXVI. Vol. I. 5 *prel. leaves, xii, and* 20 *pp.* 'The Introduction' 104 *pp.* 'The New-England Chronology' Part I. *and* Part II. 254 *pp. Old calf. Small* 8vo. (15s. 2231)

PRINCE (Thomas). Extraordinary Events the Doings of God, and marvellous in pious Eyes. Illuftrated In a Sermon At the South Church in Bofton, N. E. On the General Thanksgiving, Thurfday, July 18. 1745. Occafion'd By taking the City of Louifbourg on the Ifle of Cape-Breton, by New-England Soldiers, affifted by a Britifh Squadron. By Thomas Prince, M.A. And one of the Paftors of faid Church. *Boston:* Printed for D. Henchman in Cornhil. 1745. 2 *prel. leaves and pp.* 7-35. 8vo. (7s. 6d. 2232)

PRINCE (Thomas). Extraordinary Events the Doings of God, and marvellous in pious Eyes. Illustrated in a Sermon At the South Church in Bofton,

N. E. On the General Thanksgiving, Thursday, July 18, 1745. Occafion'd By Taking the City of Louifbourg on the Ifle of Cape-Breton, by New-England Soldiers, affifted by a Britifh Squadron. By Thomas Prince, M.A. And one of the Paftors of the faid Church. The Third Edition. Boston, Printed: *London*, Reprinted; J. Lewis, 1746. 32 pp. 8vo. (7s. 6d. 2233)

PRINCE (THOMAS). Extraordinary Events the Doings of God, and marvellous in pious Eyes. Illuftrated in a Sermon at the South Church in Bofton, N. E. On the General Thanksgiving, Thursday, July 18. 1745. Occafion'd By taking the City of Louifbourg on the Ifle of Cape-Breton, by New-England Soldiers, affifted by a Britifh Squadron. By Thomas Prince, M.A. And one of the Paftors of faid Church. *Edinburgh:* R. Fleming and Company. 1746. 3 *prel. leaves and pp.* 5-38. *Unbound.* 8vo. (5s. 6d. 2234)

PRINCE (THOMAS). The Salvation of God in 1746. In Part fet forth in a Sermon At the South Church in Bofton, Nov. 27. 1746. Being the Day of the Anniversary Thanksgiving In the Province of the Maffachufetts Bay in N.E. Wherein The moft remarkable Salvations of the Year paft, both in Europe and North-America, as far as they are come to our Knowledge, are brieflyconfidered. By Thomas Prince, M.A. And a Paftor of the faid Church. *Boston:* Printed for D. Henchman in Cornhil. 1746. *Title and pp.* 5-35. 8vo. (7s. 6d. 2235)

PRINCE (THOMAS). A Sermon Delivered At the South Church in Bofton, N. E. Auguft 14. 1746. Being the Day of General Thanksgiving for The great Deliverance of the Britifh Nations by The glorious and happy Victory near Culloden. Obtained by His Royal Highnefs Prince William Duke of Cumberland April 16. laft. Wherein The Greatnefs of the Publick Danger and Deliverance is in Part fet forth, to excite their moft grateful Praifes to the God of their Salvation. By Thomas Prince, M.A. And a Paftor of the faid Church. *Boston:* Printed for D. Henchman in Cornhil, and S. Kneeland and T. Green in Queen-ftreet. 1746. *Title and pp.* 5-39. 8vo. (7s. 6d. 2236)

PRINCE (Thomas). A Sermon Deliver'd at the South Church in Bofton, New-England, Auguft 14, 1746. Being the Day of General Thanksgiving for the Great Deliverance of the Britifh Nations, by the Glorious and Happy Victory near Culloden. Obtained by His Royal Highness Prince William Duke of Cumberland, April 16, in the fame Year. Wherein the Greatness of the Publick Danger and Deliverance is in Part fet forth, to excite their moft grateful Praifes to the God of their Salvation. By Thomas Prince, M.A. And a Paftor of the faid Church. Boston Printed: *London*, Re-printed, John Lewis, 1747. 39 pp. 8vo. (7s. 6d. 2237)

PRINCE (Thomas). The natural and moral Government and Agency of God in caufing Droughts and Rains. A Sermon At the South Church in Bofton, Thurfday, Aug. 24. 1749. Being the Day of the General Thanksgiving, In the Province of the Massachusetts, For the extraordinary reviving Rains, after the moft diftreffing Drought which have been known among us in the Memory of any Living. By Thomas Prince, A.M. And a Paftor of the faid Church. *Boston:* Printed and Sold at Kneeland and Green's, in Queen Street, 1749. 3 *prel. leaves and* 40 pp. 8vo. (4s. 6d. 2238)

PRINCE (Thomas). Six Sermons by the late Thomas Prince, A.M. one of the Ministers of the South Church In Boston. Published from his Manuscripts, By John Erskine, D.D. one of the Ministers of Edinburgh. *Edinburgh:* David Paterson, MDCCLXXXV. *xvi and text* 156 pp. *Half morocco.* 12mo. (7s. 6d. 2239)

The 16 preliminary pages are occupied with an interefting Memoir of Thomas Prince and the Prince family, By Dr. John Erskine.

PRINCE (Thomas). A Chronological History of New-England, in the form of Annals: Being A Summary and exact Account of the most material Transactions and Occurrences relating to this Country, in the order of Time wherein they happened, from the Discovery of Capt. Gosnold, in 1602, to the Arrival of Governor Belcher, in 1730. With an Introduction containing A brief Epitome of the most considerable Transactions and Events abroad, From the Creation. Including the connected line of Time, the succession of Patriarchs and Sovereigns of the most famous Kingdoms and Empires; the gradual Discoveries of America, and the Progress of the Reformation, to the Discovery of New-England. By Thomas Prince, M.A. *Boston*, N. E. Printed by Kneeland & Green, for S. Gerrish. MDCCXXXVI. A New Edition, published by Cummings, Hilliard, and Company. 1826. 439 pp. 8vo. (8s. 6d. 2240)

PRINCIPLES of Trade. Freedom and Protection are its beft Suport: Induftry, the only Means to render Manufactures cheap. Of Coins; Exchange; and Bountys; particularly on Corn. By a Well-Wifher to his King and Country. With an Appendix. Containing Reflections on Gold, Silver, and Paper paffing as Mony. The Second Edition corected and enlarg'd. *London*, Brotherton and Sewell, MDCCLXXIV. *3 prel. leaves and* 48 *pp.* 'Appendix' 16 *pp. Old tree calf.* 8vo. (15s. 2241)
This copy once belonged to William Vaughan, who has written on its fly leaf " N.B. The Notes by Dr. Franklin."

PRINCIPLES of Law and Government with an inquiry into the Justice and Policy of the Present War, [with America], and most effectual means of obtaining an honourable, permanent, and advantageous Peace. *London*: J. Murray, MDCCLXXXI. *Two Parts.* Part I. *3 prel. leaves and* 202 *pp.* Part II. *Half-title and* 127 *pp. Errata* 1 *page. Old calf.* 4to. (7s. 6d. 2242)

PROCLAMATION. By the Queen, a Proclamation, For Settling and Afcertaining the Current Rates of Foreign Coins in Her Majefties Colonies and Plantations in America: [*Colophon*]. *London*, Printed by Charles Bill, and the Executrix of Thomas Newcomb, deceas'd; Printers to the Queens moft Excellent Majefty. 1704. *A Broadside. half mor. Folio.* (4s. 6d. 2243)

PROGRESS (The) of the French In their Views of Univerfal Monarchy. *London:* W. Owen, M.D.CC. LVI. *vi and* 58 *pp.* 8vo. (4s. 6d. 2244)

PROPOSAL (A) For putting a Speedy End to the War, By Ruining the Commerce of the French and Spaniards, And Securing our Own, Without any additional Expence to the Nation. *London*, Daniel Brown, MDCCIII, *viii and pp.* 5-18. *Half morocco.* 4to. (7s. 6d. 2245)

PROPOSAL (A) For Humbling Spain. Written in 1711. By a Perfon of Diftinction. And now firft printed from the Manuscript. To which are added, Some Confiderations on the Means of Indemnifying Great Britain from the Expences of the Prefent War. *London:* J. Roberts, [1739?] *viii and 72 pp. half mor. 8vo.* (7s. 6d. 2246)

PROPOSAL (A) For Humbling Spain. Written in 1711. By a Perfon of Diftinction. And now firft printed from the Manuscript. To which are added Some Confiderations on the Means of Indemnifying Great Britain from the Expences of the Prefent War. The Second Edition. *London:* J. Roberts [1739?] *viii and 72 pp. half mor. 8vo.* (7s. 6d. 2247)

PROPOSALS Offered for the Sugar Planters Redress, And for Reviving the Britifh Sugar Commerce. In a further Letter from a Gentleman of Barbadoes, To his Friend in London. *London,* J. Wilford, M.DCC.XXXIII. *35 pp. Half morocco. 4to.* (4s. 6d. 2248)

PROPOSALS For Uniting the English Colonies on the Continent of America So as to enable them to act with Force and Vigour againft their Enemies. *London:* J. Wilkie, M.DCC.LVII. *Title, vi and 38 pp. half mor. 8vo.* (7s. 6d. 2249)

PROSPECT (A) of the Consequences of the Prefent Conduct of Great Britain towards America. *London:* J. Almon, 1776. *98 pp. Half morocco. 8vo.* (5s. 6d. 2250)

PROSPECTS on the Rubicon: Or, an Investigation into the Causes and Consequences of the Politics to be agitated at the Meeting of Parliament. *London:* MDCCLXXXVII. *iv and 68 pp. Half morocco. 8vo.* (4s. 6d. 2251)

PROTEST Against the Bill To repeal the American Stamp Act, of Last Session. *A Paris,* J. W. M.DCC. LXVI. *16 pp. 8vo.* (4s. 6d. 2252)

PROTEST (SECOND), with a List of the Voters against the Bill To Repeal the American Stamp Act, of Last Session. *A Paris,* J. W. 1766. *15 pp. With Errata to the 1st and 2nd Protest 14 lines. 8vo.* (4s. 6d. 2253)

PROTESTS. Correct Copies Of the Two Protests against the Bill To Repeal the American Stamp Act, of Last Session. With Lists of the Speakers and Voters. A *Paris*, J. W. M.DCC.LXVI. 22 *pp.* ' A List' *etc.* 8 *pp.* 8*vo.* (4s. 6d. 2254)

PROUD (ROBERT). The Hiftory of Pennfylvania, in North America, from the Original Inftitution and Settlement of that Province, under the firft Proprietor and Governor William Penn, in 1681, till after the Year 1742; with an Introduction respecting The Life of W. Penn, prior to the grant of the Province, and the religious Society of the People called Quakers;—with the firft rife of the neighbouring Colonies, more particularly of Weft-New-Jerfey, and the Settlement of the Dutch and Swedes on Delaware. To which is added, A brief Description of the said Province, and of the General State, in which it flourifhed, principally between the Years 1760 and 1770. The whole including a Variety of Things Useful and interefting to be known, refpecting that Country in early Time, &c. With an Appendix. Written principally between the Years 1776 and 1780, By Robert Proud. *Philadelphia*, Printed and Sold by Zachariah Poulson, Junior, Number Eighty, Chesnut Street, 1797. *Two Volumes.* Volume I. 508 *pp. With Portrait of Penn, and Map of Pennsylvania.* Volume II. ' Printed *etc.* No. 106, Chefnut ftreet, Nearly oppofite to the Bank of North America. 1798.' 373 *pp.* ' Appendix' *etc.* 146 *pp.* 8*vo.* (1*l.* 1s. 2255)

PSALMS. The/ Psalms,/ Hymns,/ and/ Spiritual Songs/ of the/ Old and New Teftament,/ Faithfully Tranflated into/ Englifh Metre./ For the ufe, edification, and comfort of the/ Saints in publick and private, efpe-/cially in New-England./ *Cambridge*,/ Printed for Hezekiah Usher, of Boftoo./ [1664]. 94 *pp. including the title. Imperfect, wanting all after page* 94. *Red morocco extra by Francis Bedford.* 12*mo.* (10*l.* 10s. 2256)

PSALTERIUM AMERICANUM. The Book of Pfalms, In a Tranflation Exactly conformed unto the Original; but all in Blank Verfe, Fitted unto the Tunes commonly ufed in our Churches. Which Pure Offering is accompanied with Illustrations, digging for Hidden Treafures in it; And Rules to

Employ it upon the Glorious and Various Intentions of it. Whereto are added, Some other Portions of the Sacred Scripture, to Enrich the Cantional. *Boston :* in N. E. Printed by S. Kneeland, for B. Eliot, S. Gerrish, D. Henchman, and J. Edwards, and Sold at their Shop, 1718. *Title, xxxvi and 426 pp. Imperfect, wanting pages iii and iv. Bound. Small 8vo.* (2l. 2s. 2257)

PTOLEMÆUS (CLAUDIUS). In hoc Opere/ hæc conti/nentvr Geographiæ Cl. Ptolemæi a plurimis uiris utriusſq; linguæ doctiſſ./ emēdata: & cū archetypo græco ab ipſis collata./ Schemata cū demonſtrationibus ſuis correcta a Marco Beneuentano/ Monacho cœleſtino & Joanne Cotta Veronenſi uiris Mathematicis/ conſultiſſimis./ Figura de proiectione ſpheræ in plano quæ in libro octauo deſidera/ batur ad ipſis nōdum inſtaurata ſed fere ad inuenta eius. n. ueſtigia/ in nullo etiam græco codice extabant./ Maxima quantitas diert ciuitatū : & diſtantiæ locon ab Alexādria/ Aegypti cuiuſq; ciuitatis : quæ malijs codicibus nō erant./ Planiſphærium Cl. Ptolemei nouiter recognitū & diligentiſſ. emen-/datum a Marco Beneuentano Monacho celeſtino./ Noua orbis deſcriptio ac noua Oceani nauigatio qua Liſbona ad/ Indicū peruenitur pelagus Marco Beneuentano monacho cæle-/ſtino ædita./ Noua & uniuerſalior Orbis cogniti tabula Ioā. Ruyſch Germano/ elaborata./ Sex Tabulæ nouiter confectæ uidelicet Liuoniæ : Hyſpaniæ Galliæ :/ Germaniæ : Italiæ : & Iudeæ./ Cavtvm est edicto Ivlii. II. Pont. Max./ ne q vis Imprimere avt Imprimi/ facere avdeat hoc ipsvm opvs/ pena excommvnicationis latae Sententiae/ his qvi contra Mandatvm Ivssvmqve/ conari avdebvnt./ Anno Virginei Partvs/ MDVIII./ *Rome. Signatures* A. [D & E *in six*] *to* N. *in eights,* O. *in seven, followed by 34 copperplate Maps.* ' Incipit Regiſtrum' *etc; signatures* Aa & Bb *in eights,* Cc *in four.* ' Reuerendiſſimo in Chriſto' *etc. signatures* a *in six* b *in eight. Fine copy. Vellum. Folio.* (3l. 3s. 2258)

PTOLEMÆUS (CLAUDIUS). Geo-/graphiæ/ vniversæ/ tvm veteris, tvm/ novæ absolvtissimum/ opus, duobus voluminibus distinctum,/ In quorum priore habentur/ Cl. Ptolemæi Pelvsiensis/ Geographicæ enarrationis Libri octo :/ Quorum primus, qui præcepta ipſius facultatis omnia complectitur,/

commentarijs vberrimis illuſtratus est à/ Io. Antonio Magino Patavino./ In ſecundo volumine in ſunt/ Cl. Ptolemaei, antiquæ orbis tabulæ xxvii. ad priſcas hi-/ſtorias intelligendas ſummè neceſſariæ. Et tabulæ xxxvii. recen-/tiores, quibus vniuerſi orbis pictura, ac facies, ſingularumq₃/ eius partium, regionum, ac prouinciarum ob ocu-/los patet noſtro sæculo congruens. Vnà cum ipſarum tabularum copioſiſſimis expoſitionibus, quibus ſingulæ/ orbis partes, prouinciæ, regiones, imperia, regna, ducatus, &/ alia dominia, prout nostro tempore ſe habent,/ exactè deſcribuntur/ Auctore eodem Io. Ant. Magino/ Patavino, Mathematicarum in/ Almo Bononienſi Gymnaſio publico profeſſore./ Anno 1597./ In celeberrima Agrippinensivm *Coloniæ* excvdebat/ Petrvs Keschedt./ *Two Parts.* [Part I.] 4 *prel. leaves,* 47 *and* 184 *pp. Index* 38 *pp.* [Part II]. *Title and folived leaves* 2-292. *Index* 56 *pp. Vellum.* 4to. (12s. 6d. 2259)

PUGH (ELLIS). A Salutation to the Britains, To Call them From the Many Things, to the One Thing needful, for the Saving of their Souls; Especially, To the poor unlearned Tradeſmen, Plowmen and Shepherds, thoſe that are of a low Degree like my ſelf, This, in Order to direct you to know God and Chriſt, the only wiſe God, which is Life eternal, and to learn of him, that you may become wiſer than your Teachers. By Ellis Pvgh. Tranſlated from the Britiſh Language by Rowland Ellis, Revis'd and Corrected by David Lloyd. *Philadelphia:* Printed by S. Keimer, for W. Davies, Bookbinder, in Cheſnut-Street. 1727. *xv and* 222 *pp. Old calf.* 16*mo.* (1*l.* 1s. 2260)

PULLEIN (SAMUEL). The Culture of Silk: Or, an Essay on its rational Practice and Improvement. In Four Parts. I. On the raiſing and planting of Mulberry Trees. II. On hatching and rearing the Silk-Worms. III. On obtaining their Silk and Breed. IV. On reeling their Silk-Pods. For the uſe of the American Colonies. By the Rev. Samuel Pullein. M.A. *London:* A. Millar, MDCC LVIII. *xv and* 399 *pp. With two plates. Old calf.* 8*vo.* (7s. 6d. 2261)

PULTENEY (WILLIAM). Thoughts on the present

State of Affairs with America, and the means of Conciliation. By William Pulteney, Esq: The Third Edition. *London*: J. Dodsley, MDCCLXXVIII. *Title and* 102 *pp. half mor.* 8vo. (4s. 6d. 2262)

PULTENEY (WILLIAM). Thoughts on the present state of affairs with America, and the means of conciliation. By William Pulteney, Esq. The fourth edition. *London*: J. Dodsley, MDCCLXXVIII. *Title and* 102 *pp. half mor.* 8vo. (4s. 6d. 2263)

PULTENEY (WILLIAM). Considerations on the Present State of Public Affairs, and the means of raising the necessary Supplies. By William Pulteney, Esq. The Second Edition. *London*: J. Dodsley, MDCCLXXIX. *Title and* 51 *pp. half mor.* 8vo. (4s. 6d. 2264)

PURCHAS (SAMUEL). Pvrchas his Pilgrimage./ Or/ Relations/ of the World/ and the Religions/ observed in all Ages/ And places difcouered, from the/ Creation vnto this/ present./ In foure Partes./ This first contai-/neth A Theological ànd/ Geographical Hiftorie of Afia, Africa,/ and America, with the Iflands/ Adiacent./ Declaring the Ancient Religions before the Flovd, the/ Heathnifh, Jewifh, and Saracenicall in all Ages fince, in thofe/ parts profeffed, with their feuerall Opinions, Idols, Oracles, Temples,/ Prieftes, Fafts, Feafts, Sacrifices, and Rites Religious: Their/ beginnings, Proceedings, Alterations, Sects,/ Orders and Succeffions./ With briefe Defcriptions of the Countries, Nations, States, Discoueries,/ Priuate and Publike Cuftomes, and the moft Remarkable Rarities of/ Nature, or Humane Induftrie, in the fame./ By Samvel Pvrchas, Minifter at Eftwood in Effex./ *London*,/ Printed by William Stansby for Henrie Fetherftone, and are to be/ fold at his Shoppe in Pauls Church-yard at the/ Signe of the Rofe 1613./ 14 *prel. leaves; viz. Title reverse blank;* 'The Epistle Dedicatorie.' 4 *pp*: 'To the Reader.' 4 *pp. Epigrams* 2 *pp*; 'The Contents' *etc.* 9 *pp*; 'The Catalogue of the Authors.' 6 *pp*; *Text* 752 *pp.* 'Table of the principall Matters' *etc.* 20 *pp. Fine copy. Old calf. Folio.* (18s. 2265)

PURCHAS (SAMUEL). Pvrchas his Pilgrim./ Microcosmvs,/ or/ the Historie/ Of Man./ Relating the {Wonders of his Generation,/ Vanities in his Degeneration,/ Neceffity of his Regeneration./} Meditated on the words of David. By Samuel Pvrchas, Parfon of S. Martins/ neere Lvdgate, London./ *London,*/ Printed by W. S. for Henry Fetherftone./ 1619./ 14 *prel. leaves and* 818 *pp. Old calf. Small* 8*vo.* (15*s.* 2266)

PURNELL (THOMAS). The following is a true and faithful Account of the Loss of the Brigantine Tyrrell, Arthur Coghlan, Commander; with the Misfortunes attending the faid Veffel's Crew. By Thomas Purnell, Chief Mate thereof. [*London.*] Dated 'Hoxton Sept. 1766.' *Signed* 'Thomas Purnell.' 8 *pp.* 4*to.* (7*s.* 6*d.* 2267)

PURRY (JOHN PETER). A Method For Determining the best Climate of the Earth, On a Principle to which All Geographers and Historians have been hitherto Strangers. In a Memorial prefented to the Governors of the East-India Company in Holland, for which The Author was obliged to leave that Country, By John Peter Purry. Translated from the French. *London,* M. Cooper, MDCCXLIV. 2 *prel. leaves and text* 60 *pp. Half morocco.* 8*vo.* (4*s.* 6*d.* 2268)

PYNCHON (WILLIAM). I The Time when the/ First Sabbath/ was Ordained./ 1 Negatively, Not in the Time of Adams Innocency,/ as many fay it was./ 2 Affirmatively, It was Ordained after the Time of/ Adams Fall and Re-creation./ II The Manner how the Firft Sabbath was Ordained./ 1 By bleffing the Seventh Day with many Spiritual Or-/dinances, both for publick and private ufe./ 2 By Sanctifying that Day for the Exercife of the faid Or-/dinances./ 3 By Sanctifying the outward Reft of that Day, to be a Ty-/pical Sign both of Gods Refting, and of mans Refting/ in the Seed of the Woman, that was promifed to break/ the Devils Head-plot, namely, by his Propitiatory Sacrifice./ And hence it follows,/ 1 That as the Sabbath was Ordained to be a typical Sign,/ fo it muft be abolifhed, as foon as Chrift had performed/ his faid Propitiatory Sacrifice./ 2 As it was Ordained to be the Sanctified time, for the/ Exercife of the faid bleffed Ordinances; fo the next day of/ the week, into which it was changed, muft continue with-/out intermiffion to the end of the world./ Part II. III A Treatife of Holy Time, concerning the true limits/ of the Lords Day, when it begins, and when it ends, is/ hereunto annexed/ By William Pynchon Efq./ Publifhed by Authority./ *London*, Printed by R. I. and are to be fold by T. N. at the three Lions/ in Cornhil, near the Royal Exchange 1654./ *Two Parts.* Part I. 8 *prel. leaves and* 143 *pp:* Part II. 8 *prel. leaves and* 120 *pp. Old calf.* 4*to.* (15s. 2269)

PYNCHON (WILLIAM). The Meritorious Price/ of/ Mans Redemption,/ or/ Chrifts Satisfaction difcuffed and explained./ 1 By fhewing how the Sufferings and the Sacrifice of Chrift, did fatisfie Gods/ Juftice, pacifie his Wrath, and procure his Reconciliation for mans Redemp-/tion, from Satans Headplot./ 2 By vindicating the Sufferings and the Sacrifice of Chrift, from that moft dan-/gerous Scripture-lefs Tenent, that is held forth by Mr. Norton of New-England/ in his Book of *Chrifts Sufferings*, affirming that he fuffered the Effential Tor-/ments of Hell, and the fecond death from Gods immediate vindicative wrath. 3 By fhewing that the Righteoufnefs and Obedience of Christ in relation to his/ Office of Madiatorfhip, is a diftinct fort of obedience, from his moral obedience,/ in Chapter the third and elfewhere./ 4 By fhewing that the Righteoufnefs of God (fo called in Rom. 3. 21, 22, 26/ in Rom. 10. 3, in 2 Cor. 5. 21. and in Phil. 3. 9.) is to be underftood of God the/ Fathers performance of his Covenant with Christ;/ namely, that upon Chrifts/ performance of his Covenant (by combating with Satan, and at laft by making/ his death a facrifice) he would be reconcile 1 to beleeving finners, and not im-/pute their fins to them. And therefore I. This Righteoufnefs of God muft/ needs be the formal caufe of a finners juftification. And 2. It muft needs be/ a diftinct fort of Righteoufnefs from the Righteoufnefs of Chrift contrary to/ Mr Nortons Tenent. This is evidenced in Chap. 14. and elfewhere./ 5 By Explaining Gods Declaration of the combate between the Devil and the feed/ of the woman in Gen. 3. 15. from whence (as from the foundation-principle)/ this prefent Reply doth explain all the after prophecies of Chrifts Sufferings./ 6 By clearing feveral other Scriptures of the greateft note in thefe Controverfies,/ from Mr. Nortons corrupt Expofitions, and by expounding them in their right/ fenfe; Both according to the Context, and according to fundry eminent Or-/thodox Writers./ By William Pynchon Efq; late of New England./ *London*, Printed by R. I. for Thom. Newberry, and are to be fold at his Shop in/ Cornhil, over againft the Conduit near the Royal Exchange, 1655./ 26 *prelim. leaves and text* 439 *pp. Errata* 1 *page. Old calf.* 4*to.* (3*l.* 3*s.* 2270)

QUINTANA Y GUIDO (ANTONIO DE). Epitafios/ Originales con/qve el Real Convento de Iesvs/ Maria, de esta Noble Civdad de Mexico,/ facò a luz parte del juftifsimo fentimiento, que ocultauan los generofos/ pechos de fus Religiofas hijas; los quales, en viftofas tarjas eftauan repar-/tidos por los pedeftales de doze viftofas piramides, y feis efpaciofas/ gradas (que hazian exquifita armonia) fobre que eftaua vna bien dif-/puefta Pyra que fubftituya el depofito del Mageftuofo cuerpo, con fu tum/ ba cubierta de vn paño, y dos almoadas de rica tela, ornato (fi de-cen-/te) deuido a la Real Corona, de que le confti-tuyò, y compuffo el/ fumptuofifsimo Panteon, que poblado de efquadrones de/ brillantes luzes, erigiò in honra de fu Patrona la Se-/reniffima D. Isabel de Borbon,/ Reyna de Efpaña, y Señora nueftra, a/ los 26. y 27. de Iulio del Año/ de 1645./ Al Señor Doctor Don Pedro de Barrientos/ Lomelin, del Confejo de fu Mageftad, &c./ Por el Bachiller Antonio de Qvintana/ y Guido, Capellan del Choro defta Santa Iglefia Cathedral./ Con Licencia·:/ En *Mexico*, por la Viuda de Bernardo Calderon. Año de 1645./ *Title on the reverse, Woodcut Arms.* 'Ap-rvacion del Padre/ Iuan de S. Miguel, de la Com-pañia/ de Iesvs./ 1 *page, reverse blank.* 'Al Señor Doctor D. Pedro/ de Barrientos Lomelin,' etc. 2 pp. *Text commencing* 'Titulo Dedicatorio que ocu-paua la quarta' etc. *folioed leaves 3-8, the reverse blank.* 4to. (1*l.* 11*s.* 6*d.* 2271)

QUIR (PETER FERDINAND DE). Terra Auftralis in-cognita,/ or/ A new Southerne/ Discoverie,/ con-taining/ A fifth part of the World./ Lately found out/ By Ferdinand De Qvir,/ a Spanifh Captaine./

Neuer before publifhed./ Tranflated by W. B./ London/ Printed for Iohn Hodgetts./ 1617. *Title, reverse blank, and* 27 pp. 4*to.* (4*l.* 14*s.* 6*d.* 2272)

QUEBEC. State of the present form of Government of the Province of Quebec. With a large Appendix; containing Extracts from the Minutes of an investigation into the past administration of justice in that province, instituted by order of Lord Dorchester in 1787, and from other original Papers. *London*, J. Debrett, MDCCLXXXIX. *Title, Errata, and* 176 pp. *Half morocco.* 8*vo.* (5*s.* 6*d.* 2273)

QUINCY (JOSIAH, *Junior*). Observations on the Act of Parliament, commonly called the Boston Port-Bill; with Thoughts on Civil Society and Standing Armies. By Josiah Quincy, Junior, Counfellor at Law, in Boston. Boston, N. E. Printed. *London :* Re-printed for Edward and Charles Dilly, MDCCLXXIV. 3 *prel. leaves and* 80 pp. *Half morocco.* 8*vo.* (5*s.* 6*d.* 2274)

RALEIGH (*Sir* WALTER). The/ Discoverie/ of the Large,/ Rich and Bevvtifvl/ Empire of Gviana, with/ a relation of the Great and Golden Citie/ of Manoa (which the fpaniards call El/ Dorado) And the provinces of Emeria,/ Arromaia, Amapaia and other Coun-/tries, with their riuers, ad-/ioyning/ Performed in the yeare 1595. by Sir/ W. Ralegh Knight, Captaine of her/ Majefties Guard, Lo. Warden/ of the Stanneries, and her High-/neffe Lieutenant generall/ of the Countie of/ Cornewall./ Imprinted at *London* by Robert Robinfon/ 1596./ 8 *prel. leaves*; *viz. Title, reverse blank,* 'To the Right/ Honorable my/ fingular good Lord and kinfman,/ Charles Howard, Knight of the Gar-/ter Barron, and Counceller, and of the Ad-/miralls of England the moft renow-/med: And to the Right Honorable/ Sr Robert Cecyll Knight, Councel-/ler in her Highnes priuie/ Councels.' 8 *pp*: 'To the Reader.' 6 *pp*: *Text* 112 *pp*. *Vellum.* 4*to*. (3*l*. 3*s*. 2275)

RALEIGH (*Sir* WALTER). A/ Declaration/ of the Demea-/nor and Cariage of/ Sir Walter Raleigh,/ Knight, afwell in his Voyage, as/ in, and fithence his Returne;/ And of the true motiues and induce-/ments which occafioned His Maieftie/ to Proceed in doing Iustice upon him,/ as hath bene done./ *London*, Printed by Bonham Norton/ and Iohn Bill, deputie Printers for/ the Kings moft Excellent Maieftie./ M.DC.XVIII. *Title, having on` the reverse a woodcut of the Royal Arms*; *Text* 68 *pp*. *Half calf.* 4*to*. (10*s*. 6*d*. 2276)

RALEIGH (*Sir* WALTER). Sir Walter/ Ravvleighs/ Ghost,/ or/ Englands Forewarner./ Difcouering a fecret Confultation, newly hol-/den in the Court of Spaine./ Together, with his tormenting of Count de/ Gondomar; and his ftrange affrightment, Confeffion/ and publique recantation: laying open many/ treacheries intended for the fubuer-/fion of England./ *Vtricht,*/ Printed by John Sehellem./ 1626./ *Title, reverse blank, and* 41 *pp. Wanting pages* 7 *to* 22, *inclusive.* 4*to.* (3*s.* 6*d.* 2277)

RALEIGH (*Sir* WALTER). The/ Prerogatiue/ of Parlaments/ in England:/ Proued in a Dialogue (pro &/ contra) beweene a Councellour/ of State and a Iuftice/ of Peace./ Written by the Worthy (much lacked/ and lamented) Sir W. R. K^t. deceafed./ Dedicated to the Kings Maiefty, and to/ the Houfe of Parlament now affembled./ Preferued to be now happily/ (in thefe diftracted Times)/ Publifhed, and/ Printed at *Hamburgh.*/ 1628./ 4 *prel. leaves; viz. Title, reverse blank,* ' To the King.' 5 *pp. Text* 66 *pp. half mor.* 4*to.* (10*s.* 6*d.* 2278)

RALEIGH (*Sir* WALTER). The/ Prerogative/ of/ Parliaments/ in England:/ Proued in a Dialogue (pro &/ contra) beweene a Councellour/ of State and a Iuftice/ of Peace./ Written by the worthy (much lacked and/ lamented) Sir Walter Raleigh Knight,/ deceafed./ Dedicated to the King's Maieftie, and to the/ Houfe of Parlament now affembled./ Preferued to be now happily/ (in thefe diftracted Times)/ Publifhed, and/ Printed at *Midelburge.*/ 1628./ 4 *prel. leaves ; viz. Title, reverse blank,* ' To the King.' 5*pp* : *Text* 66 *pp. half mor.* 4*to.* (7*s.* 6*d.* 2279)

RALEIGH (*Sir* WALTER). Tvbvs Historicvs:/ An Hiftoricall Perfpective ;/ Difcovering all the Empires and King-/domes of the World, as they/ flourifht refpectively under/ the foure Imperiall/ Monarchies./ Faithfully compofed out of the moft ap-/proved Authours, and exactly di-/gefted according to the fup-/putation of the beft/ Chronologers./ (With a Catalogue of the Kings and Emperours of/ the chiefe Nations of the World.)/ By the late famous and learned Knight/ Sir Walter Raleigh./ *London,*/ Printed by Thomas Harper, for Benjamin Fifher, 1636./ 13 *unnumbered leaves; viz. Title, reverse blank,* ' To the most Illuftrious and hopefull

Prince Charles,' etc. 1 *page, the reverse blank*; ' The Publifher's Advertifement to the Reader.' 3 *pp. the reverse blank*; 'Tubus Hiftoricus.' *running title* ' Sir Walter Raleigh's/ Chronologicall Tables.' 9 *pp. the reverse blank*; ' A Catalogue of the Kings and Em-/perours of the chiefe Nations/ of the World.' 7 *pp. the reverse blank*. 4*to*. (10*s*. 6*d*. 2280)

RALEIGH (*Sir* WALTER). The/ Prince,/ or/ Max-ims/ of/ State./ Written/ by Sir Walter Ravvley,/ and prefented to Prince Henry./ *London*, Printed, MDCXLII. 3 *prel. leaves and* 46 *pp. Half morocco.* 4*to*. (7*s*. 6*d*. 2281)

RALEIGH (*Sir* WALTER). Judicious/ and/ Select Effayes/ and/ Observations,/ By that Renowned and/ Learned Knight./ Sir Walter Raleigh./ upon/ The firft Invention of Shipping./ The Mifery of Invafive Warre./ The Navy Royall and Sea-Service./ With his/ Apologie for his voyage to Guiana./ *London*,/ Printed by T. W. for Humphrey Mofeley/ and are to be Sold at the Princes Armes in/ St. Pauls-Church-yard, 1650./ 5 *prel. leaves and* 42 *pp*; *Title*, 4 *pp. and* 31 *unpaged leaves*; 1 *blank leaf*; *Title and* 46 *pp*; *Title and* 69 *pp. With Portrait. Calf extra by Riviere.* 12*mo*. (12*s*. 6*d*. 2282)

RALEIGH (*Sir* WALTER). The Cabinet-Council :/ Containing the Chief Arts/ of/ Empire,/ And Mys-teries of/ State ;/ discabineted/ In Political and Po-lemical Aphorifms,/ grounded on Authority, and Experience ;/ And illuftrated with the choiceft/ Examples and Hiftorical/ Obfervations./ By the Ever-renowned Knight,/ Sir Walter Raleigh,/ Publifhed By John Milton, Efq ;/ *London*, Printed by Tho. Newcomb for Tho. John-/fon at the fign of the Key in St. Pauls Churchyard,/ near the Weft-end. 1658./ 4 *prel. leaves and* 199 *pp. Portrait of Raleigh. Old calf.* 16*mo*. (10*s*. 6*d*. 2283)

RALEIGH (*Sir* WALTER). The/ Life/ of the/ Valiant and Learned/ Sir Walter Raleigh, Knight./ With his/ Tryal/ at/ Winchester./ The Third Edition./ *London*,/ Printed for George Dawes, and Richard Tonfon within Grays-lnn-/ Gate next Grays-Inn-Lane. MDCLXXXVII. *Title and* 41 *pp. half mor. Folio.* (10*s*. 6*d*. 2284)

RALEIGH (Sir WALTER). An Introduction to a/ Breviary of the/ History of England/ With the/ Reign/ of/ King William the I./Entitled the/ Conqueror./ Written by Sr. Walter Raleigh, Kt. And/ Dedicated to the then Earl of Salisbury./ *London*,/ Printed for Sam. Keble at the Great-Turks-/Head in Fleet-ſtreet. And Dan. Brown/ at the Black-Swan and Bible without/ Temple-Bar. 1693./ 4 *prel. leaves including the Portrait, and* 77 *pp. Calf*. Small 8vo. (6s. 6d. 2285)

RAMSAY (DAVID). The History of the Revolution of South-Carolina, from a British Province to an Independent State. By David Ramsay, M.D. Member of the American Congress. In Two Volumes. *Trenton:* Printed by Isaac Collins. M.DCC.LXXXV. *Two Volumes.* Vol. I. *xx and* 453 *pp. Map and Sketch at pp.* 1, *and* 145. Vol. II. *xx and* 574 *pp. Sketches and plan at pp.* 52, 58, *and* 326. 8vo. (10s. 6d. 2286)

RAMSAY (DAVID). The History of the American Revolution. By David Ramsay, M.D. of South-Carolina. A New Edition. In Two Volumes. *London:* John Stockdale, 1793. *Two Volumes.* Volume I. 2 *prel. leaves and* 357 *pp.* Volume II. *xii and* 360 *pp.* 8vo. (8s. 6d. 2287)

RANDALL (JOHN). A brief Account of the Rise, Principles, and Discipline of the People call'd Quakers, In America, and elsewhere. Extracted from A System of Geography Lately Publiſh'd. By John Randall. *Bristol:* Sam. Farley, 1747. 24 *pp.* 12mo. (4s. 6d. 2288)

RANGEL (JOSEPH FRANCISCO DIMAS). Discurso fisico sobre la Formacion de las Auroras Boreales. Por D. Joseph Francisco Dimas Rangel, Reloxero en esta Corte. [*Colophon*] Con las Licencias Necesarias: Impreso en *México* en la Oficina de los Herederos del Lic. D. Joseph de Jauregui, Calle de San Bernardo. Año de 1789. 'I. to VII.' *pp. Half mor.* 4to. (10s. 6d. 2289)

RAYNAL (ABBE). A Philosophical and Political History of the British Settlements and Trade in North America. From the French of Abbé Raynal. In Two Volumes. *Edinburgh:* C. Macfarquhar,

M.DCC.LXXVI. *Two Volumes.* Vol. I. 240 pp. *Map of North America.* Vol. II. 231 pp. 12mo. (7s. 6d. 2290)

RAYNAL (ABBE). Révolution de l'Amérique, par M. L'Abbé Raynal, Auteur de l'Hiftoire Philofophique & Politique des Etabliffemens, & du Commerce des Européens dans les deux Indes. A *Londres,* Lockier Davis, M.DCC.LXXXI. *xvi and* 183 *pp. With Portrait of Raynal. Half morocco.* 8vo. (4s. 6d. 2291)

RAYNAL (ABBE). The Revolution of America. By the Abbé Raynal, Author of the Philosophical and Political History of the Establishments and Commerce of the Europeans in both the Indies. *Dublin:* C. Talbot, M,DCC,LXXXI. *xx and* 244 *pp. Old calf.* 12mo. (5s. 2292)

RAYNAL (ABBE). The Revolution of America. By The Abbé Raynal, Author of the Philosophical and Political History of the Establishments and Commerce of the Europeans in both the Indies. *London:* Lockyer Davis, MDCCLXXXI. *xvi and* 181 *pp.* 8vo. (4s. 6d. 2293)

RAYNAL (ABBE). The Revolution of America. By The Abbé Raynal, Author of the Philosophical and Political History of the Establishments and Commerce of the Europeans in both the Indies. A New Translation. *London:* Lockyer Davis. M.DCC. LXXXI. 2 *prel. leaves and* 199 *pp. Half morocco.* 12mo. (3s. 6d. 2294)

REAL Compañia de Comercio Para las Islas de Santo Domingo, Puerto-Rico, y la Margarita, que se ha dignado su Magestad conceder con diez Regiftros para Honduras, y Provincias de Guathemala, al Comercio de la Ciudad de Barcelona, y fu Eftablecimiento en la mifma, baxo el Patrocinio de Nueftra Señora de Monferrate, y de la Real Protecion de fu Mageftad. En *Madrid:* Joseph Rico, 1755. 2 *prel. leaves and text* 33 *pp. Calf.* 16mo. (14s. 2295)

REALES Ordenanzas para la direccion, Régimen y Gobierno del lmportante cuerpo de la Mineria de Nueva-España, y de su Real Tribunal General. De Orden de su Magestad. *Madrid.* Año de 1783. *Frontispiece, Title, xlvi and* 214 *pp. In boards.* *Folio.* (12s. 6d. 2296)

REALES (Juras). Entretenimientos de un Prisionero en las Provincias del Rio de la Plata: Por el Baron de Juras Reales, siendo Fiscal de S. M. en el Reino de Chile. *Barcelona:* José Torner. 1828. *Two Volumes.* Tomo Primero. *4 prel. leaves, viii and 334 pp. Wanting pp.* 295—302 *inclusive.* Tomo Segundo. *2 prel. leaves, and* 391 *pp.* ' Appendice.' 16 *pp.* 4*to.* (12*s.* 6*d.* 2297)

REASONS For Establishing the Colony of Georgia, With Regard to the Trade of Great Britain, the Increafe of our People, and the Employment and Support it will afford to great Numbers of our own Poor, as well as foreign perfecuted Protestants. With fome Account of the Country, and the Defign of the Trustees. *London:* W. Meadows, MDCCXXXIII. 39 *pp. Plate and Map. Half morocco.* 4*to.* (10*s.* 6*d.* 2298)

REASONS grounded on facts. Shewing, I. That a new Duty on Sugar muft fall on the Planter. II. That the Liberty of a direct Exportation to Foreign Markets will not help him in this Cafe. III. That a new Duty will not certainly increafe the Revenue. And, IV. That it will probably occafion the Defertion of our Sugar Iflands. *London:* M. Cooper, M,DCC,XLVIII. *Title and pp.* 3—21. *Half morocco.* 8*vo.* (4*s.* 6*d.* 2299)

RECENTES/ Novi Orbis/ Historiæ,/ Hoc eft,/ I. Inquifitio nauigationis Septentrionalis, an & quomodo ea feliciter perfici poffit, eáque/ figuris æneis demonftrata./ II. Relatio fuper detectione noui ad Caurum tranfitus ad terras Americanas in Chinam at-/que Iaponem ducturi./ III. Memorialis libellus Sereniffimo Hifpa-/niarum Regi oblatus fuper Detectione quar-/tæ orbis terrarum partis cui nomen Av-/stralis Incognita, eiúfque im-/menfis opibus & fertilitate./ IIII. Rerum ab Hifpanis in India Occiden-/tali hactenus geftarum, libri tres./ *Coloniæ Allobrovm,*/ Apud Petrvm de la Rouiere./ Anno M DCXII./ *Title reverse blank,* 51 *and Text* 480 *pp.* ' Elenchvs, sive Index,' 12 *pp. With* 2 *copperplate maps. Vellum.* 8*vo.* (3*l.* 3*s.* 2300)

RECIO DE LEON (Juan). [*Begins*] Ivan Recio de Leon Maeffe de Campo, *etc.* [Account of the discovery of a new route for the conveyance of

Silver from Potosi in Peru to Spain in lefs than half the time and expense of the ordinary route]. [*Madrid*, 1626.] 10 *leaves*. *Half morocco*. *Folio*.
(1*l*. 11*s*. 6*d*. 2301)

RECUEIL des Plans de L'Amerique Septentrionale, *A Paris* Chez Le S^r. Le Rouge Ingenieur Geographe du Roy, Et de S. A. S. M. le Comte de Clermont, Ruë des Augustins. 1755. *Engraved Title and* 16 *Plans*. 4*to*. (12*s*. 6*d*. 2302)

REDMAN (JOHN). Dissertatio Medica Inauguralis de Abortu. Qvam favente Deo ter Opt. Max. Ex Auctoritate Magnifici Rectoris D. Joannis Alberti, S. S. Theologiæ Doctoris, ejusdemque facultatis in Academia Lugduno Batava Professoris Ordinarii. Nec non Ampliffimi Senatus Academici Confenfu, & Nobiliffimæ Facultatis Medicæ Decreto, pro Grandu Doctoratus, Summifque in Medicina Honoribus, & Privilegiis rite, ac legitime confequendis, Eruditorum Examini fubjicit Johannes Redman, Penfylvanienfis. Ad diem 15. Julii 1748 hora locoque folitis. Nulla eft quæ pulchriora laborum præmia cultoribus perfolvit, quam medica fapientia. H. Boerhaav. De ufu ratiocin. Mechan. in Medicina p. 54. Constantia Triumphans *Lugduni Batavorum* Apud Conradúm Wishoff. 3 *prel. leaves and* 31 *pp. half morocco*. 4*to*. (7*s*. 6*d*. 2304)

REED (JOHN). An Explanation of the Map of the City and Liberties of Philadelphia. By John Reed. *Philadelphia*: Printed for the Author, and Sold by Mr. Nicholas Brooks, in Second-Street, between Market and Chesnut Streets, M.DCC.LXXIV. 24 *pp*: 'An Alphabetical List of the First Purchasers Names,' *etc*. 8 *and* 23 *pp*: 'The Date of Surveys' *etc*. 9 *pp*. 4*to*. (18*s*. 2305)

REED (JOSEPH). Joseph Reed Defendant, Ad. John Reed.} Argument for the Defendant in Error. 28 *pp*. 4*to*. (7*s*. 6*d*. 2306)

REEVES (JOHN). History of the Government of the Island of Newfoundland. With an Appendix; containing the Acts of Parliament made respecting the Trade and Fishery. By John Reeves, Esq., Chief Justice of the Island. *London*: J. Sewell, 1793. 4 *prel. leaves and* 167 *pp*. 'Appendix.' 2 *prel. leaves and* cxvi *pp*. 8*vo*. (7*s*. 6*d*. 2307)

REFLECTIONS on the Importation of Bar-Iron, From our own Colonies of North-America. In Anfwer to a late Pamphlet on that Subject. Humbly Submitted to the Confideration of the Honourable the House of Commons, March 14, 1757. 23 pp. *Half morocco.* 8vo. (10s. 6d. 2308)

REFLECTIONS Moral and Political on Great Britain and her Colonies. *London:* T. Becket. M.DCC.LXX. 3 *prel. leaves and* 66 pp. *Half morocco.* 8vo. (4s. 6d. 2309)

REFLECTIONS on the Rise, Progress, and probable consequences, of the present contentions with the Colonies. By a Freeholder. *Edinburgh:* Printed in the Year MDCCLXXVI. *iv and* 53 pp. 12mo. (4s. 6d. 2310)

REFUTATION (A) of the Letter to an Honble Brigadier-General, Commander of His Majefty's Forces in Canada. By an Officer. The Second Edition. *London:* R. Stevens, MDCCLX. [*See* LETTER]. *Half-title, title, and* 52 pp. *Half morocco.* 8vo. (4s. 6d. 2311)

REGIL (PEDRO MANUEL). Memoria Instructiva sobre el comercio general de la Provincia de Yucatan, y particular del puerto de Campeche, formada por el Señor don Pedro Manuel Regil, diputado electo para las Cortes Ordinarias por dicha Provincia. La Publica don Angel Alonso y Pantiga, diputado de las actuales Cortes, y cura Territorial y Castrense de la Parroquia de Campeche. *Madrid:* Año MDCCCXIV. En la Imprenta de Vega y Compañía. Calle de Capellanes. *Title; and* 56 pp. *Folded sheets at pp.* 42, *and* 45 (2). *Half calf.* 8vo. (15s. 2312)

REGIMENTO, & Leys sobre as Missonens do Eftado do Maranhaõ, & Parà, & fobre a liberdade dos Indios. Impreffo por ordem de El-Rey noffo Senhor. *Lisboa Occidental,* Antonio Manescal, M.DCCXXIV. 2 *prel. leaves and text* 82 pp. *Calf. Folio.* (1l. 11s. 6d. 2313)

REGISTER (A) for The State of Connecticut: With an Almanack, For the Year of our Lord, 1785. Calculated for the Meridian of New-London, Lat. 41. 25. North, By Nathan Daboll, Teacher of the Mathematics at the Academio

School in Plainfield. *New-London:* Printed and Sold by T. Green, near the Court-House. [1785]. 48 pp. [Almanac] 12 pp. 16mo. (2s. 6d. 2314)

REGULATIONS (The) Lately Made concerning the Colonies, and the Taxes Impoſed upon Them, conſidered. [By George Grenville.] *London:* J. Wilkie, 1765. *Half-title, title, and pp. 3—114.* 8vo. (6s. 6d. 2315)

RELACAM/ Verdadeira,/ e breve datomada da/ Villa de Olinda, Elvgardo Recife na Costa/ do Brazil pellos rebeldes de Olanda, tirada de huma carta que eſcreueo/ hum Religioſo de muyta authoridade, & que ſoy teſtemunha de viſta/ de quaſi todo ſocedido: & aſsi o affirma, & jura; & do mais/ que depois diſſo ſocedeo tè os dezoito de Abril/ deſte prezente, & fatal anno de 1630./ [*Colophon*] En *Lisboa.* Com todas as licenças neceſſarias Por Mathias/ Rodrigues Anno 1630./ Taixão eſta Relação em reis./ *6 unnumbered pages. Half morocco.* Folio. (1l. 11s. 6d. 2316)

RELACAÕ Abbreviada Da Republica, que os Religioſos Jeſuitas das Provincias de Portugal, e Heſpanha, eſtabelecerão nos Dominios Ultramarinos das duas Monarchias, e da Guerra, que nelles tem movido, e ſuſtentado contra os Exercitos Heſpanhoes, e Portuguezes: Formada pelos regiſtos das Secretarias dos dous reſpectivos Principaes Commiſſarios, e Plenipotentiarios; e por outros Documentos authenticos. Relation Abregée, Concernant la République que les Religieux, nommés Jéſuites, des Provinces de Portugal & d'Eſpagne, ont établie dans les Pays & Domaines d'outre mer de ces deux Monarchies, & de la Guerre qu'ils y ont excitée & ſoutenue contre les Armées Eſpagnoles & Portugaiſes: Dreſſée ſur les Regiſtres de Secrétariat des deux Commiſſaires reſpectifs Principaux & Plénipotentiaires des deux Couronnes, & ſur d'autres Pieces authentiques. [1758]. 68 pp. Memoire Pour ſervir d'addition & d'éclairciſſement à la Relation abrégée, &c. qu'on vient de donner au Public, ſur l'abominable conduite des Jéſuites, dans les pays & domaines d'outre-mer dépendans des Royaumes d'Eſpagne & de Portugal. *30 pp. Old calf.* 12mo. (8s. 6d. 2317)

636 *Bibliotheca Americana.*

RELACION de lo Svcedido/ en los Galeones y Flota de Terrafirme. [1622] 5 *folioed leaves. Unbound. Folio.* (1*l.* 11*s.* 6*d.* 2318)

RELACION de las Vito-/rias qve Don Diego de Arroy o/ y Daça, Governador y Capitan general de la prouinci/ de Cumana, tuuo en la gran Salina de Arraya, a 30. de No-/uiembre, del año paſſado de 622. y a treze de/ Enero deſte año, contra ciento y/ quatro nauios de Olan-/deſes./ ·[*Colophon*] Con Licencia/ En *Madrid*, Por la viuda de Alonſo Martin./ [1623] 4 *unnumbered pages. Unbound. Folio.* (1*l.* 1*s.* 2319)

RELACION/ de Como Martirizaron/ los Hereges Olandeses, Gelandeses,/ y Pechilingues, en odio de nueſtra ſanta Fè Catolica, al Religio-/ſo y ob-ſeruante varon el Padre Preſentado fray Alonſo Gomez/ de Enzinas, del Orden de nueſtra Señora de la Merced, Reden-/cion de Cautinos, y natural de la villa de Cuellar, en la entrada/ que hizieron eſte mes paſſado de Iunio de 1624. en la cuidad/ de Guayaquil, en la Prouincia de Quito, que es en/ las Indias, y Reynos del Perù./ [*Colophon*] Con Licencia, En *Madrid* por Iuan Delgado. Año 1625./ 4 *unnumbered pages. Folio.* (1*l.* 1*s.* 2320)

RELACION del Svcesso del Armada, y/ excercito que fue al ſocorro del Brazil, deſde que entrò en la Bahia de Todos-/ Santos, haſta que entrò en la ciudad del Saluador, que poſſeian los Rebeldes de/ Olanda, ſacada de vna carta que el ſeñor don Fadrique de Toledo eſcriuio a ſu/ Mageſtad./ [1625.] 4 *unnumbered pages. Folio.* (1*l.* 1*s.* 2321)

RELACION/ y Copia de vna Car/ ta, de las Companias de/ Infanteria, y de Acauallo, que ſu Mageſtad tiene en/ el puerto de Callao, para defenſa del dicho puerto, y/ de la Isla del Braſil. Iuntamente ſe haze rela-/cion de las nòbres de los Capitanes, y la gen/te que cada vno tiene, con las demas pre/uenciones para el dicho efeto./ [*Colophon*] Con Licencia./ Impreſſo en *Madrid*: en casa de Ber-/nardino de Guzman. Año/ de 1625./ 4 *unnumbered pages. Folio.* (1*l.* 11*s.* 6*d.* 2322)

RELACION de la Iornada qve la/ Armada de ſu Mageſtad à hecho al ſocorro del Brazil, y/ batalla que entre ella, y la de los Eſtados de Olãda ſe die/ron en doze de Septiembre defte año de 1631. en diez y/ ocho grados de altura a la bāda del Sur de la equinocial,/ y paraje de los Abrojos. [*Colophon*] Con licencia del feñor Alcalde don Alonſo de Bolañoz, En *Sevilla* por Francifco de Lyra. Año de 1631./ 4 *unnumbered pages.* *Half morocco.* *Folio.* (1*l*. 11s. 6d. 2323)

RELACION cierta y Verdadera,/ del famofo fuceffo y vitoria que tuvo el Capitan/ Benito Arias Montano, fobrino del doctifsimo/ Arias Montano, natural de Eftremadura, Gover-/nador y Capitan general de la Provincia de la nue/va Andaluzia, y cuidad de Cumana, y Alcayde de/ la fuerea de Araya, por el Rey nueftro feñor, con/tra los enemigos Olādefes, q eftavan fortificados/ en una falina que eftà riberas del rio Vnare, que es/ en efta governacion, veynte y quatro leguas de la/ ciudad de Cumana, efte año de 1633./ [*Colophon*] Con licencia, impreffo en *Sevilla* por Francifco de Lyra,/ Año de 1634./ 4 *unnumbered pages. Folio.* (1*l*. 1s. 2324)

RELACION de los/ muertos, y heridos que huuo en la Real/ Armada de la guardia de las Indias, las/ dos vezes que peleò con el enemigo,/ fobre Pan de Cauañas, año/ de 1638./ 4 *unnumbered pages.*
4to. (1*l*. 1s. 2325)

RELACION de lo Svcedido a/ la Armada Real de la guarda de la carrera de las In-/dias, defde el dia que fe hizo a la vela en la Vaia de Ca-/diz, hafta el en que dio fondo en el puerto de la Vera Cruz/ en la Nueua Efpaña. Recopilada de cartas de algunas per/fonas fidedignas y de auctoridad, que vinieron a manos de/ vna perfona graue defta Ciudad. En efte año de mil y feif-/cientos y treinta y ocho./ [*Mexico*, 1638.] 8 *folioed leaves.* 4to. (1*l*. 1s. 2326)

RELACION. Mverte de Pie de Palo./ Segvnda/ Relacion, y mvy co-/ piofa de vna carta que embiò el/feñor Duque de Medina/ a la contrataacion de/ Seuilla./ Dafe cuenta de la batalla que han tenido los Galeones con/ 40 Nauios de Olandefes, fiendo General de ellos Pie de/ Palo. Afsi mifmo fe da cuenta de fu muerte, con/ perdida de fiete nauios, en el cabo de S. Anton./ [*Colophon*] Con licencia, en *Madrid*, por Antonio Duplaftre,/ Año 1638./ 4 *unnumbered pages.* 4to. (1*l*. 1s. 2327)

RELACION/ Verdadera,/ de la Gran Vitoria qve han/ alcançado en el Brafil la gente de la Baia de/Todos Santos, contra los Olandefes. Dafe/ cuenta como les mataron dos mil hombres,/ y de la gran preffa que les tomaron, haziendo-/los embarcar, y dexar el puerto, quitando-/les todo el bagaje que/ lleuauan./ [Colophon] Impreffa con licencia en Seuilla, por Nicolas Ro-/driguez, en calle de Genoua. Año de 1638./ 4 unnumbered pages. 4to. (1l. 1s. 2328)

RELACION/ Verdadera de la/ Refriega qve Tvvieron/ nueftros Galeones de la Plata en el Ca-/bo de fan Anton, con catorze navios/ de Olāda, de que era general Pie de Pa-/lo, y da la vitoria que dellos alcançarō,/ fucedido en el mes de Agofto paffado defte prefente año de mil y feif-/cientos y treinta y/ ocho./ [Colophon] Con Licencia./ Impreffo en Sevilla, por Francifco de Lyra, Año de 1638./ 4 unnumbered pages. 4to. (1l. 1s. 2329)

RELACION Verda-/dera del viaje de los Galeones, y de las/ dos batallas que ruuieron fobre Pan de Cauañas, con los/ Olandefes, en efte año de 1638./ [Colophon] Con licencia, en Seuilla por Nicolas Rodriguez, en calle de Genoua, en efte año de 1638./ 4 unnumbered pages. 4to. (1l. 1s. 2330)

RELACION/ de la Vitoria qve/ Alcanzaron las Armas/ Catolicas en la Baîa de Todos Santos, con-/tra Olandefes, que fueron a fitiar aquella Pla-/ça, en 14. de Iunio de 1638. Siendo Go-/uernador del Eftado del Brafil/ Pedro de Silua./ [Colophon] En Madrid, Por Francifco Martinez, año 1638./ 6 folioed leaves. Half morocco.
Folio. (1l. 11s. 6d. 2331)

RELACION Verdadera de las Pazes/ que Capitvlo con el Aravcano Rebelado, el/ Marques de Baides, Conde de Pedrofo, Gouernador, y Capitan Gene-/ral del Reyno de Chile, y Prefidente de la Real Audiencia. Sacada de/ fus informes, y cartas, y de los Padres de la Compañia de Iefus, que acō-/pañaron el Real excerito en la jornada que hizo para efte efeto/ el Año paffado de 1641./ [Colophon] En Madrid, por Francifco Maroto, año de 1642./ 8 unnumbered pages. Folio. (1l. 11s. 6d. 2332)

RELACION de Todo lo Sv-/cedido en estas Provincias de la Nveva/ Efpaña, defde la formacion de la Armada Real de Barlovento, defpacho/ de Flota, y fuceffo della, hafta la falida defte primer Avifo del año de/ 1642./ 4 *unnumbered pages.* *Half morocco. Folio.* (1*l.* 11*s.* 6*d.* 2333)

RELACION de/ los Socorros,/ que ha/remitido à Tierra-Firme el Excelentifsi-/mo feñor Conde de Lemos, Virrey, Go-/vernador, y Capitan General de los Rey-/nos, y Provincias del Perù, para la reftau-/racion del Caftillo de Chagre, y/ Ciudad de Panamà, de que fe/ apoderò el Enemigo/ Inglés./ [1671]. 4 *unnumbered pages. Half morocco. Folio.* (1*l.* 11*s.* 6*d.* 2334)

RELACION de la/ Salvd Milagrosa, qve dio/ el Bienaventurado Stanislao Koft Ka, Novicio/ de la Compañia de Iesus, à otro Novicio de/ la mifma Compañia, en la Cafa de Provacion/ de San Antonio Abad de la Ciudad de/ Lima, el dia 13. de Noviembre de/ el año de 1673./ Y confta de la Proceſſo,/ que fe hizo por orden de el feñor Doctor Don/ Iofeph Davila Falcon. Provifor, y Vicario/ General de el Arçobifpado de Lima en Sede-/vacante, Canonigo Doctoral, y Catredatico/ de Prima de Canones en la Real/ Vniverfidad./ Con licencia en *Madrid:* Año de 1674./ 6 *folioed leaves. Unbound.* 4*to.* (1*l.* 1*s.* 2335)

RELACION/ del Exemplar Castigo qve/ embiò Dios a la Ciudad de Lima Cabeza del Perù,/ y fu Cofta de Barlouento con los efpantofos/ Temblores del dia 20. de Octubre/ del Año de 1687./ [*Colophon*] Con Licencia En *Lima,*/ Por Iofeph de Contreras. Año de 1687./ 8 *unnumbered pages. Folio.* (1*l.* 1*s.* 2336)

RELACION/ de lo Svcedido a la Armada de/ Barlovento à fines del año paſſado, y/ principios de efte de 1691./ Victoria, que contra los Francefes, que ocupan la Cofta/ del morte de la Ifla de Santo Domingo tuvieron,/ con el ayuda de dicha Armada, los Lauzeros, y/ milicia Efpañola de aquella Ifla, abrafando el/ Puerto de Guarico, y otras Poblaciones./ Debido todo al influxo, y providentiffimos/ ordenes del Excellentiffimo Señor/ D. Gaspar de Sandoval, Cer-/da, Silva, y Mendoza, Conde de/ Galve, &c. meritiffimo Virrey, Governador, y/

Capitan General de efta Nueva-Efpaña./ Con licencia de los Superiores en Mexico por los Herederos/ de la Viuda de Bernardo Calderon año de 1691./ 16 *unnumbered pages. Uncut and unbound.* 4to.   (2*l.* 2*s.* 2337)

RELACION./ Del Espantoso Terre-/moto que padecio efta Ciudad de los Reyes/ Lima, y fus contornos el dia 14. de Iulio de/ efte prefente año de 1699. fus laftimofos/ efectos, de muertes, y ruynas./ 7 *unnumbered pages.* 4to.   (1*l.* 11*s.* 6*d.* 2338)

RELATIONS/ Veritables/ et Cvrievses/ de l'Isle/ de Madagascar,/ et dv Bresil./ Auec l'hiftoire de la derniere Guerre faite au Brefil,/ entre les Portugais & les Hollandois./ Trois Relations d'Egypte,/ & vne du Royaume de Perfe./ *A Paris,*/ Chez Avgvstin Covrbe', au Palais, en la Gallerie/ des Merciers, à la Palme./ M. DC. LI./ Avec Privilege dv Roy. 8 *prel. leaves; the 4th blank, and* 307 *pp. Map at page* 1. *Calf.* 4to.   (10*s.* 6*d.* 2339)

RELIGIOUS INTELLIGENCE and Seasonable Advice from Abroad: Concerning Lay-Preaching and Exhortation. Collection I. [II. III. IV.] from the Connecticut Evangelical Magazine, No. 1ft, 2d & 3d. and Mr. Edwards President of Princeton College, New Jersey, his thoughts on Religion, &c. *Edinburgh:* T. Ross and Sons, 1801-2. 4 *Parts.* No. I. *Title and* 62 *pp.* No. II. 60 *pp.* No. III. *viii and pp.* 3—55. No. IV. 1802. *Title and* 58 *pp.* 12*mo.*   (6*s.* 6*d.* 2340)

REMARKS On Several Acts of Parliament Relating more efpecially to the Colonies abroad; As alfo on diverfe Acts of Assemblies there: Together with A Comparifon of the Practice of the Courts of Law in fome of the Plantations, with thofe of Westminster Hall: And a modeft Apology for the former, fo far as they materially differ from the latter. Wherein is likewife contain'd, A Difcourfe concerning the 4½ per Cent. Duty paid in Barbados, and the Leeward Iflands. *London,* T. Cooper. 1742. 3 *prel. leaves, signed* 'T. M.' *and* 125 *pp. Half morocco.* 8*vo.*   (4*s.* 6*d.* 2341)

REMARKS on the French Memorials concerning the Limits of Acadia; Printed at the Royal Printing-houfe at Paris, and diftributed by the French

Minifters at all the Foreign Courts of Europe. With two Maps, Exhibiting the Limits: One according to the Syftem of the French, as inferted in the faid Memorials; The other conformable to the English Rights, as fupported by the Authority of Treaties, continual Grants of the French Kings, and exprefs paffages of the beft French Authors. To which is added, An Answer to the Summary Discussion, &c. *London*: T. Jefferys, MDCCLVI. *Title; explanation of maps*, 1 *leaf. Text* 110 *pp.* 2 *copperplate maps. Half mor.* 8vo.   (10s. 6d. 2342)

REMARKS upon a Letter Publifhed in the London Chronicle, or Univerfal Evening Poft, N°. 115. Containing an Enquiry into the Causes of the Failure of the late Expedition againft Cape Breton. In a Letter to a Member of Parliament. *London*: M. Cooper. MDCCLVII. 30 *pp. Half morocco.* 8vo.   (5s. 6d. 2343)

REMARKS on the Letter address'd to Two Great Men. In a Letter to the Author of that Piece. *London*: R. and J. Dodsley, [1759?] *Title and pp.* 5—64. *Half morocco.* 8vo.   (4s. 6d. 2344)

REMARKS on the Review of the Controversy between Great Britain and her Colonies. In which The Errors of its Author are expofed, and The Claims of the Coloneies vindicated, Upon the Evidence of Hiftorical Facts and authentic Records. To which is fubjoined, A Proposal for terminating the prefent unhappy Dispute with the Colonies; Recovering their Commerce; Reconciliating their Affection; Securing their Rights; And eftablifhing their Dependence on a juft and permanent Basis. Humbly fubmitted to the Confideration of the British Legislature. *London*: T. Becket and P. A. De Hondt, MDCCLXIX. *Half-title, title and* 126 *pp. Half morocco.* 8vo.   (7s. 6d. 2345)

REMARKS on the New Essay of the Penfylvanian Farmer; and on the Resolves and Instructions Prefixed to that Essay; By the Author of the Right of the Britifh Legiflature vindicated. *London*, T. Becket. MDCCLXXV. *Title and* 62 *pp. Half morocco.* 8vo.   (4s. 6d. 2346)

REMARKS on the Patriot. Including some Hints respecting the Americans: With an Address to the Electors of Great Britain. *London:* Richardson and Urquhart. 1775. *Title and 46 pp. Half morocco. 8vo.* (4s. 6d. 2347)

REMARKS on the Principal Acts of the Thirteenth Parliament of Great Britain. By the Author of Letters concerning the Prefent State of Poland. Vol. I. [*all published*] Containing Remarks on the Acts relating to the Colonies. With a Plan of Reconciliation. *London*, Payne. MDCCLXXV. *xvi pp.* 'Contents' 4, *and 500 pp. 8vo.* (10s. 6d. 2348)

REMARKS on the Rescript of the Court of Madrid, and on the Manifesto of the Court of Versailles. In a Letter to the People of Great Britain. To which is added an Appendix, Containing the Rescript, the Manifesto, and a Memorial of Dr. Franklyn to the Court of Versailles. *London:* T. Cadell, MDCCLXXIX. *3 prel. leaves and 91 pp. Half morocco. 8vo.* (7s. 6d. 2349)

REMARKS on the Review of Inchiquin's Letters, published in the Quarterly Review; addressed to the Right Honorable George Canning, Esquire. By an Inhabitant of New-England. *Boston:* Published by Samuel T. Armstrong, No. 50, Cornhill. 1815. *176 pp. 8vo.* (3s. 6d. 2350)

REMEMBRANCER (THE), or Impartial Repository of Public Events. *London:* J. Almon, [*and* J. Debrett]. MDCCLXXV. *to* 1783. *Fifteen Volumes.* Vol. I. *260 pp. With 2 maps of Boston.* Vol. II. Part I. for the Year 1776. *Title and pp. 5—371. Index ii—iv.* Vol. III. Part II. For the Year 1776. *Title and 356 pp.* Vol. IV. Part III. For the Year 1776. *Title and 350 pp. Index, 6 pp. Without the two maps at pp.* 261, 290. Vol. V. For the Year 1777. *Portrait of Franklin, Title and 314 pp. Index 8 pp.* Vol. VI. For the Year 1778. *Title and 374 pp. Index 7 pp.* Vol. VII. For the Year 1778, and Beginning of 1779. *Title and 400 pp. Index 6 pp.* Vol. VIII. For the Year 1779. *Title and 386 pp. Index 4 pp. Catalogue of Books, etc. 8 pp.* Vol. IX. For the Year 1780. *Title and 384 pp. Index 6 pp.* Vol. X. For the Year 1780. Part II. *iv and 380 pp. Catalogue of Books, etc. 8 pp.* Vol. XI. For the Year 1781. Part I. *2 prel. leaves, and 375 pp.* Vol. XII. For the Year 1781. Part II.

Title and pp. 3—394 *pp. Index,* 2 *pp. Catalogue of Books, etc.* 8 *pp.* Vol. XIII. For the Year 1782. Part I. *Title and* 380 *pp. Index* 2 *pp.* ₍ Vol. XIV. For the Year 1782. Part II. 2 *prel. leaves and* 378 *pp.* Vol. XVI. For the Year 1783. Part II. *2 prel. leaves and* 380 *pp.* 8*vo.* (10*l.* 10*s.* 2351)

Vol. 15 and 17 are wanting. See No. 599.

RENEY (WILLIAM). A Narrative of the Shipwreck of the Corsair; in the month of January, 1835. On an unknown Reef near the Kingsmill Islands, in the South Pacific Ocean; with a detail of the dreadful Sufferings of the Crew. By William Reney, Chief Mate. London, Longman, 1836. *xvi and* 80 *pp.* 12*mo.* (2*s.* 6*d.* 2352)

REPONSE a la Déclaration du Congrès Américain. Traduite de l'Anglos. *A Londres.* T. Cadell, M,DCC,LXXVII. *Title, v and* 124 *pp. Index* 4 *pp. Old tree calf.* 8*vo.* (5*s.* 6*d.* 2353)

REPRESENTACION/ Politico Legal,/ que haze/ a nuestro Señor Soberano,/ Don Phelipe Quinto,/ (que Dios Guarde)/ Rey Poderoso/ de las Españas,/ y Emperador Siempre Augusto,/ de las Indias,/ para que se sirva de declarar,/ no tienen los Efpañoles Indianos obice para obte-/ner los empleos Politicos, y Militares de la Ame-/rica; y que deben fer preferidos en todos,/ aísi Eclefiafticos, como Se-/culares./ Don Juan Antonio de Ahumada,/ Colegial actual de el Mayor de Santa Maria de/ Todos Santos de Mexico, y Abogado de fu/ Real Audiencia./ 22 *Folioed leaves. Unbound. Folio.* (15*s.* 2354)

REPRESENTACION del Ilmo. Sr. Arzobispo de Mejico concerniente a algunos sucesos Anteriores a la Independencia proclamada en Aquella Capital. *Habana:* 1822. Impreso por Campe en la Oficina Liberal. 43 *pp. Half mor.* 4*to.* (3*s.* 6*d.* 2355)

REPRESENTATION (THE) and Memorial of the Council of the Ifland of Jamaica, To the Right Honourable The Lords Commiffioners for Trade and Plantations. Together with The Addreffes of the Governour and Council, and Town of Kingfton; and Affociation of the Principal Inhabitants. With a Preface, by Mr. Wood. *London:* W. Wilkins. 1716. *Title, viii and* 46 *pp.* 8*vo.* (10*s.* 6*d.* 2356)

REPRESENTATION of the Board of Trade relating to the Laws made, Manufactures set up, and Trade carried on, in His Magesty's Plantations in America. *Whitehall*, January 23, 1733-4. 20 pp. *Half morocco. Folio.* (10s. 6d. 2357)

> From this precious document of the Board of Trade we learn that several of the Colonies had, for some time previous, levied duties upon the importation of Negroes from Africa, (with a view probably of ridding themselves of so odious a traffic). "We are of opinion," says the Board, "that it would be more for the interest of the *English* Merchants that Duties upon Negroes should for the future be paid by the Purchaser than by the Importer; and His Majesty has, upon our Representation, been pleased to send an Instruction to that Effect to all his Governours in America."

REPRESENTATION from the Commissioners for Trade and Plantations, To the Right Honorable the Lords Spiritual and Temporal, In Parliament Assembled, In pursuance of their Lordships Addresses to His Majesty of the 1st and 5th of April, 1734. relating to the State of the British Islands in America, with regard to their Trade, their Strength, and Fortifications, and to what may be further necessary for the Encouragement of their Trade, and Security of those Islands: As likewise to such Encouragements as may be necessary to engage the Inhabitants of the British Colonies on the Continent in America, to apply their Industry to the Cultivation of Naval Stores of all kinds, and of such other Products as may be proper for the Soil of the said Colonies, and do not interfere with the Trade or Produce of Great Britain. *London:* John Baskett, 1734. 19 pp. 4to. (10s. 6d. 2358)

REPRESENTATION (A) on behalf of the People called Quakers, to the President and Executive Council, and the General Assembly of Pennsylvania, &c. *London:* Reprinted by James Phillips, M.DCC.LXXXII. 15 pp. 12mo. (4s. 6d. 2359)

REPRESENTATION (A) on behalf of the People called Quakers, to the President and Executive Council, and the General Assembly of Pennsylvania, &c. *York:* Reprinted by Walker and Pennington, M.DCC.LXXXII. 12 pp. 12mo. (4s. 6d. 2360)

REPUBLIK (Die) der Jesuiten, oder das Umgestürzte Paraguay, welches Eine richtige Erzählung des Krieges enthält, den diese Geistlichen gegen die Monarchen Spaniens und Portugals in Amerika zu führen gewaget. Nach den Sekretariats=Auffätzen der beyderfeitigen Konigl. Commiffarien und Bevollmächtigten der zweyen Kronen. Auf befonders ausdrücklichen Befehl des portugiefifchen Hofes an das Licht geftellt. *Amsterdam*, 1758. 36 pp. *Half morocco.* 4to. (10s. 6d. 2361)

RESENDIUS (ANGELO ANDREA). Epitome Rervm Gestarvm/ in India a Lufitanis, anno fuperiori, iuxta exem=/plum epiftolæ, quam Nonius Cugna, dux Indiæ/ max. defignatus, ad regem mifit, ex vrbe Ca=/nanorio, IIII. Idus Octobris. Anno./ M.D.XXX./ Auctore Angelo Andrea Refendio Lufitano./ *Louanii apud Seruatium Zaſſenum*, Anno/ M. D. XXXI. Menſe Iulio. Ad fi=/gnū Regni cœlorum./ 16 *leaves, including title with the reverse blank; signatures* A *to* D *in fours. Red morocco, extra, by Mackenzie.* 4to. (2l. 12s. 6d. 2362)

RESOLUTIONS (THE) of the House of Commons, on the great and constitutional questions between the Privileges of the House of Commons and the Prerogative of the Crown; From the 17th of December 1783, to the 10th of March 1784. Including the Mover and Seconder, And the Numbers in the Divifion on each Motion. Extracted verbatim from the Records of Parliament. *London*: J. Debrett. M.DCC.LXXXIV. 2 *prel. leaves and* 51 pp. *Half morocco.* 8vo. (4s. 6d. 2363)

REVIEW (A) of All that hath pafs'd between the Courts of Great Britain and Spain, Relating to Our Trade and Navigation From the Year 1721, to the Prefent Covention; With fome Particular Observations Upon it. *London:* H. Goreham 1739. *Half-title, title, and text* 60 pp. *Half morocco.* 8vo. (4s. 6d. 2364)

REVIEW (A) of The Rector Detected or the Colonel Reconnoitred. Part the First. *Williamsburg*, Printed by Jofeph Royle, MDCCLXIV. 29 pp. *Half morocco.* 4to. (10s. 6d. 2365)

REVIEW (A) of the Government and Grievances of the Province of Quebec, since the Conquest of it by the British Arms. To which is added An Appendix, containing extracts from Authentic Papers. *London:* J. Stockdale M,DCC,LXXXVIII. *Half-title, title, and text* 111 pp. *Half morocco.* 8vo. (5s. 6d. 2366)

REYNOLDS (THEOPHILUS). Cursory Observations, addressed to the Planters and Others, interested in the West India Trade; in which a more profitable mode of Territorial Appropriation is pointed out, and illustrated by example. By Theophilus Reynolds, L.L.D. *Liverpool*, F. B. Wright, 1808. 15 pp. 8vo. (3s. 6d. 2367)

RIBERA (DIEGO DE). Concentos/ Fvnebres,/ Metricos/ Lamentos, qve explican,/ Demoftraciones publicas, de reconcidos afectos, en/ los Fvnerales devidos al Illuftriffimo,/ Reverendiffimo, y Excelentiffimo Señor Maeftro/ D. Fr. Payo Enriquez/ de Ribera,/ Digniffimo Arçobifpo, que fue de efta Ciudad de/ Mexico, Virrey, y Capitan General en ella, que/ defcanza en Paz./ Escribelos/ Con memorias de fu empeñado agradecimiento,/ el Br. D. Diego de Ribera, Presbytero, y/ los dedica por la razon de juftos titulos,/ Al/ Excelentissimo Señor Conde de Paredes/ Marques de la Laguna, Virrey, y Capitan General,/ de efta Nueva-/Efpaña, y Prefidente de la Real/ Audiencia, y Chancilleria./ ¶ Con Licencia/ En *Mexico*, por la Viuda de Bernardo Calderon, año de 1684./ 22 *unnumbered leaves*. 4to. (1*l*. 1*s*. 2368)

RIBAS (ANDRES PEREZ DE). Historia/ de los Trivmphos de Nuestra/ Santa Fee entre Gentes las mas Barbaras,/ y fieras del nueuo Orbe:/ confeguidos por los Soldados, de la/ Milicia de la Compañia de Iesvs en las Mifsiones/ de la Prouincia de Nueua-/ Efpaña./ Refierense assi mismo las costvmbres,/ ritos, y fuperfticiones que vfauan eftas Gentes:/ fus pueftos, y temples:/ las vitorias que de algunas dellas alcaçaron con las armas los Ca-/tolicos Efpañoles, quando les obligaron à tomarlas : y las dichofas/ muertes de veinte Religiofos de la Compañia, que en va-/rios pueftos, y a manos de varias Naciones,/ dieron fus vidas, por la predica-/cion del fanto Euan-/gelio./ Dedicada a la mvy Catolica Magestad/ del Rey N. S. Felipe Qvarto./ Escrita por el Padre Andres Perez de Ribas,/ Prouincial en la Nueua Efpaña, natural de Cordoua./ Año 1645./ Con Privilegio./ En *Madrid*. Por Alōfo de Paredez, jūto a los Eftudios de la Cōpañia./— (History of the triumphs of our holy faith among the most barbarous and savage nations of the new world; obtained by the soldiers of the army of the Company of Jesus, in the Missions of the Province of New Spain. Likewise are reported the customs, rites and superstitions which those nations practised; their places and temples; the victories which were obtained over some of them by the arms of the Spanish Catholics, when they obliged them to take them; and the happy deaths of twenty priests of the Company, who in various places, and by the hands of various nations gave up their lives for the preaching of the holy Gospel. Dedicated to the most Catholic Majesty of the King our Lord Philip the fourth. Written by the Father Andrew Perez de Ribas, Provincial in New Spain, native of Cordova. In the year 1645. With privilege. Madrid, by Alonzo de Paredes, near the Hall of the Company.) 16 *prel. leaves and text* 756 *pp. Vellum. Folio.* (4*l*. 4*s*. 2369)

RICHSHOFFER (Ambrosius). Ambrofij Richfzhoffers,/ Brafzilianifch = und Weft Indianifche/ Reifze Befchreibung/ Stra/zburg/ Beÿ Jofzias Städeln, A°. 1677./ *2 prel. leaves; viz. Portrait of Richfhoffer, and Engraved Title: Text pp.* 3—182. *Sonnets,* 4 *pp. Errata* 1 *page. Copperplate maps and plates at pp.* 49, 57, 58, *and* 129. *Boards. Small 8vo.* (12*s*. 6*d*. 2370)

RIGHT (The) of the British Legislature To Tax the American Colonies Vindicated; and the Means of Asserting that Right proposed. *London:* T. Becket, mdcclxxiv. *Title and* 50 *pp. Half morocco.* 8*vo.* (4*s*. 6*d*. 2371)

RIGHTS (The) of Great Britain Asserted against the Claims of America: Being an Answer to the Declaration of the General Congress. [By James Macpherson, Translator of Ossian.] The Second Edition. *London:* T. Cadell, mdcclxxvi. *Title and* 92 *pp.* 'Appendix' *a folded sheet at page* 80. *Half morocco.* 8*vo.* (5*s*. 6*d*. 2372)

RIGHTS (The) of Great Britain Asserted against the Claims of America: Being an Answer to the Declaration of the General Congress. The Third Edition, with Additions. *London:* T. Cadell, mdcclxxvi. *Title and* 96 *pp. Half morocco.* 8*vo.* (4*s*. 6*d*. 2373)

RIGHTS (The) of Great Britain Asserted against the Claims of America: Being an Answer to the Declaration of the General Congress. The Fourth Edition, with Additions. *London*: T. Cadell, MDCCLXXVI. 2 *prel. leaves and* 103 *pp.* 'Appendix' *at page* 77, *a folded sheet.* 12*mo*. (4s. 6d. 2374)

RIGHTS (The) of Great-Britain Asserted against the Claims of America: Being an Answer to the Declaration of the General Congress. The Sixth Edition, with Additions. *Edinburgh*: Printed for Charles Elliot. M,DCC,LXXVI. 2 *prel. leaves and* 98 *pp.* 'Appendix' *at page* 92, *a folded sheet.* 12*mo*. (4s. 6d. 2375)

RIGHTS (The) of Great Britain Asserted against the Claims of America: Being an Answer to the Declaration of the General Congress. The Ninth Edition. To which is now added, a Further Refutation of Dr. Price's State of the National Debt. *London*: T. Cadell, MDCCLXXVI. 2 *prel. leaves and* 131 *pp.* 'Appendix' *a folded sheet at page* 99. *Half morocco.* 8*vo*. (4s. 6d. 2376)

RIGHTS (The) of Great Britain Asserted against the Claims of America: Being an Answer to the Declaration of the General Congress. The Tenth Edition. To which is now added, a Further Refutation of Dr. Price's State of the National Debt. *London*: T. Cadell, MDCCLXXVI. 2 *prel. leaves and* 131 *pp.* 'Appendix' *a folded sheet at page* 99. *Half morocco.* 8*vo*. (4s. 6d. 2377)

RIO (Antonio del). Description of the Ruins of an Ancient City, discovered near Palenque, in the Kingdom of Guatemala, in Spanish America; translated from the Original Manuscript Report of Captain Don Antonio Del Rio: Followed by Teatro Critico Americano; or, a critical investigation and research into The History of the Americans, by Doctor Paul Felix Cabrera, of the City of New Guatemala. *London*: Henry Berthoud, 1822. *xiii pp.* 'Teatro Critico' 1 *page. Text* 128 *pp.* 17 *plates.* 4*to*. (10s. 6d. 2378)

ROBERTS (George). The Four Years Voyages of Capt. George Roberts; being a Series of Uncommon Events, Which befell him In a Voyage to the Iſlands of the Canaries, Cape de Verde, and

Barbadoes, from whence he was bound to the Coaſt of Guiney. The Manner of his being taken by Three Pyrate Ships, commanded by Low, Ruſſell, and Spriggs, who, after having plundered him, and detained him 10 Days, put him aboard his own Sloop, without Provisions, Water, &c. and with only two Boys, one of Eighteen, and the other of Eight Years of Age. The Hardships he endur'd for above 20 Days, 'till he arriv'd at the Iſland of St. Nicholas, from whence he was blown off to Sea (before he could get any Suſtenance) without his Boat and biggeſt Boy, whom he had ſent aſhore; and after Four Days of Difficulty and Diſtreſs, was Shipwreck'd on the Unfrequented Iſland of St. John, where after he had remained near two Years, he built a Veſſel to bring himſelf off. With a particular and curious Deſcription and Draught of the Cape de Verd Iſlands; their Roads, Anchoring Places, Nature and Production of the Soils; The Kindneſs and Hoſpitality of the Natives to Strangers, their Religion, Manners, Cuſtoms, and Superſtitions, &c. Together with Obſervations on the Minerals, Mineral Waters, Metals, and Salts, and of Nitre with which ſome of theſe Iſlands abound. Written by Himſelf, And interſpers'd with many Pleaſant and Profitable Remarks, very inſtructive for all thoſe who uſe this Trade, or who may have the Misfortune to meet with any of the like Diſtreſſes either by Pyracy or Shipwreck. Adorn'd with ſeveral Copper Plates. *London*: A. Bettesworth, and J. Osborn, 1726. *3 prel. leaves and* 458 *pp.* 4 *Plates and Draught of all the Cape de Verd Islands. Old calf.* 8vo. (8s. 6d. 2379)

ROBERTS (William). An Account of the First Discovery of Florida. With a Particular Detail of the ſeveral Expeditions and Descents made on that Coaſt. Collected from the beſt Authorities By William Roberts. Illuſtrated by a general Map, and ſome particular Plans, together with a geographical Deſcription of that Country, By T. Jefferys, Geographer to His Majesty./ *London*: T. Jefferys, mdcclxiii. *viii pp. Contents* 2 *and* 102 *pp.* 7 *Maps and Plans.* 4to. (8s. 6d. 2380)

ROBINSON (John). Essayes;/ or,/ Observations/ Divine and/ Morall./ Collected ovt of/ holy Scriptures, Ancient and/ Moderne Writers, both di-/vine and humane./ As alfo, out of the great volume/ of mens manners: Tending to the/ furtherance of knowledge and vertue./ By Iohn Robinson./ The fecond Edition, with two Tables, the one of/ the Authours quoted; The other of the mat-/ters contained in the Obfervations./ *London,/* Printed by I. D. for I. Bellamie, at the/ three golden Lyons in Cornhill neere/ the Royall Exchange. 1638./ 16 prel. leaves and 566 pp. *Old calf.* 12mo. (2l. 12s. 6d. 2381)

ROBINSON (John). A/ Ivstification/ of/ Separation/ from the Church of England./ Againft Mr Richard Bernard his invective,/ intitvled ;/ *The Separatists schifme./* By John Robinson./ Printed in the yeere 1639./ 382 pp. followed by 3 leaves of Table. *Fine copy in old calf.* 4to. (5l. 5s. 2382)

ROBINSON (John). A/ Ivst and Necessary/ Apologie/ of certain/ Christians,/ No leffe contumelioufly then com-/monly called Brovvnists,/ or Barrovvists./ By M^r. Iohn Robin-/son, Paftor of the English/ Church at Leyden./ Publifhed firft in Latin in his and/ the Churches name over which he/ was fet: After tranflated into En-/glifh by himfelf, and now republifhed for/ the fpeciall and common good of/ our own countrymen./ [Leyden?] Printed in the yeer of our Lord,/ M,DC,XLIIII./ 72 pp. *including the Title. Red morocco extra, by Bedford.* 24mo. (5l. 5s. 2383)

ROBINSON (Matthew). Peace the best Policy or Reflections upon the Appearance of a Foreign War, the present state of Affairs at Home and the Commission for Granting Pardons in America. In a Letter to a Friend by Matt. Robinson M.? *London:* J. Almon, MDCCLXXVII. Title and 112 pp. *Half morocco.* 8vo. (4s. 6d. 2384)

ROBINSON (William). Several/ Epistles/ Given forth by Two of the/ Lords Faithful Servants,/ Whom he fent to/ New-England,/ to/ Bear Witnefs to his Everlafting Truth./ And were there (by the Priefts, Rulers, and Profeffors)/ after cruel and long Imprifonment, and inhumane/ Whippings and Banifhment, put to death; for/ no other Caufe, but for keeping the/ Commandments of God, and/ Teftimony of Jefus./ William Robinfon./ William

Leddra./ Here is alfo prefixed W. R. his Teftimony of his Call to/ that Service, for obedience unto which, he under-/went the wrath of Men, but hath obtained/ Everlafting Peace and Reft with God. *London*, Printed in the Year, 1669. 11 *pp.* 4*to.* (1*l.* 1*s.* 2385)

ROBSON (JOSEPH). An Account of six years residence in Hudson's-Bay, From 1733 to 1736, and 1744 to 1747. By Joseph Robson, Late Surveyor and Supervifor of the Buildings to the Hudfon's-bay Company. Containing a Variety of Facts, Observations, and Discoveries, tending to fhew, I. The vaft Importance of the Countries about Hudson's-Bay to Great Britain, on Account of the extenfive Improvements that may be made there in many beneficial Articles of Commerce, particularly in the Furs and in the Whale and Seal Fisheries. And, II. The interefted Views of the Hudfon's-bay Company; and the abfolute Neceffity of laying open the Trade, and making it the Object of National Encouragement, as the only Method of keeping it out of the Hands of the French. To which is added an Appendix; containing, I. A fhort Hiftory of the Difcovery of Hudfon's-bay; and of the Proceedings of the Englifh there fince the Grant of the Hudfon's-bay Charter: Together with Remarks upon the Papers and Evidence produced by that Company before the Committee of the Honourable Houfe of Commons, in the Year 1749. II. An Eftimate of the Expence of building the Stone Fort, called Prince of Wales's-fort, at the entrance of Churchill-river. III. The Soundings of Nelfon-river. IV. A Survey of the Courfe of Nelson-river. V. A Survey of Seal and Gillam's Iflands. And, VI. A Journal of the Winds and Tides at Churchill-river, for Part of the Years 1746 and 1747. The Whole illuftrated, By a Draught of Nelson and Hayes's Rivers; a Draught of Churchill-river; and Plans of York-Fort, and Prince of Wales's Fort. *London*: J. Payne. MDCCLII. *Title, vi and* 84 *pp.* 'Appendix' 95 *pp.* 3 *Maps. Old calf.* 8*vo.* (7*s.* 6*d.* 2386)

ROCHEFORT (CESAR DE). [*Engraved title*] Histoire/ Naturelle et Morale/ des/ Iles Antilles de/ l'Amerique./ A Rotterdam,/ Chez Arnout Leers.

Marchant Librair. 1658./ [*Printed title*] Histoire/ Naturelle et Morale/ des/ Iles Antilles/ de l'Amerique./ Enrichie de pluſieurs belles figures des Raretez les plus/ conſiderables qui y ſont d'écrites./ Avec vn Vocabulaire Caraïbe./ A *Roterdam*,/ Chez Arnould Leers,/ M.DC.LVIII:/ *First Edition*. 8 *prel. leaves; viz*. Two *titles*, 'Epistre.' Signed ' L. D. P.' 4 *pp*; 'Preface,' 6 *pp*; 'Avertissement,' 2 *pp*; *Text* 527 *pp*; 'Table,' 12 pp. *Fine copy. Vellum.* 4to. (1*l*. 10*s*. 6*d*. 2387)

ROCHEFORT (CESAR DE). [*Engraved title*] Histoire/ Natvrelle et Morale/ Des/ Iles Antilles de/ l'Amerique/ [*Printed title*] Histoire/ Naturelle et Morale/ des/ Iles Antilles/ de l'Amerique./ Enriche d'un grand nombre de belles Figures en taille douce,/ des Places & des Raretez les plus conſiderables,/ qui y ſont décrites./ Avec un Vocabulaire Caraïbe./ Seconde Edition./ Reveuë & augmentée de pluſieurs Deſcriptions, & de quelques/ éclairciſſemens, qu'on deſiroit en la precedente./ A *Roterdam*,/ Chez Arnout Leers,/ M.DC.LXV./ 18 *prel. leaves; viz. Two titles;* 'Epistre,' 11 *pp. Signed* ' De Rochefort'; 'Preface,' 5 *pp*; 'Avertissement,' 4 *pp*; 'Copies Lettres,' 12 *pp*; *Text* 583 *pp*; 'Table,' 13 *pp: Copperplates at pp*. 53, 332, 412. *Vellum*. 4to. (1*l*. 1*s*. 2388)

ROCHEFORT (CESAR DE). Le Tableau/ de/ L'Isle de Tabago,/ ou de la/ Nouvelle Oüalchre,/ L'unc des Iſles Antilles de/ l'Amerique,/ Dependante de la ſouveraineté des Hauts &/ Puiſſans Seigneurs les Eſtats Generaus/ des Provinces Unies des Pais-bas./ A *Leyde*/ Chez Jean Le Carpentier/ cIↃIↃCLXV./ 8 *prel. leaves and* 144 *pp. Vellum.* 8*vo*. (15*s*. 2389)

ROCHEFORT (CESAR DE). Relation/ de L'Isle/ de Tabago,/ ou de la/ Novvelle Oÿalcre,/ l'vne des Isles Antilles/ de l'Ameriqve./ Par le Sieur de Rochefort./ A *Paris*,/ Chez Lovys Billaine, au ſecond/ Pilier de la Grand' Sale du Palais. M. DC. LXVI./ Auec Permiſſion./ 8 *prel. leaves and* 128 *pp. Old calf.* 12*mo*. (10*s*. 6*d*. 2390)

ROCHEFORT (CESAR DE). Histoire/ Natvrelle/ des/ Iles Antilles/ de l'Ameriqve :/ Par Mr. De Rochfort./ A *Lyon*,/ Chez Christofle Fovrmy,/ rüe

Merciere, à la Bibliotheque./ M.DC.LXVII./ *Two
volumes.* Tome Premier, 32 *prel. leaves, the last
blank, and* 566 *pp. Copperplates at pp.* 13, 295.
Tome Second, 3 *prel.* leaves and 680 *pp. Copperplate at page* 115. *Old calf.* 12mo. (12s. 6d. 2391)

ROCHEFORT (CESAR DE). Hiſtoriſche/ Beſchrei-
bung/ Der/ Antillen Inſeln in/ America gelegen/
In ſich begreiffend deroſelben/ Gelegenheit, darinnen befindli=/chen natürlichen Sachen, ſampt
deren/ Einwohner Sitten und Gebräuchen mit/
45. Kupfferſtücken gezieret./ von/ dem Herrn de
Rochefort,/ zum zweyten mahl in Franzöſi=/ ſcher
Sprach an den Tag ge=/geben,/ nunmehr aber/ in
die Teutſche überſetzet./ *Frankfurt,*/ In Verlegung
Wilhelm Serlins, Buchdru=/ckers und Buchhand-
lers. 1668. *Two Volumes.* (Buch I.) 11 *prel.
leaves, including frontispiece, and* 430 *pp.* 'Innhalt.'
11 *pp. Copperplates at pp.* 29, 104, 105, 106, 107,
109, 111, 118, 119, 123, 124, 126, 138, 141, 142,
143, 148, 149, 153, 156, 162, 166 (2), 180, 182,
189, 192, 195, 205, 215, 233, 264, 271, 301, 307 (2),
311, 321, 335, 353. (Buch II.) 6 *prel. leaves,* 33
and 514 *pp.* 12mo. (7s. 6d. 2392)

ROCHEFORT (CESAR DE). [*Engraved title*] His-
toire/ Naturelle et Morale/ Des/ Iles Antilles de/
l'Amerique/ Derniere Edition reveuë et/ augmentée./ [*Printed title*] Histoire/ Naturelle et
Morale/ des/ Iles Antilles/ de l'Amerique,/ Enrichie d'un grand nombre de belles Figures en
taille douce, qui/ repreſentent au naturel les Places,
& les Raretez les plus/ conſiderables qui y ſont
décrites./ Avec un Vocabulaire Caraïbe./ Derniere Edition./ Reveuë & augmentée par l'Autheur
d'un Recit de l'Eſtat preſent des/ celebres Colonies
de la Virginie, de Marie-Land, de la Caroline, du/
nouveau Duché d'York, de Penn-Sylvania, & de la
nouvelle An-/gleterre, ſituées dans l'Amerique
ſeptentrionale, & qui rele-/vent de la Couronne du
Roy de la grand' Bretagne./ Tiré fidelement des
memoires des habitans des mêmes Colonies,/ en
faveur de ceus, qui auroyent le deſſein de s'y/
transporter pour s'y établie./ *A Rotterdam,*/ Chez
Reinier Leers,/ M.DC.LXXXI./ 18 *prel. leaves, including the engraved and printed titles. Text* 583 *pp;
Table,* 13 *pp. Second title,* ' Recit/ de l'Estat/ Pre-

sent des/ Celebres Colonies,' *etc.* 4S *pp. Large folding plates at pp.* 53, 332, *and* 412. *Fine copy in old red morocco.* 4to. (1*l.* 1*s.* 2393)

ROCHEFOUCAULD-LIANCOURT (Duc de la). Voyage dans les Etats-Unis d'Amérique, fait en 1795, 1796 et 1797. Par La Rochefoucauld-Liancourt. *A Paris* Du Pont, Buisson, Charles Pongens, L'an VII de la République. (1799) *Eight Volumes.* Tome Premier. *xxiv and* 365 *pp. Map at page* 1. Tome Second. *Half-title, title, iv and* 349 *pp.* Tome Troisième. *Half-title, title, iv and* 384 *pp.* Tome Quatrième. *Half-title, title, iii and* 349 *pp. Map at page* 1. Tome Cinquième. *Half-title, title, iv and* 400 *pp.* Tome Sixième. *Half-title, title, iii and* 336 *pp.* 'Tableau,' *etc. at page* 266, *a folded sheet.* Tome Septième. *Half-title, title, iv and* 366. *Map at page* 155. Tome Huitième. *Half-title, title, and* 244 *pp; folded sheets at page* 172, *numbered* I—VI. *Calf extra.* 8*vo.* (1*l.* 1*s.* 2394)

RODRIGUES DE MELLO (Joseph). Josehpi Rodrigues de Mello Lusitani Portuensis de Rusticis Brasiliæ Rebus Carminum Libri IV. Accedit Prudentii Amaralii Brasiliensis de Sacchari Opificio Carmen. *Romæ* mdcclxxxi. Ex Typographia Fratrum Puccinelliorum. *viii and* 206 *pp.* 4 *copperplates at the end. Vellum.* 8*vo.* (12*s.* 6*d.* 2395)

RODRIGUEZ (Antonio). Relacion/ de las Fiestas/ qve ala Immacv-/lada Concepcion dela Virgen N. Señora fe hizieron en la Real Ciudad de Lima en/ el Perù, y principalmente delas q hizo la Con/ gregacion dela Expectacion del Parto/ en la Cōpañia de Iefus año 1617./ Dirigida al Excelentissimo/ Señor Principe de Efquilache Virrey deftos Reynos./ Por el Bachiller Antonio Rodrigvez/ de Leon Profeffor delos derechos Pontificio y Cefareo./ ¶ Con licencia impreffo en *Lima* por Francifco del Canto./ Acofta de Iuan Fernandez Higuera mercader. Año 1618./ 2 *prel. leaves; viz. Title, the reverse blank,* 'Erratas,' *and* 'Tassa:' 1 *page;* 'Aprobacion,' 1 *page; Text* 80 *folioed leaves.* 4*to.* (1*l.* 11*s.* 6*d.* 2396)

RODRIGUEZ (Manuel). Señor./ [*Begins*] Manuel Rodriguez de la Compañia de Isevs, Procurador/ general por las Provincias de Indias, dize : *etc.*

[*Ending*] liberal Mano, y Catolico zelo de V. Mageſtad. 4 *unnumbered pages. Half morocco. Folio.* (1*l.* 1*s.* 2397)

RODRIGUEZ LAMEGO (MANUEL). ✤/ Assiento/ y Capitvlacion qve/ se tomo con Manvel Rodrigvez/ Lamego, ſobre la renta y prouiſion general de eſclauos/ negros que ſe nauegan a las Indias por tiempo/ de ocho años, y precio de ciento y veinte mil/ du cados cada año./ Año de 1623./ 17 *folioed leaves. Half mor. Folio.* (1*l.* 1*s.* 2398)

ROEBUCK (JOHN). An Enquiry, whether The Guilt of the Present Civil War in America, ought to be imputed to Great Britain or America. By John Roebuck, M. D., F. R. S. A new Edition. *London*: John Donaldson, MDCCLXXVI. *Title and* 69 *pp. Half morocco.* 8*vo.* (4*s.* 6*d.* 2399)

ROGERS (ABRAHAM). Abraham Rogers/ Offne Thür/ zu dem verborgenen/ heydenthum :/ Oder,/ Warhaftige Vorweiſung deſz/ Lebens, und der Sitten, ſamt der Religion,/ und dem Gottesdienſt der Bramines, auf der/ Cuſt Chormandel, und denen herumli=/genden Ländem :/ Mit kurtzen Anmerkungen,/ Aus dem Niederländiſchen überſetzt./ Samt/ Chriſtoph Arnolds/ Auserleſenen Zugaben,/ Von den Aſiatiſchen, Africaniſchen, und Ame-/ricaniſchen Rēligions=ſachen, ſo in XL / Capital verfaſſt./ Alles/ Mit einem nothwendigen/ Regiſter./ *Nürnberg*,/ In Verlegung, Johann Andreas Endters, und/ Wolffgang deſz Jüng-Seel. Erben./ M.DC.LXIII./ 8 *prel. leaves, including the engraved and printed titles; Text* 998 *pp. followed by* 19 *leaves of Register and one page of errata. Numerous plates. Vellum.* 8*vo.* (15*s.* 2400)

ROGERS (ROBERT). A Concise Account of North America: Containing A Deſcription of the ſeveral British Colonies on that Continent, including the Iſlands of Newfoundland, Cape Breton, &c. As to Their Situation, Extent, Climate, Soil, Produce, Riſe, Government, Religion, Preſent Boundaries, and the Number of Inhabitants ſuppoſed to be in each. Also of The Interior, or Weſterly Parts of the Country, upon the Rivers St. Laurence, the Mississipi, Christino, and the Great Lakes. To which is ſubjoined, An Account of the ſeveral

Nations and Tribes of Indians refiding in thofe Parts, as to their Cuftoms, Manners, Government, Numbers, &c. Containing many Ufeful and Entertaining Facts, never before treated of. By Major Robert Rogers. *London*: Printed for the Author, MDCCLXV. *viii and 264 pp. 8vo.* (9s. 2401)

ROGERS (ROBERT). Journals of Major Robert Rogers: Containing An Account of the feveral Excurfions he made under the Generals who commanded upon the Continent of North America, during the late War. From which may be collected The moft material Circumftances of every Campaign upon that Continent, from the Commencement to the Conclufion of the War. To which is added An Hiftorical Account of the Expedition againft the Ohio Indians in the Year 1764, under the command of Henry Bouquet, Efq; Colonel of Foot, and now Brigadier General in America, including his Tranfactions with the Indians, relative to the Delivery of the Prifoners, and the Preliminaries of Peace. With an Introductory Account of the Proceeding Campaign, and Battle at Bufhy-Run. *Dublin*: R. Acheson, M,DCC,LX,IX. *x and 218 pp.* 'An Hiftorical Account of the Expedition againft the Ohio Indians, in the year MDCCLXIV,'/ *etc. xx and 99 pp. Old calf. 12mo.* (10s. 6d. 2402)

ROGERS (WOODES). A Cruising Voyage round the World: Firft to the South-Seas, thence to the East-Indies, and homewards by the Cape of Good Hope. Begun in 1708, and finifh'd in 1711. Containing a Journal of all the Remarkable Tranfactions; particularly, Of the Taking of Puna and Guiaquil, of the Acapulco Ship, and other Prizes; An Account of Alexander Selkirk's living alone four Years and four Months in an Ifland; and A brief Defcription of feveral Countries in our Courfe noted for Trade, efpecially in the South-Sea. With Maps of all the Coaft, from the beft Spanifh Manufcript Draughts. And an Introduction relating to the South-Sea Trade. By Captain Woodes Rogers, Commander in Chief on this Expedition, with the Ships Duke and Dutchefs of Briftol. *London*: A. Bell and B. Lintot, M.DCC.XII. *xxii and 428 pp.* 'Appendix,' *56 pp.* 'Index,' *14 pp. 4 maps. Old calf. 8vo.* (10s. 6d. 2403)

ROGERS (WOODES). A Cruising Voyage round the World: Firſt to the South-Sea, thence to the East-Indies, and homewards by the Cape of Good Hope. Begun in 1708, and finiſh'd in 1711. *etc.* The Second Edition, Corrected. *London*, Andrew Bell and Bernard Lintot, M.DCC.XVIII. *xix and* 428 *pp;* 'Appendix,' 57 *pp; Index,* 7 *pp. Maps at page* 1 *of Text, and pp.* 1, 10, 33, *and* 51, *of Appendix.* *Old calf.* 8vo. (10s. 6d. 2404)

ROGERS (WOODES). A Cruising Voyage round the World: *etc.* The Second Edition, Corrected. *London*: Bernard Lintot, M.DCC.XXVI. [*The same as Second Edition, of* 1718, *except a new title, and having in addition two plates at pp.* 62 *and* 101, *representing the Aligator and Crocodile, drawn from life in London,* 1739. *Old calf.* 8vo. (10s. 6d. 2405)

ROLLE (DENYS). To the Right Honourable the Lords of His Majesty's Moſt Honourable Privy Council. The Humble Petition of Denys Rolle, Eſq; ſetting forth the Hardſhips, Inconveniencies, and Grievances, which have attended him in his Attempts to make a Settlement in Eaſt Florida, humbly praying ſuch Relief, as in their Lordſhips Wiſdom ſhall ſeem meet. [*London* 17—] 85 *pp.* *Plan at page* 72. 'Grants by the Governor of South Carolina,' *a folded sheet.* 'Copies of his Excellency Governor Grant's Letters, and alſo Copies of the rough Drafts from which Mr. Rolle's Letters to the Governor were wrote, containing the full Import of the ſame.' 47 *pp. Half morocco.* 8vo. (1*l.* 1s. 2406)

ROLT (RICHARD). A New and Accurate History of South-America: Containing A particular Account of ſome Accidents leading to the Diſcovery of the New World; of the Diſcovery made by Columbus, and other Adventures; of the ſeveral Attempts made to find out a North East and North-Weſt Paſſage; and what Parts of America are ſubject to the different European Powers. With A full Deſcription of the Spanish Provinces of Chili, Paraguay, Peru, and Terra Firma. Of Guiana; particularly of Surinam belonging to the Dutch, and of Cayenne belonging to the French; of Brazil ſubject to the Crown of Portugal; of that Part of

Paraguay poffeffed by the Jesuits, where thy have eftablifhed a New Monarchy; and of the various Nations of Indians throughout this extenfive Territory: As alfo of all the moft remarkable Iflands adjacent to its Coafts. Including the Geographical, Natural, Political, and Commercial Hiftory of every Province: With the Religion, Manners and Cuftoms of the Inhabitants. With Dissertations on the Britifh, Spanifh, Portuguefe, French, Dutch, and Indian Settlements. By Mr. Rolt. *London*: T. Gardner, M.DCC.LVI. 8 *prel. leaves and* 576 *pp. With map of South-America by Eman Bowen.* 8*vo*. (7*s*. 6*d*. 2407)

ROMERO DE MELLA (NICOLAS). Por/ Don Nicolas Romero/ de Mella, Contador de tributos, y azo-/gues de la Nueua España./ En/ El pleyto que trata con el feñor Fifcal./ Sobre/ La reftitucion del dicho oficio; y en fatisfacion de los cargos que le hi-/zo el feñor Licenciado Don Pedro de Galuez, del Confejo de fu/ Mageftad, en el Supremo de las Indias, el año de 53./ En la vifita de los Miniftros, y Oficiales/ Reales del Reyno de/ Mexico./ [1655] 26 *folioed leaves. Half mor. Folio.* (1*l*. 1*s*. 2408)

ROSS (JOHN). An Explanation of Captain Sabine's remarks on the late Voyage of discovery to Baffin's Bay. By Captain John Ross, R. N. *London*: John Murray, 1819. *Half-title, title, and* 54 *pp.* 8*vo*. (2*s*. 6*d*. 2409)

ROSS (ROBERT). A Sermon, Preached at New Town, December 8th, 1773. On Church Government and Difcipline. By Robert Ross, A. M. Paftor of the Church of Chrift in Stratfield. With A Preface and an Appendix, Containing Some Remarks on the Rev. Mr. David Judson's Reply to-faid Sermon. *New-Haven*. Printed by Thomas and Samuel Green. [1773.] 58 *pp. Unbound.* 8*vo*. (4*s*. 6*d*. 2410)

ROTHERAM (JOHN). An Essay on Faith, and its connection with Good Works. By John Rotheram, M. A. Rector of Ryton in the County of Durham, and Chaplain to the Lord Bishop of Durham. Third Edition. London, Printed: *New-York*, Reprinted and Sold by J. Parker, at the New-Printing-Office, in Beaver-Street. M.DCC.LXVII. *viii and* 126 *pp.* 8*vo*. (5*s*. 6*d*. 2411)

ROUSSIGNAC (Jacques de). The Earth twice fhaken wonderfully :/ Or, an/ Analogical Difcourfe of Earthquakes,/ its Natural Caufes, Kinds, and Manifold Effects ;/ occasioned/ By the laft of thefe, which happened on the/ Eighth Day of September 1692. at Two of the Clock/ in the Afternoon./ Divided into/ Philofophical Theorems, pick'd out of many/ Famous Modern, and Ancient Treatises,/ Tranflated into Englifh ;/ With Reference to that unufual One, that happened in/ Queen Elizabeth's Reign, on the fame Day, 8th. of September 1601./ at the fame Hour, which was fenfibly felt throughout all Europe,/ and fome part of Afia in the fame Moment, as much as it is found out./ A dorned,/ With an Account of many ftupendous and wonderful/ Events in Germany, Italy, and other Kingdoms./ Wherein/ Some Obfervations are made upon the Circumftances, wherein/ thefe Two Earthquakes agree, and in others wherein they differ./ By J.[acques] D.[e] R.[oussignac?] French Minifter./ *London*: Printed for the Author, at Sion's Colledge, near/ Cripplegate; and to be Sold at Mr. Cockrel, Bookfeller, at the Sign/ of the Three Legs in the Poultry, and at Mr. Vaillant, French Book-/feller, in the Strand, over-againft the French Savoy's Church, 169¾./ *4 prel. leaves and 47 pp. 4to.* (7s. 6d. 2412)

ROWLANDSON (Mary). A true/ History/ of the/ Captivity & Reftoration/ of/ Mrs. Mary Rowlandson,/ A Minifter's Wife in New-England./ Wherein is fet forth, The Cruel and Inhumane/ Ufage fhe underwent amongft the Heathens, for/ Eleven Weeks time : And her Deliverance from/ them./ Written by her own Hand, for her Private Ufe : And now made/ Publick at the earneft Defire of fome Friends, for the Benefit/ of the Afflicted./ Whereunto is annexed,/ A Sermon of the Poffibility of God's Forfaking a Peo-/ple that have been near and dear to him./ Preached by Mr. Jofeph Rowlandfon, Husband to the faid Mrs. Rowlandfon:/ It being his laft Sermon./ Printed firft at New-England : And Re-printed at *London*, and fold/ by Jofeph Poole, at the Blue Bowl in the Long-Walk, by Chrifts-/Church Hofpital./ 1682./ *3 prel. leaves and 36 pp. 4to.* (1l. 11s. 6d. 2413)

RUIZ DE LEON (Francisco). Hernandia, triumphos de la Fe, y gloria de las Armas Españolas. Poema Heroyco. Conquista de Mexico, cabeza del imperio Septentrional de la Nueva-España. Proezas de Hernan-Cortes, Catholicos Blasones Militares, y grandez as del Nuevo Mundo. Lo cantaba Don Francisco Ruiz de Leon, hijo de la Nueva-España, y reverente lo consagra a la Soberana, Catholica Magestad de su Rey, y Señor Natural Don Fernando Sexto, en la real Catholica Magestad de la Reyna Nuestra Señora Doña Maria Barbara, (que Dios guarde) y a las dos Magestades, Por Mano del excellentissimo Señor Duque de Alva, &c. Con Privilegio. En *Madrid:* Viuda de Manuel Fernandez, 1755. 10 *prel. leaves and* 383 *pp. Vellum.* 4*to.* (1*l.* 11*s.* 6*d.* 2414)

RULES for the St. Andrew's Society in Philadelphia. *Philadelphia:* Printed by B. Franklin, and D. Hall. MDCCLI. 16 *pp.* 8*vo.* (1*l.* 1*s.* 2415)

RULING (The) & Ordaining Power of Congregational Bishops, or Presbyters, Defended. Being Remarks on fome Part of Mr. P. Barclay's Persuasive, lately diftributed in New-England. By an Impartial Hand. In a Letter to a Friend. *Boston:* Printed for Samuel Gerrifh and Sold at his Shop near the Brick Meeting-Houfe in Cornhill, 1724. *Title and* 45 *pp.* 8*vo.* (12*s.* 6*d.* 2416)

RUMSEY (James). A Short Treatise on the application of Steam, whereby is clearly shewn, from actual experiments, that Steam may be applied to propel Boats or Vessels of any burthen againſt rapid currents with great velocity. The fame Principles are alfo introduced with Effect, by a Machine of a fimple and cheap Conſtruction, for the Purpofe of raising Water fufficient for the working of Grist-Mills, Saw-Mills, &c. And for watering Meadows and other purposes of Agriculture. By James Rumsey, Of Berkeley County, Virgina. *Philadelphia,* Printed by Joseph James: Chesnut-Street. M,DCC,LXXXVIII. 26 *pp. Uncut.* 8*vo.* (10*s.* 6*d.* 2417)

RUSSELL (William). The History of America from its Discovery by Columbus to the conclusion of the late War. With an Appendix, containing an account of the rise and progress of the present unhappy contest between Great Britain and her Colonies. By William Russell, Esq. of Gray's-Inn. *London*: Fielding and Walker, MDCCLXXVIII. *Two Volumes.* Volume I. iv and 596 pp. 28 maps and plates. Volume II. 630 pp. 'Directions for placing the Maps and Cuts.' 2 pp. 23 maps and plates. 4to. (15s. 2418)

RUTHERFURD (SAMUEL). A/ Survey/ of the/ Survey of that Summe/ of Church-Difcipline/ Penned by Mr. Thomas Hooker,/ Late Paftor of the Church at Hartford upon/ Connecticot in New England./ Wherein/ The Way of the Churches of N. England/ is now re-examined; Arguments in favour/ thereof winnowed; The Principles of that/ Way difcuffed; and the Reafons of moft/ feeming ftrength and nerves, removed./ By Samuel Rutherfurd, Profeffor of Divinity in/ the Univerfity of S. Andrews in Scotland./ *London,*/ Printed by J. G. for Andr. Crook, at the Green Dragon/ in St Pauls Church-yard. M. DC. LVIII./ *4 prel. leaves and 521 pp. Old calf.* 4to. (2l. 12s. 6d. 2419)

ABINE (EDWARD). Remarks on the Account of The late Voyage of Discovery to Baffin's Bay, published By Captain J. Ross, R. N. By Captain Edward Sabine, Royal Artillery. *London:* Richard and Arthur Taylor, 1819. *40 pp. Unbound.* 8vo. (*See* No. 2409). (3s. 6d. 2420)

SACK (ALBERT VON). A Narrative of a Voyage to Surinam; of a Residence there during 1805, 1806, and 1807; and of the Author's return to Europe by the Way of North America. By Baron Albert von Sack, Chamberlain to his Prussian Majesty. *London:* G. and W. Nicol, 1810. *7 prel. leaves, including engraved title; and 282 pp. Frontispiece. Sketch at page* 1. *Plate at page* 101. *Half calf.* 4to. (7s. 6d. 2421)

SACKVILLE (*Lord* GEORGE). The Trial Of the Right Honourable Lord George Sackville, At A Court Martial Held at the Horſe-Guards, February 29, 1760, for An Enquiry into his Conduct, Being charged with Diſobedience of Orders, While he commanded the Britiſh Horſe in Germany. Together with His Lordſhip's Defence. *London:* W. Owen, [1760.] *viii and 342 pp. Wanting pp.* 319-20. *Half morocco.* 8vo. (7s. 6d. 2422)

SAGAN/ Landnama/ vm pyrſtu bygging Iſlands af/ Nordmonnum./ Symbolum Regium./ Pieta=/ te &/ Iusti=/tia./ Skalhollte,/ Dryckt af Hendr; Kruſe/ A MDCLXXXVIII. *5 prel. leaves and 182 pp.* '*Registvr*' *etc.* 10 *leaves. Half morocco.* 4to. (2l. 2s. 2423)

Chronicle of the first Colonisation of Iceland, by the Norwegians. (Northmen).

SAGARD (GABRIEL). [*Engraved title*] Le Grand/ Voyage Dv Pays/ des Hurons, Situé en L'A=/ merique uers la mer douce/ ez dernieres confins de/ la nouuelle France/ Ou il est traicte de tout/ ce qui est du paÿs et du/ gouuernement des Sauuages/ Auec un Dictionnaire/ de la Langue huronne/ Par Fr. Gabriel Sagard/ Recollect de S^r. Francois/ de la prouince S^r. Denis./ A Paris Chez Denys/ Moreau rue S^t. Jacques à/ La Salamandre 1632/. [*Printed title*] Le Grand Voyages/ dv Pays des Hvrons,/ fitué, en l'Amerique vers la Mer/ douce, és derniers confins/ de la nouuelle France,/ dite Canada./ Où il eft amplement traité de tout ce qui eft du pays, des/ mœurs & du naturel des Sauuages, de leur gouuernement/ & façons de faire, tant dedans leurs pays, qu'allans en voya-/ges : De leur foy & croyance ; De leurs confeils & guerres, & de quel genre de tourmens ils font mourir leurs prifonniers./ Comme ils fe marient, & efleuent leurs enfans : De leurs Me-/decins, & des remedes dont ils vfent à leurs maladies : De/ leurs dances & chanfons : De la chaffe, de la pefche, & des oyfeaux & animaux terreftres & aquatiques qu'ils ont. Des/ richeffes du pays : Comme ils cultiuent les terres, & accom-/modent leur Meneftre. De leur deüil, pleurs & lamenta-/tions, & comme ils enfeueliffent & enterrent leurs morts./ Auec vn Dictionaire de la langue Huronne, pour la com-modi-/te de ceux qui ont à voyager dans le pays, & n'ont/ l'intelligence d'icelle langue./ Par F. Gabriel Sagard Theodat, Recollet de/ S. François, de la Prouince de S. Denys en France./ A *Paris*, Chez Denys Moreav, ruë S. Iacques, à/ la Salamandre d'Argent./ M.DC.XXXII./ Auec Priuilege du Roy./ 12 *prel. leaves and* 380 pp ; *followed by* 2 *blank leaves*. 'Dictionaire de la Langve' etc. 12 *pp ; and* 'Les Mots Francois tournez en Huron,' 66 *unpaged leaves ;* 'Table des choses,' etc. 14 pp. *Imperfect, wanting pp.* 150—173. *Old calf.*
8vo. (3*l*. 3*s*. 2424)

SAGITTARIUS'S Letters and Political Speculations. Extracted From the Public Ledger. Humbly Inscribed To the very Loyal and truly Pious Doctor Samuel Cooper, Paftor of the Congregational Church in Brattle Street. *Boston :* Printed : By Order of the Select Men and fold at Donation

Hall, for the Benefit of the diſtreſſed Patriots. MDCCLXXV. *Title and* 127 *pp. Calf extra, by Bedford.* 8*vo.* (15*s.* 2425)

SAINT DOMINGO. Betrachtungen über den gegenwärtigen zuſtand der franzöſiſchen Colonie zu San Domingo. Aus dem Franzöſiſchen überſetzt und mit einigen Anmerkungen verſehen. *Leipzig,* bey Johann Friedrich Junius. 1779. *Two Volumes.* Erſter Theil, 8 *prel. leaves and text* 310 *pp.* Zweyter Theil, 2 *prel. leaves and text* 332 *pp. Half calf.* 8*vo.* (7*s.* 6*d.* 2426)

SAINT DOMINGO. History of the Island of St. Domingo, from its firſt Discovery by Columbus to the present period. *London:* Printed for Archibald Constable and Co. Edinburgh: 1818. *xiv and* 446 *pp.* 8*vo.* (6*s.* 6*d.* 2427)

SAINT DOMINGO. Histoire de l'Ile de Saint-Domingue, depuis l'Epoque de sa dècouverte par Christophe Colomb Jusqu'a l'Année 1818. Publiée sur des documents authentiques, et suivie de Pièces justificatives, Telles que la Correspondance de Toussaint-Louverture avec Buonaparte; le Cérémonial de la Cour d'Haïty; la Constitution de ce royaume; l'Almanach royal d'Haïty; la Correspondance du comte de Limonade, et le Manifeste du roi Christophe. *A Paris,* Delaunay, 1819. *Half-title, title, ii pp. and text* 390 *pp. Half-calf.* 8*vo.* (5*s.* 6*d.* 2428)

SAINT JOHN (J. HECTOR). Letters from an American Farmer; describing certain Provincial Situations, Manners, and Customs, not generally known; and conveying some idea of the late and present interior circumstances of the British Colonies in North America. Written for the Information of a Friend in England, by J. Hector St. John, a Farmer in Pennsylvania. *London,* Thomas Davies, MDCCLXXXII. 8 *prel. leaves and* 318 *pp. With* 2 *maps. Half calf.* 8*vo.* (5*s.* 6*d.* 2429)

SALLE (MONSIEUR DE LA). An/ Account/ of/ Monſieur de la Salle's/ last/ Expedition and Discoveries/ in/ North America./ Preſented to the French King,/ And Publiſhed by the/ Chevalier Tonti, Governor of Fort St. Lo-/uis, in the Province of the Iſlinois./ Made Engliſh from the

Paris Original./ Also/ The Adventures of the Sieur de/ Montavban, Captain of the French/ Buccaneers on the Coaſt of Guinea, in the/ Year 1695./ *London*,/ Printed for J. Tonſon at the Judge's Head, and S. Buckly/ at the Dolphin in Fleet-ſtreet, and R. Knaplock, at the/ Angel and Crown in St. Paul's Church-Yard. 1698./ *Title and* 211 *pp.* 'A/ Relation/ of a/ Voyage/ Made by the/ Sieur de Montauban,'/ *etc.* 44 *pp. Half calf.* 8vo. (15s. 2430)

SARATE (Augustine). See ZARATE (Augustine).

SARMIENTO DE GAMBOA (Pedro). Viage al estrecho de Magallanes Por el Capitan Pedro Sarmiento de Gambóa En los años de 1579. y 1580. Y Noticia de la Expedicion Que despues hizo para poblarle. En *Madrid*: 1768. *lxxxiv and* 402 *pp.* 3 *Plates.* 'Declaration que De órden del Virréi del Perú D. Francisco de Borja,/' *etc. Title and xxxiii pp. Old calf.* 4to. (18s. 2431)

SCHEDÆ/ Ara Prests/ Froda/ Vm Island./ Prentadar i *Skalhollte* af Hendrick Kruſe./ Anno 1688./ *On the reverse of the title;* 'Ad Lectorem.' *etc. Text* 14 *pp.* 'Regiſtur' *etc;* 4 *leaves. Half morocco.* 4to. (1l. 11s. 6d. 2432)

SCHMIDEL (Huldericus). Vera hiſtoria,/ Admirandæ cvivs-/ dam nauigationis, quam Hul-/ dericus Schmidel, Straubingenſis, ab Anno 1534./ uſque ad annum 1554. in Americam vel nouum/ Mundum, iuxta Braſiliam & Rio della Plata, confecit Quid/ per hoſce annos 19. fuſtinuerit, quam varias & quam mirandas/ regiones at homines viderit. Ab ipſo Schmidelio Germanice,/ deſcripta: Nunc vero, emendatis & correctis Vrbium, Regio-/ num & Fluminum, nominibus, Adiecta etiam tabula/ Geographica, figuris & alijs notationi-/bus quibuſdam in hanc for-/mam reducta./ *Norimbergæ*,/ Impenſis Levini Hulſij. 1599./ *Title the reverse blank, and* 101 *pp. Portrait of the Author. Copperplate etchings at pp.* 6, 11, 12, 13, 15, 17, 18, 21, 25, 26, 32, 37, 40, 63, 69, 79, 97. *With the Map. Unbound.* 4to. (3l. 3s. 2433)

SCHMIDT (Ulrich). Warhafftige Be=/ſchriebunge aller/ vnd mancherley ſorgfeltigen Schif=/farten, auch viler vnbekanten erfundnen Landtſchafften, Inſu=/len, Königreichen, vnd Stedten, von derſelbigē gelegenheyt, weſen, gebreuchen,/ ſitten, Religion, Künſt vnd handtierung. Item von allerley gewächſz,/ Metallen, Specereyen, vnd anderer dinge mehr, ſo von jhnen in vnſere/ Land geführt vnd gebracht werden./ Auch von mancherley gefahr, ſtreitt vnd ſcharmützeln, ſo ſich zwiſchen jnen vnd/ den vnſern, beyde zu Waſſer vnd Lande, wunderbarlich zugetragen. Item von/ erſchrecklicher, feltzamer Natur vnd Eygenſchafft der Leuthfreſſer, Dergleichen vorhin in keinen/ Chronicken oder Hiſtorien beſchrieben, mit ſchönen Concordantzen vnd einem vol=/koṁen Regiſter, zur fürderung des gemeinen nutzes/ zuſamen getragen./ Durch Vlrich Schmidt von Straubingen, vnd andern mehr, ſodaſelbſt/ in eigener Perſon gegenwertig geweſen, vnd ſolches erfaren./ Getruckt zu *Franckfurt am Mayn*, Anno 1567/. *6 prel. leaves; viz. Title reverse blank*, ' Den Ehrneſten, Fürſichti=/gen, Erſamen vnd weiſen Herrn, Stetmeiſtern vnd/ Rath der löblichen Reichſzſtadt Schwäbiſchen Hall,/ meinen inſondern günſtigen lie=/ben Herren.'/ *8 pp. 1 blank leaf. Text*, 110 *folioed leaves;* ' Warhafftige vnd liebliche Be=/ſchreibung etlicher fürnemen Indianiſchen Landt=/ſchafften vnd Inſulen, die vormals in keiner Chronicken gedacht,/' *etc.* 59 *folioed leaves; and Colophon leaf, the reverse blank. Blue morocco extra. Folio.* (4*l.* 4*s.* 2434)

SCHOEPF (Io. Davidis). D. Io. Davidis Schœpf/ Seren. Marggrav. Brand. Onold. et Cvlmb. Med. Avl. et Milit. Coll. Med. Membr. Materia Medica Americana potissimvm Regni Vegetabilis. *Erlangue* Svmtibvs Io. Iac. Palmii. MDCCLXXXVII. *xviii and* 170 *pp. Old calf.* 8*vo.* (7*s.* 6*d.* 2435)

SCHOMBURGK (Robert H.). A Description of British Guiana, Geographical and Statistical: Exhibiting its resources and Capabilities, together with the present and future condition and prospects of the Colony. By Robert H. Schomburgk, Esq. *London:* Simpkin, Marſhall and Co. 1840. 2 *prel. leaves and text* 155 *pp. With map. Cloth.* 8*vo.* (3*s.* 6*d.* 2436)

SCHONER (Joannes). Ioannis Scho-/neri Caro-

lostadii Opvscv-/lvm Geographicvm ex Diver-
sorvm Li/bris ac cartis fumma cura & diligentia
colle=/ctum, accomodatum ad recenter ela=/boratum
ab eodem globum de=/fcriptionis terrenæ. [*Basel
1533.*] 21 *unpaged leaves including title. On the
reverse of the title is a woodcut of the Globe. Half
morocco.* 4*to.* (1*l.* 1*s.* 2437)

SCHOUTEN (Gulielmus Cornelius). Iovrnal/
ov Relation/ exacte dv voyage de Gvill. Schovten,/
dans les Indes: Par vn nouueau/ deftroit, & par
les grandes Mers/ Auftrales qu'il à defcouuert,
vers/ le Pole Antartique./ Ensemble des Nov-/
uelles Terres auparauant incognuës,/ Ifles, Fruicts,
Peuples, & Animaux/ eftranges, qu'il a trouué en
fon chemin :/ Et des rares obferuations qu'il y à
fait/ touchant la declinaifon de l'Aymant./ A
Paris./ Chez M. Gobert, au Palais eu la gallerie/
des prifonniers: Et les Cartes, chez M. Tauernier,
Graueur du Roy, de/meurant au pont Marchand./
m. dc. xviii./ 7 *prel. leaves and* 232 *pp. Maps and
plates at pp.* 9, 57, 73, 103, 113, 137, 153 *and* 169.
Calf extra by Bedford. 8*vo.* (2*l.* 2*s.* 2438)

SCHOUTEN (Gulielmus Cornelius). Iovrnal/ ov
Relation/ exacte dv Voyage/ de Gvill. Schovten,/
dans les Indes: Par vn nouueau/ deftroir, & par
les grandes Mers/ Auftrales qu'il à defcouuert,
vers/ le Pole Antartique./ Ensemble des Nov-/
uelles Terres auparuant incognuës,/ Ifles, Fruicts,
Peuples, & Animaux/ eftranges, qu'il a trouué en
fon chemin :/ Et des rares obferuations qu'il y à
fait/ touchant la declinaifon de l'Aymant./ A
Paris,/ Chez M. Gobert, au Palais en la gallerie/
des prifonniers: Et les Cartes, chez M./ Tauernier,
Graueur du Roy, de-/meurant au pont Marchand./
m.dc.xix./ 7 *prel. leaves and* 232 *pp. Without the
maps and plates.* 8*vo.* (1*l.* 11*s.* 6*d.* 2439)

SCHOUTEN (Gulielmus Cornelius). Jovrnal/
Ou/ Description/ dv merveillevx Voyage de/
Gvillavme Schovten, Hollandois natif de/ Hoorn,
fait es années 1615. 1616. & 1617./ Comme (en
circum-navigeant le Globe ter-/restre) il a def-
couvert vers le Zud du deftroit de Magellan vn/
nouveau paffage, jufques à la grande Mer de Zud./
Enfemble,/ Des avantures admirables qui luy font

advenues en/ defcouvrant du plufieurs Ifles, &
peuples eftranges./ A *Amstredam,*/ Chez Ian
Ianffon, Libraire, demeurant fur l'Eau,/ a la Carte
Marine. 1619. 4 *prel. leaves*; *viz. Title with copperplate engraving of ships in full sail, the reverse blank;*
'Preface. Au lecteur debonnaire.' 5 *pp;* 'Sur
l'amirable navigation de Gvillavme Schovten, Natif
de Hoorn.' 1 *page. Copperplate engraving of the
Globe with 6 portraits and 2 ships: Text* 80 *pp.
With copperplate engravings at pp.* 14, 24, 41, 45,
49, 51. 4to. (2*l*. 2*s*. 2440)

SCHOUTEN (Gulielmus Cornelius). Diarivm/
vel/ Defcriptio laboriofiffimi, & Moleftiffimi/ Jtin-
eris, facti à/ Gvilielmo Cornelii/ Schovtenio, Hor-
nano./ Annis 1615. 1616. & 1617./ Cum à parte
Auftrali freti Magellanici, novum ductum, aut/
fretum, in Magnum Mare Auftrale detexit, totum q/
Orbem terrarum circumnavigavit./ Quas Infulas,
& regiones, & populos viderit,/ & quæ pericula
fubierit./ *Amsterdami,* Apud Petrum Kærium. A°.
1619./ 4 *prel. leaves, and* 71 *pp.* 6 *maps and plates.*
4to. (2*l*. 2*s*. 2441)

SEABURY (Samuel). The nature and extent of
the Apostolical Commission. A Sermon, preached
at the Consecration of the Right Reverend Dr.
Samuel Seabury, Bishop of the Episcopal Church
in Connecticut. By a Bishop of the Episcopal
Church in Scotland. *London:* John, Francis, and
Charles Rivington, mdcclxxxv. 32 *pp. Unbound.*
4to. (3*s*. 6*d*. 2442)

SEASONABLE Advice, to The Members of the
Britifh Parliament, concerning Conciliatory Mea-
sures with America; and an Act of Perpetual
Insolvency, for Relief of Debtors: With Some
Strictures on the reciprocal Duties of Sovereigns,
and Senators. *London:* J. Bew, m,dcc,lxxv. *viii
and* 38 *pp. Half morocco.* 8vo. (5*s*. 6*d*. 2444)

SECKER (Thomas). A Letter To the Right Honourable Horatio Walpole, Efq; Written Jan. 9,
1750-1, By the Right Reverend Thomas Secker,
LL.D. Lord Bishop of Oxford: Concerning Bishops in America. *London:* J. and F. Rivington,
mdcclxix. 2 *prel. leaves and* 28 *pp. Unbound.*
8vo. (4*s*. 6*d*. 2445)

SELKIRK (*Earl of*). A Sketch of the British Fur Trade in North America; with Observations relative to the North-West Company of Montreal. By the Earl of Selkirk. Second Edition. *London:* James Ridgway. 1816. 3 *prel. leaves and* 130 *pp. Half calf.* 8vo. (3s. 6d. 2446)

SELLER (JOHN). America. *A small Atlas in* 28 *copperplate engravings. Calf extra by F. Bedford.* 12mo. (18s. 2447)

SENTIMENTS (THE) of a Foreigner, on the Disputes of Great-Britain with America. Translated from the French. *Philadelphia:* Printed by James Humphreys, Junior; in Front-Street. M,DCC,LXXV. 27 pp. *Half morocco.* 8vo. (4s. 6d. 2448)

SEPP (ANTONY). R. R. P. P. Antonij Sepp,/ und Antonij Böhm,/ Der Societät Jesu Prieſtern,/ Neu=vermehrte/ Reifs=Befchrei=/bung,/ Wie felbe aufs Hifpanien in Para=/quariam kommen./ Und Kurtzer Bericht der denck=/wurdigften Sachen, felbiger Land=/fchafft, Völckern, und Arbeitung der/ P. P. Miſſionariorum./ Gezogen,/ Aufs denen R. P. Sepp, Soc. Jesu mit/ eigner Hand gefchriebenen Brieffen,/ Von Steph. Ign. Sepp von Seppenb,/ und Rech: Prieſtern, J. U. C. als leib=/ lichen Brudern./ Drilte und verbefferte Edition,/ Mit Erlaubnufz der Obern./ *Passau*, Druckts und verlegts Georg Adam Höller, 1698./ 336 *pp. Old calf.* 12mo. (10s. 6d. 2449)

SEPULVEDÆ (JOANNIS GENESII) Cordubensis Opera, Cum Edita, Tum Inedita, Accurante Regia Historiæ Academia. *Matriti.* Ex Typographia Regia de la Gazeta. Anno M.DCC.LXXX. *Four Volumes.* Volumen Primum. 8 *prel. leaves, cxliv pp,* 24 *pp,* 4 *leaves, xlvi pp, Portrait of Charles 5th. and* 468 *pp.* 'Monitum ad Lectorem' 2 *pp.* Volumen Secundum. 3 *prel. leaves, lxvi and* 544 *pp.* 'Index' 75 *leaves.* Volumen Tertium. 3 *prel. leaves, xxviii and* 244 *pp.* 'Index' 9 *leaves, half-title, Summarium* 7 *leaves,* 134 *pp.* 'Index' 7 *leaves, half-title and* 399 *pp. Index* 11 *pp.* Volumen Quartum. 3 *prel. leaves, and* 591 *pp. Index* 21 *pp. Old calf.* 4to. (3l. 3s. 2450)

SERGEANT (JOHN). The Caufes and Danger of Delusions in the Affairs of Religion Confider'd and caution'd againſt, With particular Reference to the Temper of the preſent Times. In a Sermon Preach'd at Springfield, April 4. 1743. In the Audience of the aſſociated Paſtors of the County of Hampſhire. By John Sergeant, M. A. Paſtor of the Church of Chriſt in Stockbridge. Publiſh'd at the Deſire of the Hearers. *Boston*, Printed for S. Eliot in Cornhil. 1743. *36 pp. Half morocco.* 8vo. (7s. 6d. 2451)

SERGEANT (John). A Letter From the Rev^d. Mr. Sergeant Of Stockbridge, to Dr. Colman Of Boston; Containing Mr. Sergeant's Propoſal of a more effectual method for the Education of Indian Children; to raiſe 'em if poſſible into a civil and induſtrious People; by introducing the Engliſh Language among them; and thereby inſtilling into their Minds and Hearts, with a more laſting Impreſſion, the Principles of Virtue and Piety. Made publick by Dr. Colman at the Deſire of Mr. Sergeant, with some general Account of what the Rev. Mr. Isaac Hollis of - - - - has already done for the Sons of this Indian Tribe of Houſſatannoc, now erected into a Townſhip by the General Court, and called Stockbridge. *Boston,* Printed by Rogers and Fowle, for D. Henchman in Cornhill. 1743. *16 pp. Half morocco.* 8vo. (10s. 6d. 2452)

SERIOUS ADDRESS (A) To thoſe Who unneceſſarily frequent the Tavern, and Often ſpend the Evening in Publick Houſes. By ſeveral Miniſters. To which is added, A private Letter on the Subject, by the late Rev. Dr. Increaſe Mather. *Boston,* N. E. Printed for S. Gerriſh, at the lower end of Cornhill. 1726. *Title, iv, and 30 pp. Unbound.* 8vo. (7s. 6d. 2453)

SEVERAL Conferences Between ſome of the principal People amongſt the Quakers in Pennsylvania, and the Deputies from the Six Indian Nations, In Alliance with Britain; In Order to reclaim their Brethren the Delaware Indians from their Defection, and put a Stop to their Barbarities and Hoſtilities. To which is prefix'd (As introductory to the ſaid Conferences) Two Addresses from the ſaid Quakers; one to the Lieutenant-Governor, and the other to the General-Aſſembly of the Province of Pennfylvania; as alfo the Lieutenant-Governor's Declaration of War againſt the faid Delaware Indians, and their Adherents. *Newcastle upon Tyne:* I. Thompson and Company. MDCCLVI. 28 pp. 8vo. (10s. 6d. 2454)

SEWALL (JOSEPH). The Holy Spirit Convincing the World of Sin, of Righteoufnefs, and of Judgment, confidered in Four Sermons: The two former delivered at the Tuefday-Evening Lecture in Brattle-Street, January 20th, & March 3: The other at the Old-South-Church in Boston, April 17 & 26, 1741. By Jofeph Sewall, D. D. *Boston:* Printed by J. Draper, for D. Hehchman in Cornhil. 1741. *Title; vi and 134 pp. 12mo.* (10s. 6d. 2455)

SEWALL (SAMUEL). Phænomena quædam/ Apocalyptica/ Ad Afpectum Novi Orbis configurata./ Or, fome few Lines towards a defcription of the New/ Heaven/ As It makes to thofe who ſtand upon the/ New Earth/ By Samuel Sewall fometime Fellow of Harvard Colledge at/ Cambridge in New-England./ *Massachvset;/* Boston, Printed by Bartholomew Green, and John Allen,/ And are to be fold by Richard Wilkins, 1697./ 4 *prel. leaves; viz. Title the reverse blank,* 'To the Honorable, Sir William Ashvrst Knight, Governour; and the Company For the Propagation of the Gospel to the Indians in New-England, and places adjacent, in America.' 2 *pp;* 'To the Honorable William Stoughton Efq. Lieut. Governour and Commander in Chief, in and over His Majefties Province of the Maffachufets Bay in New England.' 3 *pp;* 'Pfalm 139. 7--10.' 1 *page. Text 60 pp. Morocco by Bedford.* 4to. (7l. 7s. 2456)

SEWEL (WILLIAM). The History of the Rise, Increase, and Progress, Of the Christian People called Quakers: Intermixed with several Remarkable Occurrences. Written Originally in Low-Dutch, and alfo Tranflated into Englifh, By William Sewel. The Third Edition, Corrected. *Philadelphia:* Printed and Sold by Samuel Keimer in Second Street. MDCCXXVIII. 6 *prel. leaves and* 694 *pp.* 'Index' 16 *pp. Calf extra. Imperfect, wanting 2 leaves of the Index. Folio.* (2l. 2s. 2457)

SEWEL (WILLIAM). The History of the Rise,

Increase and Progress, of the Christian People called Quakers; with several Remarkable Occurrences intermixed. Written originally in Low-Dutch, and alſo tranſlated into English, By William Sewel. The Third Edition, corrected. *Burlington,* New-Jersey: Printed and Sold by Isaac Collins, M.DCC.LXXIV. *xii and* 812 *pp.* 'Index' 16 *pp. Old calf. Folio.* (2*l.* 2*s.* 2458)

SEYBERT (ADAM). Statistical Annals: Embracing Views of the Population, Commerce, Navigation, Fisheries, Public Lands, Post-Office Establishment, Revenues, Mint, Military and Naval Establishments, Expenditures, Public Debt and Sinking Fund, of the United States of America: Founded on Official Documents: Commencing on the Fourth of March Seventeen Hundred and Eighty-nine and ending on the Twentieth of April Eighteen Hundred and Eighteen. By Adam Seybert, M. D. A Member of the House of Representatives of the United States, from the State of Pennsylvania; Member of the American Philosophical Society; Honorary Member of the Philosophical and Literary Society of New-York; Fellow of the Royal Society of Gœttingen, &c. *Philadelphia:* Thomas Dobson & Son, 1818. *xxviii and* 803 *pp. Boards.* 4*to.* (15*s.* 2459)

SEYFRIED (JOH. HEINRICH). Poliologia,/ Das iſt:/ Accurate/ Beſchreibung/ Aller vornehmſten in der ganzen Welt/ befindlichen/ Städten, Schlöſſern und Veſ=/ſtungen/ So wol was ihre Erbauung, Fortifi=/cation, Religion, Herrſchafft und Regie=/ rungs=Form, als auch Die von ihrem Urſprung an,/ bis auf gegenwärtige Zeit ſich ereignete kriegs=und/ Friedens, Freud und Leid betreffende Beg=/benheiten betrifft./ In zweyen abſonderlichen Theilen/ dergeſtalt vorgeſtellet,/ Daſz im erſten die berühmteſten Orte in ganz/ Europa, im andern aber die in Aſia, Africa und/ America befindliche, ausführlich nach dem Alphabet/ abgehandelt werden,/ Und zwar alles und jedes mit ſonderbarem Fleiſz/ zu eines jedem Leſers nutzlicher Ergötzung zuſamm/getragen, und nun zum an=dernmal verbeſſert her=/ausgeben durch/ Joh. Heinrich Seyfried, Hochfürſtl. Durchl./ zu Pfalz Sulzbach Hoſ=kammer=Rath./ *Nürnberg,/*

Verlegts Johann Leonhard Buggel, 1695./ Two Volumes. Theil I. 14 prel. leaves with folding map of the world; Text, 480 pp; and one blank leaf. Theil II. 13 prel. leaves and one blank leaf; Text, pp. 3—357. Blue morocco extra gilt, by Hayday. 8vo. (1l. 1s. 2460)

SHARP (BARTHOLOMEW). The/ Voyages/ and/ Adventures/ of/ Capt. Barth. Sharp/ And others, in the/ South Sea:/ Being/ a Journal of the fame./ Also/ Capt. Van Horn with his Buccanieres fur-/prizing of la Vera Cruz./ To which is added/ The true Relation of Sir Henry Morgan/ his Expedition againſt the Spaniards in the/ Weſt-Indies, and his taking Panama./ Together with/ The Prefident of Panama's Account of the fame/ Expedition: Tranſlated out of Spaniſh./ And Col. Beefton's adjuſtment of the Peace be-/tween the Spaniards and Engliſh in the Weſt Indies./ Publiſhed by P. A. Esq;./ London/ Printed by B. W. for R. H. and S. T. and are to be fold/ by Walter Davis in Amen-Corner. MDCLXXXIV./ 12 prel. leaves and 172 pp. Calf. 8vo. (15s. 2461)

SHARP (GRANVILLE). Extract from a Representation of the Injustice and Dangerous Tendency of tolerating Slavery; or Admitting the leaſt Claim of private Property in the Perſons of Men in England. By Granville Sharp. First printed in London. MDCCLXIX. Title, and pp. 147—198. Index, 6 pp. Half morocco. 8vo. (4s. 6d. 2462)

SHARP (GRANVILLE). A General Plan for laying out Towns and Townships on the New-Acquired Lands in the East Indies, America, or elsewhere; In order to promote Cultivation, and raise the Value of all the adjoining Land, at the Price of giving gratis the Town-Lots, and, in some Cases (as in new Colonies), also the small Out-Lots, to the first Settlers and their Heirs so long as they possess no other Land; and on equitable Conditions. First Printed in 1794. Second Edition 1804. 24 pp. With plan. 8vo. (4s. 6d. 2463)

SHARP (JOHN). A Sermon Preached at Trinity-Church in New-York, in America, Auguſt 13, 1706, At the Funeral Of the Right Honourable Katherine Lady Cornbury, Baronefs Clifton of

Leighton Bromfwold, &c. Heirefs to the moſt noble Charles Duke of Richmond and Lenox, Wife to his Excellency Edward Lord Vifcount Cornbury, Her Majeſty's Captain General, and Governor in Chief of the Provinces of New-York, New-Jerfey, and Territories depending thereon in America, &c. By John Sharp, A.M. Chaplain to the Queen's Forces in the Province of New York. *London :* Printed by H. Hills, [1708.] 16 pp. *Half morocco.* 8vo. (7s. 6d. 2464)

SHARP (JOHN). A Sermon Preached at Trinity-Church in New-York, in America, Auguſt 13. 1706. At the Funeral Of the Right Honourable Katherine Lady Cornbury, Baronefs Clifton of Leighton Bromfwold, &c. Heirefs to the moſt Noble Charles Duke of Richmond and Lenox, and Wife to his Excellency Edward Lord Vifcount Cornbury, Her Majeſty's Captain General, and Governor in chief of the Provinces of New-York, New-Jerfey, and Territories depending thereon in America, &c. By John Sharp, A.M. Chaplain to the Queen's Forces in the Province of New-York. *London:* J. Morphew, 1708. 16 pp. *Unbound.* 8vo. (7s. 6d. 2465)

SHEBBEARE (J.) An Answer to the Queries, contained in A Letter to Dr. Shebbeare, Printed in the Public Ledger, Auguſt 10. Together with Animadversions on Two Speeches In Defence of the Printers of A Paper, fubfcribed a South Briton. The First pronounced by The Right Hon. Thomas Townsend, in the Houfe of Commons, And printed in the London Packet of February 18. The Second by The Right Learned Counfellor Lee, in Guildhall, And printed in the Public Ledger of Auguſt 12. In the Examination of which a Comparifon naturally arifes between the public and private Virtues of Their Prefent Majeſties, and thofe of King William and Queen Mary. The Merits, alfo of Roman Catholics, and of Diffenters from the Church of England, refpecting Allegiance and Liberty, and their Claims to National Protection, are fairly ſtated, from their paſt and prefent Tranſ-actions. By J. Shebbeare, M.D. *London:* S. Hooper, *Title and text* 179 pp. *Half morocco.* 8vo. (4s. 6d. 2466)

SHEBBEARE (J.) An Essay on the Origin, Progrefs and Eftablifhment of National Society; in which The Principles of Government, the Definitions of phyfical, moral, civil, and religious Liberty, contained in Dr. Price's Obfervations, &c. are fairly examined and fully refuted: Together with A Juftification of the Legiflature, in reducing America to Obedience by Force. To which is added An Appendix on the Excellent and admirable in Mr. Burke's fecond printed Speech of the 22d of March, 1775. By J. Shebbeare, M.D. *London:* J. Bew, M.DCC.LXXVI. *Title and* 212 *pp. Half morocco.* 8*vo.* (4*s.* 6*d.* 2467)

SHEBBEARE (J.) An Essay on the Origin, Progrefs and Eftablifhment of National Society; in which The Principles of Government, the Definitions of phyfical, moral, civil and religious Liberty, contained in Dr. Price's Obfervations, &c. are fairly examined and fully refuted: Together with A Juftification of the Legiflature, in reducing America to Obedience by Force. To which is added an Appendix on the Excellent and admirable in Mr. Burke's fecond printed Speech of the 22d of March, 1775. By J. Shebbeare, M.D. Second Edition. *London:* J. Bew, MDCCLXXVI. *Title and* 212 *pp.* 8*vo.* (4*s.* 6*d.* 2468)

SHEFFIELD (JOHN *Lord*). Observations on the Commerce of the American States. By John Lord Sheffield. A New Edition, much enlarged. With an Appendix, Containing Tables of the Imports and Exports of Great Britain to and from all Parts. Alfo, the Exports of America, &c. With Remarks on thofe Tables, and on the late Proclamations, &c. *London:* J. Debrett, MDCCLXXXIV. 8 *prel. leaves and* 288 *pp. Tables numbered* I *to* XI. 'The Tonage' *etc.* 1 *page.* 8*vo.* (6*s.* 6*d.* 2469)

SHEFFIELD (JOHN *Lord*). Observations on the Commerce of the American States. By John Lord Sheffield. With an Appendix; Containing Tables of the Imports and Exports of Great Britain to and from all Parts, from 1700 to 1783. Alfo the Exports of America, &c. With Remarks on thofe Tables, on the Trade and Navigation of Great Britain, and on the late Proclamations, &c. The Sixth Edition, enlarged. With a Complete Index to the whole. *London:* J. Debrett, M,DCC,LXXXIV. 2 *prel. leaves;* 'Introduction' *xlvii pp;* 'Errata' 1 *page, Text* 345 *pp. Tables numbered* I *to* XVI. 'The Tonage' 1 *page;* 'Contents' 4 *pp;* 'Index' 17 *pp;* 'Errata' 1 *page.* 8*vo.* (7*s.* 6*d.* 2470)

SHELVOCKE (GEORGE). A Voyage round the World By the Way of the Great South Sea, Perform'd in the Years 1719, 20, 21, 22, in the Speedwell, of London, of 24 Guns and 100 Men, (under His Majefty's Commiffion to cruize on the Spaniards in the late War with the Spanifh Crown) till fhe was caft away on the Ifland of Juan Fernandes, in May 1720; and afterwards continu'd in the Recovery, the Jesus Maria and Sacra Familia, &c. By Capt. George Shelvocke, Commander of the Speedwell, Recovery, &c. in this Expedition. *London:* J. Senex, MDCCXXVI. 4 *prel. leaves;* 'Preface' *xxxii pp;* 'Contents' 4 *pp; Text* 468 *pp. Copperplate map: and plates at pp.* 106, 253, *and* 404 (2). *Old calf.* 8*vo.* (10*s.* 6*d.* 2471)

SHEPARD (THOMAS). The/ Sincere/ Convert/ Difcovering/ the Paucity/ of true Believers;/ And the great Difficultie of/ Saving Converfion./ By Tho. Shepheard, fometimes/ of Immanuel Colledge in Cambridge./ *London,/* Printed by T. P. and M. S. and are/ to be fold by John Sweeting, at the Angel/ in Popes-head Alley, 1643./ 9 *prel. leaves and* 266 *pp. Old morocco.* 8*vo.* (15*s.* 2472)

SHEPARD (THOMAS). The/ Sound Beleever./ Or,/ A Treatise/ of/ Evangelicall Converfion./ Discovering/ The work of Chrifts Spirit, in/ reconciling of a finner to God./ By Tho: Shepard, fometimes/ of Emmanuel Colledge in Cambridge,/ Now Preacher of Gods Word/ in New England./ *London,/* Printed for R. Dawlman 1645./ 3 *prel. leaves and* 352 *pp. Old morocco.* 8*vo.* (15*s.* 2473)

SHEPARD (THOMAS). Theses Sabbaticæ./ Or,/ The Doctrine/ of the/ Sabbath :/ Wherein/ The Sabbaths [I. Morality./ II. Change./ III. Beginning./ IV. Sanctification./] are clearly/ difcuffed./ Which were firft handled more largely in/ fundry Sermons in Cambridge in New-England/ in opening of the fourth Commandment./ In unfolding whereof many Scriptures are cleared, divers

Cafes of Con-/fcience refolved, and the Morall Law as a rule of life to a Believer,/ occafionally and diftinctly handled./ By Thomas Shepard, Paftor of the Church of/ Chrift at Cambridge in New-England./ *London*, Printed by T. R. and E. M. for John Rothwell at Sun and/ Fountaine in Pauls Church-yard. 1649./ *Four Parts*. Part I. 10 *prel. leaves and* 152 *pp*. Second Part. 32 *pp*. Third *and* Fourth Part. 50 *pp*. *Old calf*. 4*to*. (1*l*. 1*s*. 2474)

SHEPARD (Thomas). Certain/ Select Cases/ Refolved./ Specially, tending to the right/ ordering of the heart, that/ we may comfortably walk/ with God in our general/ and particular Callings./ By Thomas Shephard,/ Sometimes of Emanuel-Colledge/ in Cambridge, Now Preacher of/ Gods Word in New-/England./ *London*, Printed by W. H. for John Rothwell, at the Sun/ and Fountain in Pauls Church-yard, near/ the little North-door. 1650./ 4 *prel. leaves and* 87 *pp*. *Old calf*. 8*vo*. (10*s*. 6*d*. 2475)

SHEPARD (Thomas). Subjection/ to/ Chrift/ in all his/ Ordinances,/ and Appointments,/ The beft means to preferve our/ Liberty./ Together with a/ Treatife/ Of Ineffectual Hearing the Word;/ How we may know whether we have heard/ the fame effectually: And by what means it may/ become effectual unto us./ With fome remarkable Paffages of his life./ By Tho. Shephard, late Paftor of the Church/ of Chrift in Cambridge in New-England./ Now published by Mr. Jonathan Michell/ Paftor of the faid Church in New-England./ *London*, Printed for John Rothwell and are to be fold by/ Tho. Brewfter, at the three Bibles, in Pauls Church-/yard neer the Weft end 1652./ 8 *prel. leaves and* 195 *pp*. *Table* 11 *pp*. *Old calf*. 8*vo*. (15*s*. 2476)

SHEPARD (Thomas). The/ Sound Beleever./ A/ Treatife/ of/ Evangelicall Converfion./ Discovering/ The work of Chrifts Spirit, in/ reconciling of a Sinner to God./ By Thomas Shepard,/ fometimes of Emmanuel Coledge in Cam-/bridge, now Preacher of Gods Word in/ New-England./ *London*,/ Printed for Andrew Crooke at the/ Green-Dragon in Pauls-church-yard,/ M.DC.LIII./ Title,

3 *prel. pp ; and Text* 317 *pp.* *Table 3 pp.* *Calf.*
8*vo.* (12*s.* 6*d.* 2477)

SHEPARD (Thomas). Subjection to Chrift,/ in all his/ Ordinances/ and/ Appointments,/ The beft means to preferve our Liberty./ Together with a/ Treatife/ of/ Ineffectual hearing the Word ;/ How we may know whether we/ have heard the fame effectually :/ And by what means it may become/ effectual unto us./ With fome remarkable paffages of his life/ By Tho. Shephard late Paftor of the Church/ of Chrift in Cambridge in New-England./ Now publifhed by Mr. Jonathan Michel,/ Paftor of the faid Church in New-England./ *London*, Printed for Tho. Brewfter, at the three Bibles in Pauls Church-yard. 1654./ 6 *prel. leaves and* 195 *pp.* 'Table' 11 *pp. Calf. Small* 8*vo.* (15*s.* 2478)

SHEPARD (Thomas). The/ Sincere Convert :/ Discovering/ The fmall number of true/ Beleevers,/ And the great difficulty of Saving/ Converfion./ Wherein is excellently and plainly opened/ thefe choice and Divine Principles ;/ Viz. [1. That there is a God, and this God is moft glorious./ 2. That God made man in a bleffed eftate./ 3. Man's mifery by his Fall./ 4. Chrift the only Redeemer by price./ 5. That few are faved, and that with difficulty./ 6. That mans perdition is of himfelf./ Whereto is now added the Saints Jewell,/ fhewing how to apply the Promifes; And/ the Souls Invitation unto Jefus Chrift./ By Tho. Sheppard, fometimes of Emanuel/ Colledge in Cambridge./ Corrected and much amended by the Author./ *London*, Printed by E. Cotes, for John Sweeting,/ at the Angel in Popes-head Alley, 1655./ 8 *prel. leaves and* 247 *pp. Calf.* 8*vo.* (10*s.* 6*d.* 2479)

SHEPARD (Thomas). Theses Sabbaticæ./ Or,/ The Doctrine/ of the/ Sabbath./ Wherein/ The/ Sabbaths/ [1. Morality,/ 11. Change,/ III. Beginning,/ IV. Sanctification,] are clear-/ly difcuf-/fed./ Which were firft handled more largely/ in fundry Sermons in Cambridg in New-Eng-/land, in opening of the fourth Commandment./ In unfolding whereof many Scriptures are cleared, di-/vers Cafes of Confcience refolved, and the Moral/ Law as a rule of Life to a Believer, occafional-/ly and dif-

tinctly handled./ By Thomas Shepard, Paftor of the
Church of/ Christ at Cambridge in New-England./
London, Printed by S. G. for John Rothwel at the
Foun-/tain and Bear in Goldfmiths row in Cheap-
fide./ 1655./ 14 *prel. leaves and* 320 *pp. followed
by* 3 *prel. leaves and* 32 *pp. with* 2 *prel. leaves,* 1 *and*
17 *pp. Old calf.* 8*vo.* (10*s.* 6*d.* 2480)

SHEPARD (Thomas). The/ Parable/ of the/ Ten
Virgins/ opened & applied:/ Being the Sub-
ftance of divers/ Sermons/ on Matth. 25. 1,—13./
Wherein, the Difference between the Sincere
Chriftian and/ the moft Refined Hypocrite, the
Nature and Characters of Saving/ and of Common
Grace, the Dangers and Difeafes incident to/ moft
flourifhing Churches or Chriftians, and other Spi-
ritual/ Truths of greateft importance, are clearly/
difcovered, and practically Improved./ By/ Thomas
Shepard/ late Worthy and Faithfull Paftor of the
Church of Chrift at/ Cambridge in New-England./
Now Publifhed from the Authors own Notes, at
the defires of/ many, for the common Benefit of the
Lords people,/ By/ Jonathan Mitchell Minifter at
Cambridge,/ Tho: Shepard, Son to the Reverend
Author,/ now Minifter at Charles-Town in New-
England./ *London,*/ Printed by J. H. for John
Rothwell, at the Fountain in Goldfmiths-Row in
Cheap-fide,/ and Samuel Thomfon at the Bifhop's
Head in Pauls Church-yard. 1660./ *Two Parts.*
Part I. 4 *prel. leaves and* 240 *pp.* Part II. 203 *pp.
Table.* 5 *pp. Old calf. Folio.* (18*s.* 2481)

SHEPARD (Thomas). The/ Sincere Convert,/
Discovering/ The fmall number of true/ Beleevers,/
And the great difficulty of Saving/ Converfion./
Wherein is excellently and plainly opened/ thefe
choice and Divine Principles:/ Viz. [1. That there
is a God, and this God is moft glorious./ 2. That God
made man in a bleffed eftate./ 3. Mans mifery by
his fall./ 4. Chrift the only Redeemer by Price./
5. That few are faved, and that with difficulty./
6. That mans perdition is of himfelf./ Whereto is
now added the Saints Jewel, fhewing/ how to
apply the promife; And the Souls Invi-/tation
unto Jefus Chrift./ By Tho. Shepherd, fometimes
of Emanuel/ Colledge in Cambridge./ Corrected
and much amended by the Author./ *London,*

Printed by Tho: Mabb, for Robert Horne,/ at the Angel in Popes-head-alley. 1664./ 8 *prel. leaves* and 216 pp. *Half calf.* 8vo. (10s. 6d. 2482)

SHEPARD (THOMAS). The/ Sincere Convert:/ Difcovering the fmall number of/ True Believers,/ And the great difficulty of/ faving Converfion./ Wherein are excellently and plainly opened thefe/ choice and Divine Principles:/ Viz. 1. That there is a God, and this God is moft glorious./ 2. That God made Man in a blefled eftate./ 3. Mans mifery by his Fall./ 4. Chrift the onely Redeemer by price./ 5. That few are faved, and that with difficulty./ 6. That Mans perdition is of himself./ Whereto is now added/ The Saint's Jewel, fhewing how to/ apply the Promifes; and/ The Soul's Invitation unto/ Jefus Chrift./ By Tho. Sheppard, fometimes of Emanuel/ College in Cambridge./ Corrected and much amended by the Author./ *London,*/ Printed by J. Flefher for Robert Horne at Grefham-college, in/ the first Court in Bifhopf-gate-ftreet. 1667./ 8 *prel. leaves and* 237 *pp. Old calf.* 8vo. (10s. 6d. 2483)

SHEPARD (THOMAS). The/ Sincere Convert:/ Difcovering the fmall number of/ True Believers,/ And the great difficulty of/ Saving Converfion./ Wherein are excellently and plainly opened thefe/ choice and Divine Principles:/ Viz. 1. That there is a God, and this God is moft glorious./ 2. That God made Man in a blefled eftate./ 3. Man's mifery by his Fall./ 4. Chrift the onely Redeemer by price./ 5. That few are faved, and that with difficulty./ 6. That Man's perdition is of himfelf./ Whereto is now added/ The Saint's Jewel, fhewing how to/ apply the Promifes; and/ The Soul's Invitation unto/ Jefus Chrift./ By Tho. Sheppard, fometimes of Emanuel/ Colledge in Cambridge./ *London,*/ Printed by E. Flefher for Robert Horn at the South En-/trance of the Royal Exchange. 1672./ 8 *prel. leaves and* 223 *pp. Calf.* 8vo. (10s. 6d. 2484)

SHEPARD (THOMAS). The/ Parable/ of the/ Ten Virgins/ Opened & Applied:/ Being the Sub-ftance of divers/ Sermons/ on Matth. 25. 1,---13./ Wherein, the Difference between the Sincere Chriftian and/ the moft Refined Hypocrite, the

Nature & Characters of Saving/ and of Common Grace, the Dangers and Difeafes incident to/ moft flourifhing Churches or Chriftians, and other Spiritual/ Truths of greateft importance, are clearly/ difcovered, and practically Improved,/ By/ Thomas Shepard/ Late Worthy and Faithful Paftor of the Church of Chrift at/ Cambridge in New-England./ Now publifhed from the Authors own Notes, at the defires of/ many, for the common Benefit of the Lords people,/ By/ Jonathan Mitchell Minifter at Cambridge./ Tho. Shepard, Son to the Reverend Author,/ now Minister at Charles-Town. in New-England./ Re-printed, and carefully Corrected in the Year,/ 1695./ *Two Parts.* Part I. 4 *prel. leaves and* 232 *pp.* Part II. 190 *pp. Table,* 5 *pp. Old calf. Folio.* (18s. 2485)

SHEPARD (THOMAS). The Sound Believer. A Treatise of Evangelicall Converfion. Discovering The Work of Chrift's Spirit, in reconciling of a Sinner to God. By Tho. Shepherd, fometimes of Emanuel Colledge in Cambridge, Now Preacher of God's Word in New-England. *Aberdeen,* Printed by James Nicol, 1730. 325 *pp. Table* 3 *pp.* 12*mo.* (15s. 2486).

[SHERMAN (ROGER).] A Sermon, of a new kind, Never preached, nor ever will be; Containing a Collection of Doctrines, Belonging to the Hopkintonian Scheme of Orthodoxy; Or the Marrow of the moft Modern Divinity. And an Addrefs to the Unregenerate, agreeable to the Doctrines. *New-Haven;* Printed and Sold by T. and S. Green. 28 *pp. Half mor.* 12*mo.* (10s. 6d. 2487)

SHIPLEY (JONATHAN). A Sermon Preached before the Incorporated Society for the Propagation of the Gofpel in Foreign Parts; at their Anniversary Meeting in the Parifh Church of St. Maryle-Bow, On Friday February 19, 1773. By the Right Reverend Jonathan Lord Bifhop of St. Asaph. London Printed: *Boston,* New-England, Re-Printed: And to be Sold by Thomas and John Fleet, at the Heart and Crown in Cornhill, 1773. 17 *pp. Half morocco.* 8*vo.* (4s. 6d. 2488)

SHIRLEY (WILLIAM). A Letter from William Shirley, Efq; Governor of Maffachufet's Bay, To his Grace the Duke of Newcaſtle: With A Journal of the Siege of Louisbourg, and other Operations of the Forces, during the Expedition againſt the French Settlements on Cape Breton; Drawn up at the Defire of the Council and Houſe of Repreſentatives of the Province of Maſſachuſet's Bay; approved and atteſted by Sir William Pepperrell, and the other Principal Officers who commanded in the faid Expedition. Publiſhed by Authority. *London:* E. Owen. 1746. 32 *pp. Half morocco.* 8*vo.* (7*s.* 6*d.* 2489)

SHIRLEY (WILLIAM). A Letter from William Shirley, Efq; Governor of Maſſachufetts-Bay, To His Grace the Duke of Newcaſtle: With A Journal of the Siege of Louiſbourg, and other Operations of the Forces, during the Expedition againſt the French Settlements on Cape-Breton; drawn up at the Defire of the Council and Houſe of Repreſentatives of the Province of Maſſachuſetts-Bay; approved and atteſted by Sir William Pepperrell, and the other Principal Officers who commanded in the faid Expedition. Publiſhed by Authority. London: Printed 1746. *Boston:* Re-printed by Rogers and Fowle, for Joshua Blanchard, at the Bible and Crown in Dock-Square. 1746. 16 *pp.* 8*vo.* (10*s.* 6*d.* 2490)

SHIRLEY (WILLIAM). The Conduct of Major Gen. Shirley, Late General and Commander in Chief of His Majesty's Forces in North America. Briefly stated. *London:* R. and J. Dodsley, 1758. *viii and* 131 *pp. Half mor.* 8*vo.* (10*s.* 6*d.* 2491)

SHORT/ (A) Account/ of the/ Manifeſt Hand of God/ That hath Fallen upon Several/ Marſhals and their Deputies/ Who have made Great Spoil and Havock of the/ Goods of the People of God called/ Quakers,/ in the/ Iſland of Barbadoes,/ For their Testimony againſt Going or Sending/ to the Militia./ With a Remarkable Account of some others of the Perſe-/cutors of the fame People in the fame Iſland. Together/ with an Abſtract of their Sufferings./ *London,* Printed and Sold by T. Sowle, near the/ Meeting-houſe in White-hart-court in Gracious-street. 1696./ 23 *pp.* 'An Abstract' *etc. a folded sheet.* 4*to.* (1*l.* 1*s.* 2492)

SHORT (A) Account of the Interest and Conduct of the Jamaica Planters. In an Address to the Merchants, Traders, and Liverymen of the City of London. *London:* M. Cooper, MDCCLIV. *Title and* 21 *pp.* 8*vo.* (4*s.* 6*d.* 2493)

SHORT (A) History of the Conduct of the Present Ministry, With Regard to the American Stamp Act. *London:* J. Almon, 1766. 21 *pp. Half morocco.* 8*vo.* (4*s.* 6*d.* 2494)

SHORT (A) History of the Conduct of the present Ministry, With Regard to the American Stamp Act. The Second Edition. *London:* J. Almon, 1766. 21 *pp. Half morocco.* 8*vo.* (4*s.* 6*d.* 2495)

SHORT (A) Account Of that Part of Africa Inhabited by the Negroes. With Refpect to the Fertility of the Country, the good Difpofition of many of the Natives, and the Manner by which the Slave Trade is carried on. Extracted from divers Authors, in order to fhew the Iniquity of that Trade, and the Falfity of the Arguments ufually advanced in its Vindication. With Quotations from the Writings of feveral Perfons of Note, viz. George Wallis, Francis Hutcheson, and James Foster, and a large Extract from a Pamphlet, lately publifhed in London, on the Subject of the Slave Trade. The Third Edition. Philadelphia: Printed *London:* Reprinted by W. Baker and J. W. Galabin, MDCCLXVIII. 80 *pp.* 8*vo.* (7*s.* 6*d.* 2496)

SHORT Address to the Government, the Merchants, Manufacturers, and the Colonists in America, and the Sugar Islands, On the prefent State of Affairs. By a Member of Parliament. *London,* G. Robinson, MDCCLXXV. *Title and* 40 *pp. Half morocco.* 8*vo.* (5*s.* 6*d.* 2497)

SHORT (A) History of the Opposition during the Laft Seffion of Parliament. The Third Edition. *London:* T. Cadell, MDCCLXXIX. 58 *pp. Unbound.* 8*vo.* (4*s.* 6*d.* 2498)

SHORT (A) History of the Oppofition during the Laft Seffion of Parliament. The Third Edition. *London:* T. Cadell, MDCCLXXIX. *vi and* 58 *pp. Half morocco.* (4*s.* 6*d.* 2499)

SHOWER (JOHN). Practical Reflections on the Earthquakes That have happened in Europe and

America, But chiefly in the Islands of Jamaica, England, Sicily, Malta, &c. With a Particular and Hiſtorical Account of them, and divers other Earthquakes. By John Shower. The Second Edition. *London:* Cook, James, and Kingman, MDCCL. Title, viii, and 98 pp. 8vo. (4s. 6d. 2500)

SIGFRID (ISAAC). Theological Theses, Containing the chief Heads of the Christian Doctrine, Deduced from Axioms; Compoſed and publickly defended in Preſence and under the Direction of the very reverend and moſt judicious John Henry Ringier, V. D. M. And Profeſſor of controverſial Divinity in the Academy At Bern. By Isaac Sigfrid, of Zoffingen in Bern, and Daniel Wyttenbach, of Bern, In Order to obtain the Honour of the S. Ministry. 1747. (Tranſlated from Latin.) To which is added a Diſcourse by Gerrit Lydekker. A.B. *New-York.* Printed and Sold by Samuel Brown at the Foot of Botbaker's-Hill, between the New-Dutch Church and Fly-Market. 1766. 6 prel. leaves and 55 pp. 'A Discourse' etc. Title and 113 pp. 'Advertiſement.' 4 pp. 8vo. (10s. 6d. 2501)

SIGNS (THE) of the Times consider'd: Or, The high Probability, that the preſent Appearances in New-England, and the Weſt of Scotland, are a Prelude of the Glorious Things promiſed to the Church in the latter Ages. *Edinburgh,* T. Lumisden and J. Robertson; MD.CC.XLII. 3 prel. leaves; Text, pp. 5—34. 8vo. (5s. 6d. 2502)

SILLERY (MADAME). A Selection from the Annals of Virtue, of Madame Sillery: Containing the Moſt important and Intereſting Anecdotes from the Histories of Spain, Portugal, China, Japan, and America: With ſome Account of the Manners, Customs, Arts and Sciences of France. Translated from the French By Elizabeth Mary James. *Bath.* S. Hazard, M.DCC.XCIV. 4 prel. leaves and text 255 pp. 'Subscribers.' and 'Errata.' 8 pp. Old calf. 8vo. (7s. 6d. 2503)

SIMON (PEDRO). ✠/ Primera Parte/ De las Noticias hiſtoriales/ de las Conquiſtas de tier/ra firme en las Indias/ Occidentales./ Compvesto por el Padre/ Fray Pedro Simon Prouincial/ de la Serafico Orden de San Fran=/cisco, del Nueuo Reyno de Granada/ en las Indias, Lector Jubilado en

Sa=/cra Theologia, y qualificador del San^{to}/ Officio, hijo de la Prouincia de Car/thagena en Caſtilla, Natural de/ la Parrilla Obiſpado de/ Cuenca./ Dirigido/ A nvestro invic=/tiſſimo y maior Monarca/ del Antiguo y nuebo Mun/do Philippo quarto en ſu/ Real y supremo Conſejo/ de las Indias./ [*Colophon*] Con Privilegio,/ Del Rey nueſtro Señor, en *Cuenca* por/ Domingo de la Iglesia, Año./ de 1627./ 7 *prel. leaves including engraved title, text* 671 *pp*; *Table* 11 *leaves*; *Table de Vocablos* 9 *leaves*. 2 *of the* 7 *prel. leaves are wanting. Vellum. Folio.* (2*l*. 2504)

SIMONDE DE SISMONDI (J. C. L.) De l'Intérêt de la France a l'égard de la Traite des Nègres, par J. C. L. Simonde de Sismondi. A *Genève*, J. J. Paschoud, et a *Paris*, 1814. 59 *pp*. 8*vo*. (2*s*. 6*d*. 2505)

SIVERS (HENRICH). Bericht/ Von/ Gröhnland,/ Gezogen aus zwo Chroniken: Einer alten Ihs=/ landiſchen, und einer neuen Däniſchen; übergeſand/ in Frantzöſiſcher Sprahche/ An/ Herren von der Mote den Wayer von einem/ unbenandten Meiſter, und gedruckt zu/ Parihs bey Auguſtin kürbe in s./ Anno 1647./ Jetzo aber Deutſch gegäben, und, um deſto fartiger ihn/ zu gebrauchen, unterſchihdlich eingeteihlet/ Von/ Henrich Sivers./ *Hamburg./* In Verlägung Johan Naumans und Jurgen Wolfs./ Gedruckt im Jahr Chriſti/ 1674./ 3 *prel. leaves and* 70 *pp. with* 2 *seq. pp. Copperplate map of Greenland, engraved by J. Wichman. Half Russia.* 4*to*. (15*s*. 2506)

SLADE (WILLIAM). Vermont State Papers; being a Collection of Records and Documents, connected with the Assumption and Establishment of Government by the People of Vermont; together with the Journal of the Council of Safety, the First Constitution, the Early Journals of the General Assembly, and the Laws from the Year 1779 to 1786, inclusive. To which are added the Proceedings of the First and Second Councils of Censors. Compiled and Published by William Slade, Jun: Secretary of State. *Middlebury*: J. W. Copeland, Printer. 1823. *ii and pp*. 9—568. *Calf extra by Bedford.* 8*vo*. (15*s*. 2507)

SMALLEY (John). The Consistency of the Sinner's Inability to comply with the Gospel; with his inexcusable Guilt in not complying with it, illustrated and confirmed: In two Discourses, On John vi[th], 44th. By John Smalley, A. M. Paftor of a· Church in Farmington. *Hartford:* Printed by Green & Watson, near the Great Bridge. m,dcc,lxix. 71 pp. 8vo. (4s. 6d. 2508)

SMITH (Aaron). The Atrocities of the Pirates; being a Faithful Narrative of the Unparalleled Sufferings enduded by the Author during his Captivity among the Pirates of the Island of Cuba; with an account of the excesses and barbarities of those Inhuman Freebooters. By Aaron Smith, (Who was himself afterwards tried at the Old Bailey as a Pirate, and acquitted.) *London:* G. and W. B. Whittaker, 1824. *xi pp. and text 214 pp. Boards.* 12mo. (4s. 6d. 2509)

SMITH (John). A Map of Virginia./ VVith a Descripti-/on of the Covntrey, the/ Commodities, People, Govern-/ment and Religion./ VVritten by Captaine Smith, fometimes Go-/vernour of the Countrey./ Wherevnto is annexed the/ proceedings of thofe Colonies, fince their firft/ departure from England, with the difcourfes,/ Orations, and relations of the Salvages,/ and the accidents that befell/ them in all their Iournies/ and difcoveries./ Taken faithfvlly as they/ were written out of the writings of/ Doctor Rvssell. Richard Wiffin./ Tho. Stvdley. Will. Phetti Place./ Anas Todkill. Nathaniel Povvell./ Ieffra Abot. Richard Pots./ And the relations of divers other diligent obfervers there/ prefent then, and now many of them in England./ By VV[illiam]. S[trackey]. At *Oxford,/* Printed by Jofeph Barnes. 1612./ *4 prel. leaves and 39 pp; Second title and* ' To the Reader ' *2 leaves, and 110 pp. Map of Virginia. Fine copy in blue morocco by Bedford.* 4to. (12l. 12s. 2510)

SMITH (John). The/ Generall Historie/ of/ Virginia, New-England, and the Summer/ Ifles: with the names of the Adventurers,/ Planters, and Governours from their/ firft beginning An°: 1584. to this/ prefent 1624./ With the Procedings. of those Severall Colonies/ and the Accidents that befell them in all their/ Journyes and Difcoveries./ Alfo the Maps and Defcriptions of all thofe/ Countryes, their Commodities, people,/ Government, Cuftomes, and Religion/ yet knowne./ Divided into sixe Bookes./ By Captaine Iohn Smith fometymes Governour/ in thofe Countryes & Admirall./ of New England./ London./ Printed by I. D. and/ I. H. for Michael/ Sparkes./ 1624./ *Engraved title and 6 prel. leaves. Text pp. 1 to 96 and 105 to 248 ; und Errata. With the 4 maps complete. Folio.* (10*l*. 10*s*. 2511)

SMITH (JOHN). A Sea Grammar,/ With/ the Plaine Exposition/ of Smiths Accidence for young/ Sea-men, enlarged./ Diuided into fifteene Chapters : What they are you/ may partly conceive by the Contents. Written by Captaine Iohn Smith, fometimes/ Governour of Virginia, and Admirall of/ New-England./ London,/ Printed by Iohn Haviland,/ 1627./ *6 prel. leaves and text 86 pp.* 4to. (3*l*. 3*s*. 2512)

SMITH (JOHN). The/ True Travels,/ Adventvres,/ and/ Observations/ of/ Captaine Iohn Smith,/ In Europe, Afia, Affrica, and America, from Anno/ Domini 1593. to 1629./ His Accidents and Seafights in the Straights ; his Service/ and Stratagems of warre in Hungaria, Tranfilvania, Wallachia, and/ Moldavia, againft the Turks, and Tartars ; his three fingle combats/ betwixt the Chriftian Armie and the Turkes./ After how he was taken prifoner by the Turks, fold for a Slave, fent into/ Tartaria ; his defcription of the Tartars, their ftrange manners and cuftomes of/ Religions, Diets, Buildings, Warres, Feafts, Ceremonies, and/ Living ; how hee flew the Bafhaw of Nalbrits in Cambia,/ and efcaped from the Turkes and Tartars./ Together with a continuation of his generall Hiftory of Virginia,/ Summer-Iles, New England, and their proceedings, fince 1624. to this/ prefent 1629 ; as alfo of the new Plantations of the great/ River of the Amazons, the Iles of S^t. Chriftopher, Mevis,/ and Barbados in the Weft Indies./ All written by actuall Authours whofe names/ you shall finde along the Hiftory./ London,/ Printed by J. H. for Thomas Slater, and are to bee/ fold at the Blew Bible in Greene Arbour./ 1630./ 6

prel. leaves and 60 *pp. wanting the large copperplate engraving in six compartments. Cloth.*
Folio. (1*l.* 11s. 6d. 2513)

SMITH (John). Advertisements/ For the unexperienced Planters of/ New-England, or any where./ Or,/ The Path-way to experience to erect a/ Plantation./ With the yearely proceedings of this Country in Fiſhing/ and Planting, ſince the yeare 1614. to the yeare 1630./ and their preſent eſtate./ Alſo how to prevent the greateſt inconveniences, by their/ proceedings in Virginia, and other Plantations,/ by approved examples./ With the Countries Armes, a deſcription of the Coaſt,/ Harbours, Habitations, Land-markes, Latitude and/ Longitude: with the Map, allowed by our Royall/ King Charles./ By Captaine Iohn Smith, ſometimes Governour of Virginia, and Admirall of New-England./ *London,*/ Printed by Iohn Haviland, and are to be ſold by/ Robert Milbovrne, at the Grey-hound/ in Pauls Church-yard. 1631./ 4 *prel. leaves and* 40 *pp. Map.* 4*to.* (5*l.* 5s. 2514)

SMITH (John). The/ Generall Historie/ of/ Virginia, New=England, and the Summer/ Iſles: with the names of the Adventurers,/ Planters, and Governours from their/ firſt beginning An°: 1584. to this/ preſent 1626./ With the Procedings of those Severall Colonies/ and the Accidents that befell them in all their/ Journyes and Diſcoveries./ Alſo the Maps and Deſcriptions of all thoſe/ Countryes, their Commodities, people,/ Government, Cuſtomes, and Religion/ yet knowne./ Divided into sixe Bookes./ By Captaine Iohn Smith ſometymes Governour/ in thoſe Countryes & Admirall/ of New England./ *London./* Printed by I. D. and/ I. H. for Edward/ Blackmore/ Anno 1632./ *Engraved frontispiece, and in every other respect the same as the first Edition of* 1624, *with the* 4 *maps.*
Folio. (10*l.* 10s. 2515)

SMITH (John). Reiſen, Entdeckungen und Unternehmungen des Schifs=Capitain Johann Schmidt oder John Smith; welche den wahren Urſprung derer Engliſchen Colonien in Nord=Amerika bewirkt haben, und ihn deutlich vor Augen ſtellen: Erdſtentheils aus deſſelben ligenen Schriften beſchrieben von Carl Friedrich Scheibler, Paſtor zu Hansfelde, Zartzig und Schwend in Preuffifch Pommern. *Berlin,* bei Siegismund Friedrich Heffe. 1782. 232 *pp. and* 1 *leaf of Errata. Half calf.* 8*vo.* (10s. 6d. 2516)

SMITH (JOHN). The Trve Travels, Adventvres and Observations of Captaine Iohn Smith, in Europe, Asia, Africke, and America: Beginning about the yeere 1593, and continued to this present 1629. From the London Edition of 1629. *Richmond:* Republished at the Franklin Press. William W. Gray, Printer. 1819. *Two Volumes.* Vol. I. 7 *prel. leaves and* 247 *pp. Portrait of Smith, plates at pp.* 14, 113, *map at* 149. Vol. II. *Frontispiece; xi and* 282 *pp. Calf.* 8*vo.* (18s. 2517)

SMITH (JOHN). An Authentic Copy of the Minutes of Evidence on the Trial of John Smith, a Missionary, in Demerara; Held at the Colony House, in George Town, Demerara, on Monday, the 13th Day of October, 1823, and 27 following Days; on a Charge of exciting the Negroes to Rebellion; copied verbatim, From a Report as Ordered to be printed, by the House of Commons, 22d of March, 1824. With an Appendix, including The Affidavit of Mrs. Jane Smith, the Petition presented to the House of Commons, from the Directors of the London Missionary Society, Letters of Mr. John Smith. And other interesting Documents. *London:* Samuel Burton, 1824. 179 *pp. Boards.* 8*vo.* (4s. 6d. 2518)

SMITH (JOSHUA HETT). An Authentic Narrative of the causes which led to the death of Major Andrè, Adjutant-General of his Majesty's Forces in North America. By Joshua Hett Smith, Esq. Counsellor at Law, late Member of the Convention of the State of New York. To which is added a Monody on the death of Major Andrè. By Miss Seward. *London:* Mathews and Leigh, 1808. *vii and* 358 *pp. Portrait, map, and plate. Half calf.* 8*vo.* (7s. 6d. 2519)

SMITH (JOSHUA TOULMIN). The Discovery of America by the Northmen in the Tenth Century. By Joshua Toulmin Smith, Author of "Progress of Philosophy among the Ancients;" "Comparative view of ancient History, with explanation of Chronological Eras;" etc. With Two Maps. *London:* Charles Tilt, 1839. *xii and* 344 *pp.* 2 *maps and* 2 *plates.* 8*vo.* (4*s.* 6*d.* 2520)

SMITH (SAMUEL). The History of the Colony of Nova-Cæsaria, or New-Jersey: Containing, an Account of its First Settlement, Progressive Improvements, the Original and present Constitution, and other events, to the Year 1721. With some particulars since; and a short view of its present state. By Samuel Smith. *Burlington, in New-Jersey:* Printed and Sold by James Parker: Sold also by David Hall, in Philadelphia. M,DCC,LXV. *x and* 574 *pp. Fine copy. Old calf.* 8*vo.* (2*l.* 2*s.* 2521)

SMITH (WILLIAM). A New Voyage to Guinea: Describing The Cuſtoms, Manners, Soil, Climate, Habits, Buildings, Education, Manual Arts, Agriculture, Trade, Employments, Languages, Ranks of Diſtinction, Habitations, Diverſions, Marriages, and whatever elſe is memorable among the Inhabitants. Likewise, An Account of their Animals, Minerals, &c. With great Variety of entertaining Incidents, worthy of Obſervation, that happen'd during the Author's Travels in that large Country. Illuſtrated with Cutts, engrav'd from Drawings taken from the Life. With an Alphabetical Index. By William Smith, Eſq; Appointed by the Royal African Company to ſurvey their Settlements, make Diſcoveries, &c. *London:* John Nourse, MDDCXLIV. [1744] *iv and* 276 *pp. Index* 8 *pp. Frontispiece and plates at pp.* 8, 147, 148, 151. *Tree calf.* 8*vo.* (7*s.* 6*d.* 2522)

SMITH (WILLIAM). A Natural History of Nevis, And the reſt of the Engliſh Leeward Charibee Iſlands in America. With many other Obſervations on Nature and Art; Particularly, An Introduction to The Art of Decyphering. In Eleven Letters from the Rev^d Mr. Smith, ſometime Rector of St. John's at Nevis, and now Rector of St. Mary's in Bedford; to the Rev^d Mr. Mason, B.D. Woodwardian Profeſſor, and Fellow of Trinity-College, in Cambridge. *Cambridge:* J. Benthan, MDCCXLV. 3 *prel. leaves (with errata) and* 318 *pp.* 'Index' 9 *pp. Old calf.* 8*vo.* (5*s.* 6*d.* 2523)

SMITH (WILLIAM). Histoire de la Nouvelle-York, depuis la Découverte de cette Province jusqu'a notre Siécle, Dans laquelle on rapporte les démêlés qu'elle a eus avec les Canadiens & les Indiens; les Guerres qu'elle a foutenues contre ces Peuples; les Traités & les Alliances qu'elle a faits avec eux, &c. On y a joint Une Defcription Géographique du Pays, & une Hiftoire Abrégée de fes Habitans, de leur Religion, de leur Gouvernement Civil & Eccléfiaftique, &c. Par William Smith. Traduite de l'Anglois par M. E*** A Londres. M.DCC. LXVII. xvi and 415 pp. old calf. 8vo. (8s. 6d. 2524)

SMITH (WILLIAM). A Sermon On the Present Situation of American Affairs. Preached in Christ-Church. June 23, 1775, At the Requeft of the Officers of the Third Battalion of the City of Philadelphia, and Diftrict of Southwark. By William Smith, D.D. Provost of the College in that City. Philadelphia Printed: London Re-printed, Edward and Charles Dilly. M.DCC.LXXV. 2 prel. leaves, iv and 32 pp. 8vo. (3s. 6d. 2525)

SMITH (WILLIAM). The History of the Province of New-York, from the first discovery. To which is annexed A Defcription of the Country, an Account of the Inhabitants, their Trade, Religious and Political State, and the Conftitution of the Courts of Juftice in that Colony. By William Smith, A.M. London: J. Almon, MDCCLXXVI. viii and 334 pp. Calf extra by Bedford. 8vo. (15s. 2526)

SMITH (WILLIAM). Eulogium on Benjamin Franklin, LL.D. President of the American Philosophical Society, &c. &c. Delivered March 1, 1791, in Philadelphia, before both Houses of Congress, and the American Philosophical Society, &c. By William Smith, D.D. One of the Vice-Prefidents of the faid Society, and Provoft of the College and Academy of Philadelphia. London: T. Cadell, MDCCXCII. Half-title, title, and 39 pp. 8vo. (4s. 6d. 2527)

SMYTH (J. F. D.) A Tour in the United States of America: Containing An Account of the Present Situation of that Country; The Population, Agriculture, Commerce, Customs and Manners of the Inhabitants; Anecdotes of feveral Members of the Congress, and General Officers in the American

Army; and Many other very fingular and interefting Occurrences. With A Defcription of the Indian Nations, the general Face of the Country, Mountains, Forefts, Rivers, and the moft beautiful, grand, and picturefque Views through-out that vaft Continent. Likewise Improvements in Husbandry that may be adopted with great Advantage in Europe. By J. F. D. Smyth, Esq. *London*, G. Robinson, MDCCLXXXIV. *Two Volumes*. Vol. I. 12 *prel. leaves, and* 400 *pp.* Vol. II. 6 *prel. leaves and* 456 *pp.* 8*vo.* (8*s.* 6*d.* 2528)

SNOWDEN (RICHARD). The American Revolution: Written in Scriptural, or, Ancient Historical Style. By Richard Snowden. *Baltimore*: Printed by W. Pechin, No. 10, Second-street. [   ] 360 *pp.* 'The Columbiad; or a Poem on the American War, in Thirteen Cantoes. By Richard Snowden. *Baltimore*: Printed by W. Pechin, No. 10, Second-street.' 44 *pp. Old calf. Small* 8*vo.* (10*s.* 6*d.* 2529)

SOBER Remarks on a Book lately Reprinted at Bofton, Entituled, A Modeft Proof Of the Order and Government fettled by Christ and his Apoftles in the Church. In a Letter to a Friend. The Second Edition. *Boston* in N. E. Printed for Samuel Gerrifh, and Sold at his Shop near the Brick Meeting-Houfe in Cornhill. 1724. 4 *prel. leaves and* 126 *pp.* 8*vo.* (15*s.* 2530)

SOLIS Y RIBADENEYRA (ANTONIO DE). Historia/ de la Conqvista/ de Mexico,/ Poblacion, y Progrefsos/ de la America Septentrional,/ conocida por el nombre/ de/ Nveva Eſpaña./ Escriviala/ Don Antonio de Solis,/ Secretario de fu Mageftad, y su Chronifta/ mayor de las Indias./ Y/ la pone a los pies del/ Rey Nvestro Señor,/ por mano del/ Excelentissimo Señor/ Conde de Oropefa./ En *Madrid*./ En la Imprenta de Bernardo de Villa-Diego, Impreſſor de fu Mageftad./ Año M.DC. LXXXIV./ *First Edition.* 17 *prel. leaves including the engraved title containing the portrait of the Author. Text* 548 *pp.* 'Indice' 15 *pp. old calf. Large Paper. Folio.* (1*l.* 5*s.* 2531)

SOLIS Y RIBADENEYRA (ANTONIO DE). Historia/ de la Conqvista/ de Mexico,/ Poblacion, y Progressos/ de la America Septentrional,/ conocida por el nombre/ de Nveva España./ Escriviala/ Don Antonio de Solis,/ Secretario de sv Magestad, y sv Chronista/ mayor de las Indias,/ Dedicase al Illvstrissimo Señor/ Don Gvillen de Rocafvll/ y Rocaberti, por la gracia de Dios vizconde/ de Rocaberti, Conde de Peralada, y de Albatera, &c./ Año 1691./ *Barcelona*./ En la Imprenta de Ioseph Llopis, Impreffor de Libros; y à fu cofta./ Vendefe en fu Cafa, en la calle de Santo Domingo./ 10 *prel. leaves and text* 548 *pp*. 'Indice' 15 *pp*. *Old calf*. Folio. (15s. 2532)

SOLIS Y RIBADENEYRA (Antonio de). Histoire/ De la Conqnête du/ Mexique,/ Ou de la Nouvelle/ Espagne./ Par Fernand Cortez./ Traduite de l'Efpagnol de Don/ Antonio de Solis,/ par l'Auteur du Triumvirat./ A la *Haye*,/ Chez Adrian Moetjens,/ Marchand Libraire prés la Cour, à la/ Libraire Françoife./ M.DC.XCII./ *Two Volumes*. Tom. I. 18 *prel. leaves and* 412 *pp*. 'Table.' 15 *pp. Copperplates at pp*. 1, 35, 44, 184, 341, 342, 344, 345, 350, 365, 409. Tome II. 6 *prel. leaves and* 378 *pp*. 'Table' 15 *pp. Copperplates at pp*. 176, 336, 371. 12mo. (10s. 6d. 2533)

SOLIS Y RIBADENEYRA (Antonio de). Histoire de la Conquête du Mexique, ou de la Nouvelle Espagne, par Fernand Cortez, Traduite de l'Efpagnol de Dom Antoine de Solis, par l'Auteur du Triumvirat. *A Paris*, Par la Compagnie des Libraires. M.DCC.IV. *Two Volumes*. Tome I. 18 *prel. leaves and* 412 *pp*. 'Table' 20 *pp. Copperplate Map and plates at pp*. 1, 35, 44, 184, 341, 345, 346, 348, 365, 408. Tome II. 6 *prel. leaves and* 380 (379) *pp*. 'Table' 15 *pp. Plates at pp*. 177, 243, 336, 372. *Old calf. Small 8vo*. (7s. 6d. 2534)

SOLIS Y RIBADENEYRA (Antonio de). Historia de la Conqvista de Mexico, Poblacion, y Progressos de la America Septentrional, conocida por el Nombre de Nueva España, escriviala Don Antonio de Solis, Secretario de fu Mageftad, y fu Choronifta mayor de las Indias. Dedicada al Excelentissimo Señor Don Joseph de Solis Val-Derrabano Pacheo Giron Guzman y Luzon, Cavallero del Abito de Santiago, Conde de Montellano, Adelantado de la Provincia de Yucatan, Governador del Confejo Real de Caftilla, &c. Con Privilegio:

En *Madrid*: Antonio Gonçalez de Reyes. 1704. 12 *prel. leaves and text* 352 *pp.* ' Indice,' 15 *pp.* *Folio.* (15s. 2535)

SOLIS Y RIBADENEYRA (Antonio de). Histoire de la Conqueste du Mexique, ou de la Nouvelle Espagne, par Fernand Cortez, Traduite de l'Efpagnol de Dom Antoine de Solis, par l'Auteur du Triumvirat. Quatrie'me Edition, A *Paris*, Par la Compagnie des Libraires. MDCCXIV. *Two Volumes.* Tome 1. 17 *prel. leaves and text* 537 *pp. Table* 19 *pp. Map and plates at pp.* 1, 43, 243, 412, 435, 447, 452, 454, 476. 534. Tome II. 7 *prel. leaves and text* 494 *pp. Table* 15 *pp.* ' Privilege du Roy.' *3 pp. Plates at pp.* 229, 435, 485. *Old calf. Small 8vo.* (7s. 6d. 2536)

SOLIS Y RIBADENEYRA (Antonio de). The History of the Conqueft of Mexico by the Spaniards. Done into English from the Original Spanish of Don Antonio de Solis, Secretary and Hiftoriographer to His Catholick Majefty. By Thomas Townsend, Efq; *London*: T. Woodward, M.DCC. XXIV. *Portrait of Cortes.* 9 *prel. leaves, Text, Books* 1 *and* 2, 163 *pp. Plate and Map at pp.* 1 *and* 31. *Books* 3 *and* 4, 252 *pp. Plates at pp.* 50, 69, 70, 72. *Book* 5, 152 *pp. Plates at pp.* 124 *and* 146. *Old calf. Folio.* (10s. 6d. 2537)

SOLIS Y RIBADENEYRA (Antonio de). The History of the Conqueft of Mexico by the Spaniards. Done into English from the Original Spanish of Don Antonio de Solis, Secretary and Hiftoriographer to His Catholick Majefty. By Thomas Townsend, Efq; Illuftrated with Copper Plates. *Dublin*: S. Powell, MDCCXXVII. *Two Volumes.* Vol. I. 18 *prel. leaves and pp.* 25-455. *Plates at pp.* 383, 396, 417, 422. Vol. II. *Title and pp.* 457-970. *With map. Old calf. 12mo.* (7s. 6d. 2538)

SOLIS Y RIBADENEYRA (Antonio de). Histoire de la Conqueste du Mexique ou de la Nouvelle Espagne, par Fernand Cortez, Traduite de l'Efpagnol de Dom Antoine de Solis, par l'Auteur du Triumvirat. Cinquième Edition. A *Paris*, Par la Compagnie des Libraires. M.DCC.XXX. *Two Volumes.* Tome 1. 16 *prel. leaves and* 606 *pp. Table and Privilege* 26 *pp. Map and Plates at pp.* 1, 49,

62, 274, 466, 504, 505, 511, 514, 528. Tome II. 6 prel. leaves and 560 pp. Table 22 pp. Plates at pp. 261, 494, 549. Old calf. Small 8vo. (7s. 6d. 2539)

SOLIS Y RIBADENEYRA (ANTONIO DE). The History of the Conquest of Mexico by the Spaniards. Tranflated into English from the Original Spanish of Don Antonio de Solis, Secretary and Historiographer To His Catholick Majesty, By Thomas Townsend, Efq; Late Lieutenant Colonel in Brig. Gen. Newton's Regiment. The whole Tranflation Revised and Corrected By Nathanael Hooke, Efq; Tranflator of The Travels of Cyrus, and The Life of the Archbishop of Cambray. *London:* T. Woodward, and H. Lintot, MDCCXXXVIII. Two Volumes. Vol. I. 3 prel. leaves, r and 479 pp. Portrait of Cortes: Plates at pp. 1, 52, 359, 393, 4, 398. Vol. II. xii and 475 pp. Plates at pp. 430, 465. Old calf. 8vo. (7s. 6d. 2540)

SOLIS Y RIBADENEYRA (ANTONIO DE). *Another copy, the same as above, Printed for* 'John Osborn.' (7s. 6d. 2541)

SOLIS Y RIBADENEYRA (ANTONIO DE). The History of the Conquest of Mexico by the Spaniards. Tranflated from the Original Spanish of Don Antonio de Solis, Secretary and Hiftoriographer to His Catholick Majefty, By Thomas Townsend, Efq; The whole Tranflation Revifed and Corrected By Nathanael Hooke, Efq; Author of The Roman History, &c. The Third Edition. *London:* H. Lintot; J. Whiston and B. White. MDCCLIII. Two Volumes. Vol. I. xvi and 384 pp. Portrait of Cortes and Plates at pp. 1, 17, 290, 318, 321. Vol. II. x and 386 pp. Plates at pp. 317 and 377. Boards. 8vo. ·(7s. 6d. 2542)

SOLIS Y RIBADENEYRA (ANTONIO DE). Histoire de la Conquête du Mexique, ou de la Nouvelle Espagne. Par Fernand Cortez, Traduite de l'Efpagnol de Dom Antoine de Solis, par l'Auteur du Triumvirat. Sixième Edition. A *Paris,* M. DCC. LIX. Two Volumes. Tome I. xxxi and 606 pp. Table and Privilege 26 pp. Map and plates at pp. 1, 49, 274, 504, 5, 511, 514, 529. Tome II. 6 prel. leaves and 560 pp. Table 22 pp. Plates at pp. 261, 494, 549. Old calf. Small 8vo. (7s. 6d. 2543)

SOLIS Y RIBADENEYRA (Antonio de). Historia de la Conquista de Mexico, Poblacion, y Progressos de la America Septentrional, conocida por el nombre de Nueva España. Escrivala Don Antonio de Solis y Rivadeneyra, Secretario de fu Mageftad, y fu Chronifta Mayor de las Indias. En *Madrid*, Juan de San Martin. 1763. 12 *prel. leaves and* 476 *pp. Vellum.* 4*to.* (10s. 6d. 2544)

SOLIS Y RIBADENEYRA (Antonio de). Historia de la Conquista de Mexico, Poblacion, y Progressos de la America Septentrional, conocida por el nombre de Nueva España. Escriviala Don Antonio de Solis y Rivadeneyra, Secretario de su Magestad, y su Chronista Mayor de las Indias. En *Madrid;* Don Antonio Mayoral. 1768. 12 *prel. leaves and* 549 *pp. Vellum.* 4*to.* (10s. 6d. 2545)

SOLIS Y RIBADENEYRA (Antonio de). Historia de la Conquista de Mexico, Poblacion, y Progresos de la America Septentrional, conocida por el Nombre de Nueva España. Escribiala Don Antonio de Solis y Ribadeneyra, Secretario de su Magestad, y su Cronista Mayor de las Indias. Dividida en dos Tomos, e Ilustrada con Laminas finas. Con las licentias Necesarias. *Barcelona:* Por Thomas Piferrer. 1771. *Two Volumes.* Tomo I. 12 *prel. leaves and* 479 *pp. Map and plates at pp.* 1, 48, 390, 395, 397, 464. Tomo II. 6 *prel. leaves and* 488 *pp. Plates at pp.* 199, 264. 8*vo.* (10s. 6d. 2546)

SOLIS Y RIBADENEYRA (Antonio de). Historia de la Conquista de Mexico, poblacion y progresos de la America Septentrional, conocida por el nombre de Nueva España. Escribiala D. Antonio de Solis y Rivadeneyra, Secretario de su Magestad, y su Chronista Mayor de las Indias. En *Madrid,* D. Antonio Fernandez. 1790. 10 *prel. leaves and* 549 *pp. Old calf.* 4*to.* (10s. 6d. 2547)

SOLIS Y RIBADENEYRA (Antonio de). Historia de la Conquista de Mexico, Poblacion, y Progresos de la América Septentrional, conocida por el Nombre de Nueva-España. Escribiala Don Antonio de Solis, Secretario de su Magestad, y Cronista mayor de las Indias. Dividida en Tres Tomos. *Madrid:* mdccxci. Don Placido Barco

Lopez. *Three Volumes.* Tomo I. 16 prel. *leaves and* 357 pp. *Indice* 9 pp. Tomo II. 2 prel. *leaves and* 500 pp. Tomo III. 2 prel. *leaves and* 364 pp. *Small* 8vo. (10s. 6d. 2548)

SOLORZANO PEREIRA (Juan de). [*Engraved title*] Politica Indiana/ de/ el D^or. D. Jvan de Solorzano/ Pereira Cavallero del Orden de/ Santiago, del Confejo del Rey/ N. S^r. elos Supremos de Cas/tilla y de la/ Indias/ Dirigida/ Al Rey Nvestro S^r,/ en fu Real y Supremo Confejo/ de las Indias/ por mano del Exmo./ S^r. Conde de Castrillo/ Prefidente delmefmo/ Confejo &c./ Con Privilegio en Madrid en la Officina/ de Diego diaz de la Carrera/ An'o de 1647./ [*Printed title*] Politica Indiana./ Sacada en Lengva Castellana de/ los dos tomos del derecho, i govierno mvnicipal/ de las Indias Occidentales qve mas copiosamente/ escribio en la Latina./ El Dotor Don Ivan de Solorzano Pereira/ caballero del orden de Santiago, del/ Confejo del Rey Nueftro Señor en los Supremos/ de Caftilla, i de las Indias./ Por el Mesmo Avtor,/ Dividida en feis Libros./ En los qvales con gran distincion, i estvdio/ fe trata, i refuelve todo lo tocante al Defcubrimiento, Defcripcion, Adqui-/ficion, i Retencion de las mefmas Indias, i fu govierno particular, afsi cerca/ las Perfonas de los Indios, i fus Servicios, Tributos, Diezmos, i Encomien-/das, como de lo Efpiritual, i Eclefiaftico, cerca de fu Dotrina, Patronazgo/ Real, Iglefias, Prelados, Prebendados, Curas Seculares, i Regulares, Inqui-/fidores, Comiffarios de Cruzada, i de las Religiones. I en lo Temporal, cerca/ de todos los Magiftrados feculares, Virreyes, Prefidentes, Audiencias,/ Confejo Supremo, i Iunta de Guerra dellas, con infercion, i/ declaracion de las muchas cedulas Reales que/ para efto fe han defpachado./ Añadidas/ mvchas cosas, que no estan en los tomos/ Latinos, i en particular todo el Libro Sexto, que en diez i fiete Capitulos trata de/ la Hazienda Real de las Indias, Regalias, Derechos, i Miembros de que fe/ compone, i del modo en que fe adminiftra; i de los Oficiales/ Reales, Tribunales de Cuentas, i Cafa de la/ Contratacion de Sevilla./ Obra de svmo trabaio, i de igval importancia,/ i utilidad, no folo para los de las Provincias de las Indias, fino de las de Efpa-/ña, i otras Naciones, de qualquier Profefsion que fean, por la gran va-/riedad de cofas que comprehende, adornada de todas/ letras, i efcrita con el metodo, claridad,/ i lenguaje que por ella/ parecerà./ Con dos Indices muy diftintos, i copiofos, uno de los Libros, i Capitulos en que fe/ divide : i otro de las cofas notables que contiene./ Con Privilegio,/ En *Madrid*. Por Diego Diaz de la Carrera./ Año M.DC. XLVIII./ 24 *prel. leaves* ; *viz. Engraved and printed titles* 2 *leaves* ; ' Censvra del Señor *etc.* Licencias ' *etc.* 2 *leaves*; ' Al Rei Nro Sor Don Felipe IV.' *etc.* 7 *leaves* ; ' Al Excelentissimo Señor Don Garcia de Haro i Avellaneda,' *etc.* 3 *leaves* ; *copperplate engraved portrait*, 1 *leaf* ; ' Al Retrato del Autor defte libro.' *etc.* 1 *leaf* ; ' Al Lector.' 3 *leaves* ; 'Indice de los Libros,' *etc.* 5 *leaves* : *Text* 1040 *pp*. ' Indice mvy Copioso ' *etc.* 52 *leaves*. *Vellum. Fine copy. Folio.* (1*l.* 1*s.* 2549)

SOLORZANO PEREIRA (JUAN DE). D. D. Ioannis/ de Solorzano/ Pereira,/ I.V. D. ex eqvestri Militia/ D. Iacobi, et in supremis Castellæ,/ & Indiarum Confiliis Senatoris ;/ de Indiarum Ivre ;/ sive/ de jvsta Indiarum Occidentalium/ Inquifitione, Acquifitione, & Retentione./ Cui acceffit alia ejusdem avthoris/ Difputatio de Parricidii Crimine./ Cum duplici Indice, primo Librorum & Capitum ; altero Rerum notabilium abfolutiffimo./ Editio nouiffima ab innumeris, quibus priores deformatæ erant mendis emaculata./ *Lugduni,*/ Sumptibus Lavrentii Anisson./ M.DC.LXXII./ Cvm Svperiorvm Permissu./ *Two Volumes*. Tomvs Primvs. 12 *prel. leaves and* 438 *pp. Indexes* 44 *leaves ; followed by* 64 *pp. of text, and* 8 *leaves of Index.* Tomvs Secvndvs. 6 *prel. leaves, and* 858 *pp. Index* 71 *leaves. Folio.* (10*s.* 6*d.* 2550)

SOME Account of the North-America Indians; their Genius, Charaƈters, Cuftoms, and Difpofitions, towards the French and Englifh Nations. To which are added, Indian Miscellanies, viz. 1. The Speech of a Creek-Indian againft the immoderate Ufe of Spirituous Liquors; delivered in a National Affembly of the Creeks, upon the breaking out of the late War. 2. A Letter from Yariza, an Indian Maid of the Royal Line of the Mohawks, to the principal Ladies of New-York. 3. Indian

Songs of Peace. 4. An American Fable. Collected by a learned and ingenious Gentleman in the Province of Penfylvania. *London:* R. Griffiths, [1754] 68 pp. *Half mor. 8vo.* (10s. 6d. 2551)

SOME Remarks on a Pamphlet, call'd, Reflections, on the Conftitution and Management of the Trade to Africa, Demonstrating the Author's abufive Afperfions therein contained, to be ill-Grounded, the Matters of Fact wrong Reprefented, and the late Management of that Trade fet in a True Light. With An Account, of the Needful Charge of the Britifh Settlements in Africa; in what manner they may be beft Maintain'd, and the Trade carry'd on to the Benefit of this Nation, and our Plantations in America. [*London*] Printed in the Year, MDCCIX. 32 pp. *Half mor. 8vo.* (4s. 6d. 2552)

SOME Considerations on the Consequences Of the French Settling Colonies on the Mississippi, With refpect to the Trade and Safety of the English Plantations in America and the Weft-Indies. From a Gentleman of America, to his Friend in London. *London:* J. Roberts, 1720. *Half-title, title, and* 60 pp. *With map. Half mor. 8vo.* (7s. 6d. 2553)

SOME Observations on the Affiento Trade, As it has been Exercifed by the South-Sea Company; proving the Damage Which will accrue thereby to the Britifh Commerce and Plantations in America, And particularly to Jamaica. To which is annexed A Sketch of the Advantages of that Ifland to Great Britain, by its annual Produce, and by its Situation for Trade or War. Addressed to His Grace the Duke of Newcastle, One of his Majefty's Principal Secretaries of State. By a Perfon who refided feveral Years at Jamaica. *London:* H. Whitridge, MDCCXXVIII. *iv and text* 38 pp. *Half morocco. 8vo.* (5s. 6d. 2554)

SOME Observations on Extracts taken out of the Report from the Lords-Commiffioners for Trade and Plantations. [*London*, 1730] 4 pp. *folded and bound in calf. Folio.* (8s. 6d. 2555)

SOME Considerations Humbly offer'd upon the Bill Now depending in the Houfe of Lords, Relating to the Trade between the Northern Colonies and the Sugar-Iflands. In a Letter to a Noble Peer. [*London*], MDCCXXXII. 19 *pp. Half morocco.* 8*vo.* (4*s.* 6*d.* 2556)

SOME Fruits of Solitude, in Reflections and Maxims, Relating to the Conduct of Human Life. In Two Parts. The Eight Edition. *Newport*, Rhode-Ifland: Printed by James Franklin, at the Town-School-Houfe, 1749. 6 *prel. leaves and* 158 *pp. Table 7 pp.* 'More Fruits of Solitude: Being The Second Part of Reflections and Maxims, Relating to the Conduct of Human Life. *Newport*, Rhode Ifland: Printed by James Franklin, at the Town School-Houfe, 1749.' 3 *prel. leaves: imperfect, wanting all after page* 106. 12*mo.* (10*s.* 6*d.* 2557)

SOME Observations on the Bill, Intitled, "An Act for granting to His Majefty an Excife upon Wines, and Spirits diftilled, fold by Retail or confumed within this Province, and upon Limes, Lemons, and Oranges." *Boston:* Printed in the Year, 1754. *Title and text* 12 *pp. Half morocco. Small* 8*vo.* (2*l.* 2*s.* 2558)

SOME Hints to People in Power, on the Prefent Melancholy Situation of our Colonies in North America. *London:* J. Hinxman MDCCLXIII. *Half morocco.* 48 *pp.* 8*vo.* (5*s.* 6*d.* 2559)

SOME Thoughts on the Method Of Improving and Securing the Advantages which accrue to Great-Britain from the Northern Colonies. *London:* J. Wilkie, MDCCLXV. 23 *pp. Half morocco.* 8*vo.* (4*s.* 6*d.* 2560)

SOME Important Observations, Occafioned by, and adapted to, The Publick Fast, Ordered by Authority, December 18th, A.D. 1765. On Account of the Peculiar Circumstances of the prefent Day. Now humbly offered to the Publick, By the Author. *Newport:* Printed and fold by Samuel Hall. 1766. *Half-title, title, and pp.* 3—61. *Half mor.* 4*to.* (10*s.* 6*d.* 2561)

SOME Candid Suggestions towards Accommodation of Differences with America. Offered to Consideration of the Public. *London:* T. Cadell, MDCCLXXV. 33 *pp. Half mor.* 8*vo.* (4*s.* 6*d.* 2562)

SOME Reasons for approving of the Dean of Gloucester's Plan, of separating from the Colonies; with a Proposal for a further Improvement. *London:* N. Conant, M.DCC.LXXV. 32 *pp. Half morocco. 8vo.* (4s. 6d. 2563)

SOME Seasonable Observations and Remarks upon The State of our Controversy with Great Britain; And on the Proceedings of the Continental Congress: Whereby many interefting Facts are related, and Methods propofed for our fafety and an Accommodation. By a Moderate Whig. *America:* Printed and fold in the Year MDCCLXXV. 14 *pp. Half morocco. 8vo.* (7s. 6d. 2564)

SOME Transactions between the Indians and Friends in Pennsylvania, In 1791 & 1792. *London:* James Phillips, MDCCXCII. 14 *pp. Half morocco. 8vo.* (3s. 6d. 2565)

SOME Considerations on this question; Whether the British Government acted wisely in granting to Canada her present constitution? With an Appendix; containing Documents, &c. By a British Settler. *Montreal:* Printed and Sold by J. Brown/ No. 20, St. François Xavier Street. 1810. 26 *pp. Half morocco. 8vo.* (4s. 6d. 2566)

SOME Account of the conduct of the Religious Society of Friends towards the Indian Tribes in the Settlement of the Colonies of East and West Jersey and Pennsylvania: with a brief narrative of their labours for the Civilization and Christian Instruction of the Indians, from the time of their settlement in America, to the year 1843. Published by the Aborigines Committee of The Meeting for Sufferings. *London:* Edward Marsh, 1844. 2 *prel. leaves and text* 247 *pp. With two coloured maps. 8vo.* (4s. 6d. 2567)

SOMER-ISLANDS. A True/ Relation/ of the/ Illegal Proceedings/ of the/ Somer-Islands-Company/ in their/ Courts at London./ And the like done by their Governour/ Sir John Heydon, Knight, and his Council, in the/ Somer-Islands./ In all Humility prefented to the Honourable Knights,/ Citizens and Burgeffes Affembled in Parliament./ Craving from them to be Relieved from the following/ Oppressions./ *London:* Printed in the

Year 1678./ *Title, the reverse blank;* 'Contents' *on* A 2, 1 page, *the reverse blank ; Text pp.* 1 *to* 12 ; *Contents* 1 *page, the recto blank ; continuation of text* (A 2) *pp.* 13 *to* 26. *Calf extra by Bedford.*
4to. (2l. 2s. 2568)

SOTO (FERNANDO DE). A/ Relation/ of the/ Invafion and Conqueſt/ of/ Florida/ by the/ Spaniards Under the Command of/ Fernando de Soto./ Written in Portuguele by a Gentleman/ of the Town of Elvas./ Now Englished./ To which is Subjoyned Two Journeys of the/ prefent Emperour of China into Tartary/ in the Years 1682, and 1683./ With fome Difcoveries made by the Spaniards in/ the Iſland of California, in the Year 1683./ *London:* Printed for John Lawrence, at the Angel in the Poultry/ over againſt the Compter. 1686./ 7 *prel. leaves and* 272 *pp. Calf.* 8vo. (1l. 1s. 2570)

SOTWEED REDIVIVUS: Or the Planters Looking-Glafs. In Burlefque Verfe. Calculated for the Meridian of Maryland. By E. C. Gent. *Annapolis:* Printed by William Parks, for the Author. M.DCC.XXX. *viii and text* 28 *pp. Half morocco.*
4to. (15s. 2571)

SOULES (FRANÇOIS). Histoire des Troubles de L'Amérique Anglaise, Ecrite fur les Mémoires les plus authentiques; Dédiée a sa Majesté Très-Chrétienne; Par François Soulés. Avec des Cartes. A *Paris,* Buisson, 1787. *Three Volumes.* Tome Premier. 4 *prel. leaves and* 379 *pp.* Tome Second. *Half-title, title, and* 365 *pp.* Tome Troisième. *Half-title, title, and* 420 *pp.* 8vo. (10s. 6d. 2572)

SOUSA COUTINHO (FRANCISCO DE). Propoſitie/ Ghedaen/ Ter Vergaderinge van hare Hoogh Mog. d'Hee-/ren Staten Generael der Vereenigde Neder-/landen, In's Graven-Hage den 16 Au-/guſti, 1647./ Door den Heer/ Francisco de Sousa Coutinho,/ Raedt van ſijn Coninckl. Majeſt. van/ Portvgal: Sijnen Gouverneur ende Capiteyn Ghenerael van de/ Vlaemſche Eylanden./ Geno emt/ Met den ſelven Tijtel van den Staet van Braſil./ Ende/ Ambaſſadeur by Hare Hoogh Moogende./ Gedruckt, Anno 1647./ 4 *leaves. Calf by Hayday.* 4to. (10s. 6d. 2573)

SOUTH CAROLINA. A True State of the Cafe between the Inhabitants of South Carolina, and the Lords Proprietors of that Province; containing an Account of the Grievances under which they labour. 4 pp. Folio. (7s. 6d. 2574)

SOUTH CAROLINA. A New and Accurate Account of the Provinces of South-Carolina and Georgia: With many curious and ufeful Obfervations on the Trade, Navigation and Plantations of Great-Britain, compared with her moft powerful maritime Neighbours in antient and modern Times. London, J. Worrall, 1732. Half-title, title, and 76 pp. Half morocco. 8vo. (10s. 6d. 2575)

SOUTH CAROLINA. A New and Accurate Account of the Provinces of South-Carolina and Georgia: With many curious and ufeful Obfervations on the Trade, Navigation and Plantations of Great-Britain, compared with her moft powerful maritime Neighbours in antient and modern Times. London: J. Worrall, 1733. Half-title, title, and 76 pp. 8vo. (10s. 6d. 2576)

SOUTH CAROLINA. An Historical Account of the Rise and Progress Of the Colonies of South Carolina and Georgia. In Two Volumes. Alexander Donaldson, London. M.DCC.LXXIX. Two Volumes. Vol. I. xiv and 347 pp. Vol. II. ix and 329 pp. Calf. 8vo. (16s. 6d. 2577)

SOUTHERNE (THOMAS). Oroonoko:/ A/Tragedy/ As it is Acted at the/ Theatre=Royal,/ By His Majesty's Servants./ Written by Tho. Southerne./ London:/ Printed for H. Playford in the Temple=Change. B. Tooke/ at the Middle=Temple=Gate. And S. Buckley at the/ Dolphin againft St. Dunftan's Church in Fleetftreet./ MDCXCVI./ 4 prel. leaves and 84 pp. 'Epiloge.' 2 pp. Half morocco. 4to. (7s. 6d. 2578)

SPAFFORD (HORATIO GATES). A Gazetteer of the State of New-York; carefully written from original and authentic materials arranged on a new plan, In Three Parts: Comprising, First—A comprehensive geographical and statistical view of the whole state, conveniently disposed under separate heads: Second—An ample general view of each county, in alphabetical order, with topographical and statistical tables, showing the civil and political divisions, population, post-offices, &c: Third—A very full and minute topographical description of each town or township, city, borough, village, &c. &c. In the whole state, Alphabetically arranged; as also its lakes, rivers, creeks, with every other subject of topographical detail; forming a complete Gazetteer or Geographical Dictionary of the State of New York. With an accurate Map of the State. By Horatio Gates Spafford, A.M. Author of a Geography of the United States, a Member of the New-York Historical Society, and a Corresponding Secretary of the Society of Arts. *Albany:* Printed and published by H. C. Southwick, No. 94, State-Street. 1813. 334 *pp. Appendix, ii pp.* 8vo. (4s. 6d. 2579)

SPANIARDS/ (The)/ Cruelty and Treachery to the/ English/ In the time of/ Peace and War,/ Discovered,/ Being the Council of a Perfon of/ Honour to King James, then upon Treaty/ of Peace with them, for to infift upon a/ Free Trade in the Weft-Indies/ With fome Expedients for the fub-/jecting of the Spaniard in America, to/ the Obedience of England./ Now tendred to the Confideration of His Highnefs/ The Lord Protector, and his Council./ *London./* Printed by J. M. for Lodowick Lloyd and are to be fold at his/ Shop, at the Sign of the Caftle in Cornhil, 1656./ *2 prel. leaves, viz. Title and Dedication, signed* ' D. K.' *Text 56 pp. Half morocco.* 4to. (1l. 1s. 2580)

SPANISH AMERICA. Observations on the present state of Spanish America, and on the most effectual method of terminating the present commotions there. By a Spaniard, a Lover of his Country. Translated from the Spanish. *London:* R. Wilks, 1817. *Title, and text 45 pp. Half morocco.* 8vo. (3s. 6d. 2581)

SPANISH EMPIRE (The) in America. Containing, A fuccinct Relation of the Difcovery and Settlement of its feveral Colonies; a View of their refpective Situations, Extent, Commodities, Trade, &c. And A full and clear Account of the Commerce with Old Spain by the Galleons, Flota, &c. Also of the Contraband Trade with the English,

Dutch, French, Danes, and Portuguefe. With An exact Defcription of Paraguay. By an English Merchant. *London:* M. Cooper. 1747. 6 *prel. leaves and* 330 *pp. Old calf.* 8*vo.* (10s. 6d.   2582)

SPARKS (JARED). The Library of American Biography. Conducted By Jared Sparks. *Boston:* Hilliard, Gray, and Co. London: Richard James Kennett. 1834—9. *Ten Volumes, original Editions.* 12*mo.* (1*l.* 11s. 6d.   2583)

SPECIMEN (A) of Naked Truth, from a British Sailor, A fincere Wellwifher, to the Honour, and Profperity of the prefent Royal Family, and his Country. *London:* W. Webb, MDCCXLVI. 30 *pp. Half morocco.* 8*vo.* (4s. 6d.   2584)

SPEECH (THE) of a Creek-Indian, against the Immoderate Use of Spirituous Liquors. Delivered In a National Affembly of the Creeks upon the breaking out of the late War. To which are added, 1. A Letter from Yariza, an Indian Maid of the Royal Line of the Mohawks, to the principal Ladies of New York. 2. Indian Songs of Peace. 3. An American Fable. Together with Some Remarks upon the Characters and Genius of the Indians, and upon their Cuftoms and Ceremonies at making War and Peace. *London:* R. Griffiths, M.DCC.LIV. 68 *pp.* 8*vo.* (*See* 2551)   (7s. 6d.   2585)

SPEECH (THE) of Mr. P------ And feveral others, In a certain auguft Affembly On a late important Debate: With an Introduction of the Matters preceding it. [*London*] Printed in the Year —66. [1766] *Title and pp.* 5—34. *Unbound.* 8*vo.* (4s. 6d.   2586)

SPEECH (A) intended to have been spoken on the Bill for altering the Charters of the Colony of Massachusett's Bay. [By Dr. Shipley Bishop of St. Asaph.] *London:* T. Cadell, MDCCLXXIV. *vii and* 36 *pp. Half morocco.* 8*vo.* (4s. 6d.   2587)

SPEECH (A) intended to have been spoken on the Bill for altering the Charters of the Colony of Massachusett's Bay. The Second Edition. *London:* T. Cadell, MDCCLXXIV. *vii and* 36 *pp. Half morocco.* 8*vo.* (3s. 6d.   2588)

SPEECH (A) intended to have been spoken on the

Bill for altering the Charters of the Colony of Massachusett's-Bay. The Fourth Edition. *London:* T. Cadell, M DCC LXXIV. *vii and 36 pp. Half morocco. 8vo.* (3s. 6d. 2589)

SPEECH (A) intended to have been spoken on the Bill for altering the Charters of the Colony of Massachusett's Bay. The Sixth Edition. London, Printed. *Boston:* Reprinted, and Sold by Edes and Gill, in Queen-Street. M.DCC.LXXIV. *24 pp. Half morocco. 8vo.* (4s. 6d. 2590)

SPEECH (A) never intended to be Spoken, in answer to a Speech intended to have been Spoken on the Bill for altering the Charter of the Colony of Massachusett's Bay. Dedicated to the Right Reverend The Lord Bishop of St. A——. *London:* J. Knox, MDCCLXXIV. *iv and 34 pp. Errata 1 page. Half morocco. 8vo.* (4s. 6d. 2591)

SPEECH (A) never intended to be Spoken, in answer to a Speech intended to have been Spoken on the Bill for altering the Charter of the Colony of Massachusett's Bay. Dedicated to the Right Reverend The Lord Bishop of St. A——. *London:* J. Knox, MDCCLXXIV. *iv and 35 pp. Half morocco. 8vo.* (4s. 6d. 2591*)

SPEECH (THE) of a Scots Weaver: Dedicated to Richard Glover, Efq. *London:* W. Nicoll, MDCCLXXIV. *65 pp. At the end of the Dedication signed* 'Thermopilæ.' *Half morocco. 8vo.* (4s. 6d. 2592)

SPEECH (A) intended to have been delivered in the House of Commons in Support of the Petition from the General Congress at Philadelphia. By the Author of an Appeal to the Justice and Interests of Great-Britain. *London:* M.DCC.LXXV. *Half-title, title, and 67 pp. Half mor. 8vo.* (4s. 6d. 2593)

SPEECH (A) on some Political Topics, The substance of which Was intended to have been Delivered in the House of Commons, On Monday the 14th of December, 1778, When the Estimates of the Army were agreed to in the Committee of Supply. *London:* T. Cadell, MDCCLXXIX. *4 prel. leaves and 71 pp. Half mor. 8vo.* (4s. 6d. 2594)

SPEILBERGEN (JORIS VAN). Ooft ende Weft-Indifche/ Spieghel/ Waer in Befchreven werden de twee laetfte Na=/vigatien, ghedaen inde Jaeren 1614.1615.1616.1617. ende 1618. De/ eene door den vermaerden Zee-Helt Ioris van Speilbergen door de/ Strate van Magallanes, ende foo rondtom den gantfchen Aerdt-/Cloot, met alle de Batallien foo te Water als te Lande ghefchiet./ Hier fyn mede by ghevoecht tvvee Hiftorien, de eene vande Oost ende de andere vande West-/Indien, met het ghetal der Schepen, Forten, Soldaten ende Gefchut./ De andere ghedaen by Iacob le Maire, de welcke in't Zuyden/ de Straet Magellanes, een nieuwe Straet ontdeckt heeft, met de Befchrijvinghe/ aller Landen, Volcken ende Natien. Alles verciert met fchoone Caerten ende figueren hier toe dienftelijck./ *'t Amstelredam./* By Jan Janffz, Boeckvercooper op't Water inde Pas-Caert./ Ao. M. DC. XXI./ *4 prel. leaves and pp. 9-192. Copperplates numbered 2-18, and 20-25. Vellum. Oblong 4to.* (2l. 2s. 2595)

SPENCER (Thomas). A True and Faithful/ Relation/ of the/ Proceedings/ of the/ Forces of Their Majesties/ K. William and Q. Mary,/ In their Expedition againft the French,/ in the/ Caribby Iflands/ in the/ West-Indies :/ Under the Conduct of His Excellency Chriftopher/ Codrington, Captain General and Comman-/der in Chief of the faid Forces,/ In the Years 1689. and 1690./ Written by Thomas Spencer, Jun. Secretary to/ the Honourable Sir Timothy Thornhil Baronet, to whofe Re-/giment he was Mufter-Mafter, and fupplied the Place of/ Commiffary./ *London,* Printed for Robert Clavel at the Peacock, at the Weft-/End of St. Paul's Church-yard, 1691./ *Reverse of title blank; Dedication to Admiral Edward Russell,* 2 *pages. Text* 12 *pp. in very close type. Fine copy.* 4to.   (1l. 11s. 6d.   2596)

SPITILLI (Gaspar). Brevis et/ Compendiosa Nar-/ratio Missionvm Qva-/rvndam Orientis et/ Occidentis./ Excerpta ex quibufdam litteris a PP. Petro/ Martinez Prouinciali Indiæ Orientalis, P./ Ioanne de Atienza Prouinciali Peruanæ, P. Pietro Diaz Prouinciali Mexcicanæ Pro-/uinciarum, datis anno 1590 & 1591. Ad/ Reueren. P. Generalem. Societatis Iesv./ Et collecta per P.

Gasparum Spitilli/ eiusdem Societatis./ *Antverpiæ*./ Excudebat Martinus Nutius ad insigne dua-/rum Cyconiarum. Anno 1593./ 52 *pp*. *Calf extra by Riviere.* 12*mo.* (15s. 2597)

SPIZELIUS (THEOPHILUS). Theophili Spizelii/ Elevatio/ Relationis/ Monteziniana/ de Repertis in America/ Tribubus Israeliticis ;/ et Discussio/ Argumentorum./ Pro Origine Gentium Ameri-/ canarum Israelitica/ A/ Menasse Ben Israel/ in מקוה ישראל Seu Spe/ Israelis/ Conquisitorum/. Cum celeberrimi viri/ Johannis Buxtorfii/ de Judaico isto conatu ad/ Theophilum Spizelium/ Epistola./ *Basileæ*./ Apud Joannem König, 1661./ 12 *prel. leaves and text* 128 *pp*. *Calf extra by Riviere.* Small 8*vo.* (18s. 2598)

SPOTORNO (GIAMBATTISTA). Della Origine e della Patria di Cristoforo Colombo libri tre di Don Giambattista Spotorno Barnabita, *Genova* 1819. Andrea Frugoni, 247 *pp*. *Uncut. Half mor.* 8*vo.* (10s. 6d. 2599)

SPRENGEL (MATTHIAS CHRISTIAN). Briefe über Portugal, nebst einem Anhang über Brasilien. Aus dem Französischen. Mit Anmerkungen herausgegeben von Matthias Christ. Sprengel, Professor der Geschichte in Halle. *Leipzig,* in der Weygandschen Buchhandlung, 1782. 6 *prel. leaves and* 290 *pp. half calf.* Small 8*vo.* (4s. 6d. 2600)

STADEN (HANS). Warhaftig/ Historia vnd beschreibung eyner Landt=/schafft der Wilden, Nacketen, Grimmigen Menschfresser/ Leuthen, in der Newenwelt America gelegen, vor vnd nach/ Christi geburt im Land zü Hessen vnbekant, bisz vff dise ij./ nechst vergangene jar, Da sie Hans Staden von Hom=/berg aufz Hessen durch sein eygne erfarung erkant,/ vnd yetzo durch den truck en tag gibt./ Dedicirt dem Durchlenchtigen Hochgebornen herrn,/ H. Philipsen Landtgraff zü Hessen, Graff zü Catzen/ elnbogen, Dietz, Ziegenhain vnd Nidda, seinem G. H./ Mit eyner vorrede D. Joh. Dryandri, genant Eychman,/ Ordinarij Professoris Medici zü Marpurgk./ Inhalt des Büchlins volget nach den Vorreden./ Getruckt zü *Marpurg,* im jar M. D. LVII./ [*Colophon*] Zü Marpurg im Kleeblatt,

bei/ Andres Kolben, vff Faſtnacht. 1557./ 8 *prel.
leaves;* viz. *Title the reverse blank,* ' Dem Durchleuchtigen vnd Hoch⸗/gebornen Fürſten vnd Herrn, Herrn Philipſen/ Landtgrauen zü Heſſen, Grauen zü/ Catzenelnbogen, Diez, Ziegenhain/ vnd Nidda, τc. Meinem/ gnedigen Fürſten/ vnd Herrn,'/ *2 pp.*
' Dem Wolgebornen hern H. Philipſen/ Graff zü Naſſaw vnd Sarprück τc. meinem in Gne⸗/digen Hern. Wünſcht D. Dryander viel heyls/ mit erbietunge feiner Dienſte./ 10 *pp.* ' Inhalt des büchs'/ 1 *page.* ' Was hilfft ' *etc. underneath a large woodcut of a Ship in full sail;* ' Die Landtſchafft mit den genanten hauingen,' *etc. a folded woodcut map of* ' Amerika ooer Praſilien.' *Text in 81 leaves, signatures* a *to* t *in fours,* v *in five; many woodcuts with the text. Fine copy. Vellum.* 4to. (8*l.* 8*s.* 2601)

STADEN (HANS). Varhaftige./ be⸗/ſchreibung eyner Landſchaffe der wilden/ nacketen/ grimmigen menſchenfreſſer leuthen, in der newen/ welt America gelegen. Vor vnd nach Chriſti geburt imland/ zü Heſſen vnbekant, biſz vff! diſe zwey negſt vergangene jar,/ Daſie Hans Staden von Homberg aufz Heſſen durch ſein/ eygne erfarung erkant, vnd ytzt durch den truck an tag gibt. Vnd zum andern mal fleiſſig corrigirt vnd gebeſſert./ Dedicirt dem Durchleuchtigen hochgebornen fürſten/ H. Philipſen Landtgraue zü Heſſen, Graff zü Catzen⸗/elubogen, Dietz, Ziegenhain vñ Nidda, ſeinem G. H./ Miteyner verrede D. Ioh. Dryandri, genant Eychman,/ Ordinarij Profeſſoris Medici zü Marpurg./ Inhalt des büchlins volget nach den vorreden./ [*Colophon*] Getruckt zü *Marpurg* im/ Heſſen land, bei Andres Colben,/ Vff Mariæ Geburts tag,/ Anno M. D. LVII. *Very poor copy.* 4to. (2*l.* 2*s.* 2602)

STAMLER (JOHN). Dialogvs. Iohannis Stamler. Avgvstn./ De Diversarvm Gencivm Sectis/ et Mvndi Religionibvs./ Regiſtrū operis reſpice in fine./ [*Colophon*] Impreſſum *Auguste:* per Erthardum oglin. & Jeorgiū Nadler Cura/ correctōne et diligentia venerabilis domini Wolfgangi Aittinger/ pſpiteri Auguſteñ. ac bonarum Artium zc. Magiſtri Collonienſs/ Anno noſtre ſalutis. 1. 50. &. 8. die. 22. menſis May. zc./ *2 prel. leaves;* viz. *Title engraved both sides,*' Reverendo . in . Christo . Patri .

et . Domino.' *etc.* 1 *page*; ' ⁋ Germani . Freidancer . et . Trviecrart . ad . Lectorem ' *etc.* 1 *page. Text XXXII folined leaves*; ' Registrvm.' 3 *pp. Calf by Hayday. Folio.* (1*l.* 11*s.* 6*d.* 2603)

STANHOPE (George). The early Converfion of Iflanders, a wife Expedient for propagating Chriftianity. A Sermon, Preached before the Incorporated Society for the Propagation of the Gofpel in Foreign Parts; at their Anniversary Meeting in the Parifh-Church of St. Mary-le-Bow; On Friday the 19th of Feb. 1713-14. By George Stanhope, D.D. Dean of Canterbury, and Chaplain in Ordinary to Her Majesty. *London:* J. Downing, 1714. 39 *pp. With* 2 *Plans at pp.* 36 *and* 37. *Half mor.* 8*vo.* (4*s.* 6*d.* 2604)

STATE (The) of the Sugar-Trade; shewing the Dangerous Consequences that Muft attend any additional Duty thereon. *London:* E. Say, 1747. 24 *pp. Half mor.* 4*to.* (4*s.* 6*d.* 2605)

STATE of the Britifh and French Colonies in North America, With Refpect to Number of People, Forces, Forts, Indians, Trade and other Advantages. In which are confidered, I. The defencelefs Condition of our Plantations, and to what Caufes owing. II. Pernicious Tendency of the French Encroachments, and the fitteft Methods of fruftrating them. III. What it was occafioned their prefent Invafion, and the Claims on which they ground their Proceedings. With a Proper Expedient propofed for preventing future Difputes. In Two Letters to a Friend. *London:* A Millar, mdcclv. *Title and* 150 *pp.* 8*vo.* (10*s.* 6*d.* 2606)

STATE (A) of the Claim of His Majefty's Bermuda Subjects to the Right of Gathering Salt at Turks Iflands, Referred to by the Governor, Council, and Affembly of Bermuda, in their Memorial of the 7th Day of May, 1790, to the Right Honourable William Wyndham Grenville, His Majefty's Secretary of State for the American Department. *London:* Printed in the Year 1790. *Title and* 26 *pp. half morocco.* 4*to.* (7*s.* 6*d.* 2607)

STEARNS (Samuel). The American Oracle. Comprehending An Account of Recent Discoveries in the Arts and Sciences, with a variety of Religious, Political, Physical, and Philosophical subjects, Neceffary to be known in all Families, for the Promotion of their prefent Felicity and future Happiness. By the Honourable Samuel Stearns, LL.D. and Doctor of Physic; Astronomer to his Majesty's Province of Quebec, and New Brunswic; also to the Commonwealth of Massachusetts, and the State of Vermont, in America. *London:* J. Lackington, 1791. *viii and text* 627 *pp. Index xviii pp. Bound.* 8*vo.* (7*s.* 6*d.* 2608)

STEDMAN (C.) The History of the Origin, Progress, and Termination of the American War. By C. Stedman, who served under Sir W. Howe, Sir H. Clinton, and the Marquis Cornwallis. In Two Volumes. *London:* Printed for the Author; 1794. *Two Volumes.* Vol. I. *xv and* 399 *pp.* 7 *Plates at pp.* 127, 195, 210, 214, 352, 362, 377. Vol. II. *xv and* 449 *pp.* 'Index.' 13 *pp.* 8 *Plates at pp.* 132, 185, 210, 329, 342, 358, 400, 412. *Old calf.* 4*to.* (1*l.* 11*s.* 6*d.* 2609)

STEPHEN (JAMES). The Speech of James Stephen, Esq. In the Debate in the House of Commons, March 6, 1809, on Mr. Whitbread's Motion relative to the late overtures of the American Government: With supplementary remarks on the recent Order in Council. *London:* J. Butterwor), and J. Hatchard, 1809. *iv and* 126 *pp. Half morocco.* 8*vo.* (4*s.* 6*d.* 2610)

STEPHENS (WILLIAM). The Castle-Builders; or, the History of William Stephens, of the Ifle of Wight, Efq; lately deceafed. A Political Novel, Never before publifhed in any Language. *London:* Printed for the Author. MDCCLIX. *xv and* 198 *pp.* 'Contents.' *pp. ix, and x.* 8*vo.* (10*s.* 6*d.* 2611)

STEPHENSON (MARMADUKE). A Call/ from/ Death to Life,/ and/ Out of the Dark wayes and Worfhips of the World where/ the Seed is held in Bondage under the Merchants of/ Babylon, Written by Marmaduke Stephenson ;/ Who (together with another dear Servant of the Lord called/ William Robinson) hath (fince the Writing hereof) fuffer-/ed Death, for bearing Witneffe to the fame

Truth,/ amongſt the Profeſſors of Boſtons Juriſdic-tion/ in New England./ With a True Copy of Two Letters, which they Writ to the Lords/ People a little before their Death./ And alſo the True Copy of a Letter as it came to our hands, from/ a Friend in New England, which gives a brief Relation of the/ manner of their Martyrdom, with ſome of the Words which they/ expreſt at the time of their ſuf-fering./ *London*, Printed for Thomas Simmons, at the Sign of the/ Bull and Mouth near Alderſgate. 1660./ 32 pp. half mor. 4to.   (1*l*. 11s. 6d.   2612)

STEUART (ADAM). Some/ Observations/ and/ Annotations/ Upon the/ Apologetical Narration,/ Humbly ſubmitted to the Honour-/able Houses of Parliament;/ The moſt Reverend and Learned/ Divines/ of the/ Assembly,/ And all the Proteſtant Churches here/ in this Iſland, and abroad./ Lon-don,/ Printed for Chriſtopher Meredith, and are to be ſold in/ Pauls Church-yard at the ſign of the Crane. 1643./ 4 prel. leaves, signed ' A. S.' and 71 pp. half mor. 4to.   (7s. 6d.   2613)

STEUART (ADAM). An/ Answer/ to a/ Libell/ Intituled,/ A Coole Conference/ Betweene the cleered/ Reformation/ and the/ Apologetical Nar-ration,/ Brought together by a Wel-willer to both ;/ Wherein are cleerely refuted what ever he bringeth a-/gainſt the Reformation cleared, moſt humbly ſub-/mitted to the judgement of the Honorable Houſes/ of Parliament, the moſt Learned and Re-/ verend Divines of the Aſſembly,/ and all the Re-formed/ Churches./ By Adam Stevart./ Imprinted at *London*, 1644./ 3 prel. leaves and 62 pp. half mor. 4to.   (7s. 6d.   2614)

STEVENS (JOHN). A New Collection of Voyages and Travels, Into ſeveral Parts of the World, none of them ever before Printed in Engliſh. Contain-ing, 1. The Deſcription, &c. of the Molucco and Philippine Iſlands, by L. de Argenſola. 2. A new Account of Carolina, by Mr. Lawſon. 3. The Travels of P. de Cieza, in Peru. 4. The Travels of the Jeſuits in Ethiopia. 5. The Captivity of the Sieur Mouette in Fez and Morocco. 6. The Travels of P. Teixeira from India to the Low-Countries by Land. 7. A Voyage to Madagaſcar by the Sieur

Cauche. In Two Volumes, Illuftrated with feveral Maps and Cuts. London, J. Knapton, 1711. *Two Volumes.* Vol. I. 6 *prel. leaves including the collective title,* 'Molucco and Philippine Iflands, &c.' 260 *pp. Index.* 8 *pp.* 'A New Voyage to Carolina;' *etc.* 3 *prel. leaves and* 258 *pp. Lately publish'd etc.* 1 *page. With map and* 2 *plates.* Vol. II. 5 *prel. leaves including collective title* 'Travels of P. de Cieza, &c.' 244 *pp. The contents and Index* 11 *pp.* 'The Travels of the Jesuits in Ethiopia:' *etc.* 2 *prel. leaves and* 264 *pp. The contents and Index* 16 *pp.* 'The Travels of the Sieur Mouette,' *etc.* 115 *pp. The contents and Index* 5 *pp.* 'The Travels of Peter Teixeira,' *etc.* 81 *pp. The contents and Index* 6 *pp.* 'A Voyage to Madagascar, *etc.* By Francis Cauche,' 77 *pp. Index.* 3 *pp. With* 2 *maps and plate. Large Paper, calf extra, gilt edges by F. Bedford.* 4to. (10*l.* 10*s.* 2615)

STIGLIANI (Tomaso). Del/ Mondo/ Nvovo/ del Cavalier/ Tomafo Stigliani./ Venti Primi Canti./ Co i sommarii dell' istesso/ Autore dietro à ciafchedun d' effi, e/ con vna lettera del medefimo in fine,/ la qual difcorre fopra d' alcuni riceuu-/ti auuertimēti intorno à tutta l' opera./ Con Priuilegio del Sereniffimo di P. P./ In *Piacenza* por Aleffandro Bazacchi. 1617./ 700 *pp.* 'Gli Errori dell Stampa' *etc.* 6 *pp.* 12*mo.* (2*l.* 2*s.* 2616)

STILES (Ezra). A Discourse on the Christian Union: The Subftance of which was delivered before The Reverend Convention of the Congregational Clergy In the Colony of Rhode-Island; Affembled at Bristol April 23. 1760. By Ezra Stiles, A.M. Pastor of the fecond Congregational Church in Newport. *Boston:* N. E. Printed and fold by Edes and Gill. mdcclxi. 139 *pp. Half morocco.* 8vo. (4*s.* 6*d.* 2617)

STILES (Ezra). The United States elevated to Glory and Honor. A Sermon, Preached before His Excellency Jonathan Trumbull, Esq. L.L.D. Governor and Commander in Chief, And the Honorable The General Assembly of The State of Connecticut, Convened at Hartford, At the Anniverfary Election, May 8th, 1783. By Ezra Stiles,

D.D. President of Yale-College. *New-Haven:* Printed by Thomas & Samuel Green. M,DCC, LXXXIII. 96 pp. half mor. 8vo. (4s. 6d. 2618)

STILES (EZRA). A History of three of the Judges of King Charles I. Major-General Whalley, Major-General Goffe, and Colonel Dixwell: Who, at the Restoration, 1660, Fled to America; and were secreted and concealed, in Massachusetts and Connecticut, for near thirty years. With an Account of Mr. Theophilus Whale, of Narraganfett, Suppofed to have been alfo one of the Judges. By President Stiles. *Hurtford:* Printed by Elisha Babcock. 1794. 357 pp. *Erratu, and Advertisement* 1 *page. Portrait of Stiles facing Title,* 8 *plates at pp.* 129, 77, 80, 114, 126, 136, 202, 345, *numbered I to IX. Calf extra by Bedford.* 8vo. (1l. 1s. 2619)

STITH (WILLIAM). The History of the Firft Discovery and Settlement of Virginia: Being An Essay towards a General History of this Colony. By William Stith, A. M. Rector of Henrico Parifh, and one of the Governors of William and Mary College. *Williamsburg:* Printed by William Parks, M,DCC,XLVII. *viii and* 331 pp. 'An Appendix to the Firft Part of the History of Virginia,' *etc. v and* 34 *pp. Old calf.* 8vo. (1l. 11s. 6d. 2620)

STITH (WILLIAM). The History of the Firft Discovery and Settlement of Virginia. By William Stith, A.M. Prefident of the College of William and Mary in Virginia. Virginia, Printed: *London*, Reprinted for S. Birt in Ave-Mary-Lane. M.DCC. LIII. *viii and* 331 pp. 'An Appendix to the First Part of the History of Virginia,' *etc. v and* 34 *pp. Old calf.* 8vo. (1l. 11s. 6d. 2621)

STODDARD (SOLOMON). Gospel Order/ Revived,/ Being an Anfwer to a Book lately fet forth by the Reverend Mr. Increafe Mather, Prefident/ of Harvard Colledge, &c./ Entituled,/ The Order of the Gofpel, &c./ Dedicated to the Churches of Chrift in New-England./ By fundry Minifters of the Gofpel in New-England./ Printed in the Year 1700./ 6 *prel. leaves; viz.* 'Advertifement.' *facing title; title,* 'The Epiftle Dedicatory, To the Churches of Chrift in N. England.' 8 *pp. Text*

40 pp. *Fine copy in morocco by Francis Bedford.*
4to. (4*l.* 4*s.* 2622)

<blockquote>
The Advertisement facing the title is as follows: "The *Reader* is defired to take Notice that the Prefs | in *Boston* is fo much under the aw of the Reverend | Author, whom we anfwer, and his Friends that we | could not obtain of the Printer there to print the fol-/ lowing Sheets, which is the only true Reafon why we | have fent the Copy fo far for its Impreffion and where | it printed with fome Difficulty."
</blockquote>

STODDARD (SOLOMON). The/ Doctrine/ of/ Inftituted Churches/ Explained and Proved/ from the/ Word/ of/ God./ By Solomon Stoddard, A.M. Minifter of the Gofpel in/ Northampton, New-England./ *London:* Printed for Ralph Smith, at the Bible under the Piazza of the Royal/ Exchange in Cornhil. 1700./ *Title and* 34 *pp. morocco by Bedford.* 4to. (2*l.* 12*s.* 6*d.* 2623)

STODDARD (SOLOMON). The/ Way for a People/ To Live Long in the Land that/ God/ Hath given them./ A Sermon/ Preached before His Excellency,/ The Governour, the Honoured/ Council and Affembly of the Province/ of the Maffachufetts-Bay in New-England,/ on the 26. of May 1703. At the Election/ of Her Majefties Council By Solomon Stoddard, / And Paftor of Northampton./ *Boston:/* Printed by Bartholomew Green and John Allen, for B / and are to be Sold at his Shop under the Weft End of the/ Town Houfe. 1703./ *Title and* 25 *pp. morocco by Bedford.* 4to. (2*l.* 2*s.* 2624)

STODDARD (SOLOMON). An Answer/ to some/ Cafes of Confcience/ Refpecting the Country./ By Solomon Stoddard, A.M. Paftor in Northampton./ [*Colophon*] *Boston* in New-England:/ Printed by B. Green: Sold by Samuel Gerrifh, at his Shop near the/ Brick Meeting-Houfe in Corn Hill. June 25th. 1722./ 15 *pp. morocco extra by Bedford.* 4to. (2*l.* 2*s.* 2625)

STORIES of popular Voyages and Travels; with illustrations. Containing abridged Narratives of recent Travels of some of the most popular writers on South America. With a preliminary sketch of the Geography, History, and Productions of that Country. New Edition. *London:* Whittaker, Treacher, and Co., MDCCXXX. *Half-title, title, iv*

and 259 pp. *With Engraved title, map and 3 Plates.*
12mo. (2s. 6d. 2626)

STORK (Dr.) An Extract from the Account of East Florida, Publifhed by Dr. Stork, who refided a confiderable Time in Augustine, the Metropolis of that Province. With the observations of Denys Rolle, who formed a Settlement on St. John's river, in the fame Province. With his Proposals to Such Perfons as may be inclined to fettle thereon. *London:* Printed in the year MDCCLXVI. *Title and* 39 *pp. half mor.* 8vo. (7s. 6d. 2627)

STORK (WILLIAM). A Description of East-Florida, with a Journal, kept by John Bartram of Philadelphia, Botanist to his Majesty for The Floridas; upon A Journey from St. Augustine up the River St. John's, as far as the Lakes. With Explanatory Botanical Notes. Illuftrated with an accurate Map of East-Florida, and two Plans; one of St. Augustine, and the other of the Bay of Espiritu Santo. The Third Edition, much enlarged and improved. *London:* W. Nicoll, MDCCLXIX. *2 prel. leaves, viii and* 40 *pp.* ' A Journal,' *etc. Title, xii and* 36 *pp. Map and 2 Plans.* 4to. (8s. 6d. 2628)

STORY (THOMAS). A Determination of the Case of Mr. Thomas Story, and Mr. James Hoskins, Relating to an Affair of the Pennfylvania Company, &c. *London:* J. Roberts, 1724. 11 *pp. Unbound.* 4to. (15s. 2629)

STOUGHTON (WILLIAM). An/ Assertion/ for/ True and Christian/ Church-Policie :/ Wherein/ Certain Politike Objections made against/ the Planting of Pastors and Elders in/ every Congregation are suffici=/ently answered. &c./ By/ William Stoughton/ Fellow of New Coll. Oxon./ and Magistrate of the Colony of Mas=/sachusets, New Eng./ *London :/* Printed in the Yeare, 1642./ *5 prel. leaves and* 178 *pp. The Title Written. Calf.* 4to. (1l. 1s. 2630)

SUAREZ DE FIGUEROA (CHRISTOVAL). Hechos/ de Don Garcia/ Hvrtado de Mendoça,/ [Quatro] Marques de Cañete./ A Don Ivan Andres/ Hurtado de Mendoça/ su hijo Marques de Cañete,/ Señor de las Villas de Argete/ y su partido, Mon-tero mayor/ del Rey ñro señor, Guarda/ mayor de la ciudad/ de Cuenca, ett²./ Por el Doctor Christoval/ Suarez de Figueroa./ En *Madrid*, en la Imprenta Real./ Año 1616./ *Engraved title*, 8 *prel. leaves and* 324 *pp. old calf.* 4*to.* (2*l.* 12*s.* 6*d.* 2631)

<small>Mendoza, the 4th Marquis di Canete, was Captain General of Chile, and afterwards Viceroy of Peru.</small>

SUCCINCT Account of the Treaties and Negociations between Great Britain and the United States of America, relating to the Boundary between the British possessions of Lower Canada and New Brunswick, in North America, and the United States of America. [*London.*] 206 *pp. Contents* 1 *page. Map of North America.* 8*vo.* (7*s.* 6*d.* 2632)

<small>Privately printed, and having the autograph of the Earl of Anglesey.</small>

SUCCINCT (A) View of the Origin of our Colonies, with Their Civil State, Founded by Queen Elizabeth, Corroborated by Succeeding Princes, and Confirmed by Acts of Parliament; whereby The Nature of the Empire eftablifhēd in America, And the Errors of various Hypotheses formed thereupon, may be clearly understood with Obfervations on the Commercial, Beneficial and Perpetual Union of the Colonies with this Kingdom. Being An Extract from an Essay lately publifhed, Entitled The Freedom of Speech and Writing, &c. *London:* MDCCLXVI. *Title and* 46 *pp.* 8*vo.* (7*s.* 6*d.* 2633)

SUMMARY (A) View of the Rights of British America, Set forth in fome Resolutions intended for The Inspection of the prefent Delegates of the People of Virginia, now in Convention. By a Native, and Member of the Houfe of Burgeffes. Williamsburg, Printed. *London*, Re-printed for G. Kearsly, 1774. 2 *prel. leaves, viz. Title and Preface; Dedication* 'To the King' *pp. v—xvi, Signed* 'Tribunus.' *Text pp.* 5—44. *Half morocco.* 8*vo.* (4*s.* 6*d.* 2634)

SUMMARY (A) Account of the present flourishing State of the Island of Tobago, with a Plan of the Island. *London:* S. Hooper, MDCCLXXVII. *iv and pp.* 7—80. 8*vo.* (4*s.* 6*d.* 2635)

SUMMERSETT (JAMES, *a Negro*). The Original

Report of the celebrated Case of James Summersett which decided that American Slaves on reaching English ground are Free. *Manuscript.* 132 pp. 4to. (1*l*. 11*s*. 6*d*. 2635*)

SUPREMACY (The) of the British Legislature over the Colonies candidly discussed. *London:* J. Johnson, MDCCLXXV. *2 prel. leaves and* 38 *pp. Half morocco.* 8*vo.* (4*s*. 6*d*. 2636)

SUTCLIFF (Robert). Travels in some parts of North America, in the years 1804, 1805, & 1806, by Robert Sutcliff. *York:* C. Peacock, 1811. *xi and* 293 *pp. With* 6 *plates. Calf.* 12*mo.* (5*s*. 2637)

SYMMES (Thomas). Utile Dulci. Or, A Joco-Serious Dialogue, Concerning Regular Singing: Calculated for a Particular Town, (where it was publickly had, On Friday Oct. 12. 1722.) but may ſerve ſome other places in the ſame Climate. By Thomas Symmes, Philomuſicus. *Boston:* Printed by B. Green, for Samuel Gerriſh, near the Brick Meeting Houſe in Cornhill. 1723. *Title,* ii *and* 59 *pp. Half morocco. Small* 8*vo.* (15*s*. 2638)

AILFER (PATRICK). A True and Historical Narrative Of the Colony of Georgia In America, From the firſt Settlement thereof until this preſent Period: Containing The moſt authentick Faɕts, Matters and Tranſaɕtions therein; together with His Majeſty's Charter, Repreſentations of the People, Letters, &c. And a Dedication to his Excellency General Oglethorpe. By Pat. Tailfer, M.D. Hugh Anderson, M.A. Da. Douglas, and others, Land-holders in Georgia, at preſent in Charles-Town in South-Carolina. *Charles-Town, South-Carolina*: Printed by P. Timothy, for the Authors, M.DCC.XLI. *xviii and* 118 pp. *Half-mor.* 8vo. (7s. 6d. 2639)

TALBOT (EDWARD ALLEN). Five Years Residence in the Canadas: Including a Tour through Part of the United States of America, in the Year 1823. By Edward Allen Talbot, Esq., of the Talbot Settlement, Upper Canada. In Two Volumes. *London*: Longman, 1824. *Two Volumes.* Vol. I. *xvi and* 419 pp. 1 *plate.* Vol. II. 400 pp. 1 *plate. Boards.* 8vo. (7s. 6d. 2640)

TAMAIO DE VARGAS (THOMAS). Restavracion/ de la Civdad del Salvador,/ i baia de Todos-Sanctos,/ en la Provincia del Brasil./ Por las Armas de/ Don Philippe iv. el Grande,/ Rei Catholico/ De las Espanas i Indias, &c./ A Sv Magestad/ Don Thomas Tamaio de Vargas/ ſu Chroniſta./ Año 1628./ Con Privilegio./ En *Madrid*: Por la vivda de Alonso Martin./ 8 *prel. leaves, the eighth blank, and* 178 *folioed leaves.* 'Svmma de lo Particvlar' *etc.* 8 pp. *Vellum.* 4to. (2l. 2s. 2641)

TAXATION no Tyranny; an Answer to the Resolutions and Address of the American Congress. [By Dr. Samuel Johnson.] *London*, Cadell, MDCCLXXV. *Half-title, title, and* 91 *pp. Half mor.* 8*vo.* (4*s.* 6*d.* 2642)

TAXATION no Tyranny; an Answer to the Resolutions and Address of the American Congress. The Third Edition. *London:* T. Cadell, MDCCLXXV. *Half-title, title, and* 91 *pp.* 8*vo.* (4*s.* 6*d.* 2643)

TAXATION. The Pamphlet, entitled, "Taxation no Tyranny," candidly considered, and it's arguments, and pernicious doctrines, Exposed and Refuted. *London:* W. Davis, [1775.] *Half-title, title, and text* 132 *pp. Calf extra by F. Bedford.* 8*vo.* (2*l.* 2*s.* 2644)
With many manuscript additions and corrections in the handwriting of Burke.

TAXATION. An Answer to a Pamphlet, entitled Taxation no Tyranny. Addressed to the Author, and to Persons in Power. *London:* J. Almon, MDCCLXXV. 63 *pp.* 8*vo.* (4*s.* 6*d.* 2645)

TAXATION, Tyranny. Addressed to Samuel Johnson, L.L.D. *London:* J. Bew, M.DCC.LXXV. *Title and* 80 *pp. Half morocco.* 8*vo.* (4*s.* 6*d.* 2646)

TEMPLEMAN (THOMAS). A New Survey of the Globe: Or, an Accurate Mensuration of all the Empires, Kingdoms, Countries, States, principal Provinces, Counties, & Islands in the World. The Area is given in Square Miles, by which the Extent, Magnitude, and true Proportion, that one Country bears to another, are exactly known. The Diftant and Separate Territories, of every Prince, and State, are collected together, and fo regularly plac'd, that at one View, their whole Dominions may be seen. The chief City, or Town, of every Kingdom, Province, and Island, the Longitude, Latitude, & nearest Distance from London in British Miles. The Protestant Kingdoms and States, distinguish'd from thofe of the Roman Catholicks; a Comparifon between the greatnefs and extent of their feveral Dominions, the difference ballanc'd and demonftrated. Also the Antient Perfian and Roman Empires, compar'd with the present Rufsian, Turkish and other great Empires:

And what Proportion the Known and Habitable Earth bears to ye Seas and unknown Parts. A Collection of all the Noted Sea-Ports in the World, ſhewing in what Country they are, & to whom Subject, with their Longitude, Latitude, and diſtance from the Port of London, by Sea; Alſo the Settlements & Factories, belonging to the English, Dutch, French, Portugueſe, Spaniards, &c. in the East and West-Indies, Africa, and other Parts. With Notes Explanatory & Political, wherein the Number of People in all ye principal Countries and Cities of Europe are severally calculated from the Number of Houses or Bills of Mortality. By Thomas Templeman of S^t. Edmunds-Bury, Suffolk. Engraved by T. Cole in Great Kirby Street Hatton Garden *London*. [1776?] *Engraved title*, 'To the Honble James Reynolds, Eſq;' etc. 1 *page, Introduction, List of Subscribers and Table x pp. Plates numbered 1 to 35. Old calf. Oblong 4to.* (15s. 2647)

TENNENT (GILBERT). The Neceſſity of holding faſt the Truth repreſented in Three Sermons on Rev. iii. 3. Preached at New-York, April 1742. With an Appendix, Relating to Errors lately vented by ſome Moravians in thoſe Parts. To which are added, A Sermon on the Prieſtly-Office of Chriſt, And another, On the Virtue of Charity. Together with A Sermon of a Dutch Divine on taking the little Foxes; faithfully tranſlated. By Gilbert Tennent, M.A. Miniſter of the Goſpel at New-Brunſwick, in New-Jerſey. *Boston*: Printed and Sold by S. Kneeland and T. Green in Queen-Street, over againſt the Priſon. M<small>DCCXLIII</small>. *Title, vi and* 110 pp. 'Two Sermons' *etc. Title and* 37 *pp.* 'A Sermon By Abraham Hellenbrock,' *etc. Title and 31 pp. 8vo.* (10s. 6d. 2648)

TENNENT (GILBERT). Sermons on Important Subjects; adapted To the Perilous State of the British Nation, lately preached in Philadelphia. By Gilbert Tennent, A.M. Miniſter of the Gospel. *Philadelphia*: Printed by James Chattin, at the Neweſt-Printing-Office, on the South Side of the Jerſey-Market. 1758. *xxxvii pp. one blank leaf, and text* 425 *pp. Calf extra by F. Bedford. 8vo.* (15s. 2649)

TERNAUX-COMPANS (HENRI). Notice sur la Colonie de la Nouvelle Suède. Par H. Ternaux-Compans. *Paris.* Arthur Bertrand, 1843. *Half-title, title, text 29 pp. and map. Half morocco.* 8vo. (5s. 2650)

TESTIMONY (THE) of the People called Quakers, given forth by a Meeting of the Reprefentatives of faid People, in Pennsylvania and New-Jersey, held at Philadelphia the twenty-fourth Day of the firft Month, 1775. *Signed* 'James Pemberton.' *Single sheet. Folio.* (2s. 6d. 2651)

THACHER (PETER). A Sermon, preached to the Society in Brattle Street, Bofton, November 14, 1790. And occasioned by the Death of The Hon. James Bowdoin, Efq. L.L.D. F.R.S. Lately Governor of the Commonwealth of Massachusetts. By Peter Thacher, A.M. Pastor of the Church in Brattle Street. Printed at *Boston*, by I. Thomas and E. T. Andrews, Faust's Statue, Nº. 45, Newbury Street. MDCCXCI. 27 *pp. Half morocco.* 4to. (4s. 6d. 2652)

THATCHER (B. B.) Indian Biography or an Historical Account of those individuals who have been distinguished among the North American Natives as Orators, Warriors, Statesmen, and other remarkable Characters. By B. B. Thatcher, Esq. In Two Volumes. *New-York*: J. & J. Harper, 1832. *Two Volumes.* Vol. I. *Title and pp. 5—324. With plate, and Portrait of Red Jacket.* Vol. II. *Title and pp. 5—320.* 12mo. (5s. 2653)

THEVENOT (MELCHISADEC). Recueil/ de Voyages/ de Mr/ Thevenot./ Dedié au Roy./ A *Paris,*/ Chez Estienne Michallet/ ruë S. Jaques à l' Image S. Paul./ M.DC.LXXXI./ Avec Privilege du Roy./ *Title, on the reverse* 'Suite du Recueil.' *and* 16 *pp. Map at page* 10. 'Découverte de quelques pays et Nations de l'Amerique Septentrionale.' 43 *pp. with* 'Carte, *etc.* 1673.' 'Voyage d'un Ambassadevr que le Tzaar de Moscovie envoya par Terre a la Chine l' Année 1653. 18 *pp.* 'Explication des Lettres de la Figure fuivante.' 2 *pp. with map.* 'Discours sur l'Art de la Navigation,' *etc.* 32 *pp.* 'Histoire Naturelle de l'Ephemere.' 20 *pp.* 'Table' *etc. engraved figures* 13 *pp. with* 2 *folded plates.* 'Histoire Naturelle du Cancellus, ou Bernard l'Hermite, Reprefentée par Figures.' 8 *pp. with plate.* 'Le Cabinet de Mr. Svvammerdam, Docteur en Medecine,' *etc.* 16 *pp. Old calf.* 8*vo.* (5*l.* 5*s.* 2654)

This little volume is particularly valued on account of its containing Father Marquette's Relation of his voyage down the Mississippi River in 1673, with the map of his route, &c.

THEVET (ANDREW). Historia/ dell' India America/ detta Altramente/ Francia Antartica,/ di M. Andrea Tevet ;/ Tradotta di Francese in/ Lingva Italiana, da/ M. Givseppe Horologgi./ Con Privilegio./ In *Vinegia* Appresso Gabriel/ Giolito de' Ferrari/ MDLXI./ 16 *prel. leaves; viz. Title, reverse blank,* 'All' Illvstriss. et Eccellentissimo Signore, Il Signor Paolo Giordano Orsino, Givseppe Horologgi.' 14 *pp.* 'Tavola' 16 *pp. Text* 363 *pp.* 'Registro' 1 *page, followed by one leaf with Printer's device. Vellum. Small* 8*vo.* (2*l.* 2*s.* 2655)

THEVET (ANDREW). ¶ The Nevv/found vvorlde, or/ Antarctike, wherin is contai-/ned wöderful and ftrange/ things, as well of humaine crea=/tures, as Beaftes, Fifhes, Foules, and Ser-/pents, Trees, Plants, Mines of/ Golde and Siluer: garnished with/ many learned aucthorities,/ trauailed and written in the French/ tong, by that excellent learned/ man, mafter Andrevve/ Thevet./ And now nevvly tranflated into Englifhe,/ wherein is reformed the errours of/ the auncient Cofmo-/graphers./ ¶ Imprinted at *London,*/ by Henrie Bynneman, for/ Thomas Hacket./ And are to be fold at his fhop in Poules Church/ yard, at the figne of the Key./ [*Colophon*] '¶ Imprinted at London, in Knight-/rider ftrete, by Henry Bynneman, for/ Thomas Hacket./ 1568./ 8 *prel. leaves; viz. Title in a broad type metal border, the reverse blank,* '¶ To the right honorable Sir Henrie Sidney, Knight of the moft Noble order of the Garter, Lorde Prefident of Wales, and Marches of the fame, Lord Deputie Generall of the Queenes Maiefties Realme of Ireland, Your humble Orator Thomas Hacket wifheth the fauoure of God, long and happy life, encreafe of honor, continuall health and felicitie.' 4 *pp.* '¶ An Admonition to the Reader.' 1 *page.* 'In prayfe of the Author.' 1 *page.* '¶ To my Lord the Right reuerend Cardinall of Sens, keper of the great feales of France : Andrew Theuet wifheth peace and felicitie.' 8 pp. Text 138 folioed leaves. ' ¶ The Table of the Chapters of this prefent Boke.' 4 pp. Fine copy. 4to. (10l. 10s. 2656)

THEY Run and We Run Written on the late Engagement between Admiral Keppel & the Duc de Chartres July 27th. 1778 off Ushant. *A song, with music.* Single sheet, half mor. Folio. (3s. 6d. 2657)

THOM (ADAM). The Claims to the Oregon Territory considered. By Adam Thom, Esq., Recorder of Rupert's Land. London : Smith, Elder and Co., 1844. iv and 44 pp. 8vo. (2s. 6d. 2658)

THOMAS (DALBY). An/ Hiftorical Account/ of the/ Rife and Growth of the/ Weft-India/ Colonies,/ And of the Great Advantages they/ are to England, in refpect/ to Trade/. Licenced According to Order/. London,/ Printed for Jo Hindmarfh at the Golden-Ball, over/ againft the Royal-Exchange. 1690./ 3 prel. leaves and 53 pp. Half calf. 4to. (1l. 11s. 6d. 2659)

THOMAS (GABRIEL). An Hiftorical and Geographical Account/ of the/ Province and Country/ of/ Pensilvania;/ and of/ Weft-New-Jerfey/ in/ America./ The Richnefs of the Soil, the Sweetnefs of the Situation,/ the Wholefomenefs of the Air, the Navigable Rivers, and/ others, the prodigious Encreafe of Corn, the flourifhing/ Condition of the City of Philadelphia, with the ftately/ Buildings, and other Improvements there. The ftrange/ Creatures, as Birds, Beafts, Fifhes, and Fowls, with the/ feveral forts of Minerals, Purging Waters, and Stones,/ lately difcovered. The Natives, Aborigines,/ their Lan-/guage, Religion, Laws, and Cuftoms ; The firft Planters,/ the Dutch, Sweeds, and Englifh, with the number of/ its Inhabitants; As alfo a Touch upon George Keith's/ New Religion, in his fecond Change fince he left the/ Quakers./ With a Map of both Countries./ By Gabriel Thomas,/ who refided there about Fifteen Years./ London, Printed for, and Sold by A. Baldwin, at/ the Oxon Arms in Warwick-Lane, 1698./ 4 prel. leaves followed by map and ' Hiftory of Penſilvania,' 55 pp. 'History of New-Jersey,' 6 prel. leaves and 34 pp. 8vo. (1l. 11s. 6d. 2660)

THOMAS (Pascoe). A True and Impartial Journal of a Voyage to the South-Seas, and Round the Globe, In His Majesty's Ship the Centurion, Under the Command of Commodore George Anſon. Wherein All the material Incidents during the ſaid Voyage, from its Commencement in the Year 1740 to its Concluſion in 1744, are fully and faithfully related, having been Committed to Paper at the Time they happen'd. Together with ſome hiſtorical Accounts of Chili, Peru, Mexico, and the Empire of China; exact Deſcriptions of ſuch Places of Note as were touch'd at. And Variety of occaſional Remarks. To which is added, A large and General Table of Longitudes and Latitudes, aſcertain'd from accurate obſervations, or (where thoſe are wanting) from the beſt printed Books and Manuſcripts taken from the Spaniards in this Expedition: Alſo the Variations of the Compaſs throughout the Voyage, and the Soundings and Depths of Water along the different Coaſts: And laſtly, several curious Observations on a Comet ſeen in the South Seas, on the Coaſt of Mexico. By Pascoe Thomas, Teacher of the Mathematicks on board the Centurion. *London*, S. Birt. MDCCXLV. 8 prel. leaves and 347 pp. Appendix 39 pp. Old calf. 8vo. (10s. 6d. 2661)

THOMPSON (Thomas). An Account of Two Missionary Voyages By the Appointment of the Society for the Propagation of the Goſpel in Foreign Parts. The one to New Jersey in North America, the other from America to the Coaſt of Guiney. By Thomas Thompson, A.M. Vicar of Reculver in Kent. *London:* Benj. Dod, MDCCLVIII. 2 prel. leaves and 87 pp. 8vo. (10s. 6d. 2662)

THOROWGOOD (Thomas). Ievvs in America,/ or,/ Probabilities/ That the Americans are of/ that Race./ With the removall of ſome/ contrary reaſonings, and earneſt de/ſires for effectuall endeavours to make them Chriſtian./ Propoſed by Tho: Thorovvgood, B.D. one of the/ Aſſembly of Divines./ *London*, Printed by W. H. for Tho. Slater, and are be to ſold/ at his ſhop at the ſigne of the

Angel in Duck lane, 1650./ *20 prel. leaves; viz.
Title, the reverse blank,* ' To the Honovrable Knights
and Gentlemen that have refidence in, and relation
to the County of Norfolk, Peace, from the God of
Peace.' 14 *pp.* 'The Preface to the Reader.' 8 *pp.*
' An Epiftolicall Difcourfe Of Mr. Iohn Dvry, To
Mr. Thorowgood.' 16 *pp.* Text 139 *pp.* *Half mo-
rocco.* 4*to.* (4*l.* 4*s.* 2663)

THOROWGOOD (THOMAS). Jews/ in/ America,/
or/ Probabilities, that thofe Indians are/ Judaical,
made more probable by fome Ad-/ditionals to the
former Conjectures./ An Accurate Discourse is
premifed of/ Mr. John Elliot, (who firft preached
the Gofpel/ to the Natives in their own Language)
touching/ their Origination, and his Vindication of
the/ Planters./ Tho. Thorowgood S. T. B. Nor-
folciencis./ *London,/* Printed for Henry Brome at
the Gun in Ivie-lane. 1660./ 5 *prel. leaves; viz.
Title, reverse blank,* ' To the King's Most Excellent
Majesty.' 8 *pp*; 'To the Noble Knights, Ladies,
and Gentlemen of Norfolk,' *etc.* 33 *pp.* 'Jevves in
America. Summe of the firft Treatife.' 2 *pp; half-
title,* 'Jewes in America.' 'The learned Conjectures of Reverend Mr. John Eliot touching the
Americans,' *etc.* 28 *pp.* ' Chap. I. A short Difcourfe,
concerning the New World, or America." 67 *pp.*
4*to.* (4*l.* 4*s.* 2664)

THOUGHTS on Trade in General, our West-Indian
in Particular, our Continental Colonies, Canada,
Guadaloupe, and the preliminary Articles of Peace.
Addressed to the Community. *London:* John
Wilkie, MDCCLXIII. 86 *pp; dated* ' December 1762.'
and signed ' Ignotus.' *half mor.* 8*vo.* (4*s.* 6*d.* 2665)

THOUGHTS on the Origin and Nature of Government Occafioned by The late Difputes between
Great Britain and her American Colonies. Written
in the Year 1766. *London:* T. Becket and P. A.
de Hondt, MDCCLXIX. 64 *pp.* *Half morocco.*
8*vo.* (4*s.* 6*d.* 2666).

THOUGHTS on the Cause of the present Discontents. The Fourth Edition. *London,* J. Dodsley,
MDCCLXX. Title and 118 *pp.* *Half morocco.*
8*vo.* (5*s.* 6*d.* 2667)

THOUGHTS on the Late Transactions respecting Falkland's Iflands. [By Dr. Samuel Johnson.] *London:* T. Cadell, MDCCLXXI. *Title and 75 pp. Half morocco. 8vo.* (4s. 6d. 2668)

THOUGHTS on the Late Transactions respecting Falkland's Iflands. The Second Edition. *London:* T. Cadell, MDCCLXXI. *Half-title, title, and 75 pp. Half morocco. 8vo.* (4s. 6d. 2669)

THOUGHTS on the Late Transactions respecting Falkland's Iflands. London: Printed, *New-York:* Re-printed, by H. Gaine, at his Book-Store and Printing-Office, at the Bible and Crown, in Hanover-Square. M, DCC, LXXI. *48 pp. Half morocco. 8vo.* (7s. 6d. 2670)

THOUGHTS on the Act For making more Effectual Provifion for the Government of the Province of Quebec. *London:* T. Becket, MDCCLXXIV. *Title and pp. 5-39. Half morocco. 8vo.* (5s. 6d. 2671)

THOUGHTS upon the Political Situation of the United States of America, in which that of Massachusetts Is more particularly confidered. With some Observations on the Constitution for a Federal Government. Addressed to the People of the Union. By a Native of Boston. Printed at Worcester, Massachusetts, by Isaiah Thomas. MDCCLXXXVIII. *209 pp.* (7s. 6d. 2672)

THOUGHTS On Civilization, And the gradual Abolition of Slavery in Africa and the Weft Indies. Printed for J. Sewell, No. 32, Cornhill. [*London*, 1790?] *12 pp. Half mor. 8vo.* (3s. 6d. 2673)

THOUGHTS on the Canada Bill, now depending in Parliament. *London:* J. Debrett, M.DCC.XCI. *Half-title, title, and 50 pp. half mor. 8vo.* (4s. 6d. 2674)

THREE Letters to a Member of Parliament, On the Subject of the Present Dispute with our American Colonies. *London,* T. Lowndes, MDCCLXXV. *Title and 74 pp. Half mor. 8vo.* (4s. 6d. 2675)

THROOP (BENJAMIN). Religion and Loyalty, the Duty and Glory of a People; Illustrated in a Sermon. From 1 Peter 2. 17. Preached before the General Assembly of the Colony of Connecticut, at Hartford, On the Day of the Anniverſary Election, May 11th, 1758. By Benjamin Throop, A.M. Paſtor of a Church in Norwich. *New-London*: Printed by Timothy Green, Printer to the Governor and Company, MDCCLVIII. *Title and pp. 5-37. 12mo.* (7s. 6d. 2676)

THUMB (THOMAS). The Monster of Monsters: A true and faithful Narrative of a moſt remarkable Phænomenon lately ſeen in this Metropolis; to the great Surprize and Terror of His Majesty's good Subjects: Humbly Dedicated to all the Virtuoſi of New-England. By Thomas Thumb, Eſq. [*Boston*], Printed in July 1754. 24 pp. *Red morocco gilt*. 12mo. (2l. 2s. 2677)

THYSIUS (ANTONIUS). Antonii Thysii JC./ Historia Navalis,/ Sive/ Celeberrimorvm/ Præliorum,/ quæ/ Mari ab antiquiſſimis temporibus uſque ad Pacem Hi-/ſpanicum Batavi, Fœderatiq; Belgæ, utplurimum victores/ geſſerunt, luculenta deſcriptio./ *Lugduni Batavorum,/* Ex Officina Joannis Maire, cIɔ Iɔcɪ.vɪɪ./ *4 prel. leaves, 305 pp. and 7 pp. of Index. Calf extra. 4to.* (1l. 1s. 2678)

TITFORD (W. J.) Sketches towards a Hortus Botanicus Americanus; or, Coloured Plates (with a Catalogue and concise and familiar description of many species) of New and Valuable Plants of the West Indies and North and South America. Also of several others, Natives of Africa and the East Indies: Arranged after the Linnæan System. With a concise and comprehensive Glossary of terms, prefixed, and a general Index. By W. J. Titford, M. D. Corresponding Member of the Society for the Encouragement of Arts, &c. *London:* Printed for the Author, by C. Stower, Hackney: 1811. *15 prel. leaves including colored Frontispiece, and pp. 4-137. 17 colored plates; Text to plates 30 pp. English Index, 4 pp. Addenda, iv pp. List of Subscribers, 4 pp. 4to.* (10s. 6d. 2679)

TJASSENS (JOHAN). Zee-Politie,/ Der/ Vereenigde Nederlanden,/ Vertoont in een Tafel,/ Ende in twee Boecken beſchreven,/ door/ Johan Tjassens,/ Waer achter gevoecht zijn eenige Saecken tot on-/derrechtnge, en Kenniſſe, tot de Politie dienende. In 'sGraven-Hage,/ By Johan Vely Boeck-

verkooper, A°. 1669./ 24 prel. leaves and 391 pp.
Large paper. Vellum. 4to. (2l. 2s. 2680)

TOUCH STONE (A) for the Clergy. To which is added, a Poem, wrote By a Clergyman in Virginia, In a Storm of Wind and Rain. Printed in the Year 1771. 16 pp. 8vo. (4s. 6d. 2681)

TRACTS (SELECT) relating to Colonies. Consisting of I. An Eſſay on Plantations. By Sir Francis Bacon Lord Chancellor of England. II. Some Paſſages taken out of the Hiſtory of Florence, &c. III. A Treatiſe. By John De Witt Penſioner of Holland. IV. The Benefit of Plantations of Colonies. By William Penn. V. A Diſcourſe concerning Plantations. By Sir Josiah Child. *London*, J. Roberts. 4 prel. leaves and 40 pp. Unbound. 8vo. (7s. 6d. 2682)

TRATADO de Amistad, Límites y Navegacion concluido entre el Rey Nuestro Señor y los Estados Unidos de América: Firmado en San Lorenzo el Real à 27 de Octubre de 1795. *Madrid*, 1796. *Title and 54 pp. In double columns, in Spanish and English,*' Modelo del Pasaporte'(2). *Half morocco.* 4to. (7s. 6d. 2683)

TRAVELLER'S DIRECTORY (THE), and Emigrant's Guide; containing general descriptions of different routes through the States of New-York, Ohio, Indiana, Illinois, and the Territory of Michigan, with short descriptions of the Climate, Soil, Productions, Prospects, &c. *Buffalo*: Steele & Faxon. 1832. 82 pp. *Contents 2 pp. Boards.* 12mo. (2s. 6d. 2684)

TRAVELLER'S GUIDE (THE) to America; comprehending a concise and accurate description of the Western States of Alabama Mississippi, Louisiana, Tennessee, Kentucky, Michigan, Indiana, Missouri, and the Territory of Illinois, with necessary instructions and advice to Settlers and Emigrants, also, an Account of Upper and Lower Canada, With much useful Information concerning the State of the Country, Soil, Provisions, &c. and Two Letters from Mr. Emmett, Containing interesting and valuable remarks on the State of Society, pointing out those Trades and qualifications which prove most advantageous in the United

States. *Cork:* John Bolster, Patrick Street. 1818. 71 pp. 12mo. (4s. 6d. 2685)

TRAVELS (The) Of feveral Learned Miffioners of the Society of Jesus, into Divers Parts of the Archipelago, India, China, and America. Containing a general Defcription of the moft remarable Towns; with a particular Account of the Cuftoms, Manners and Religion of thofe feveral Nations, the whole interfpers'd with Philofophical Obfervations and other curious Remarks. Tranflated from the French Original publifh'd at Paris in the Year 1713. *London:* R. Gofling, MDCCXIV. *8 prel. leaves and 336 pp. Index, Books Printed, etc. 16 pp. 2 plates at pp. 176 and 215. Old calf.* 8vo. (7s. 6d. 2686)

TRAVELS in North America. *Dublin:* Printed by Brett Smith, Mary-Street. 1824. *180 pp. including Frontispiece and Title; woodcuts on pp. 93, 123, 140, 145.* 12mo. (2s. 6d. 2687)

TREATIES/ (Several)/ of/ Peace and Commerce/ Concluded between the late/ King/ Of Bleffed Memory Deceafed,/ and other/ Princes and States;/ with/ Additional Notes in the Margin, Referring/ to the feveral Articles in each Treaty, and a Table./ Reprinted and Publifhed by His Majefties/ Efpecial Command./ *London/* Printed by His Majefties Printers, and fold by/ Edward Poole at the Sign of the Ship over a-/gainft the Royal Exchange. 1686./ *2 prel. leaves; viz. Title, reverse blank,* 'Table of the Treaties.' *1 page. Text 269 pp. Half morocco.* 4to. (10s. 6d. 2688)

TREATIES. A General Collection of Treatys Declarations of War, Manifeftos, and other Publick Papers, Relating to Peace and War, Among the Potentates of Europe, from 1648 to the prefent Time. Particularly The Treaty of Munfter 1648. The Pyrenean Treaty, with the French King's and the Infanta's Renunciation of the Spanifh Dominions, 1659. The Sale of Dunkirk 1662. The Peace betwixt England and France, and England and Holland in 1667. The Treaty of Aix-la-Chapelle. The Triple League 1668. Treatys of Commerce between England, France, Spain and Holland. Treaty of Nimeguen 1678. Defenfive Alliance betwixt England and Holland 1678./ Declarations of War by the Allys againft France 1688, 1689 and 1702. The firft Grand Alliance 1689. The feparate Peace betwixt France and Savoy 1696. Treaty of Refwick 1697. Treatys of Partition 1698, &c. The fecond Grand Alliance. Treaty for fecuring the Hanover Succeffion. Ufurpations of France fince the Treaty of Munfter. The Right of the Crown of England to Hudfon's-Bay. With many others, to be feen in the Contents. To which is prefix'd, An Hiftorical Account of the French King's Breach of the moft Solemn Treatys. *London:* J. Darby 1710. 44 *and* 448 *pp. Old calf.* 8*vo.* (7*s.* 6*d.* 2689)

TREATIES. A General Collection of Treatys, Declarations of War, Manifeftos, and other Publick Papers, relating to Peace and War. In Four Volumes. *etc.* The Second Edition. *London:* J. J. and P. Knapton, *etc.* M.DCC.XXXII. *Four Volumes.* Vol. I. 32 *and* 448 *pp.* Vol. II. *xxii, Errata i, and* 560 *pp.* 'The Contract of Marriage of the moft Chriftian King with the moft Serene Infanta, eldeft Daughter of the Catholick King. The 7th of November, 1659.' 23 *pp.* Vol. III. *xxxix and* 492 *pp.* Vol. IV. 4 *prel. leaves and* 458 [490] *pp.* 'Catalogue' *etc.* 13 *pp. Old calf.* 8*vo.* (1*l.* 1*s.* 2690)

TREATISE (A) on the Cotton Trade: In twelve Letters. Addressed to the Levant Company, West-India Planters, and Merchants. By Experience. Printed for the Author, *London;* [17—]. *Half-title, title, iii to vi and* 63 *pp.* 12*mo.* (3*s.* 6*d.* 2691)

TREATY/ Of Peace,/ Good Correfpondence & Neutrality/ in/ America,/ Between the moft Serene and Mighty Prince/ James II./ By the Grace of God,/ King of Great Britain, France and Ireland,/ Defender of the Faith, &c./ And the moft Serene and Mighty Prince/ Lewis XIV./ The Moft Chriftian King:/ Concluded the $\frac{6}{16}$th Day of Novemb. 1686./ Publifhed by His Majefties Command./ *In the Savoy:* Printed by Thomas Newcomb, One of/ His Majefties Printers. MDCLXXXVI./ 20 *pp. Half morocco.* 4*to.* (7*s.* 6*d.* 2692)

TREATY (THE) Held with the Indians of the Six Nations at Philadelphia, in July 1742. To which is Prefix'd An Account of the firſt Confederacy of the Six Nations, their preſent Tributaries, Dependents, and Allies. *London:* Re-printed. T. Sowle Raylton and Luke Hinde, [1743?] *xii and 38 pp. Half morocco. 8vo.* (10s. 6d. 2693)

- TREATY of Amity, Commerce, and Navigation, between His Britannic Majesty and the United States of America; by their President, with the advice and consent of the Senate, Nov. 19, 1794. *London:* J. Debrett, 1795. *25 pp. Half morocco. 8vo.* (2s. 6d. 2694)

TROTT (NICHOLAS). The Laws of the Britiſh Plantations in America, Relating to the Church and the Clergy, Religion and Learning. Collected in One Volume. By Nicholas Trott, LL.D. Chief Juſtice of the Province of South-Carolina. *London:* B. Cowse. MDCCXXI. *13 prel. leaves and 435 pp. Large paper. Calf. Folio.* (1l. 11s. 6d. 2695)

TRVE (THE)/ Relation/ of that vvor-/thy Sea Fight, which/ two of the Eaſt India Shipps, had/ with 4 Portingals, of great force and bur-/then, in the Perſian Gulph./ With the Lamentable/ Death of Captaine Andrew/ Shilling./ With/ other Memorable Ac-/cidents, in that/ Voiage./ Printed this 2. of Iuly./ *London./* Printed by I. D. for Nathaniel Newbery and William/ Sheffard, and are to be ſold in Popes-head Alley./ 1622./ *Title, and 22 pp. 4to.* (2l. 2s. 2696)

TRUE (A) State Of the Preſent difference between the Royal African Company, and the Separate Traders: Shewing The Irregularities and Impoſitions of the Joint-Stock Managers; the Uſeleſneſs of their Forts; the Expence they are at in the Maintenance of the ſame; the Charge of ſupporting them in a Condition of Defence; the vaſt Sums they have receiv'd by the Ten per Cent. Duty in order thereunto, and what has been miſapply'd to their own private Uſes; the Advantages and Reaſonableneſs of an Open Trade to Africa; and, laſtly, the Danger of an Excluſive Trade, not only to the Traders of South and North Britain, but, to our American Plantations. Written by a True Lover of his Country, and humbly ſubmitted to the Wife Confideration of Both Houfes of Parliament. London: Printed in the Year 1710. 40 pp. *With plan at page 5.* 4to. (10s. 6d. 2697)

TRUE (A) Account of the Aloe Americana or Africana, Which is now in Blossom in Mr. Cowell's Garden at Hoxton; Which is upwards of Twenty Foot high, and has already put forth Thirty Branches for Flowers, all upon one Stem, Twelve whereof are already fairly Opened and Blown out. As also Of Two other Exotick Plants, call'd, the Cereus, or Torch-Thiftle, Which have likewife put forth their Bloffoms in Mr. Cowell's faid Garden. The like whereof has never been feen in England before. *London:* T. Warner, 1729. *4 prel. leaves and text 44 pp. With copperplate of the Torch-Thistle at page 40. Half morocco.* 8vo. (7s. 6d. 2698)

TRUE (A) State of the Case Between the Britifh Northern-Colonies and the Sugar Islands In America, Impartially Confidered, With Refpect to the Bill now depending in the Right Honourable the Houfe of Lords, Relating to the Sugar Trade. M.DCC.XXXII. *Title and text 46 pp. Half morocco.* 4to. (10s. 6d. 2699)

TRUE (A) and Particular Relation Of the Dreadful Earthquake Which happen'd At Lima, the Capital of Peru, and the neighbouring Port of Callao, On the 28th of October, 1746. With an Account likewife of every Thing material that paffed there afterwards to the end of November following. Publifhed at Lima by Command of the Viceroy, And Tranflated from the Original Spanifh, By a Gentleman who refided many Years in thofe Countries. To which is added, A Description of Callao and Lima before their Deftruction; and of the Kingdom of Peru in general, with its Inhabitants; fetting forth their Manners, Cuftoms, Religion, Government, Commerce, &c. Interfperfed with Paffages of Natural Hiftory and phyfiological Difquifitions; particularly an Enquiry into the Cause of Earthquakes. The Whole illuftrated with a Map of the Country about Lima, Plans of the Road and Town of Callao, another of Lima; and feveral Cuts of the Natives, drawn on the Spot by the Tranflator. The Second Edition. *London:* T. Osborne, MDCCXLVIII. *xxiii and text* 341 *pp. Map of Lima, and plates numbered 1 to IX. Old calf.* 8vo. (7s. 6d. 2700)

TRVE (THE) Sentiments of America: Contained in a Collection of Letters sent from the Hovse of Representatives of the Province of Massachvsetts Bay to several Persons of High Rank in this Kingdom. Together with certain Papers relating to a svpposed Libel on the Governor of that Province and a Dissertation on the Canon and the Fevdal Law. *London*, I. Almon, 1768. *Title,* 'The following refolution' *etc.* 1 *page: Text pp.* 5-158. *Half morocco.* 8vo. (7s. 6d. 2701)

TRUE (THE) Conftitutional Means For putting an End to the Disputes between Great-Britain and her American Colonies. *London*, T. Becket and P. A. De Hondt, MDCCLXIX. *Title and* 38 *pp. Half morocco.* 8vo. (4s. 6d. 2702)

TRUTH Triumphant or a Defence of the Church of England, against The Second Solemn League and Covenant, published under the Title of the Glorious Combination &c. With Addresses to the Members of the Dutch Churches, and To all Friends of Religion, Liberty, and Peace. *New-York*, MDCCLXIX. *Title, Preface, and text* 64 *pp. Half morocco.* 4to. (1l. 1s. 2702*)

TRUMBULL (JOHN). Autobiography, Reminiscences and Letters of John Trumbull, from 1756. to 1841. *New-York & London:* Wiley and Putnam. New-Haven: B. L. Hamlen. 1841. *xvi and* 439 *pp. With* 23 *plates.* 8vo. (7s. 6d. 2703)

TRYON (THOMAS). Tryon's Letters, Domeftick and Foreign, To feveral Perfons of Quality: Occafionally diftributed in Subjects, Viz. Philofophical, Theological, and Moral. By Tho. Tryon. Author of the Way to Health, Long Life, and Happinefs. *London:* Geo. Conyers, and Eliz. Harris, 1700. *Title and* 240 *pp.* 8vo. (10s. 6d. 2704)

TRYON (THOMAS). Tryon's Letters upon Several Occafions. viz. 1. Of Hearing. 2. Of Smelling. 3. Of Tafting. 4. Of Seeing. 5. Of Feeling. 6. Of the Making of Coal-Fires. 7. Of the Making of

Bricks, Tyles, &c. 8. Of Religion. 9. Of Dropfies. 10. Of various Opinions in Religion. 11. Of the Humanity of Chrift. 12. Of an Afflicted Mind. 13. Of Faith, Hope and Charity. 14. Of God's Permiffion for Killing and Eating of Beafts. 15. Of a Soldier's Life. 16. Of the Fountain of Darkness. 17. Of the Fountain of Love and Light. 18. Of Cleannefs. 19. Of Flefh-Broaths, &c. 20. Of the Right and Left Hands. 21. Of Corpulency of the Body. 22. Of Fevers. 23. Of Education. 24. Of Smells. 25. Of Predeftination. 26. Of Death. 27. Of Judicial Astrology. 28. Of Perpetual Motion. 29. Of Mufick. 30. Of Languages. 31. Of Times for Eating. 32. To a Planter of Sugar. 33. To a Gentleman in Barbadoes. 34. To a Planter, about the Manufactury of Cotton. 35. Of the Making of Sugar. 36. Of the Burial of Birds. 37. Of Fermentation. By Tho. Tryon. Author of the Way to Health, Long Life, and Happinefs. *London*: Geo. Conyers, and Eliz. Harris, 1700. 7 *prel. leaves and* 240 *pp.* 8*vo.* (7*s.* 6*d.* 2705)

TUCKER (GEORGE). The Life of Thomas Jefferson, Third President of the United States ; with parts of his Correspondence never before Published, and notices of his Opinions on Questions of Civil Government, National Policy, and Constitutional Law. By George Tucker, Professor of Moral Philosophy in the University of Virginia. In Two Volumes. *London:* Charles Knight, MDCCCXXXVII. *Two Volumes.* Vol. 1. *xxii and* 612 *pp. Portrait of Jefferson.* Vol. II. *x and* 587 *pp. Cloth boards.* 8*vo.* (10*s.* 6*d.* 2706)

TUCKER (JOHN). A Sermon Preached at Cambridge, before his Excellency Thomas Hutchinson, Efq; Governor: His Honor Andrew Oliver, Efq; Lieutenant-Governor, The Honorable His Majesty's Council, And the Honorable House of Representatives, of the Province of the Maffachufetts-Bay in New-England, May 29th. 1771. Being the Anniverfary for the Election of His Majesty's Council for faid Province. By John Tucker, A.M. Paftor of the Firft Church in Newbury. *Boston:* New-England: Printed by Richard Draper, Printed to His Excellency the Governor, and the Honorable His Majefty's Council. MDCCLXXI. 63 *pp. Half morocco.* 8*vo.* (7*s.* 6*d.* 2707)

TUCKER (Josiah). An Humble Address and earnest Appeal to those respectable personages in Great-Britain and Ireland, who, by their great and permanent interest in Landed property, their liberal education, elevated rank and enlarged views, are the ablest to judge, and the fittest to decide, whether a connection with, or a separation from the Continental Colonies of America, be most for the national advantage, and the lasting benefit of their Kingdoms. By Josiah Tucker, D.D. Dean of Glocester. *Glocester:* R. Raikes, M.DCC.LXXV. 93 pp. 'An Account' etc. *folded sheet at page 49. Half morocco.* 8vo. (4s. 6d. 2708)

TUCKER (Josiah). An Humble Address and earnest appeal to those respectable personages in Great-Britain and Ireland, who, by their great and permanent Interest in Landed property, their liberal education, elevated rank, and enlarged views are the ablest to judge, and the fittest to decide, whether a connection with, or a separation from the Continental Colonies of America, be most for the national advantage, and the lasting benefit of these Kingdoms. Second Edition, Corrected. By Josiah Tucker, D.D. Dean of Glocester. *Glocester:* R. Raikes; M.DCC.LXXV. 93 pp. 'An Account' etc. *folded sheet at page 49. Half morocco.* 8vo. (4s. 6d. 2709)

TUCKER (Josiah). A Letter to Edmund Burke, Efq; Member of Parliament for the City of Bristol, and Agent for the Colony of New York, &c. in answer to his Printed Speech, said to be spoken in the House of Commons on the Twenty-Second of March, 1775. By Josiah Tucker, D.D. Dean of Glocester. *Glocester:* R. Raikes; M.DCC.LXXV. 58 pp. *Half morocco.* 8vo. (4s. 6d. 2710)

TUCKER (Josiah). A Series of Answers to certain popular Objections against separating from the Rebellious Colonies, and discarding them entirely; being the concluding Tract of the Dean of Glocester, on the Subject of American Affairs. *Glocester;* R. Raikes; M,DCC,LXXVI. 108 pp. Contents 5 pp. *Half morocco.* 8vo. (4s. 6d. 2711)

TUCKER (Josiah). Cui Bono? or, an Inquiry, what benefits can arise either to the English or the

Americans, the French, Spaniards, or Dutch, from the greatest Victories, or Successes in the present War, being a series of Letters addressed to Monsieur Necker, late controller General of the Finance of France. Third Edition, with an additional preface. With a plan for a general pacification. By Josiah Tucker, D.D. Dean of Glocester. *London:* T. Cadell, M.DCC.LXXXII. *Title and pp. v-xxv. Text pp. 3-141. Half mor. 8vo.* (7s. 6d. 2712)

TUCKER (JOSIAH). Four Letters on important National Subjects, addressed to the Right Honourable the Earl of Shelburne, His Majesty's First Lord Commissioner of the Treasury. By Josiah Tucker, D.D. Dean of Glocester. *Glocester:* R. Raikes. M DCC LXXXIII. *vii and 119 pp.* 'At a Meeting, *etc.* January 24th, 1783. Resolved, That the following Letter, *etc.* be Printed,' *etc.* 23 pp. *Half morocco. 8vo.* (4s. 6d. 2713)

TUDOR (WILLIAM). The Life of James Otis, of Massachusetts: Containing also, Notices of some contemporary Characters and events from the year 1760 to 1775. By William Tudor. *Boston:* Wells and Lilly. 1823. *ix and 508 pp. With portrait of Otis. Half morocco. 8vo.* (7s. 6d. 2714)

TUMULTIBUS (DE)ª Americanis de que Eorum conciliatoribus meditatio Senilis. *Oxonii:* E Typographeo Clarendoniano. J. Fletcher, and D. Prince; B. White, Londini. M DCC LXXVI. *2 prel. leaves and 36 pp. Half mor. 8vo.* (4s. 6d. 2715)

TUTCHIN (MR.). The/ Earth-quake/ of/ Jaimaca,/ Defcrib'd in a/ Pindarick Poem./ By Mr. Tutchin./ *London,*/ Printed, and are to be fold by R. Baldwin, near the/ Oxford-Arms in Warwick-Lane, 1692./ *8 pp. Half morocco. Folio.* (7s. 6d. 2716)

TVVO/ Famovs/ Sea-Fights./ Lately made,/ Betwixt the Fleetes of the King of/ Spaine, and the Fleetes of the/ Hollanders./ The one, in the Weft-Indyes :/ The other,/ The Eight of this prefent moneth of/ February, betwixt Callis and/ Gravelin./ In the former, the Hollander fuffered./ In the latter, the Spaniard lost./ Two Relations not vnfit for thefe Times to animate/ Noble Spirits to attempt and accomplifh/ brave Actions./ *London,*/ Printed for Nath: Bvtter and Nic: Bovrne,/ with Priviledge. 1639./ *16 unnumbered pages. Half morocco. 4to.* (1*l.* 11*s.* 6*d.* 2717)

TWO Papers On the Subject of Taxing the British Colonies in America. The First entitled, "Some "Remarks on the moſt rational and effectual "Means that can be uſed in the preſent Conjunc- "ture for the future Security and Preſervation of "the Trade of Great-Britain, by protecting and "advancing her Settlements on the North Conti- "nent of America." The other, "A Proposal for "eſtabliſhing by Act of Parliament the Duties "upon Stampt Paper and Parchment in all the "Britiſh American Colonies." *London*: J. Almon, 1767. 22 *pp. Half morocco.* 8vo. (7*s.* 6*d.* 2718)

CHTERITZ (Heinrich von). Kurtze/ Reise Beschreibung/ Hr. Heinrich von Uchteritz,/ Lieutenants, Erbsassen auff Modelwitz/ in Meissen, rc./ Worinnen vermeldet, was er auf derselben für Unglück und/ Glück gehabt, sonderlich wie er gefangen nach West-Indien geführet,/ zur Sclaverey verkaufft, und auff der/ Insel Barbados/ Durch den namen seines Herrn Vettern Johann Christoff von Uchteritz,/ uff Medewitz und Spansdorff Erbgesessen, Cammer=Junckern auff/ Gottorff, wunderlich errettet und erlöset worden./ *Weissenfels* bey Johann Christian Wohlfarten, Im Jahr 1705./ 32 pp. 4to. (1l. 1s. 2719)

ULLOA (Antonio de). Noticias Americanas: Entretenimientos Phisicos-Historicos, sobre La América, Meridional, y la Septentrional Oriental. Comparacion General De los Territorios, Climas, y Produciones en las tres especies, Vegetales, Animales, y Minerales: Con Relacion Particular De las Petrificaciones de Cuerpos Marinos de los Indios naturales de aquellos Paises, sus costumbres, y usos: De las Antiguedades: Discurso sobre la Lengua, y sobre el modo en que pasaron los primeros Pobladores. Su Autor Don Antonio de Ulloa, Comendador de Ocaña, en el Orden-de Santiago, Gefe de Esquadra de la Real Armada, de la Real Sociedad de Londres, y de las Reales Academias de las Ciencias de Stockolmo, Berlín, &c. En *Madrid*: Don Francisco Manuel de Mena, MDCCLXXII. 12 prel. leaves and 407 pp. 'Erratas,' 1 page. *Vellum*. 4to. (15s. 2720)

ULTIMAS noticias del Reino de Nueva-España. [*Colophon*] *Habana.*—1821. Diaz de Castro. 8 pp. Half morocco. 4to. (2s. 6d. 2721)

UMFREVILLE (EDWARD). The Present State of Hudson's Bay. Containing a full description of that Settlement, and the adjacent Country; and likewise of the Fur Trade, with hints for its improvement, &c. &c. To which are added, Remarks and Observations made in the Inland parts, during a residence of near Four Years; a specimen of Five Indian Languages; and a Journal of a Journey from Montreal to New-York. By Edward Umfreville; Eleven Years in the service of the Hudson's Bay Company, and Four Years in the Canada Fur Trade. *London:* Charles Stalker, MDCCXC. *Half-title, title, vii and* 230 pp. 'An Account' *etc. at page* 82. 'Plan of a Buffalo Pound,' *at page* 160. 'A Specimen of sundry Indian Languages,' *etc. at page* 202. 8vo. (7s. 6d. 2722)

USSELYNX (WILLIAM). Argonavtica Gvstaviana;/ Das ift:/ Nothwendige Nach Richt/ Von der Yewen Seefahrt vnd/ Kauffhandlung;/ So von dem Weilandt Allerdurchleuchtigften, Grofzmäch=/tigften vnd Siegreicheften Fürften vnnd Herrn, Herrn Gvstavo/ Adolpho Magno, der Schweden, Gothen vnd Wenden König Grofz=/ Fürften in Finnlandt, Hertzogen zu Eheften vnd Carelen, Herrn zu Inger=/manlandt, rc. Allerglorwürdigften Seeligften Andenckens,/ durch aurichtung einer/ General Handel=Compagnie,/ Societet oder Gefellfchafft,/ In dero Reich vnd Landen, zu derfelben fonderbahrem Auff=/nehmen vnd Flor, aufz hohem Verftandt vnd Rath, vor wenig Jahren/ zu ftifften angefangen:/ Anietzo aber der Teutfchen Evangelifchen Nation, infonder=/heit den jenigen welche fich in S. K. M. Freundfchafft, devotion, oder Ver=/bündnufz begeben, vnd fich diefes groffen Vortheils, bey fo ftattlicher Gelegenheit, gebrauchen/ wollen, zu vnermefzlichem Nutz vnd Frommen, ufz Königlicher Mildigkeit, zuneigung vnd Gnade,/ mitgetheilet worden: vnd mit dem förderlichften, vermittels gnädiger verleihung defz/ Allerhöchften, fortgefetzet vnd völlig zu Werck gerichtet/ werden foll./ Daraufz denn ein jedweder claren, gründlichen, vnd zu feinem Behuff fatfamen Bericht vnd Wiffenfchafft diefes Hochwichtigen Wercks einnehmen, vnd wie daffelbe nicht al=/lein an fich felbft fondern auch diefes orths, Chriftlich, hochrühmlich, Rechtmäffig vnd hocnützlich,/ auch practicierlich vnd ohne groffe difficulteten fey, zur gnüge verftehen kan,/ Dabey auch zugleich vernünfftig erachten vnnd ermeffen mag: Ob jhme vnd den feinigen, welz/ Standes oder Condition er jmmer feyn möchte, diefes hiemit jhme angewiefeñen vorhabens, zwifchen diefem vnd dem, ge=/liebts Gott, nächft kommenden Newen Jahrs Tage, durch einfchreibung feines Namens vnd einer gewiffen Poft/ Geldes, es fey fo viel es wolle, fich theilhafftig zu machen rathfam vnd thunlich/ erfunden werden möchte./ Was aber für allerhandt vnterfchiedene Schrifften, diefe Sache betreffendt,/ allhier beyfamen vorhanden; folches wird die nächftfolgende Seite zeigen./ Gedruckt zu *Franckfurt am Mayn*, bey Cafpar Rödteln,/ Im Jahr Chrifti 1633. Menfe Junio./ Mit der Cron Schweden Freyheit./ 10 *prel. leaves; viz. Title, on the reverse* ' Verzeichnufz derer Sachen vnd Schrifften,' *etc.* ' Der Königlichen May. vnd Reiche Schwe=/den Rath,' *etc.* 3 *pp.* ' Kurtzer Extract ' *etc.* 2 *pp.* ' Ne pagina vacaret;' *etc.* 1 *page*. ' Oct Roy Vnd Privilegivm,' *etc.* 8 *pp.* ' Ampliatio Oder Erweiterung Defz Privilegii,' *etc.* 4 *pp.* ' Formular/ Defz/ Manifest/ Vnd/ Vergleich=oder Contract=brief=/fes,' *etc.* 56 *pp.* ' Mercvrivs Germaniæ,' *etc.* 51 *pp. Bound. Folio.* ˜(10*l.* 10*s.* 2723)

UTENHOVE (Jan). Commenta=/riolvs/ Parallelos,/ sive/ Libellvs Affertorius (quo Principum im-/primis duorum, Hifpaniarum fcilicet/ & Indiarum Regis auguftiffimi,/ Regis Philippi inquā Secundi, & Turcici/ Magni Imperatoris Mahumetis Tertij/ Vires, opes, prouiuciæ, atque forma eas/ bene adminiftrandi & regendi tempore/ belli atque pacis explicantur, armaq;, &/ arcana deteguntur infinita) nunc/ primùm ex Iohannis Boteri Itali libris/ ideoma verfus in Latinum ex Italo/ fermone, nullius antea excufus typis./ *Coloniæ Agrippinæ*,/ Apud Lambertum Andreæ. Anno M. D. XCVII./ 26 *leaves, the* 16*th and the last blank.*

'Typis Orbis Terrarvm.' *on the reverse of 3rd, and recto of the 4th leaves.* 'Tvrcici Imperii Descriptio' *on the reverse of the 17th and recto of the 18th leaves. Half morocco.* 4to.   (1*l*. 1*s*.   2724)

VALDES (Antonio). Derrotero de las Costas de España en el Océano Atlántico, y de las Islas Azores ó Terceras para inteligencia y uso de las Cartas Esféricas Presentadas al Rey Nuestro señor por el Exc^{mo}. Sr. Boylio Fr. Don Antonio Valdés, Teniente General de la Real Armada, del Consejo de Estado, Secretario de Estado, y del Despacho Universal de Marina. Y Construidas de Orden de S. M. Por el Brigadier de la Real Armada Don Vicente Tofiño de San Miguel, Director de las Academias de Guardias Marinas, de la Real de la Historia, correspondiente de la de las Ciencias de Paris, Socio de la de Lisboa, Socio Literato de la Sociedad Bascongada, y de mérito de la de los Amigos del Pais de Palma. De Orden Superior. *Madrid.* Por la Viuda de Ibarra, Hijos y Compañia. Año MDCCLXXXIX. *Title, xviii and* 247 *pp. Large paper. Calf. 8vo.* (15s. 2725)

VALLE (Alonso del). Memorial y Carta en que/ el Padre Alonso del Valle Procvrador/ general de la Prouincia de Chile, reprefenta a N. muy Reuerendo Padre/ Mucio Vitilefqui, Prepofito general de la Compañia de Iesvs, la ne-/cefsidad que fus mifsiones tienen de fujetos para los glorio-/fos empleos de fus Apoftolicos/ minifterios./ [*At the end*] *Seuilla* y Março 12. de 1642./ 10 *unnumbered leaves. Folio.* (1*l.* 11*s.* 6*d.* 2726)

VALLETTE (Elie). The Deputy Commissary's Guide Within the Province of Maryland together With plain and sufficient directions for Testators to form, and Executors to perform their Wills and Testaments; for administrators to compleat their Administrations, and for every Person any way concerned in deceased Person's Estates, to proceed therein with Safety to themselves and others. by Elie Vallette. Register of the Prerogative.—*Annapolis.* Printed by Ann C——, MDCC—. *Engraved title, iv and* 248 *pp. Index* 9 *pp. Contents of the Appendix* 2 *pp.* 'Table of Descent.' *at page* 106. *Title-page mutilated.* 8*vo.* (15*s.* 2727)

VANDER DONCK (ADRIAEN). Beschryvinge/ Van/ Nieuvv-Nederlant,/ (Gelijck het tegenwoordigh in Staet is) Begrijpende de Nature, Aert, gelegentheyt en vruchtbaerheyt/ van het felve Landt; mitfgaders de proffijtelijcke ende gewenfte toevallen, die/ aldaer tot onderhondt der Menfchen, (foo uyt haer felven als van buyten inge-/bracht) gevonden worden. Als mede de maniere en ongemeyne Eygenfchap-/pen vande Wilden ofte Naturellen vanden Lande. Ende een byfonder verhael/ vanden wonderlijcken Aert ende het Weefen der Bevers./ Daer noch by-gevoeght is/ Een Difcours over de gelentheyt van Nieuw-Nederlandt,/ tuffchen een Nederlandts Patriot, ende een Nieuw Nederlander./ Befchreven door/ Adriaen vander Donck, Beyder Rechten Doctoor, die tegenwoordigh/ noch in Nieuw-Nederlandt is./ En hier achter by gevoeght/ Het voordeeligh Reglement vande Ed: Hoog. Achtbare/ Heeren de Heeren Burgermeefteren defer Stede,/ betreffende de faken van Nieuw Nederlandt./ Den tweeden Druck./ Met een pertinent Kaertje van 'tzelve Landt verçiert,/ en van veel druck-fouten gefuyvert./ *'t Aemsteldam,* By Evert Nieuwenhof, Boeck-verkooper, woonende op/'t Ruflandt, in 't Schrijf-boeck, Anno 1656./ Met Privilegie voor 15 Jaren./ 4 *prel. leaves ; viz. Title, on the reverse* 'Extract uyt Privilege.' *etc. Four woodcuts of coats of arms,* 'Opdracht, Aen De Hoogloffelijcke, Wel-wijze en voor zienige Heeren,' *etc. Signed* 'E. Nieuwenhof.' 2 *pp.* 'Mitsgaders, Aen de Erentfefte, Wijfe ende feer Waerdige Heeren,' *etc.* 2 *pp.* 'Aan de Leeser.' 1 *page,* 'Op de Voorftanders en de Befchrijvinge.' *etc.* 1 *page. Map,* 'Nova Belgica five Nieuw Nederlandt.' *Text* 100 *pp.* 'Register,' 4 *pp.* 'Conditien,/ Die door de Heeren Burgermeesteren der Stade/ Amfterdam; volgens 't gemaecte Accoort met de Weft-Indifche/ Compagnie, ende d'Approbatie van hare Hog : Mog : de Heeren/ Staten General der Vereenighde Nederlanden, daer/ op gevolght, geprefenteert werden aen alle de gene, die/ als Coloniers na Nieuw-Nederlandt willen vertrecken ;/ welcke haer fullen hebben te addrefferen aen de E. E. Hee-/ren Coenraed Burgh, Raedt ende Ond-Schepen, Henrick Roeters, Opper-Commiffaris van de Wiffelbanck, Eduart/ Man, Ifaac van Beeck, Hector Pieterfz. ende Ioan Tayfpil, als/ Commiffarifen ende Directeurs, hier toe by de Heeren/ Burgermeefteren vernoemt, &c./ t' *Amsterdam*,/ Met confent vande Ed. Hoog. Achtbare Heeren, de Heeren Borgermeefteren,/ By Evert Nieuwenhoff Boeckverkooper opt Ruflandt/ in 't Iaer. 1656./ *Title, reverse blank, text 5 pp.* ' Lyfte.' *1 page. Fine copy in blue mor. extra, by Bedford.* 4to. (16*l*. 2728)

VARENIUS (BERNHARDUS). Geographia/ Generalis,/ In qua affectiones generales/ Telluris explicantur/ Autore/ Bernh: Varenio/ Med: D./ *Amstelodami.*/ Ex Officina Elzeviriana. 1671./ *Engraved title,* 19 *prel. leaves and* 784 *pp. Folded sheets at pp.* 8(2), 66, 126, 172. *Vellum.*
12mo. (10*s.* 6*d.* 2729)

VARGAS (MANUEL DE). ✤/ Relacion de los Milagros qve/ Dios nuefiro feñor ha obrado por vna Image del gloriofo P. S. Frā/ cifco de Borja en el nueuo Reyno de Granada, facada de los procef/fos originales de la informacion, y aprouaciõ que dellos hizo el Iluf/triffimo feñor D. Iulian de Cortazar Arçobifpo de Santa Fè,/ Por el P. Manuel de Vargas de la Compañia de Iefus./ [*Colophon*] Con licencia del Ordinario, En *Madrid* por Andres de Para,/ Año de 1629./ *2 leaves. Folio.* (1*l.* 1*s.* 2730)

VAUGHAN (SAMUEL). A Refutation of a False Aspersion first thrown out upon Samuel Vaughan, Efq. In the Public Ledger of the Twenty-third of Auguft 1769, And fince that Time induftrioufly Propagated, with an intent to Injure Him in the Eye of the Public. *London*: E. and C. Dilly, MDCCLXIX. *2 prel. leaves and* 26 *pp. Half morocco.*
8*vo.* (3*s.* 6*d.* 2731)

VAZQUEZ DE MEDINA (JUAN). Por/ Ivan Vazqvez de/ Medina, vezíno de la Ciudad de Me-/xico, y Teforero de la Cafa de/ la moneda de ella./

En el Pleyto/ con/ D. Iuan Francifco Centeno, y D. Iuan/ Anfaldo de Vera./ Sobre/ la confirmacion del dicho oficio./ [1662.] 24 folioed leaves.
Folio. (12s. 6d. 2732)

VEITIA LINAGE (Joseph de). Norte/ de la contratacion/ de las Indias/ Occidentales./ Dirigido Al Exc^{mo}. Señor/ D. Gaspar/ de Bracamonte/ y Gvzman,/ Conde de Peñaranda, Gentilhombre de la Camara del Rey/ Nueftro Señor, de fus Confejos de Eftado, y Guerra,/ y de la Iunta del Govierno Vniverfal/ deftos Reynos./ Y/ Presidente antes del Consejo Svpremo/ de las Indias, ya del de Italia./ Por/ D. Ioseph de Veitia Linage,/ Cavallero de la Orden de Santiago, Señor de la Cafa de Veitia,/ del Confejo de fu Mageftad, fu Teforero, Juez Oficial de la Real/ Audiencia de la Cafa de la Contratacion/ de las Indias./ Con Privilegio :/ En *Sevilla*, Por Iuan Francifco de Blas, Impreffor mayor de dicha Ciudad. Año 1672./ 16 prel. leaves; Libro Primero 299 pp. Libro Segvndo 264 pp. Indice 70 pp; and Colophon leaf. Fine copy.
Folio. (1l. 11s. 6d. 2734)

VELASQUEZ DE CARDENAS, Y LEON (Carlos Celedonio). Breve Practica, y Regimen del Confessonario de Indios, en Mexicano, y Castellano ; para instruccion del Confessor Principiante, Habilitacion, y examen del Penitente, que dispone Para los Seminaristas El Br. D. Carlos Celedonio Velasquez de Cardenas, y Leon, Colegial Real del Pontificio, y Real Colegio Seminario, y fu Vice-Rector, Cathedratico dos vezes de Philofophia, de Mayores, Rhetorica, y Letras Humanas, Examinador Synodal de efte Arzobifpado, Cura del Partido de S. Miguel Xaltocan, y Juez Eclefiaftico de él, y fus anexos Quantitlan, y Tultitlan. De Zumpahuacan, Capuluac, y ahora de la Concepcion de Otumba, Cura por S. M. y Juez Eclefiaftico por el Ilmô. Sr. Dr. Don Manuel Jofeph Rubio, y Salinas, de la Santa Sede Apoftolica, del Confejo de S. M. Digniffimo Arzobifpo de Mexico. Y la Dedica al Eminentiffimo Señor San Carlos Borromeo, Cardenal de Santa Praxede, Vigilantiffimo Arzobifpo de Milan. Con las Licencias Necessarias. 12 prel. leaves and 54 pp. Small 8vo. (4l. 4s. 2735)

VENEGAS (MIGUEL). Noticia de la California, y de su Conquista temporal, y espiritual hasta el tiempo presente. Sacada de la Historia Manuscrita, formada en Mexico año de 1739. por el Padre Miguel Venegas, de la Compañia de Jesus; y de otras Noticias, y Relaciones antiguas, y modernas. Añadida de algunos Mapas particulares, y uno general de America Septentrional, Afsia Oriental, y Mar del Sùr intermedio, formados fobre las Memorias mas recientes, y exactas, que je publican juntamente. Dedicada al Rey N^{tro}. Señor por la Provincia de Nueva-Efpaña, de la Compañia de Jefus. En *Madrid:* Viuda de Manuel Fernandez, M.D.CCLVII. *Three Volumes.* Tomo Primero, 12 *prel. leaves and* 240 *pp. with map at page* 1. Tomo Segundo, 4 *prel. leaves and* 564 *pp.* Tomo Tercero, 4 *prel. leaves and* 436 *pp. with maps at pp.* 194, 236, *and* 436. *Old calf extra.* 4to. (3*l.* 3*s.* 2736)

VENEGAS (MIGUEL). A Natural and Civil History of California: Containing An accurate Defcription of that Country, Its Soil, Mountains, Harbours, Lakes, Rivers, and Seas; its Animals, Vegetables, Minerals, and famous Fifhery for Pearls. The Customs of the Inhabitants, Their Religion, Government, and Manner of Living, before their Converfion to the Chriftian Religion by the miffionary Jesuits. Together with Accounts of the feveral Voyages and Attempts made for fettling California and taking actual Surveys of that Country, its Gulf, and Coaft of the South Sea. Illuftrated with Copper Plates and an Accurate Map of the Country and the adjacent Seas. Tranflated from the original Spanifh of Miguel Venegas, a Mexican Jefuit, publifhed at Madrid 1758. In Two Volumes. *London,* James Rivington, 1759. *Two Volumes.* Vol. 1. 10 *prel. leaves and* 455 *pp. Frontispiece, map at page* 13, *and plate at page* 36. Vol. II. 4 *prel. leaves and* 387 *pp. Frontispiece and plate at p.* 141. *Fine copy, calf.* 8vo. (1*l.* 1*s.* 2737)

VERNON (ADMIRAL). A New Ballad On the Taking of Porto-Bello, By Admiral Vernon. *London:* R. Dodsley, 1740. 7 *pp. Folio.* (7*s.* 6*d.* 2738)

VERNON (ADMIRAL). The Genuine Speech Of the Truly Honourable Adm -------- l V -------- N, to the Sea-Officers, at a Council of War, Just before The Attack of C--------- A. As communicated by a Perfon of Honour then prefent, in a Letter to his Friend. *London:* T. Cooper, M,DCC,XLI. *Half-title, title, and* 19 *pp. Unbound.* 8vo.   (4s. 6d. 2739)

VERY (A) short and candid Appeal to Free Born Britons. By An American. *London:* Printed for the Author, MDCCLXXIV. *Title and* 28 *pp. Signed,* 'A Carolinian.' *Half morocco.* 8vo. (4s. 6d. 2740)

VESPUCCI (AMERIGO). Alberic⁹ vefpucci⁹ laurētio/ petri francifci de medicis Salutem plurimā dicit/ Felix/ Jehan lambert/ [*Paris* 1505] *Title with woodcut figures, the reverse blank; text in* 9 *unnumbered pages, signature* a. *Fine copy in brown morocco extra, by Bedford.* 4to. (21l. 2741)

VESPUCCI (AMERIGO). De ora antarctica/ per regem Portugallie/ pridem inuenta./ [*Colophon*] Impreſſum *Argentine* per Mathiam hupfuff. M.vᶜ.v./ 6 *leaves, with woodcut of figures and ships on the title, signature* A. *Fine copy with rough leaves, in brown morocco extra, by Bedford.* 4to. (21l. 2742)

VESPUCCI (AMERIGO). Cum Privilegio/ ✠ Paefi Nouamente retrouati. Et Nouo Mondo oa A berico vefputio Fiorentino intitulato. [*Colophon*] ¶ Stampato in *Vicentia* cū la impenfa de Mgro/ Henrico Vicentino: & diligente cura & indu/ ſtria de Zāmaria fuo fiol nel. M.ccccvii. a/ di. iii. de Nouembre. Cum gratia &/ priuilegio p āni. x. como nella/ fua Bolla appare: che p/ fōa del Dominio Ve/ neto nō ardifca ī/ primerlo./ *Title, reverse blank;* 'Tabula Cōmunis.' 9 *pp;* Montalboddo Fracan. al fuo amiciſſimo Ioānimaria/ Anzolello Vicentino. S.'/ 1 *page. Text in* 120 *leaves, Primo Libro to Libro Sexto, signatures* a *to* D *in fours, the last leaf blank. Two leaves in facsimile, viz. Title and last leaf of the Table. morocco.* 4to. (21l. 2743)

VESPUCCI (AMERIGO). Cosmographiæ/ Introdvctio/ cvm qvibvs/dam Geome/triæ/ ac/ Astrono/miæ principiis ad/ eam rem necessariis/ Infuper quattuor Americi/ Vefpucij nauigationes./ Vniuerfalis Cofmographiæ defcriptio tam/ in folido qzplano, eis etiam infetjs/ quæ Ptholomeo ignota a nu/peris reperta funt./ Disthycon¹ Cum deus aftra regat, & terræ climata Cæfar Nec tellus, nec eis fydera maius habent./ *20 unnumbered leaves, signatures* A, B *in* 6, *and* C *and* D *in four leaves; on the reverse of the title, commencing* ' Divo Maximiliano Cæsari sem/per Avgvsto Gymnasivm/ vosagense' *etc. ending on the last leaf* ' Hactenus exequuti capita *etc.* Finis introductionis.' *the reverse blank. Wanting a folded sheet in signature* C, *counted as two leaves, with a woodcut of the globe, on the reverse, commencing* ' Propofitum eft hoc libello quandam Cosmographie introductionē fcribere: quam nos tam '/ *ending* ' fignauimus fed hæc iam miffa facientes.'/ ' Qvattvor Americi/ Vespvtii Navi/gationes/' *etc.* [*Colophon*] Finitū. iiij. kl. Septē/bris Anno fupra fef/quimillefimū. vij./ [*Guatier Lud, St Dié*] 32 *unnumbered leaves, signatures* A (a) *to* f, *the reverse of the last leaf blank. Unbound.* 4to. (10*l.* 10*s.* 2744)

VESPUCCI (AMERIGO). Cosmographæ Introdv=/ ctio, cvm qvibvs/dam Geome/triæ/ ac/ Astrono/ miæ principiis ad/ eam rem necessariis./ Infuper quatuor Americi Ve=/fpucij nauigationes./ Vniuerfalis Cofmographie defcriptio/ tam in folido qz plano, eis etiam/ infertis que Ptholomeo/ ignota a nuperis/ reperta funt./ Distichon./ Cum deus aftra regat, & terræ climata Cæfar/ Nec tellus nec eis fydera maius habent./ 18 *unnumbered leaves* [1*st,* 2*nd,* 5*th, and* 6*th, are of the first Edition, May* 7*th,* 1507 ?] *the remainder are of the edition as above. On the reverse of the title* ' Maximiliano Cæsari Avgvsto/ Philesivs Vogesigena.' 4*to.* (8*l.* 8*s.* 2745)

VESPUCCI (AMERIGO). Cofmographie intro/ductio: cum quibufdam Geome=/trie ac Aftronomie princi/pijs ad eam rem/ neceffarijs./ Infuper quattuor Americi Ve/fpucij nauigationes./ Vniuerfalis Cofmographie defcriptio/ tam in folido qz plano, eis etiam/ infertis que Ptholomeo/ ignota, a nuperis/ reperta funt./ Cum deus aftra regat, et terre climata Cefar/ Nec tellus, nec eis fydera maius babent./ [*Colophon*] Preffit apud *Argentora,*/ cos hoc opus Ingeniofus vir Joannes/ grüniger. Anno poft natu fal=/uatorē fupra fefquimil=/lefimū Nono./ Joanne Adelpho Mulicho Argentineñ Caftigatore./ 32 *leaves, the reverse of the last leaf blank. Signatures* A *to* F. A, B, D, *and* E, *in fours,* C *in six,* F *in eight leaves. Fine copy. Unbound.* 4*to.* (10*l.* 10*s.* 2746)

VESPUCCI (AMERIGO). Paefi nouamente ritrouati per/ la Nauigatione di Spagna in Calicut. Et da Alber/tutio Velputio Fiorentino intitulato Mon/do Nouo: Ncuamente Imprefla./ [*Colophon*] ❡ Stampata in *Venetia* per Zorzi de Rufconi milla-/nefe: Nel. M.ccccc.xyii. a di. xyiii. Agofto./ *124 unnumbered leaves, with woodcut of the City of Venice on the title; the reverse of the last leaf blank; signatures A in four, b to q in eights. Blue morocco extra.* 8vo. (31*l.* 10s. 2747)

VESPUCCI (AMERIGO). Paefi nouamente retrouati. & Nouo Modo da Alberico Velputio Flo=/retino intitulato./ [*Colophon*] ❡ Stampato in *Milano* con la impenfa de lo. Iacobo & fratelli da/ Lignano: & diligente cura & induftria de Ioanne Angelo fcinzen/ zeler: nel. M.ccccxix. a di. v. de Mazo./ *Title with woodcut of figures and ships, on the reverse,* 'Tabvla;' '❡ Montalboddo Fracan,' *etc. 7 pp. Text in 79 leaves, Libro Primo to Libro Sexto, signatures a to u in fours, the last leaf blank. Vellum.* 4to. (21*l.* 2748)

VESPUCCI (AMERIGO). Vita di Amerigo Vespucci. *pp.* 25—35. *With portrait of* ' Americ. Vespuccius.' *Half morocco.* 4to. (7s. 6d. 2749)

VETANCURT (AUGUSTIN DE). Arte/ de lengva/ Mexicana, /✤ dispvesto ✤/ Por orden, y mandato de N. R^{mo} P./ Fr. Francisco Treviño, Predica-/dor Theologo, Padre de la fanta Provincia de Burgos, y Comiffario/ General de todas las de la Nueva-Efpaña, y por el Reverendo,/ y Venerable Diffinitorio de la Provincia del Santo Evangelio./ Dedicado al Bienventvrado/ S. Antonio de Padva./ Por el P. Fr. Auguftin de Vetancurt hijo de/ la dicha Provincia del Santo Evangelio, Predicador jubilado, ex/ lector de Theologia, y Preceptor de la lengua Mexicana, Vicario/ de la Capilla de S. Joseph de los Naturales en el Convento/ de N. P. S. Francisco de Mexico./ Con licencia, *Mexico* por Francifco Rodriguez Lupercio. 1673./ *6 prel. leaves; viz. Title, the reverse blank;* 'Approbabion del R. P. Fray Damian de la Serna,' *etc. 2 pp;* 'Parecer del Doctor, y Maestro Don Antonio de la Torre, y Arellano,' *etc.* 1 *page;* 'Licencia del Ordinario,' 1 *page;* 'Censvra del Doctor, y Maestro

Don Ygnacio de Hoyos, Santillana,' etc. 1 *page*; Patente de N. M. R. P. Provincial.' 1 *page*; 'Al Lector.' 1 *page*; 'Dedicatoria,' 3 *pp*: Te*x*t 49 *folioed leaves, for 5.*); 2 *folios* 14. 'Instrvccion Breve Para/ adminiſtrar los Santos Sacramētos/ de la Conſeſſion, Uiatico, Matrimonio, y Vela-/ciones en la la lengua Mexicana.' 13 *pp*; 'Catecismo Mexicano.' 3 *pp*. 4*to*. (5*l*. 5*s*. 2750)

VETANCURT (Avgvstin de). Teatro/ Mexicano/ Descripcion Breve/ de los Svcessos Exemplares,/ Historicos,/ Politicos,/ Militares, y Religioſos del nuevo mundo/ Occidental de las Indias,/ Dedicado/ Al Eſpoſo de la que es del miſmo Dios Eſpoſa,/ Padre putativo del Hijo, que es Hijo del miſmo/ Dios Christo, Dios, y hombre verdadero./ Al que con el ſudor de ſu reſtro ſustentó al que/ todo lo ſuſtenta: Al que fue Angel de Guarda de/ la Ciudad de Dios milagro de ſu Omnipotencia,/ y abiſmo de la gracia./ Maria Señora Nvestra./ Al glorioso Patriarca de la casa de Dios Señor S. Joseph./ Dispvesto/ Por el R. P. Fr. Avgvstin de Vetancvrt, Mexicano, hijo de la miſma Provincia, Difinidor actual, Ex-Lector/ de Theologia, Predicador Jubilado General, y ſu Chroniſta/ Apoſtolico, Vicario, y Cura Miniſtro, por ſu Mageſtad, de/ la Igleſia Parrochial de S. Joseph de los Naturales/ de Mexico./ Con Licencia de los Svperiores./ En *Mexico* por Doña Maria de Benavides Viuda de Iuan de Ribera, Año de/ 1698./ 6 *prel. leaves. Parts* 1 *and* 2, 66 *pp. and* 168 *pp*; *Indice* 2 *pp*; 'Tratado de la Ciudad de Mexico,' *etc.* 56 *pp. Followed by the title to the Second Volume:* 'Chronica/ de la/ Provincia del Santo Evangelio/ de Mexico./ Quarta parte del Teatro Mexicano de los/ ſucceſſos Religioſos./ Compuesta/ por el Reverendo Padre/ Fray Auguſtin de Vetancur, Mexicano, hijo de la miſma/ Provincia, Definidos actual, Ex-Lector de Theologia,/ Predicador Iubilado General, y ſu Chroniſta Appostolico,/ Vicario y Cura Miniſtro, por ſu Magestad,/ de la Igleſia Parrochial de San Ioseph/ de los Naturales de Mexico./ *etc.* Con licencia de los Svperiores./ En *Mexico*, por Doña Maria de Benavides Viuda de Iuan de Ribera. Año de/ 1697./ 6 *prel. leaves and* 138 *pp*; 'Menologio Franciscano de los varones masseñalados, que con ſus vadas exemplares,' *etc.* 1 *page, the reverse blank, and* 156 *pp. Two volumes.* Vellum. Folio. (6*l*. 16*s*. 6*d*. 2751)

VIAGE, y svcesso de los Cara-/uelones, Galeoncetes de la guarda de Cartagena de las/ Indias, y fu cofta. Y la grandiofa victoria que han tenido cōtra los Coffarios Piratas en aquel Mar,/ efte año 1621. los quales en el hazian grandes robos, y por efto ceffauan las contrataciones,/ con gran daño de las coftas y vezinos de tierra firme./ [*Colophon:*] Con licencia, Impreffa en *Madrid*, por la viuda de Cofme Delgado. Año de mil/ y feyfcientos y veinte y vno./ *2 leaves. Half mor. Folio.* (1*l.* 1*s* 2752)

VIAGGIO (IL)/ fatto da gli Spa/gnivoli a/ torno a'l/ Mondo./ Con Gratia per Anni. XIIII./ MDXXXVI./ *4 prel. leaves; viz. Title, the reverse blank,* 'A'l Lettore.' *4 pp. and a half ; Text 47 unnumbered leaves ;* 'Capitolo. VI.' *1 page, the reverse blank. Signatures A to M in fours. Half mor. 4to,* (10*l.* 10*s*. 2753)

VIAUD (PIERRE). The Shipwreck and Adventures of Monsieur Pierre Viaud, A Native of Bourdeaux, and Captain of a Ship. Tranflated from the French, By Mrs. Griffith. *London*, T. Davies, MDCCLXXI. *xii and 276 pp. Frontispiece. 8vo.* (4*s*. 6*d*. 2754)

VEITIA LINAGE (JOSEPH DE). The/ Rule/ Eftablifh'd in Spain,/ for the/ Trade/ in the/ Weft Indies./ Being a proper Scheme for Direct-/ing the Trade to the/ South Sea,/ Now by Act of Parliament to be/ Eftablifh'd in Great Britain./ Tranflated from the Spanifh by Captain/ John Stevens./ To which are Added,/ Two Compleat Lifts: One, of the Goods Tranfported/ out of Europe to the Spanifh West Indies; the other, of/ Commodities brought from thofe Parts into Europe./ *London*, Printed for Samuel Crouch, at the corner of/ Popes-Head Alley in Cornhill./ [1700?] *13 prel. leaves, and text 367 pp. Index 9 pp. Old calf. 8vo.* (15*s*. 2755)

VIEW (A) of the Depredations and Ravages Committed by the Spaniards on the British Trade and Navigation. Moft humbly offer'd to the Confideration of the Parliament of Great Britain. *London:* W. Hinchliffe, 1731. *Title, ix and 44 pp. Half morocco. 8vo.* (5*s*. 6*d*. 2756)

VIEW (A) of the Controversy between Great-Britain and her Colonies: Including a Mode of Determining their prefent Difputes, Finally and Effectually; and of preventing All Future Contentions. In a Letter to the Author of a full Vindication of The Meafures of the Congrefs, from the Calumnies of their Enemies. By A. W. Farmer. Author of Free Thoughts, &c. *New-York*: Printed by James Rivington, M,DCC,LXXIV. 37 pp. *Half morocco.* 8vo. (7s. 6d. 2757)

VIEW (A) of the Controversy between Great-Britain and her Colonies: Including a Mode of Determining their Prefent Difputes, Finally and Effectually; and of preventing all future contentions. In a Letter to the Author of A Full Vindication of the Meafures of the Congrefs, from the Calumnies of their Enemies. By A. W. Farmer, Author of Free Thoughts, &c. New-York, Printed: *London* Reprinted Richardson and Urquhart, 1775. *Half-title, title and* 90 pp. 8vo. (7s. 6d. 2758)

VIEW (A) of the History of Great-Britain, during the Administration of Lord North, to the Second Session of the Fifteenth Parliament. In Two Parts. With Statements of the Public Expenditure in that Period. *London:* G. Wilkie, MDCCLXXXII. *Title, ii and* 412 pp. 8vo. (8s. 6d. 2759)

The First Part was publifhed in the preceding year, under the title of the Hiftory of Lord North's Adminiftration.

VIEW (A) of the State of Parties in the United States of America; being an Attempt to Account for the present Ascendancy of the French, or Democratic Party, in that Country; in two Letters to a Friend. By a Gentleman who has recently visited the United States. *Edinburgh:* John Ballantyne and Co. 1812. 110 pp. 8vo. (2s. 6d. 2760)

VIEWS of Society and Manners in America; in a series of letters from that country to a friend in England, during the years 1818, 1819, and 1820. By an Englishwoman. *London:* Longman, 1821. *x and* 523 pp. *Half calf.* 8vo. (6s. 2761)

VILBAO (LUIS DE). Sermon de la Fe/ en el Solene/ y General Avto, qve/ fu Tribunal Santo celebrò en la/ Ciũdad de Lima./ El Domingo tercero de Aduiento, que fue dia de Santo/ Tomas Apoftol, à 21. de Diziembre, de 1625. años./ Por el Padre Maeftro Fray Luis de Vilbao, de la Sagra/ da Orden de Predicadores, Calificador del Santo Ofi-/cio, y

Catredatico proprietario de Prima de Teo-/logia en la Real Vniuerſidad de los Reyes./ Al Excelentiſſimo Señor D. Diego Ferdinandez de Cordoua Marques/ de Guadalcazar, Virrey, y Capitan General deſlos Reynos/ del Piru, &c./ Año de 1626./ Impreſſo en *Lima*; Con licencia de ſu Excelencia./ *Title and folioed leaves 2 to 18. Calf extra by Bedford. 4to.* (1*l*. 11*s*. 6*d*. 2762)

VILLAGOMEZ (PEDRO DE). Discvrso/ Ivridico/ sobre/ Que pertenece a la Dignidad Arçobiſpal, ò/ Epiſcopal, el nombrar, y remover' los Colecto-/res delas Igleſias Catedrales de las Indias,/ ſin dependencia del Real Pa-/tronazgo./ Por/ El Ilvstrissimo Señor Don/ Pedro de Villagomez, Arçobiſpo de la Santa/ Igleſia Metropolitana de la ciudad de los Re-/yes, del Conſejo de ſu/ Mageſtad./ Capitvlo I./ Relacion del caſo, motivos, intento, y diuiſion/ de eſte diſcurſo./ [*End*] Annuat Deus per Chriſtum Dominum no-/ſtrum, Amen. Lima y Diziembre 10. de 1653./ Pedro Arçobiſpo de Lima./ *60 folioed leaves. 4to.* (1*l*. 11*s*. 6*d*. 2763)

VILLAGRA (GASPAR DE). Historia/ de la Nveva/ Mexico, del Capitan/ Gaspar de Villagra./ Dirigida al Rey D. Felipe/ nueſtro ſeñor Tercero deſte nombre./ Año 1610./ Con privilegio./ En *Alcala*, por Luys Martinez Grande./ A coſta de Baptiſta Lopez mercador de libros./ [*Colophon*.] Impreſſo en Alcala de/ Henares, por Luys/ Martinez Grāde./ Año. 1610./ *24 prel. leaves including portrait of author: Text 287 folioed leaves, and Colophon one leaf. Blue morocco extra by Bedford. Very fine copy. Small 8vo.* (4*l*. 14*s*. 6*d*. 2764)

VILLE (JEAN BAPTISTE DE). Histoire des Plantes de l'Europe, et des plus Usite'es qui viennent d'Aſie, d'Afrique, & d'Amerique. Où l'on voit leurs Figures, leurs noms, en quel temps elles fleuriſſent, & le lieu où elles croiſſent. Avec un Abrégé de leurs qualitez, & de leurs Vertus ſpecifiques. Diviſée en deux Tomes, & rangée ſuivant l'ordre du Pinax de Gaſpard Baubin. *A Lyon*, Chez Nicolas De Ville, MDCCVII. *Two Volumes. Tome Premier. 24 prel. leaves and 442 pp. Tome II. Title and pp. 445—866. Table 80 pp. Old calf. 12mo.* (10*s*. 6*d*. 2765)

VINCENT (Thomas). An Explicatory Catechiſm:
Or, an Explanation of the Assemblies Shorter
Catechiſm. Wherein all the Anſwers in the Aſſem-
blies Catechiſm are taken abroad in Under-Queſ-
tions and Anſwers, the Truth explain'd and proved
by Reaſon and Scripture ſeveral Caſes of Conſcience
reſolv'd ſome chief Controverſies in Religion ſtated,
with Arguments againſt divers Errors. Uſeful to
be read in private Families, after Examination in
the Catechism itſelf, for the more clear and thorough
underſtanding of what is therein Learn'd. By
Thomas Vincent, ſometimes Miniſter of Maudlin
Milk-ſtreet in London. *Boston* in New-England:
Printed for D. Henchman, over againſt the Brick-
Meeting Houſe in Cornhill, John Phillips, at the
Stationers-Arms, and T. Hincock, at the Bible and
Three Crowns near the Town-Dock. 1729. *Title,
viii and 315 pp. 12mo.* (10s. 6d. 2766)

VINDICATION (A) of The Proceedings of The
Eastern Association In Fairfield County; and of
The Council that cenſured Mr. White, And diſmiſſed
him from his Paſtoral Relation to The First Church
in Danbury: In a Letter To The Reverend Mr.
Joseph Bellamy, In which the whole Proceſs is
fairly repreſented, contrary to the falſe Repreſen-
tations and abuſive Reflections contained in a
Pamphlet called A Brief Narrative of their Proceedings. By the Committee Of the First Society
in Danbury. *New-Haven:* Printed by B. Mecom.
1764. 78 *pp.* 8*vo.* (7s. 6d. 2767)

VIRGINIA. The/ New Life/ of Virginea:/ Declaring the/ former svccesse and pre-/ſent eſtate of
that plantation, being the ſecond/ part of Noua
Britannia./ Publiſhed by the authoritie of his
Maieſties/ Counſell of Virginea./ *London,/* Imprinted by Felix Kynston for William Welby,
dwelling at the/ ſigne of the Swan in Pauls Church-
yard. 1612./ *Title (facsimile) with woodcut, portrait,
and coat of arms, the reverse blank;* 'To the Right/
Worshipful and/ Worthie Knight Sir/ Thomas
Smith of London, Gouernour of the/ Moſcouia and
Eaſt Indie Companies, one of/ his Maieſties Counſell for Virginea,/ and Treaſurer for the Colony:/
Peace and health in Chriſt./ 4 *pp.* *Signed* 'R. I.'
Text, 'The New Life of Virginea.' *in 24 unnumbered leaves. 4to.* (5*l.* 5*s.* 2768)

VIRGINIA. A Perfect Defcription of/ Virginia :/ Being,/ A full and true Relation of the prefent State/ of the Plantation, their Health, Peace, and Plenty: the number/ of people, with their abundance of Cattell, Fowl, Fifh, &c. with feverall/ forts of rich and good Commodities, which may there be had, either/ Naturally, or by Art and Labour. Which we are fain to/ procure from Spain, France, Denmark, Swedeland, Germany,/ Poland, yea, from the Eaft-Indies. There/ having been nothing related of the/ true eftate of this Planta-/tion thefe 25 years./ Being fent from Virginia, at the requeft of a Gentleman of worthy note, who defired to know the true State of Virginia as it now ftands./ Also,/ A Narration of the Countrey, within a few/ dayes journey of Virginia, Weft and by South, where people come/ to trade: being related to the Governour, Sir William Berckley,/ who is to go himfelfe to difcover it with 30 horfe, and 50 foot,/ and other things needfull for his enterprize./ With the manner how the Emperor Nichotawance/ came to Sir William Berckley, attended with five petty Kings,/ to doe Homage, and bring Tribute to King Charles. With his folemne Proteftation, that the Sun and Moon fhould lofe/ their Lights, before he (or his people in that Country), fhould prove difloyall, but ever to keepe Faith/ and Allegiance to King Charles./ *London*, Prind for Richard Wodenoth, at the Star under Peters/ Church in Cornhill. 1649./ *2 prel. leaves; viz. 1st. on verso the royal arms: 2nd. Title, reverse blank; text 19 pp. Morocco extra by Bedford, fine copy. 4to. (10l. 10s. 2769)*

VIRGINIA. The Case of the Planters of Tobacco in Virginia, As reprefented by Themselves; figned by the Prefident of the Council, and Speaker of the Houfe of Burgeffes. To which is added, a Vindication Of the faid Reprefentation. *London:* J. Roberts, 1733. *64 pp. Half mor. 8vo. (7s. 6d. 2770)*

VIRGINIAN. The American Wanderer, through Various Parts of Europe, in a series of Letters to a Lady, (Interfperfed with a Variety of interesting Anecdotes,) By a Virginian. *Dublin*, B. Smith, MDCCLXXXIII. *xxiii & 288 pp. 12mo. (7s. 6d. 2771)*

VOLNEY (C. F.) View of the Climate and Soil of the United States of America: To which are annexed some Accounts of Florida, The French Colony of the Scioto, certain Canadian Colonies, and the Savages or Natives: Tranflated from the French of C. F. Volney, Member of the Conservative Senate, and the French National Institute, and Honorary Member of the American Philosophical Society at Philadelphia, the Asiatic Society at Calcutta, the Atheneums of Avignon, Alençon, &c. With Maps and Plates. *London:* J. Johnson, 1804. *xxiv pp. Table of Contents, pp. iii-vi. Text* 504 *pp. Plates at pp.* 59, 99. *Two maps at the end.* 8*vo.* (6s. 6d. 2772)

VOYAGE dans la Haute Pensylvanie et dans l'Etat de New York, Par un Membre adoptif de la nation Onéida. Traduit et publié par l'auteur des Lettres d'un Cultivateur Américain. De L'emprimerie de Crapelet. A *Paris* Au IX—1801. *Three Volumes.* Tome Premier. *xxxii pp. including Frontispiece; Text* 427 *pp. Plates at pp.* 115, 119, 253. *Map at the end.* Tomo Second. *xiv and* 434 *pp. Plates at pp.* 131, 182, 192. *Map at the end.* Tome Troisième. *xii and* 410 *pp.* 'Indication' *etc. folded sheet at page* 166, *folded sheet at page* 173. *Plates at pp.* 197, 199. 'Tableau' *etc. at pp.* 252, 253. *Half calf.* 8*vo.* (12s. 6d. 2773)

VOYAGES. An Historical Account of all the Voyages round the World, performed by English Navigators; including those lately undertaken By Order of his Present Majesty. The whole Faithfully Extracted from the Journals of the Voyagers. Drake, undertaken in 1577-80. Cavendish, 1586-88. Cowley, 1683-86. Dampier, 1689-96. Cooke, 1708-11. Rogers, 1708-11. Clipperton and Shelvocke, 1719-22. Anson, undertaken in 1740-44. Byron, 1764-66. Wallis, 1766-68. Carteret, 1766-69, and Cook, 1768-71. Together with that of Sydney Parkinson, Draftfman to Joseph Banks, Efq; who circumnavigated the Globe with Capt. Cook, in his Majefty's Ship the Endeavour. And The Voyage of Monf. Bougainville round the World, Performed by Order of the French King. Illuftrated with Maps, Charts, and Hiftorical Prints. In Four Volumes. To which is added,

An Appendix. Containing the Journal of a Voyage to the North Pole, by the Hon. Commodore Phipps, and Captain Lutwidge. *London:* F. Newbery, MDCCLXXIV. *Four Volumes.* Volume the First. Title, 1 prel. pp. List of Subscribers, 5 pp. Directions to the Bookbinder for placing the plates, 1 page; Text 480 pp; 1 map and 15 plates. Volume the Second. *Title and* 440 pp. 8 *plates.* Volume the Third. MDCCLXXIII. *viii and* 470 pp. 4 *Charts and* 15 *Plates,* 1 *wanting at page* 327. Volume the Fourth. MDCCLXXIII. *Title and* 364 pp. *The Bookseller's Advertisement,* 2 pp; 'Supplement, containing the Journal of a Voyage,' etc. *Title and* 118 pp. 5 *plates, map, and chart. Half calf.* 8vo. (1l. 1s. 2774)

VOYAGES. A new Collection of Voyages, Discoveries and Travels: Containing Whatever is worthy of Notice, in Europe, Asia, Africa and America: In respect to The Situation and Extent of Empires, Kingdoms, and Provinces; their Climates, Soil, Produce, &c. With the Manners and Cuſtoms of the ſeveral Inhabitants; their Government, Religion, Arts, Sciences, Manufactures, and Commerce. The whole conſiſting of ſuch English and Foreign Authors as are in moſt Eſteem; including the Deſcriptions and Remarks of ſome late celebrated Travellers, not to be found in any other Collection. Illuſtrated with a Variety of accurate Maps, Plans, and elegant engravings. In Seven Volumes. *London:* J. Knox, MDCCLXVII. *Seven Volumes.* Vol. I. 8 *prel. leaves and* 515 pp. Vol. II. 2 *prel. leaves and* 496 pp. Vol. III. 2 *prel. leaves and* 520 pp. Vol. IV. 2 *prel. leaves and* 464 pp. Vol. V. 2 *prel. leaves and* 472 pp. Vol. VI. 2 *prel. leaves and* 543 pp. Vol. VII. 2 *prel. leaves and* 528 pp. *Old calf.* 8vo. (1l. 10s. 2775)

There is in the first Volume a list of 49 maps and plates.

VOYAGES. Interesting Account of the Early Voyages, made by the Portugueſe Spaniards, &c. To Africa, East and West-Indies. The Diſcovery of Numerous Iſlands; with Particulars of the Lives of thoſe Eminent Navigators. Including the Life and Voyages of Columbus. To which is prefixed the Life of that Great Circumnavigator Captain Cook, with particulars of his Death. Extracted from Dr. Kipps's. *London:* Printed for the Pro-

prietors, M,DCC,XC. 12 prel. leaves and pp. 7-276.
Plates and maps at pp. 7, 8, 17, 25, 32, 40, 48. Old
calf. 4to. (10s. 6d. 2776)

VOYAGES. A General Collection of Voyages and
Discoveries, made by the Portuguese and the
Spaniards during the Fifteenth and Sixteenth Centuries. Containing the interesting and entertaining
Voyages of the Celebrated Gonzalez and Vaz,
Gonzalez Zarco, Lanzerota, Diogo Gill, Cada
Mosto, Pedro di Sintra, Diogo d'Azambuza Bartholomew Diac, Vasco de Gama, Voyages to the
Canary Islands, Voyages of Columbus, Nino and
Guierra, Ojeda and Vespusius Cortereal, Alvarez
Cabral, Francis Almeed, Albuquerque, Andrea
Corsali, Voyage to St. Thomas, Voyage of de Solis,
Pinzon, &c. Voyage of John Ponce, Grijalva,
Nicuessa, Cortes, Ojeda and Ocampo, Magellan.
With other Voyages, to the East-Indies, the West-Indies, Round the World, &c. Adorned with
Copper-Plates, Maps, &c. London: W. Richardson, MDCCLXXXIX. 5 prel. leaves and pp. 7-518.
Plates and maps. 4to. (12s. 6d. 2777)

VUE de la Colonie Espagnole du Mississipi, ou des
Provinces de Louisiane et Floride Occidentale, en
l'Année 1802. Par un observateur résident sur les
lieux: Ouvrage accompagné de deux cartes dressées avec soin, et artistement gravées et enluminées. B......- Duvallon, Editeur. Paris. 1803.
xx and 318 pp. Table Abrégée 5 pp. Avis au Relieur,
& Errata et Additions. 4 pp. With 2 colored maps.
Half calf. 8vo. (5s. 6d. 2778)

ADSWORTH (Benjamin). An Eſſay, for the Charitable Spreading of the Gospel into Dark Ignorant Places: Being a Sermon (now ſomething Inlarged) Preach'd at the Lecture in Boſton, Octob. 16. 1718. By Benjamin Wadſworth, A.M. Paſtor of a Church of Chriſt in Boſton, N.E. *Boston*: Printed by B. Green, for Benj. Eliot, at his Shop. 1718. *Title and 36 pp. Unbound.* 12mo. (10s. 6d. 2779)

WADSWORTH (Benjamin). The Gospel not Oppoſed, but by the Devil and Mens Luſts. A Lecture Sermon Preach'd at Boſton, Jan. 8. 1718, 19. From Mat. x. 34. By Benjamin Wadſworth, A.M. Paſtor of a Church of Chriſt in Boſton, N.E. *Boston*, N.E. Printed by B. Green, for Benj. Eliot, at his Shop. 1719. *Title, and 46 pp. Unbound.* 12mo. (10s. 6d. 2780)

WADSWORTH (Benjamin). Vicious Courſes, Procuring Poverty. Deſcrib'd and Condemn'd. A Lecture Sermon, Preach'd at Boſton, Feb. 19. 1718, 19. By Benjamin Wadſworth, A.M. Paſtor of a Church of Chriſt in Boſton, N. E. *Boston*, Printed by John Allen, for Benjamin Eliot, at his Shop in King ſtreet, 1719. *Title and 32 pp. Unbound.* 12mo. (10s. 6d. 2781)

WAFER (Lionel). A New/ Voyage/ and/ Deſcription/ of the/ Iſthmus of America,/ Giving an Account of the/ Author's Abode there,/ The Form and Make of the Country,/ the Coaſts, Hills, Rivers, &c. Woods,/ Soil, Weather, &c. Trees, Fruit, Beaſts,/ Birds, Fiſh, &c./ The Indian Inhabitants, their Features,/ Complexion, &c. their Manners, Cu-/ftoms, Employments, Marriages, Feasts,/ Hunting, Computation, Language, &c./ With Remarkable Occurrences in the South/ Sea, and elfewhere./ By Lionel Wafer. Illuſtrated with feveral Copper=Plates./ *London*: Printed for James Knapton, at the Crown in/ St. Paul's Church-yard, 1699./ 4 *prel. leaves and 224 pp. Index* 14 *pp. Books, etc.* 2 *pp. Map at page* 1, *plates at pp.* 28, 103, 141. *Old calf.* 8*vo.* (18*s.* 2782)

WAFER (LIONEL). A New Voyage and Description of the Isthmus of America. Giving An Account of the Author's Abode there, The Form and Make of the Country, the Coafts, Hills, Rivers, &c. Woods, Soil, Weather, &c. Trees, Fruit, Beasts, Birds, Fish, &c. The Indian Inhabitants their Features, Complxion, &c their Manners, Cuſtoms, Employments, Marriages, Feafts, Hunting, Computation, Language, &c. With Remarkable Occurrences in the South-Sea and elfewhere. By Lionel Wafer. The Second Edition To which are added, The Natural Hiftory of thofe Parts, By a Fellow of the Royal Society: And Davis's Expedition to the Gold Mines in 1702. Illuſtrated with feveral Copper-Plates. *London*, Printed for James Knapton, At the Crown in St. Pauls Church-Yard. MDCCIV. 8 *prel. leaves and* 283 *pp: Index.* 12 *pp: Map and* 3 *plates. Old calf.* 8*vo.* (15*s.* 2783)

WAGHENAER (L. J.) The Mariners Mirrovr/ Wherein may playnly be feen the courfes, heights, dif=/tances, depths, foundings, flouds and ebs, rifings of/ lands, rocks, fands and fhoalds, with the marks for th'en=/trings of the Harbouroughs, Havens and Ports of the greateft part of Europe: their feueral traficks and commodities: Together w.th the Rules and inftrumēts/ of Navigation./ Firſt made & fet fourth in diuers exact Sea-Charts, by that famous/ Nauigator Lvke Wagenar of Enchuifen And now fitted with necefsarie/ additions for the ufe of Englifhmen by/ Anthony Ashley./ Herein alfo may be underſtood the exploits lately atchiued by the right/ Honorable the L. Admiral of Englād with her Ma.ties Nauie; and fome/ former feruices don by that worthy Knight/ Sr. Fra : Drake./ [*London,* 1588.] 24 *leaves of preliminary matter, including engraved title. Copperplate maps* (1) *to* (22) *with description printed on each map.* 'The Second Part/ of the Mariners Mirrovr/ conteining in diuers perfect plots & fea Charts boeth the Northern and Eaftern/ Navigation :/ viz. From the Streights between Douer and Callis, the/ coasts of England, Scotland, Norway, Emden, Yut=/land ct. with all the founds of Denmark & the Baltick/ fea unto Wiburgh and the Narue/ With their particular descriptions/ trafiks and commodities./ *Engraved title and copperplate maps* I *to* XXIII, *with description printed on each map. And* 12 *copperplate maps of the various engagements between the English and Spanish Fleets, the last being a map of* 'Anglia' *Without descriptions and unnumbered. Unbound.* Folio. (3*l.* 13*s.* 6*d.* 2784)

WALKER (HOVENDEN). A Journal: Or full Account Of the late Expedition to Canada. With an Appendix Containing Commiffions, Orders, Inftructions, Letters, Memorials, Courts-Martial, Councils of War, &c. relating thereto. By Sir Hovenden Walker, K*t*. London: Printed for D. Browne at the Black-Swan, W. Mears at the Lamb, without Temple Bar, and G. Strahan at the Golden Ball againft the Exchange in Cornhill, 1720. 2 prel. leaves and text 304 *pp. Old calf.* 8*vo.* (1*l.* 1*s.* 2785)

WALKER (JAMES). Letters on the West Indies. By James Walker. *London:* Rest Fenner, 1818. *xvi and* 268 *pp.* 8*vo.* (4*s.* 6*d.* 2786)

WALLACE (EDWARD J.) The Oregon Question determined by the Rules of International Law. By Edward J. Wallace, M.A., Barrister-at-Law, Bombay. London: A. Maxwell & Son, 1846. 39 *pp.* 8*vo.* (2*s.* 6*d.* 2787)

WALLER (WILLIAM). An/ Efsay/ on the/ Value of the Mines,/ late of Sir Carbery Price./ By William Waller, Gent./ Steward of the said Mines./ Writ for the private Satisfaction of/ all the Partners./ *London:/* Printed in the Year, MDCXCVIII./ 12 *prel. leaves, and* 55 *pp. With two folding sheets, one a woodcut plan of Potosi. Old red morocco, fine copy.* 8*vo.* (12*s.* 6*d.* 2788)

WALTER (THOMAS). Flora Carolina, secundum

Systema Vegetabilium Perillustris Linnæi digesta; Characteres essentiales Naturalesve et diferentias veras exhibens; cum emendationibus numerosis: Descriptionum antea evulgatarum: Adumbrationes stirpium plus mille continens: Necnon, generibus novis non paucis, speciebus plurimis novisq. Ornata. Auctore Thomas Walter, Agriola. *Londini*: J. Fraser: M,DCC,LXXXVIII. *viii and* 263 *pp. Plate facing title.* 8vo. (7s. 6d. 2789)

WANSEY (HENRY). The Journal of an Excursion to the United States of North America, in the Summer of 1794. Embellished with The Profile of General Washington, and an Aqua-tinta View of the State House, at Philadelphia. By Henry Wansey, F.A.S. A Wiltshire clothier. *Salisbury*: J. Easton; 1796. *xiii pp. half-title and* 290 *pp: Index,* 12 *pp: Errata,* 1 *page. Profile facing title, and plate at page* 131. 8vo. (6s. 6d. 2790)

WARD (NATHANIEL). The/ Simple Cobler/ Of/ Aggavvam in America./ Willing/ To help'mend his Native Country, la-/mentably tattered, both in the upper-Leather/ and fole, with all the honeſt ſtiches he can take./ And as willing never to bee paid for his work,/ by Old Engliſh wonted pay./ It is his Trade to patch all the year long, gratis./ Therefore I pray Gentlemen keep your purſes./ By Theodore de la Guard./ *London,*/ Printed by John Dever & Robert Ibbitſon, for Stephen Bowtell, at the/ ſigne of the Bible in Popes Head-Alley, 1647./ 2 *prel. leaves; viz. Title, the reverse blank*; 'To the Reader.' 1 *page; Text,* 80 *pp. Fine large and clear copy, with rough leaves. Morocco by Bedford.* (5l. 5s. *Others* 3l. 3s. *and* 2l. 2s. 2791)

WARD (NATHANIEL). *Another copy, very fine, in calf extra by Bedford, having on the title-page the autograph of White Kennet.* (5l. 5s. 2792)

WARDEN (D. B.) A Chorographical and Statistical Description of the District of Columbia, the seat of the General Government of the United States, with an engraved plan of the District, and view of the Capitol. *Paris*: printed and sold by Smith, Rue Montmorency. 1816. *vii and* 212 *pp. Index,* 2 *pp. Plan at page* 1. *Plate at page* 34. *Calf.* 8vo. (12s. 6d. 2793)

WARREN (GEORGE). An Impartial/ Description/ of/ Surinam/ upon/ The Continent of Guiana/ in/ America./ With a Hiftory of feveral ftrange Beafts, Birds,/ Fifhes, Serpents, Infects, and Cuftoms of/ that Colony, &c./ Worthy the Perufal of all, from the experience of/ George Warren Gent./ *London*, Printed by William Godbid for Nathaniel Brooke/ at the Angel in Grefham-Colledge, in the fecond yard/ from Bifhopfgate-ftreet. 1667./ *2 prel. leaves; viz. Title the reverse blank.* 'To the Reader.' *2 pp. Text*, 28 *pp. 4to.* (1*l.* 11*s.* 6*d.* 2794)

WASHINGTON. The Campaigns of the British Army at Washington and New Orleans, in the Years 1814-1815. By the Author of the Subaltern. Fourth Edition, corrected and revised. *London:* John Murray, MDCCCXXXVI. *iv and* 389 *pp. Cloth. Uncut. 12mo.* (3*s.* 6*d.* 2795)

WASHINGTON (GEORGE). The Journal of Major George Wafhington, sent by the Hon. Robert Dinwiddie, Efq; His Majefty's Lieutenant-Governor, and Commander in Chief of Virginia, to the Commandant of the French Forces on Ohio. To which are added, the Governor's Letter: and a translation of the French Officer's Anfwer. With a New Map of the Country as far as the Mississippi. Williamsburgh Printed, *London*, Reprinted for T. Jefferys, MDCCLIV. 32 *pp. With the map. Half morocco. 8vo.* (1*l.* 1*s.* 2796)

WASHINGTON (GEORGE). Letters from General Washington, To feveral of his Friends in the Year 1776. In which are set forth A fairer and fuller View of American Politics, Than ever yet transpired, Or the Public could be made acquainted with through any other Channel. *London:* J. Bew, M.DCC.LXXVII. *Title, and* 73 *pp. Half morocco. 8vo.* (10*s.* 6*d.* 2797)

WASHINGTON (GEORGE). A Poetical Epistle to his Excellency George Washington, Esq. Commander in Chief of the Armies of the United States of America, from An Inhabitant of the State of Maryland. To which is annexed, A Short Sketch of General Washington's Life and Character. Annapolis Printed 1779: *London:* Reprinted for C. Dilly, MDCCLXXX. 24 *pp. Unbound. 4to.* (10*s.* 6*d.* 2798)

WASHINGTON (George). A Message of the President of the United States to Congress relative to France and Great-Britain. Delivered December 5, 1793. With the Papers therein referred to. To which are added the French originals. Published by order of the House of Representatives. *Philadelphia:* Printed by Childs and Swaine. M,DCC,XCIII. 103 pp. *half mor. 8vo.* (10s. 6d. 2799)

WASHINGTON (George). Official Letters to the Honorable American Congress, Written during the War between the United Colonies and Great Britain, by his Excellency, George Washington, Commander in Chief of the Continental Forces, now President of the United States. Copied by Special Permiffion from the Original Papers preserved in the Office of the Secretary of State, Philadelphia. *London:* Cadell Junior and Davies, 1795. *Two Volumess.* Vol. I. *viii and* 364 *pp.* Vol. II. *Half-title, title, and* 384 *pp. Uncut.* 8vo. (10s. 6d. 2800)

WASHINGTON (George). Memory of Washington: Comprising a sketch of his Life and Character; and the National Testimonials of Respect. Also, a collection of Eulogies and Orations. With a copious Appendix. *Newport. R. I.* Printed by Oliver Farnsworth. 1800. 246 *pp. Subscribers' Names,* 6 *pp. Portrait of G. Washington. Calf.* 12mo. (10s. 6d. 2801)

WASHINGTON (George). Letters from his Excellency General Washington, to Arthur Young, Esq. F.R.S. Containing an Account of his Husbandry, with a Map of his Farm; his Opinions on various Questions in Agriculture; and many particulars of the Rural Economy of the United States. *London:* B. M'Millan, 1801. *vi and* 172 *pp. With the map. 8vo.* (7s. 6d. 2802)

WATERTON (Charles). Wanderings in South America, the North-West of the United States, and the Antilles, in the years 1812, 1816, 1820 and 1824. With original instructions for the perfect preservation of Birds, &c. for Cabinets o. Natural History. By Charles Waterton, Esq. *London:* J. Mawman, 1825. *vii and* 326 *pp. Plate facing title. Large paper.* 4to. (7s. 6d. 2803)

WATTS (ISAAC). A Guide to Prayer. Or, A Free and Rational Account of the Gift, Grace and Spirit of Prayer, With plain Directions how every Chriftian may attain them. By I. Watts, D.D. The Eighth Edition Corrected. *Boston:* Printed by J. Draper, for D. Henchman in Cornhil. M DCC. XXXIX. *Title, x and 228 pp. Table 4 pp. 12mo.* (1*l.* 1*s.* 2804)

WEBB (JOHN). The Young-Mans Duty, Explained and Preffed upon Him. In A Sermon From Eccles. XII. I. Preached to a Society of Young Men, On a Lords-Day Evening: And now Publifhed at their Requeft. By John Webb, A.M. and Paftor of a Church of Chrift in Bofton. Recommended by the Reverend, Increase Mather, D.D. *Boston:* Printed by S. Kneeland, for D. Henchman, at the Corner Shop over againft the Brick Meeting-Houfe. 1718. *Title, ii pp. and wanting all after page 32. Small 8vo.* (8*s.* 6*d.* 2805)

WEBSTER (PELATIAH). Political Essays on the Nature and Operation of Money, Public Finances, and other Subjects: Publifhed during the American War, and continued up to the prefent Year, 1791. By Pelatiah Webster, A.M. *Philadelphia:* Printed and sold by Joseph Crukshank, No. 91, High-Street. M DCC XCI. *viii and 504 pp. Half calf. 8vo.* (8*s.* 6*d.* 2806)

WELCH-COBLER. The honeft/ Welch-Cobler,/ for her do fcorne to call her/felfe the fimple Welch-Cobler :/ Although her thinkes in all her/ Confciences, if her had as many as would ftand/ betweene Paules and Sharing-Croffe that her have/ not fo much wit as her Prother Cobler of A-/merica, yet her thinke her may have as much/ knavery; and though her have not fo much Creek,/ which her holds to be Heathenifh; nor Hebrew,/ which her holds to be Shewifh Language; nor/ Latine, which is the Language of Rome, yet her/ fhall endever her felfe to teliver her felfe in as/ cood Tialect as her can for her hart plood, for the/ petter underftanding of all her friends and kind-/red, whether Comro or Sifs, wherein her fhall/ find variety of counfells, profitable inftructions, feafonable cautions, to prevent tangers that may come/ upon all her countrymen here; Her alfo fhall find fome/ truth, little honefty, fome wit, and a creat teale of kna-/verie./ By Shinkin ap Shone, ap Griffith, ap Gearard, ap Shiles, ap/ Shofeph, ap Lewis, ap Laurence, ap Richard, ap Tho-/mas, ap Sheffre, ap Sheames, ap Taffie, ap Harie,/ All Shentleman in Wales./ [London] Printed by M. Shinkin, Printer to S. Taffie, and/ are to be fold at the Signe of the Goat on the/ Welch Mountaine. 1647./ 8 pp. 4to. (1*l*. 1*s*. 2807)

WELD (ISAAC). Travels through the States of North America, and the Provinces of Upper and Lower Canada, during the Years 1795, 1796, and 1797. By Isaac Weld Junior. Illustrated and embellished with Sixteen Plates. *London*: John Stockdale, 1799. *xxiv and 464 pp. Books, etc. 8 pp.* ' Erratum.' *pasted at the bottom of the list of plates. With the 16 plates. Half calf.* 4to. (10*s*. 6*d*. 2808)

WELD (ISAAC). Travels through the States of North America, and the Provinces of Upper and Lower Canada, during the Years 1795, 1796, and 1797. By Isaac Weld, Junior. Third Edition. Illustrated and embellished with sixteen plates. In Two Volumes. *London*: John Stockdale, 1800. *Two Volumes. Vol. I. xx and 427 pp. 2 maps and 9 plates. Vol. II. viii and 376 pp. 5 plates. Half calf.* 8vo. (7*s*. 6*d*. 2809)

WELD (ISAAC). Travels through the States of North America, and the Provinces of Upper and Lower Canada, during the Years 1795, 1796, and 1797. By Isaac Weld, Jun. Fourth Edition. Illustrated and Embellished with Sixteen Plates. In two Volumes. *London*: John Stockdale, 1807. *Two Volumes. Vol. I. xx and 427 pp. 2 maps and 9 plates. Vol. II. viii and 376 pp. 5 plates. Half calf.* 8vo. (7*s*. 6*d*. 2810)

WELDE (T.) A/ Short Story/ of the/ Rife, reign, and ruine of the Antinomians,/ Familifts & Libertines, that infected the Churches/ of/ New-England:/ And how they were confuted by the Affembly of Mi-/nifters there: As alfo of the Magiftrates proceedings/ in Court againft them./ Together with Gods ftrange and remarkable judge-/ ments from Heaven upon fome of the chief fomenters of/ thefe Opinions; And the lamentable death of M^s. Hutchifon./ Very fit for thefe times; here being the fame errours amongſt/ us, and acted by the fame fpirit./ Publiſhed at the inſtant requeſt of fundry, by one that was an eye/ and eare-witneſſe of the carriage of matters there./ *London,*/ Printed for Ralph Smith at the figne of the Bible in Cornhill/ neare the Royall Exchange. 1644./ 10 *prel. leaves; viz.* Title in a metal type border, *the reverse blank;* 'To the Reader.' *Signed* 'T. W.' 1 *page.* 'The Preface.' *Signed* 'T. Welde.' 16 *pp:* Text 66 *pp. Calf extra by Bedford.* 4to. (2l. 12s. 6d. 2811)

WEMMS (WILLIAM). The Trial of William Wemms, James Hartegan, William M'Cauley, Hugh White, Mathew Killroy, William Warren, John Carrol, and Hugh Montgomery, Soldiers in his Majeſty's 29th Regiment of Foot, For the Murder of Criſpus Attucks, Samuel Gray, Samuel Maverick, James Caldwell, and Patrick Carr, On Monday Evening, the 5th of March, 1770, at the Superior Court of Judicature, Court of Aſſize, and general Goal Delivery, held at Boston. The 27th Day of November, 1770, by Adjournment. Before the Hon. Benjamin Lynde, John Cushing, Peter Oliver, and Edmund Trowbridge, Esquires, Justices of faid Court. Publiſhed by Permiſſion of the Court. Taken in Short Hand by John Hodgson. *Boston:* Printed by J. Fleeming, and fold at his PrintingOffice, nearly oppoſite the White-horſe Tavern in Newbury-ſtreet. M,DCC,LXX. 217 *pp. Calf extra by Bedford.* 8vo. (18s. 2812)

WESLEY (JOHN). An Old Fox Tarr'd and Feathered. Occasioned by what is called Mr. John Wesley's Calm Addreſs to our American Colonies. By an Hanoverian. A Calm Addreſs to our American Colonies. *London:* Printed for the Author; [1775.] 16 *pp. Half mor.* 8vo. (4s. 6d. 2813)

WESLEY (JOHN). A Calm Address to our American Colonies. By John Wesley, M.A. *London,* R. Hawes, [1775.] 23 *pp. Half morocco.* 12mo. (4s. 6d. 2814)

WESLEY (JOHN). A Calm Address to our American Colonies. By John Wesley, M.A. *London:* R. Hawes, MDCCLXXV. 23 *pp. Half morocco.* 12mo. (3s. 6d. 2815)

WESLEY (JOHN). A Calm Address to our American Colonies. By John Wesley, M.A. A New Edition, Corrected, and Enlarged. London, Robert Hawes, [1776.] 22 pp. 12mo. (4s. 6d. 2816)

WESLEY (John). A Calm Addreſs to the Inhabitants of England. By John Wesley. London: J. Fry and Co. M.DCC.LXXVII. 21 pp. Half morocco. 12mo. (3s. 6d. 2817)

WESLEY (John). Some Observations on Liberty: Occaſioned by a late Tract. By John Wesley, M.A. London, R. Hawes, 1776. 36 pp. Half morocco. 12mo. (3s. 6d. 2818)

WEST (John). The Substance of a Journal during a residence at the Red River Colony British North America: And frequent excursions among the North West American Indians, in the years 1820, 1821, 1822, 1823. Second Edition, enlarged with a Journal of a Mission to the Indians of New Brunswick, and Nova Scotia, and the Mohawks on the Ouse or Grand River, Upper Canada. 1825-1826. By John West, A.M. Late Chaplain to the Hon. The Hudson's Bay Company. L. B. Seeley and Son, London. MDCCCXXVII. xvi and 326 pp. With 4 plates. Cloth. 8vo. (5s. 2819)

WEST INDIA COMPANY. Nader Prolongatie van het Octroy voor de Westindische Compagnie. en van de eerſte prolongatie van dien, voor den tyd van nog dertig jaaren. Gearreſteert den 8 Auguſty 1730. In 's Gravenhage, By Jacobus Scheltus, Anno 1730. 20 pp. Calf, by Hayday. 4to. (10s. 6d. 2820)

WEST-INDIES. Weſt-vnnd Oſt Indiſcher/ Luſtgart:/ Das iſt,/ Eygentliche Erzehlung,/ Wann vnd von wem die Newe Welt erfunden,/ beſägelt, vnd eingenommen worden, vnd was ſich Denck-/ würdiges darbey zugetragen./ Neben Beſchreibung aller deren Landſchafften,/ Inſeln, Völcker, Thieren, Früchten, Gewächſen, ſo/ beydes in Weſt=vnd Oſt Indien zu finden./ Wie auch Verfaſſung der fürnembſten Schiffahrten ſo/ nicht allein dahin, ſonderen auch vmb die gantze Welt von den Spa=/nieren, Engelländeren, Holländeren, &c. verrichter/ worden./ Aufz glaubwürdigen Schrifften zuſamen gezogen./ Gedruckt zu Cöllen,/ Bey Wilhelm Lützenkirchen,/ Anno MDCXVIII./ 4 *prel. leaves; viz. Title, the reverse blank.* ' Dem Hochwürdigen in Gott Vatter vnnd Herren, Herren Hugoni,' *etc.* 4 *pp, signed* ' Gaſpar Ens L. Wilhelm Lutzenkirchen.' ' An den Günſtigen Leſer.' 2 *pp: Text,* 436 *pp.* ' Des Oſt Indiſchen Luſtgar=/tens/ Erſter Theil:/' 236 *pp. Vellum.* 4to. (2*l.* 2*s.* 2821)

WEST INDIES. [*Printed title*] West-Indische/ Spieghel,/ 't *Amstelredam,* By Broer Ianſz. ende Iacob Pieterſz. Wachter, Boeck-/vercooper op den Dam, inde Wachter. Anno 1624./ [*Engraved title*] Weſt-Indiſche/ Spieghel,/ Waer inne men ſien kan,/ Alle de Eylanden, Provintien, Lant-ſchappen, het/ Machtige Ryck van Mexico, en 't Gout/ en Silver-rycke Landt van Peru./ 'Tſampt/ De Courſen, Havenen, Klippen,/ Koopmanschap-pen, etc. ſoo wel inde Noort als in/ de Zuyt-zee. Als mede hoe die vande/ Spanjaerden eerſt ge in-vadeert ſyn./ Door/ Athanasium Inga,/ Peruaen, van Cuſco./ 4 *prel. leaves; viz. Engraved and printed titles,* ' Toe eyghen-Brief.' 4 *pp: Text* 435 *pp.* ' Regiſter des Boecks:' 7 *pp.* 2 *maps,* 't Noorder deel van West Indien' *and* 't Zuyder deel van West-Indien.' *Vellum.* 4to. (1*l.* 11*s.* 6*d.* 2822)

WETMORE (JAMES). A Vindication of The Pro-feſſors of the Church of England in Connecticut. Againſt The Invectives contained in a Sermon preached at Stanford by Mr. Noah Hobart, Dec. 31. 1746. In a Letter to a Friend. By James Wetmore, A.M. Rector of the Pariſh of Rye, and Miſſionary from the venerable Society for the Pro-pagation of the Goſpel in foreign Parts. *Boston:* N. E. Printed and Sold by Rogers and Fowle in Queen-ſtreet. MDCCXLVII. 45 *pp. Half morocco.* 8*vo.* (10*s.* 6*d.* 2823)

WHAT think ye of the Congress now? Or, an En-quiry, how far the Americans Are bound to abide by, and execute, the Decisions of the late Conti-nental Congress. With a Plan, By Samuel Gallo-way, Eſq; for a Proposed Union between Great-Britain and the Colonies. To which is added, An Alarm to the Legislature of the Province of New-York. Occaſioned by the preſent Political Dis-turbances. Addreſſed to the Representatives in General Assembly convened. New York, *Printed by J. Rivington: London,* Reprinted for Richardson Urquhart, 1775. *Title and* 90 *pp.* *Half morocco.* 8*vo.*   (7*s.* 6*d.* 2824)

WHEATLEY (PHILLIS). Poems on various subjects, religious and moral. By Phillis Wheatley, Negro Servant to Mr. John Wheatley, of Boston, in New England. *London:* Printed for A. Bell, Bookseller, Aldgate; and sold by Messrs. Cox and Berry, King Street, Boston. MDCCLXXIII. 124 *pp.* *Contents,* 3 *pp. With frontispiece portrait. Calf.* 8*vo.*   (10*s.* 6*d.* 2825)

WHEELOCK (ELEAZAR). A plain and faithful Narrative of the Original Design, Rise, Progress and present State of the Indian Charity-School At Lebanon, in Connecticut. By Eleazar Wheelock, A.M. Pastor of a Church in Lebanon. *Boston:* Printed by Richard and Samuel Draper, in Newbury-street. M.DCC.LXIII. 55 *pp. Half morocco.* 8*vo.*   (7*s.* 6*d.* 2826)

WHEELOCK (ELEAZAR). A Brief Narrative of the Indian Charity-School, In Lebanon in Connecticut, New England. Founded and Carried on by That faithful Servant of God The Rev. Mr. Eleazar Wheelock. *London:* J. and W. Oliver, MDCCLXVI. 48 *pp. Half mor.* 8*vo.*   (5*s.* 6*d.* 2827)

WHITAKER (NATHANAEL). Two Sermons: On the Doctrine of Reconciliation. Together with an Appendix, in answer to a Dialogue wrote to discredit the main Truths contained in these Discourses, By the Reverend William Hart, Of Saybrook, in Connecticut. By Nathanael Whitaker, D.D. Minister of the Gospel in Salem, in Massachusetts-Bay. *Salem*, New-England: Printed by Samuel Hall, in the main Street. MDCCLXX. 168 *pp.* 8*vo.*   (6*s.* 6*d.* 2828)

WHITBOURNE (RICHARD). A/ Discovrse/ and Discovery/ of Nevv-fovnd-land, with/ many reasons to prooue how worthy and be-/neficiall a Plantation may there be made,/ after a far better manner than/ now it is./ Together with the Lay-/ ing open of certaine enor-/mities and abuses committed by some that trade/ to that Countrey, and the meanes laide/ downe for reformation/ thereof./ Written by Captaine Richard Whitbourne of/ Exmouth, in the County of Deuon, and pub-/lished by Authority./ Imprinted at *London* by *Felix Kyngston*, for/ William Barret. 1620./ 9 *prel. leaves*; *viz. Title, on the reverse the royal arms*; 'To the High/ and Mightie Prince,/ Iames, By the Grace of/ God, King of Great Brittaine, France/ and Ireland, Defender of the/ Faith, &c.'/ (A 3) 4 *pp*; *signed* 'Richard Whitbovrne.' 'To his Maieſties good/ Subiects.' (B) 4 *pp*: *signed* 'R. W.' 'The Preface be-/ing an Indvction to/ the following Diſcourſe.'/ (B 3) 8 *pp. in italics*; *Text,* (D) 69 *pp. followed by one blank page*; 'A concluſion to the Reader, containing/ a particular Deſcription, and relation/ of ſome things omitted in the for-/mer Diſcourſe.'/ 4 *pp. Fine copy, in calf extra, by Bedford.* 4*to.* (4*l.* 4*s.* 2829)

WHITBOURNE (RICHARD). A/ Discovrse/ And Discovery/ of Nevv-found-land, with/ many reaſons to prooue how worthy and bene-/ficiall a Plantation may there be made, after a far/ better manner than now it is./ Together with the laying/ open of certaine enormities/ and abuſes committed by ſome that trade to that/ Countrey, and the meanes laid downe for/ reformation thereof./ Written by Captaine Richard Whitbourne of/ Exmouth, in the County of Deuon, and pub-/liſhed by Authority./ As alſo, an Inuitation: and likewiſe certaine Letters ſent/ from that Countrey; which are printed in the/ latter part of this Booke./ Imprinted at *London* by Felix Kingſton./ 1622./ 11 *prel. leaves*; *viz. Title, on the reverse the royal arms*; 'At Theobalds, the 12. of Aprill 1622.' 1 *page*; 'After our very hearty Commendations to your good Lordſhips,' *etc.* 1 *page*; 'The names of ſome, who haue vndertaken to/ helpe and aduance his Maieſties Plantation in/ the New-found-land. viz.' 2 *pp*; *signed* 'R. W.' 'To the High/ and Mightie Prince,/ Iames, by the Grace of/ God, King of great Brittaine, France/ and Ireland, Defender of the/ Faith, &c./ 4 *pp*; *signed* 'Richard Whitbovrne.' 'To his Maieſties good/ Subiects.'/ 4 *pp*; *signed* 'R. W.' 'The Preface,/ being an indvc-/tion to the following/ Diſcourse / 8 *pp* : *Text* 107 *pp.* 'A Concluſion to the former Diſcourſe,' *etc.* 5 *pp*; *signed* 'R. W.' 'A Letter from Captaine Edward Wynne, Go-/uernour of the Colony at Ferryland, within the/ Prouince of Aualon, in

Newfound-land, vnto/ the Right Honorable Sir George Calvert/ Knight, his Maiefties Principall Secre-/tary. Iuly 1622,/ *and 3 other Letters, pp. 1 to* 15. (*pp.* 35, 70, *and* 71, *are paged* 3, 100, *and* 101.) *Calf extra, by Bedford.* 4*to.* (4*l.* 4*s.* 2830)

WHITBOURNE (RICHARD). A/ Difcovrfe/ and Discovery/ of nevv - fovnd - land, with/ many reafons to prooue how worthy and'bene-/ficial a Plantation may there be made, after a/ better manner than it was./ Together with the laying/ open of certain enormities/ and abufes committed by fome that trade to that/ Countrey, and the meanes laid downe for/ reformation thereof./ Written by Captaine Richard Whitbourne of/ Exmouth, in the County of Deuon, and pub-/lifhed by Authority./ As alfo a louing Inuitation and likewife the copies of certaine/ Letters fent from that Countrey; which are printed in/ the latter part of this Booke. Imprinted at *London* by Felix Kingston. 1623./ *9 prel. leaves; viz. Title, on the reverse the royal arms, and* ' Moft humbly,' *etc.* 'At Theobalds, the 12. of Aprill 1622.' 1 *page,* ' After our very hearty Commendations to your good Lordfhips,' *etc.* 1 *page;* [' The names of fome, who haue vndertaken to helpe and aduance his Maiefties Plantation in the New-found-land. viz.' 2 *pp. signed* ' R. W.' *wanting.*] 'To the High/ and Mightie Prince,/ Iames, by the Grace of God,/ King of great Brittaine, France and Ireland,/ Defender of the Faith, &c.'/ 2 *pp.* 'To his Maiefties good Subiects.' 3 *pp;* 'The Preface,' 7 *pp. Text,* 97 *pp;* 'A Conclufion to the former Difcourfe,' *etc.* 4 *pp.* 'A Letter from Captaine Edward Wynne,' *etc. and 3 other Letters, pp.* 1 *to* 15. 4*to.* (3*l.* 2831)

WHITEFIELD (GEORGE). A Journal of a Voyage from London to Savannah in Georgia. In Two Parts. Part I. From London to Gibraltar. Part II. From Gibraltar to Savannah. By George Whitefield A.B. of Pembroke College, Oxford. [With a fhort Preface, fhewing the Reafons of its Publication. London, James Hutton, 1738.] *Title, iv and* 58 *pp. Title-page mutilated. Half morocco.* 8*vo.* (4*s.* 6*d.* 2832)

WHITEFIELD (GEORGE). A Journal of a Voyage from London to Savannah in Georgia. In Two

Parts. Part I. From London to Gibralter. Part II. From Gibralter to Savannah. By George Whitefield, A. B. of Pembroke-College, Oxford. With a ſhort Preface, ſhewing the Reaſon of its Publication. The Fifth Edition. *London*, James Hutton, MDCCXXXIX. 55 *pp.* 8*vo.* (4s. 6d. 2833)

WHITEFIELD (GEORGE). A Continuation Of the Reverend Mr. Whitefield's Journal, From his Arrival at Savannah, To his Return to London. *London*, James Hutton, M.DCC.XXXIX. *2 prel. leaves and* 38 *pp.* 'Advertiſement.' 1 *page. Half morocco.* 8*vo.* (5s. 6d. 2834)

WHITEFIELD (GEORGE). A Continuation Of the Reverend Mr. Whitefield's Journal From his Arrival at Savannah, To his Return to London. The Second Edition. *London:* W. Strahan, MDCCXXXIX. *2 prel. leaves and* 38 *pp.* 8*vo.* (5s. 6d. 2835)

WHITEFIELD (GEORGE). [*First title*] The Rev. Mr. Whitefield's Answer to the Bishop of London's last Pastoral Letters. The Second Edition. With the Supplement. [*Second title*] The Rev. Mr. Whitefield's Answer to the Bishop of London's last Pastoral Letter. *London :* W. Strahan, MDCCXXXIX. *Text, pp.* 3-28. 'A Supplement to The Rev. Mr. Whitefield's Answer,' *etc.* 8 *pp.* 8*vo.* (2s. 6d. 2836)

WHITEFIELD (GEORGE). The heinous Sin of Drunkenness A Sermon Preached on Board the Whitaker. By George Whitefield, A. B. of Pembroke College, Oxford. *London:* C. Whitefield, MDCCXXXIX. *Wanting all after page* 20. *Unbound.* 8*vo.* (2s. 6d. 2837)

WHITEFIELD (GEORGE). Thankfulneſs for Mercies received a neceſſary Duty A Farewel Sermon Preached on Board the Whitaker, At Anchor near Savannah in Georgia, On Sunday May the 17th, 1738. By George Whitefield, A. B. of Pembroke College, Oxford. *London :* C. Whitefield, MDCCXXXIX. *Title and pp.* 3-24. 8*vo.* (2s. 6d. 2838)

WHITEFIELD (GEORGE). A Continuation Of the Reverend Mr. Whitefield's Journal, From his Embarking after the Embargo, To his Arrival at Savannah in Georgia. *London:* W. Strahan 1740. 88 *pp.* 8*vo.* (5s. 6d. 2839)

WHITEFIELD (GEORGE). An Account of Money Received and Diſburſed for the Orphan-House in

Georgia. By George Whitefield, A. B. Late of Pembroke-College, Oxford. To which is prefixed A Plan of the Building. *London:* W. Strahan for T. Cooper, 1741. *Title and* 45 *pp. With the Plan.* 8vo. (7s. 6d. 2840)

WHITEFIELD (GEORGE). A Letter To the Reverend Mr. John Wesley: In Answer to his Sermon, entituled, Free-Grace. By George Whitefield, A. B. Late of Pembroke-College, Oxford. *London:* W. Strahan for T. Cooper, 1741. 31 *pp.* 8vo. (2s. 6d. 2841)

WHITEFIELD (GEORGE). A Continuation of the Account of the Orphan-House in Georgia. From January 1740, to June 1742. To which are alfo fubjoin'd, Some Extracts from an Account of a Work of a like Nature, carried on by the late Profeffor Franck in Glaucha near Hall in Saxony. By George Whitefield, A. B. Late of Pembroke-College in Oxford. *Edinburgh,* T. Lumisden and J. Robertson; M.DCC.XLII. 85 *pp. Unbound.* 12mo. (4s. 6d. 2842)

WHITEFIELD (GEORGE). A Continuation Of the Reverend Mr. Whitefield's Journal, From a few Days after his Return to Georgia To his Arrival at Falmouth, on the 11th of March, 1741. Containing An Account of the Work of God at Georgia, Rhode-Ifland, New-England, New-York, Pennfylvania and South-Carolina. The Seventh Journal. The second Edition. *London:* W. Strahan; MDCCXLIV. 88 *pp. Half mor.* 8vo. (5s. 6d. 2843)

WHITEFIELD (GEORGE). A Short Account of God's Dealings With the Reverend Mr. George Whitefield, A. B. late of Pembroke-College, Oxford, from His Infancy to the Time of his entring into Holy Orders. Written by Himself, on board the Elizabeth, Captaine Stephenfon, bound from London to Philadelphia and fent over by him to be publifhed for the Benefit of the Orphan Houfe in Georgia. The Second Edition. *London:* W. Strahan, MDCCXLIV. 46 *pp. Half morocco.* 12mo. (4s. 6d. 2844)

WHITEFIELD (GEORGE). Britain's Mercies, and Britain's Duty; Reprefented in a Sermon Preach'd at the New-Building in Philadelphia, On Sunday

Auguft 24, 1746. Occafioned by the Suppreffion of the late Unnatural Rebellion. By George Whitefield, A. B. Late of Pembroke - College, Oxon. The Second Edition. *Boston*: Printed and Sold by S. Kneeland and T. Green in Queen-Street. 1746. *Title and pp.* 5-22. 8*vo.* (2s. 6d. 2845)

WHITEFIELD (GEORGE). Britain's Mercies, and Britain's Duty. Represented in a Sermon Preach'd at Philadelphia, On Sunday Auguft 24, 1746. And occafioned by the Suppression Of the late Unnatural Rebellion. By George Whitefield, A. B. Late of Pembroke College, Oxon. Philadelphia Printed: *London* Re-printed, For J. Robinson, 1746. 24 *pp. Half morocco.* 8*vo.* (2s. 6d. 2846)

WHITEFIELD (GEORGE). The Two First Parts of his Life, with his Journals, Revifed, correčted, and abridged, By George Whitefield, A. B. Chaplain to the Right Hon. the Countefs of Huntingdon. *London*: W. Strahan, MDCCLVI. 3 *prel. leaves and* 446 *pp. Old calf.* 12*mo.* (7s. 6d. 2847)

WHITELOCKE (JOHN). Trial of Lieutenant General John Whitelocke, Commander in Chief of the Expedition against Buenos Ayres. By Court-Martial, held in Chelsea College, On Thursday, the 28th January, 1808, and succeeding days. *London*: Samuel Tipper, 1808. *Half-title, title, and* 214 *pp.* 1 *blank leaf.* 'Appendix,' 12 *pp. Plan of the march, etc.* 8*vo.* (4s. 6d. 2848)

WHITNEY (PETER). The History of the County of Worcester, in the Commonwealth of Massachusetts: With a Particular Account of every Town from its tirst Settlement to the prefent Time; Including its Ecclesiastical State, together with a Geographical Description of the same. To which is prefixed, a Map of the County, at Large, from actual Survey. By Peter Whitney, A. M. Minifter of the Gofpel in Northborough, in faid County. Printed at *Worcester*, Massachusetts, by Isaiah Thomas, Sold by him in Worcester, by faid Thomas and Andrews, in Boston, and by faid Thomas and Carlisle, in Walpole, Newhampfhire. MDCCXCIII. 339 *pp. With the map. Calf.* 8*vo.* (12s. 6d. 2849)

WHOLSOME Severity reconciled with/ Christian Liberty./ Or,/ The true Refolution of a prefent

Con-/troverſie concerning Liberty of/ Conſcience./ Here you have the Queſtion ſtated, the middle/ way betwixt Popiſh Tyrannie and Schiſmatizing/ Liberty approved, and alſo confirmed from/ Scripture, and the teſtimonies of Divines,/ yea of whole Churches :/ The chiefe Arguments and Exceptions uſed in The/ Bloudy Tenent, The Compaſsionate Samaritane,/ M. S. to A. S. &c. examined./ Eight Diſtinctions added for qualifying and/ clearing the whole matter./ And in concluſion a Parænetick to the five Apo-/logiſts for chooſing Accommodation rather/ then Toleration./ Imprimatur. Ia. Cranford. Decemb. 16. 1644./ *London*,/ Printed for Chriſtopher Meredith, and are to be ſold/ at the Signe of the Crane in Pauls Churchyard. 1645./ 4 *prel. leaves and* 40 *pp. half mor.* 4*to.* (1*l.* 1*s.* 2850)

WIGGLESWORTH (EDWARD). The Bleſſedneſs of the Dead who die in the Lord. A Sermon Preached at the Publick Lecture, Tueſday, April 6. 1731. In the Hall of Harvard=College, In Cambridge, N. E. Upon the News of the Death of Thomas Hollis, Eſq; of London, The moſt bountiful Benefactor to that Society. By Edward Wigglesworth, D. D. And Hollis-Profeſſor of Divinity. Publiſhed at the Deſire of the Preſident and Fellows of Harvard-College. *Boston* in New-England : Printed for S. Gerriſh, at the lower End of Cornhil. 1731. *Title, iv and* 23 *pp. Unbound.* 8*vo.* (4*s.* 6*d.* 2851)

WIGGLESWORTH (EDWARD). A Letter To the Reverend Mr. George Whitefield, By Way of Reply To his Anſwer to the College Teſtimony againſt him and his Conduct. By Edward Wigglefworth, D. D. Profeſſor of Divinity in ſaid College. To which is added, The Reverend Preſident's Answer To the Things charg'd upon Him by the ſaid Mr. Whitefield, as Inconſiſtences. *Boston*, N. E. Printed and ſold by T. Fleet, at the Heart and Crown in Cornhill. 1745. 61 *pp.* 'Poſtcript.' 2 *pp.* 'The Reverend Preſident's Answer,' 5 *pp.* *signed* 'Edward Holyoke.' 4*to.* (7*s.* 6*d.* 2852)

WIGGLESWORTH (EDWARD). Calculations on American Population, with A Table for eſtimating the annual Increase of Inhabitants in the Britiſh Colonies : The Manner of its Conſtruction Explained; and Its Ufe Illuftrated. By Edward Wigglesworth, M.A. Hollis Profeffor of Divinity at Cambridge. *Boston:* Printed and Sold by John Boyle in Marlboro' Street. MDCCLXXV. 24 pp. Half morocco. 8vo. (7s. 6d. 2853)

WILBERFORCE (SAMUEL). A History of the Protestant Episcopal Church in America. By Samuel Wilberforce, M.A. Chaplain to H. R. H. Prince Albert, and Archdeacon of Surrey. *London:* James Burns, 1844. xvi and 456 pp. *Map and table.* Cloth, uncut. 12mo. (3s. 6d. 2854)

WILCOCKE (SAMUEL HULL). History of the Viceroyalty of Buenos Ayres; containing the most accurate details relative to the Topography, History, Commerce, Population, Government, &c. &c. Of that Valuable Colony. By Samuel Hull Wilcocke. Illustrated with plates. *London:* Sherwood, Neely, and Jones, [1806]. 2 prel. leaves and 576 pp. *Map facing title, chart and plates at pp. 58, 172, 336, 415, 418, 457.* 8vo. (7s. 6d. 2855)

WILKES (CHARLES). Narrative of the United States' Exploring Expedition, during the Years 1838, 1839, 1840, 1841, 1842. By Charles Wilkes, U. S. N. Commander of the Expedition, Member of the American Philosophical Society, &c. Condensed and Abridged. *London:* Whittaker and Co., [1845.] 4 prel. leaves and 372 pp. Half calf. 8vo. (5s. 2856)

WILKINSON (JAMES). Burr's Conspiracy exposed; and General Wilkinson vindicated against the slanders of his Enemies on that important occasion. 1811. *Title, Advertisement 1 page, Introduction, pp. 3-18. Text, pp. 3-99. Appendix 136 pp.* Half calf. 8vo. (7s. 6d. 2857)

WILKINSON (JAMES). Memoirs of My own Times. By General James Wilkinson. In Three Volumes. *Philadelphia:* Printed by Abraham Small. 1816. *Two Volumes.* Vol. I. xv and 855 pp. 7 Returns A to G. 'Appendix,' 42 pp. 'Errata,' 2 pp. facsimile letters at pp. 282, 283. Vol. II. Title and 578 pp. 'Appendix.' 260 pp. [Vol. 3 wanting] Half calf. 8vo. (1l. 1s. 2858)

WILLARD (SAMUEL). A/ Sermon/ Preached upon Ezek. 22. 30, 31./ Occafioned by the Death of the/

much honoured/ John Leveret Efq;/ Governour of the Colony of the/ Mattachufets. N. E./ By S. W. Teacher of the South Church/ in Bofton./ *Boston ;/* Printed by John Fofter, in the Year 1679./ *Title in a type metal border, the reverse blank, and text,* 13 *pp. Fine copy, in morocco, by Bedford.* 4*to.* (3*l.* 3*s.* 2859)

WILLARD (SAMUEL). The Duty of a People that have Renewed/ their Covenant with God./ Opened and Urged in/ A Sermon/ Preached to the fecond Church in Bofton in/ New-England, March 17. 16$^{79}_{80}$. after/ that Church had explicitly and moft/ folemnly renewed the Ingagement/ of themfelves to God, and one to another./ By Samvel VVillard, Teacher of a Church in/ Bofton in New-England./ *Boston,* Printed by John Fofter. 1680. *Title, reverse blank, and* 13 *pp. Fine copy in morocco, by Bedford.* 4*to.* (3*l.* 3*s.* 2860)

WILLARD (SAMUEL). Ne Sutor ultra Crepidam./ Or brief/ Animadverfions/ Upon the New-England/ Anabaptifts/ late fallacious/ Narrative ;/ Wherein the Notorious Miftakes/ and Falfhoods by them Publifhed, are detected./ By Samuel Willard, Teacher of a Church in Bofton in New-England. *Boston* in New-England,/ Printed by S. Green upon Affignment of S. Sewall. And are to be Sold/ by Sam. Philips, at the Weft end of the Exchange: 1681./ 4 *prel. leaves; viz. Title, reverse blank,* ' To the Reader.' 5 *pp. signed* ' Increase Mather.' *Text* 27 *pp. Fine copy in morocco, by Bedford.* 4*to.* (4*l.* 4*s.* 2861)

WILLARD (SAMUEL). The Movrners/ Cordial/ Againft Exceffive/ Sorrovv/ Difcovering what grounds of Hope/ Gods People have concerning their/ dead/ Friends/ By Samuel Willard, Teacher of a/ Church in Boston./ *Boston,* Printed by Benjamin Harris, and/ John Allen. 1691./ Very Suitable to be given at Funerals./ 4 *and* 138 *pp.* 16*mo.* (1*l.* 1*s.* 2862)

WILLARD (SAMUEL). Love's/ Pedigree./ Or/ A Difcourfe fhewing the Grace of/ Love in a Believer to be of/ A Divine Original/ Delivered in a/ Sermon/ Preached at the Lecture in Boston,/ Febr. 29. $^{1699}_{1700}$./ By S. Willard, Teacher of a Church there./ *Boston*, in N. E. Printed by B. Green, and/ J. Allen. Sold by Benjamin Eliot, at his Shop/ under the Weſt End of the Town Houſe. 1700./ *Title & pp*. 3-28. 16*mo*. (10*s*. 6*d*. 2863)

WILLARD (SAMUEL). The Peril/ of the/ Times Diſplayed./ Or,/ The Danger of Mens taking up/ with a/ Form of Godlineſs,/ But Denying the Power of it./ Being/ The Subſtance of ſeveral Sermons/ Preached :/ By Samuel Willard,/ Teacher of a Church in Boſton. N. E. *Boſton*, Printed by B. Green, & J. Allen,/ Sold by Benjamin Eliot. 1700./ 168 *pp*. 12*mo*. (1*l*. 1*s*. 2864)

WILLARD (SAMUEL). A Compleat Body of Divinity in Two Hundred and Fifty Expository Lectures on the Aſſembly's Shorter Catechiſm wherein The Doctrines of the Christian Religion are unfolded, their Truth confirm'd, their Excellence diſplay'd, their Uſefulneſs improv'd ; contrary Errors & Vices refuted & expos'd, Objections anſwer'd, Controverſies ſettled, Caſes of Conſcience reſolv'd ; and a great Light thereby reflected on the preſent Age. By the Reverend & Learned Samuel Willard, M. A. Late Paſtor of the South Church in Boſton, and Vice-Preſident of Harvard College in Cambridge, in New-England. Prefac'd by the Paſtors of the ſame Church. *Boston* in New-England : Printed by B. Green and S. Kneeland for B. Eliot and D. Henchman, and Sold at their Shops. MDCCXXVI. *Title, iv*, 6, *and* 914 *pp*. *A Catalogue, etc*. 1 *page*. *Folio*. (3*l*. 3*s*. 2865)

WILLIAMS (DANIEL). Man made Righteous/ by/ Chriſt's Obedience./ Being two/ Sermons/ at/ Pinners-Hall./ With Enlargements, &c./ Alſo ſome/ Remarks/ on/ Mr. Mather's Poſtſcript, &c./ By Daniel Williams./ *London*/ Printed for J. Dunton at the Raven/ in the Poultry, 1694./ 6 *prel. leaves and* 238 *pp*. *Old calf*. 8*vo*. (7*s*. 6*d*. 2866)

WILLIAMS (EDWARD). Virginia :/ More eſpecially the South part thereof,/ Richly and truly valued : viz./ The fertile Carolana, and no leſſe excellent Iſle of Roa-/noak, of Latitude from 31. to 37. Degr. relating the/ meanes of rayſing infinite profits to the Adventu-/rers and Planters./ The ſecond Edition, with Addition of/ The Discovery

of Silkworms,/ with their benefit./ And Implanting
of Mulbury Trees./ Also/ The Dreffing of Vines,
for the rich Trade of ma-/king Wines in Virginia./
Together with/ The making of the Saw-mill, very
ufefull in Virginia,/ for cutting of Timber and
Clapbord to build with-/all, and its Converfion to
many as profitable Ufes./ By E. W. Gent./ *London,/* Printed by T. H. for John Stephenfon, at the
Signe of/ the Sun below Ludgate. 1650./ *6 prel.
leaves; viz. Title, the reverse blank,* ' To the worthy
Gentlemen, Adventurers and Plan-/ters in Virginia.'/ *2 pp;* 'To the Supreme Authority of this
Nation, The/ Parliament of England.'/ 8 *pp; signed*
' Ed. Williams.' *Text,* 47 *pp.* 'The Table.' 8 *pp.*
'Virginias/ Difcovery of/ Silke-Wormes,/ with
their benefit./ And/ The Implanting of Mulberry
Trees./ Alfo/ The dreffing and keeping of Vines,
for the rich Trade/ of making Wines there./ Together with/ The making of the Saw-mill, very
ufefull in Virginia,/ for cutting of Timber and
Clapboard, to build with-/all, and its converfion to
other as profitable Ufes./ *London,*/ Printed by T.
H. for John Stephenfon, at the figne of/ the Sun,
below Ludgate. 1650./ *4 prel. leaves; viz. one blank
leaf; Title, reverse blank;* 'To all the Virginia
Merchants, Adventures, and Planters.' 4 *pp. signed*
' Ed. Williams.' *Text,* 78 *pp. 2 maps, one with and one
without the portrait of Drake.* 4to. (15*l.* 15*s.* 2867)

WILLIAMS (GRIFFITH). An Account Of the Island
of Newfoundland, With the Nature of its Trade,
And Method of carrying on the Fishery. With
Reasons for the great Decreafe of that moft valuable
Branch of Trade. By Capt. Griffith Williams, Of
the Royal Regiment of Artillery, who refided in
the Ifland Fourteen Years when a Lieutenant, and
now has a Command there. To which is annexed,
A Plan To exclude the French from that Trade.
Propofed to the Adminiftration in the Year 1761,
By Capt. Cole. [*London*], Printed for Capt. Thomas
Cole, M.DCC.LXV, *Half-title, title, and* 35 *pp. Half
morocco.* 8*vo.* (4*s.* 6*d.* 2868)

WILLIAMS (JOHN). An Enquiry into the Truth
of the Tradition, concerning the Difcovery of
America, By Prince Madog ab Owen Gwynedd,
about the year, 1170. By John Williams, L.L.D.

London: J. Brown, M.DCCXCI. *viii and* 82 *pp.*
'Appendix.' 3 *pp.* 8*vo.* (10*s.* 6*d.* 2869)

WILLIAMS (JOHN). Farther Observations, on the Dilcovery of America, by Prince Madog ab Gwynedd, about the year, 1170. Containing the account given by General Bowles, the Creek or Cherokee Indian, lately in London, and by leveral others, of a Wellh Tribe or Tribes of Indians, now living in the Weltern parts of North America. By John Williams, L.L.D. *London:* J. Brown, M.DCCXCII. *ix and* 51 *pp.* 8*vo.* (7*s.* 6*d.* 2870)

WILLIAMS (JONATHAN). Thermometrical Navigation. Being A Series of Experiments and Observations, tending to Prove, that by ascertaining The Relative Heat of the Sea-Water from time to time, The Paflage of a Ship through the Gulph Stream, and from deep water into soundings, May be discovered in Time to avoid Danger, although (owing to tempestuous weather,) it may be impossible To heave the Lead or obferve the Heavenly Bodies. Extracted from the American Philosophical Transactions. Vol. 2 & 3. With Additions and Improvements. *Philadelphia:* Printed and Sold by R. Aitken, No. 22, Market Street. 1799. *xii and* 98 *pp.* 'Postcript,' 4 *pp. With map. Old calf.* 8*vo.* (7*s.* 6*d.* 2871)

WILLIAMS (ROGER). The/ Blovdy Tenent,/ of Persecution, for caufe of/ Conscience, difcuffed, in/ A Conference betweene/ Trvth and Peace./ VVho,/ In all tender Affection, prefent to the High/ Court of Parliament, (as the Refult of/ their Difcourfe) thefe, (amongſt other/ Paffages) of higheft confideration./ [*London*] Printed in the Year 1644./ 12 *prel. leaves; viz. Title, the reverse blank;* 'Firſt, That the blood of fo many hundred thoufand fouls of Proteftants and Papifts,' *etc.* 4 *pp;* 'To the Right Honorable, both Houſes of the High Court of Parliament.' 4 *pp;* 'To every Courteous Reader.' 3 *pp.;* 'A Table of the principall Contents of the Booke.' 10 *pp: Text* 247 *pp. Red morocco by F. Bedford.* 4*to.* (7*l.* 7*s.* 2872)

WILLIAMS (ROGER). The/ Bloody Tenent/ yet/ More Bloody:/ by/ Mr. Cottons endevour to wafh it white in the/ Blood of the Lambe;/ Of whofe precious Blood, fpilt in the/ Blood of his Servants; and/ Of the blood of Millions fpilt in former and/ later Wars for Confcience fake,/ that/ Moft Bloody Tenent of Perfecution for caufe of/ Confcience, upon a fecond Tryal, is found now more/ apparently and more notoriously guilty./ In this Rejoynder to Mr. Cotton, are principally/ I. The Name of Perfecution,/ II. The Power of the Civill Sword/ in Spirituals/] Examined/ III. The Parliaments permiffion of/ Diffenting Confciences/] Juftified./ Alfo (as a Teftimony to M^r. Clarks Narrative) is added/ a Letter to Mr Endicot Governor of the Maffachufets in N.E./ By R. Williams of Providence in New-England./ *London*, Printed for Giles Calvert, and are to be fold at/ the black-fpread-Eagle at the Weft-end of Pauls, 1652./ 20 prel. leaves; viz. Title in a type metal border, the reverse blank; ' To the Most Honorable the Parliament of the Common-wealth of England.' signed ' Roger Williams,' 18 pp; 'To the feveral Refpective General Courts, efpecially that of the Maffachufets in N. England.' signed ' Roger Williams.' 7 pp; 'To the Merciful and Compafsi-nate Reader.' signed 'Roger Williams.' 12 pp: Text 320 pp. 'The Principal Contents.' 16 pp. Old calf. 4to. (7l. 7s. 2873)

WILLIAMS (Roger). The Bloudy Tenant of Presecution for Cause of Conscience Discused: And Mr. Cotton's Letter examined and answered. By Roger Williams. Edited for The Hanserd Knollys Society, by Edward Bean Underhill. *London:* J. Haddon, 1848. xlvi pp. Title and 440 pp. 'Second Annual Report,' etc. 8 pp. Cloth. 8vo. (7s. 6d. 2874)

WILLIAMS (Roger). To the King's Moft Excellent Majesty./ The Humble Petition of Roger Williams of London, Mariner, Your Majefty's moft Loyal and Dutiful Subject./ [*London.* 1680?] Single sheet. Half morocco. Folio. (7s. 6d. 2875)

WILLIAMS (Samuel). The Natural and Civil History of Vermont. By Samuel Williams, LL.D. Member of the Meteorological Society in Germany of the Philosophical Society in Philadelphia and of the Academy of Arts and Sciences in Massachusetts. Publiſhed according to Act of Congress. Printed at *Walpole*, Newhampshire, by Isaiah Thomas and David Carlisle, Jun. Sold at their Bookstore, in Walpole, and by ſaid Thomas, at his Bookstore, in Worceſter. MDCCXCIV. *xvi and* 416 *pp. Map of Vermont. Calf.* 8*vo.* (7*s.* 6*d.* 2876)

WILLSON (MARCIUS). American History: Comprising Historical Sketches of the Indian Tribes; a description of American Antiquities, with an inquiry into their origin and the origin of the Indian Tribes; History of the United States, with appendices shewing its connection with European History: History of the present British Provinces; History of Mexico; and History of Texas, brought down to the time of its admission into the American Union. By Marcius Wilson, Author of School History of the United States, comprehensive Chart of American History etc. *New York:* Mark H. Newman & Co. No. 199 Broadway. 1847. 672 *pp. Cloth.* 8*vo.* (8*s.* 6*d.* 2878)

WILMORE (JOHN). The/ Case/ of/ John Wilmore/ Truly and Impartially Related:/ Or, a/ Looking= Glaſs/ for all/ Merchants and Planters/ That are Concerned in the/ American Plantations./ *London,*/ Printed for Edw. Powell at the White Swan in/ Little Brittain, MDCLXXXII./ *Title and* 17 *pp; signed* 'John Wilmer.' *Folio.* (1*l.* 1*s.* 2879)

WILMOT (JOHN EARDLEY -). Historical View of the Commission for enquiring into the Losses, Services, and Claims, of the American Loyalists, at the close of the War between Great Britain and her Colonies, in 1783: With an Account of the Compensation granted to them by Parliament in 1785 and 1788. By John Eardley - Wilmot, Esq. *London*, J. Nichols, 1815. *viii und* 204 *pp. With plate of the* 'Reception of the American Loyalists by Great Britain, in the year 1783.' *Half calf.* 8*vo.* (7*s.* 6*d.* 2880)

WILSON (H.) The Shipwreck of the Antelope Eaſt-India Packet, H. Wilson, Eſq. Commander, on the Pelew Islands, ſituate in the Weſt Part of the Pacific Ocean; In August 1783. Containing the subsequent Adventures of the Crew with a ſingular Race of People hitherto unknown to Europeans. With Interefting Particulars of Lee Boo, Second Son of the Pelew King, To the Time of his Death, at Capt. Wilson's Houfe at Rotherhithe. By One of the Unfortunate Officers. *London :* D. Brewman, MDCCLXXXVIII. *viii and* 134 *pp. With plate.* 8*vo.* (4*s.* 6*d.* 2881)

WILSON (JAMES). Commentaries on the Constitution of the United States of America. With that Constitution prefixed, in which are unfolded, the Principles of Free Government, and the Superior Advantages of Republicanism demonstrated By James Wilson, LL.D. Profeffor of Laws in the College and University of the Commonwealth of Pennfylvania, one of the Affociate Judges of the Supreme Court of the United States, and appointed by the Legiflature of Pennfylvania to form a Digeft of the Laws of that State; and By Thomas M'Kean, LL.D. Chief Juftice of the Commonwealth of Pennfylvania. The whole extracted from Debates, publifhed in Philadelphia, By T. Lloyd. *London :* J. Debrett, 1792. 4 *prel. leaves and pp.* 4-147. *Index,* 2 *pp. Errata,* 1 *page.* 8*vo.* (7*s.* 6*d.* 2882)

WILSON (THOMAS). The Knowledge and Practice of Christianity Made Easy To the Meaneft Capacities : Or, an Essay towards an Instruction for the Indians; Which will likewife be of Ufe To all fuch who are called Christians, but have not well confidered the Meaning of the Religion they profefs : Or, who profess to know God, but in Works do deny Him. In Twenty Dialogues. Together with Directions and Prayers, for The Heathen World, Missionaries, Catechumens, Private Persons, Families, Of Parents for their Children, For Sundays, &c. The Twelfth Edition. By the Right Reverend Father in God, Thomas, Lord Bifhop of Sodor and Man. *London :* John Rivington M,DCC,LXXVI. 4 *prel. leaves, xxiv and* 280 *pp. Calf.* 12*mo.* (7*s.* 6*d.* 2883)

WILSON (THOMAS W.) An Authentic Narrative of the Piratical Descents upon Cuba made By hordes from the United States, headed by Narciso Lopez, a native of South America ; to which are added some interesting letters and declarations from the prisoners, with a list of their names, &c. By Thomas W. Wilson. *Havana* September 1851. 44 *pp.* 4*to.* (2*s.* 6*d.* 2884)

WINCHESTER (ELHANAN). The Gospel of Christ No Caufe of Shame: Demonftrated in two Difcourfes on the Subject. By Elhanan Winchester. *Philadelphia:* Printed by B. Towne. 1783. 140 *pp.* 8vo. (4s. 6d. 2885)

WINCHESTER (ELHANAN). An Oration on the Discovery of America. Delivered in London, October the 12th, 1792, being Three Hundred Years from the day on which Columbus landed in the New World. By Elhanan Winchester. *London:* Printed for the Author, MDCCXCII. 32 *pp.* 8vo. (2s. 6d. 2886)

WINCHESTER (ELHANAN). An Oration on the Discovery of America. Delivered in London, October the 12th, 1792, being Three Hundred Years from the day on which Columbus landed in the New World. The Second Edition, with an Appendix, containing among other Things a description of the City of Washington, in the District of Columbia; illustrated with an accurate engraving. By Elhanan Winchester. *London:* Printed for the Author, [1792.] 77 *pp. Schedule, a folded sheet; A List of the Publications of the Author, etc.* 2 *pp. With the Plan of Washington. Half morocco.* 8vo. (5s. 6d. 2887)

WINSLOW (EDWARD). New-Englands/ Salamander,/ discovered/ By an irreligious and fcornefull/ Pamphlet, called New-Englands Jonas/ caft up at London, &c. Owned by Major Iohn/ Childe, but not probable to be written by him./ Or,/ A fatisfactory anfwer to many afperfi-/ons caft upon New-England therein./ Wherein our government there is fhewed to/ bee legall and not Arbitrary, being as neere the Law/ of England as our condition will permit./ Together/ With a briefe Reply to what is written in an-/fwer to certaine paffages in a late Booke called/ Hypocrifie unmasked./ By Edw. Winflow./ *London:* Printed by Ric. Cotes, for John Bellamy, and are to bee/ fold at his fhop at the figne of the three Golden Lions in/ Cornehill neare the Royall Exchange, 1647./ *Title in a narrow type metal border, the reverse blank: Text* 29 *pp. Fine large copy, with rough leaves. Red morocco extra, by Bedford.* 4to. (21*l.* 2888)

WINTERBOTHAM (W.) An Historical Geographical Commercial, and Philosophical View of the American United States, and of the European Settlements in America and the West-Indies. by W. Winterbotham. In Four Volumes. *London:* J. Ridgway, 1795. *Four Volumes. Vol. I. 9 prel. leaves, and 591 pp. Portrait of Washington, 2 maps and 1 plate. Vol. II. 2 prel. leaves, and 493 pp. Portrait of Penn, 2 maps and 1 plate. Vol. III. 2 prel. leaves, and 525 pp. Portrait of Franklin, 2 maps and 6 plates. Vol. IV. 2 prel. leaves, and 415 pp. 'Appendix,' 54 pp. 'Index,' 9 pp. 'Directions to the Binder,' 2 pp. Portrait of Winterbotham, maps, tables, and plates. Calf. 8vo.* (18s. 2889)

> Accompanied by Winterbotham's American Atlas; viz.
> 1. General Map of North America
> 2. Map of the United States
> 3. Map of the Northern or New England States
> 4. Map of the Middle States
> 5. Map of the Southern States
> 6. Plan of the City of Wafhington
> 7. Map of Kentucky
> 8. General Map of South America
> 9. Map of the West Indies.

WINTHROP (John). A Journal Of the Transactions and Occurrences in the fettlement of Maffachufetts and the other New-England Colonies, from the year 1630 to 1644: Written by John Winthrop, Efq. Firft Governor of Maffachufetts: And now firft publifhed from a correct copy of the original Manufcript. *Hartford:* Printed By Elisha Babcock. M,DCC,XC. *3 prel. leaves and 364 pp; Contents, 4 pp. Calf.* (15s. 2890)

WIRT (William). Sketches of the Life and Character of Patrick Henry. By William Wirt, of Richmond, Virginia. Second Edition, Corrected by the Author. *Philadelphia:* James Webster, 1818. *iv and 427 pp. 'Appendix,' xii. With portrait of Patrick Henry. Calf. 8vo.* (7s. 6d. 2891)

WISDOM (The), and Policy of the French in the Construction of their Great Offices, So as beft to anfwer the Purpofes of extending their Trade and Commerce, and enlarging their Foreign Settlements. With Some Observations in relation to the Disputes now fubfifting between the English and French Colonies in America. *London:* R. Baldwin, MDCCLV. *Title, text and 133 pp. Half morocco. 8vo.* (7s. 6d. 2892)

WITHERSPOON (John). An Address to the Natives of Scotland residing in America. Being an Appendix to a Sermon preached at Princeton on a General Fast. By John Witherspoon, D. D. Prefident of the College at New Jersey. *London:* Fielding and Walker, M,DCC,LXXVIII. *iv and 24 pp. Half morocco. 8vo.* (2s. 6d. 2893)

WITHERSPOON (John). The Dominion of Providence over the Passions of Men. A Sermon, preached at Princeton, May 17, 1775, being the General Fast Appointed by the Congress through the United Colonies. By John Witherspoon, D.D. Prefident of the College of New Jersey. Philadelphia printed; *London* reprinted, For Fielding and Walker, M,DCC,LXXVIII. *iv and 44 pp. Half morocco. 8vo.* (2s. 6d. 2894)

WITHERSPOON (John). Christian Magnanimity: A Sermon, Preached at Princeton, September, 1775—the Sabbath preceding the Annual Commencement; And again with Additions, September 23. 1787. To which is added, an Address to the Senior Class Who were to receive the Degree of Bachelor of Arts. By John Witherspoon, D.D. L.L.D. Prefident of the College of New-Jerfey. *Princeton:* Printed by James Tod. M.DCC.LXXXVII. *iv and 44 pp. 8vo.* (2s. 6d. 2895)

WITHERSPOON (John). A Sermon on the Religious Education of Children. Preached, in the Old Presbyterian Church in New-York, to a very numerous Audience, on the Evening of the second Sabbath in May. By the Rev. John Witherspoon, D. D. President of Princeton College. *Elizabeth-Town:* Printed by Shepard Kollock, M,DCC,LXXXIX. *24 pp. 8vo.* (2s. 6d. 2896)

WOLCOTT (Roger). Poetical/ Meditations,/ being the/ Improvement/ of some/ Vacant Hours,/ By Roger Wolcott, Efq;/ With a/ Preface/ By the Reverend/ Mr. Bulkley of Colchefter./ New London:/ Printed and Sold by T. Green,/ 1725./ *Half-title,* 'Mr. Wolcott's/ Poetical Meditations.'/ *Title, reverse blank;* 'The Preface,' *lvi pp. signed* 'John Bulkley,' *and dated* 'Colchefter, December 24./ 1724./' 'To the Reverend/ Mr. Timothy Edwards./ *ii pp. signed* 'R. W.' *and duted* 'Windfor, January

4th./ 1722,3.'/ Text, 'Some Improvement of vacant Hours,/ By Roger Wolcott, Efq;'/ 18 *pages, containing six minor poems on religious subjects.* Then comes 'A Brief Account/ of the/ Agency/ Of the Honourable/ John Winthrop, Efq;/ in the Court of/ King Charles the Second,/ Anno Dom. 1662./ When he Obtained for the Colony of Con-/necticut His Majefty's Gracious Charter.'/ *pages* 19 *to* 78, ' Finis.' *Then follows* ' Errata,' *one page;* ' Advertisement' 3 *pages, signed* ' Joseph Dewey,' *and dated* ' Colchefter/ 1725./' Red morocco extra by Bedford. 8vo. (7l. 17s. 6d. 2899)

It has been stated that Mr. Dewey, a maker of woollen cloth, in Colchester, Connecticut, was at the expense of printing this book, on the condition of inserting his advertisement at the end. Indeed the worthy clothier intimates as much in his advertisement: "having been fomething at Charge in promoting the Publifhing the fore-going Meditations, do here take the Liberty to Advertife my Country-People of fome Rules which ought to be obferved, in doing their part, that fo the Clothiers might be affifted in the better perfoimance of what is expected of them, that the Cloth which is made among us may both Wear and Laft, better, than it can poffibly do, Except thefe following Directions are Obferved by us." Then follow his feven Rules.

The interest of this book centres in the historical poem upon Winthrop's obtaining of Charles II. the Charter of Connecticut. After the Restoration, the "Sages of Connecticut" fent Winthrop their Governor to England to present an address, and

"To ask the King for CHARTER Liberties."

Soon after, it was announced to Charles who "was in his Council sat," that

"An Agent from Connecticut doth wait,
With an Addrefs before your Palace Gate."

Winthrop admitted, difcharges himfelf in homespun numbers, redolent rather of truth than poetry, filling some sixty pages, in which he recounts the national, civil, political, and military history of the Colony from the earliest time till " great Safacus and his Kingdom fell," lingering long about that beautiful river, that

"Calmly on a gentle wave doth move;
As if 'twere drawn to Thetis house by love.
The Waters Frefh and Sweet, & he that fwims
In it, Recruits and Cures his Surfeit Limbs.
The Fisherman the Fry with Pleafure gets,
With Seins, Pots, Angles, and his Tramel-nets.
In it swim Salmon, Sturgion, Carp and Eels.
Above fly Cranes, Geefe, Duck, Herons and Teals;
And Swans which take fuch Pleafure as they fly,
They sing their Hymns oft long before they Dy."

After reciting the exploits of Capt. John Mason, the Pequot War, and the fall of Saracus, the Agent concludes:—

" And we Your Supplyants before the Throne,
Beg leave to hope while all your Favours Taft,
Connecticut will not be overpaft."

" Great CHARLES who gave attention all the while,
Looking on Winthrop with a Royal Smile,
Until that of his Fathers woes he fpeaks,
Which drew the Chriftal Rivers down his Cheeks.

But feeing Winthrop his Addrefs had clos'd,
The King his Mind and Countenance Compos'd,
And with as bright an Air of Majesty,
As Phœbus fhews when he Serenes the Sky,
Made this Refolve upon the Agency,

Be it so then, and WE OUR SELF *Decree*
CONNECTICUT *shall be a* COLONY:
Enfranchis'd with such Ample Liberties
As Thou, Their Friend, *shalt best for them Devise;*
And further know Our Royal Pleasure thus,
And so it is Determined by US;
Chief in the Patent WINTHROP *Thou shalt stand,*
And Valiant Mason *next at thy right Hand.*
And for Chief Senators and Patentees,
Take Men of Wealth and known Abilities;
Men of Estates and Men of Influence,
Friends to their Country and to US *Their Prince.*

And may the People of that Happy Place
Whom thou hast so Endeared to My Grace;
Till times last Exit, through Succeeding Ages,
Be Blest with Happy English Privileges.
And that they may be so, bear thou from hence
To them these Premonitions from their Prince.

First, *Let all Officers in Civil Trust*
Always Espouse their Countrys Interest.
Let Law and Right be Precious in their Eyes,
And hear the Poor Mans Cause when e're he Crys.
Preserve Religion Pure and Understand,
That is the Firmest Pillar of the Land:
Let it be kept in Credit in the Court
And never fail for want of due Support.

And let the Sacred Order of the Gown,
With Zeal apply the Business that's their own.
So Peace may Spring from th' Earth & Righteousness,
Look down from Heaven, Truth and Judgment Kiss.

Then, *Let the Freemen of your Corporation,*
Always beware of the Insinuation,
Of those which always Brood Complaint and Fear,
Such Plagues are Dangerous to Infect the Air:
Such Men are Over-Laden with Compassion
Having Mens Freedom in such Admiration:
That every Act of Order or Restraint
They'll Represent as matter of Complaint.
And this is no New Doctrine, 'tis a Rule
Was taught in Satans first Erected School.
It serv'd his turn with wonderful Success,
And ever since has been his Master-piece.
'Tis true the sleight by which that field was won,
Was argued from man's benefit alone.
But these outdo him in that way of Evil,
And will sometimes for God's sake play the Devil.

And Lastly, *Let Your New* English *Multitude,*
Remember well a bond of Gratitude
Will Lye on them and their Posterity
Do bear in mind their Freedom came by Thee."

WOLLASTON (WILLIAM). The Religion of Nature delineated. *London:* Samuel Palmer, 1726. 219 pp. *Index* 11 pp. *Calf extra, by F. Bedford.* 4to. (1*l.* 11*s.* 6*d.* 2900)

This is the Book which Franklin mentions in his Autobiography as having worked upon, while a press-man with Samuel Palmer, in London.

WOOD (WILLIAM). Nevv/ Englands/ Prospect./ A true, lively, and experimen-/tall defcription of that part of America,/ commonly called ˋNevv-England :/ difcovering the ftate of that Coun-/trie, both as it ftands to our new-come/ Englifh Planters: and to the old/ Native Inhabitants./ Laying downe that which may both enrich the/ knowledge of the mind-travelling Reader,/ or benefit the future Voyager./ By William Wood./ Printed at *London* by Tho. Cotes, for Iohn Bellamie, and are to be fold/ at his fhop, at the three Golden Lyons in Corne-hill, neere the/ Royall Exchange. 1634./ 4 *prel. leaves*; *viz. Title, the reverse blank*, 'To the Right Worfhip-/full, my much honored Friend,/ Sir William Armyne,/ Knight and Baronet.'/ 2 *pp. signed* 'W. W.' 'To the Reader,' 2 *pp. signed* 'W. W.' 'To the Author, his fingular good/ Friend, M^r. William Wood.'/ 1 *page, signed* 'S. W.' 'The Table' *and* 'Errata,' 1 *page. Text,* 98 *pp.* 'Becaufe many have defired to heare fome of the Na-/tives Language, I have here inferted a fmall Nomen-/clator,' *etc.* 5 *pp. With map of* 'The South part of Nevv-England, as it is Planted this yeare, 1634.' 4*to.* (5*l.* 5*s.* 2901)
With the Autograph of White Kennett.

WOOD (WILLIAM). Nevv/ Englands/ Prospect./ A true, lively, and experimen-/tall defcription of that part of America,/ commonly called Nevv-England :/ difcovering the ftate of that Coun-/trie, both as it ftands to our new-come/ Englifh Planters; and to the old/ Native Inhabitants./ Laying downe that which may both enrich the/ knowledge of the mind-travelling Reader,/ or benefit the future Voyager,/ By William Wood./ Printed at *London* by Tho. Cotes for Iohn Bellamie, and are to be fold/ at his fhop, at the three Golden Lyons in Corne-hill, neere the/ Royall Exchange. 1635./ 4 *prel. leaves*; *viz. Title, the reverse blank,* 'To the Right Worfhipfull,/ my much honoured friend, Sir/ William Armyne, Knight/ and Baronet,'/ 2 *pp. signed* 'W. W. 'To the Reader,' 2 *pp. signed* 'W. W.' 'To the Author, his fingular good Friend, M^r. William Wood,' 1 *page, signed* 'S. W.' 'The Table,' 1 *page. Text* 83 *pp.* 'Becaufe many have defired to heare fome of the Na-/tives Language,' *etc.* 5 *pp. With map of* 'The South part of

Nevv-England, as it is Planted this yeare, 1635.'
Old calf. 4to. (4l. 14s. 6d. 2902)

WOOD (WILLIAM). New/ Englands/ Prospect./ A true, lively, and experimentall/ defcription of that part of America com-/monly called New-England: dif-/covering the ftate of that Country, both as/ it ftands to our new-come Englifh Plan-/ters; and to the old Native/ Inhabitants./ Laying down that which may both en-/rich the knowledge of the mind-travelling/ Reader, or benefit the future Voyager./ By William Wood/ London,/ Printed by Iohn Dawfon, and are to be fold by Iohn Bellamy/ at his fhop, at the three Golden Lyons in Corne-/hill, neere the Royall Exchange,/ 1639./ 4 prel. leaves; viz. Title, the reverse blank, 'To the Right Worfhipfull, my/ much honoured friend, Sir William/ Armyne, Knight and Baronet,'/ 2 pp. signed 'W. W.' 'To the Reader,' 2 pp. signed 'W. W.' 'To the Author, his fingular good Friend M^r. William Wood,' 1 page, signed 'S. W.' 'The Table,' 1 page. Text, 83 pp. 'Becaufe many have defired to heare fome of the Natives language,' etc. 5 pp. With map of 'The South part of New-England, as it is Planted this yeare 1639.'/ Brown morocco extra. 4to. (4l. 14s. 6d. 2903)

WOOD (WILLIAM). William Wood; - - - - - Appellant. David Polhill, Efq; and others, on Behalf of themfelves, and other, the Proprietors of Gold and Silver Mines in Jamaica Refpondents. The Appellant's Case. To be Heard at the Bar of the House of Lords, on [Wednesday] the [Fourth] Day of [February] Day of [February] 1746. [London. 1746.] 3 pp. Folio. (4s. 6d. 2904)

WOOLMAN (JOHN). Considerations on keeping Negroes; Recommended to the Professors of Christianity, of every Denomination. Part Second. By John Woolman. Philadelphia: Printed by B. Franklin, and D. Hall. 1762. 52 pp. Unbound. 8vo. (10s. 6d. 2905)

WOOLMAN (JOHN). A Journal of the Life, Gospel Labours, and Christian Experiences of that Faithful Minister of Jesus Christ, John Woolman, Late of Mount-Holly, in the Province of New-Jersey, North-America. To which are added, His Works, containing his laſt Epiſtle and other Writings. *Dublin: R. M. Jackson, 1794. xv and 464 pp. Calf.* 8vo. (7s. 6d. 2906)

WORD (A) of Comfort to a Melancholy Country. Or the Bank of Credit Erected in the Maſſachuſetts-Bay, Fairly Defended by a Diſcovery of the Great Benefit, accruing by it to the Whole Province; With a Remedy for Recovering a Civil State when Sinking under Deſperation by a Defeat on their Bank of Credit. By Amicus Patriæ. *Boston: Printed in the Year, 1721. 2 prel. leaves and 58 pp.* 16mo. (1l. 1s. 2907)

WORSLEY (ISRAEL). A View of the American Indians, their General Character, Customs, Language, Public Festivals, Religious Rites, and Traditions: Shewing them to be the Descendants of The Ten Tribes of Israel. The Language of Prophecy concerning them, and the course by which they travelled from Media into America. By Israel Worsley. *London:* June, MDCCCXXVIII. Printed for the Author. *Half-title, title, xii and 185 pp.* 12mo. (3s. 6d. 2908)

WRIGHT (EDWARD). Certain Errors/ in/ Navigation./ Detected and Corrected/ By Edw. Wright./ With many Additions that were not/ in the former Editions./ *London./* Printed by joſeph Moxon,/ and ſold at his Shop at the Atlas on Corn-hill. 1657./ *Engraved title, 12 prel. leaves, and 224 pp;* 'The Division of the whole Art of Navigation.' 110 pp: 'Made and ſold by Joſeph Moxon,' etc. 1 *page*; 'The Haven-finding Art,' *etc.* 20 pp. *Diagrams at pp.* 38, 57, 65, 148. *Platt for sailing to the Azores, on copper, at page* 91, 2d. Part. *Calf.* 4to. (1l. 11s. 6d. 2909)

WRIGHT (JOHN). The American Negotiator, or the Various Currencies of the British Colonies in America; As well the Islands, as the Continent. The Currencies of Nova Scotia, Canada, New England, New York, East Jersey, Penſylvania, West Jersey, Maryland, Virginia, North Carolina, South Carolina, Georgia, &c. And of the Islands of Barbadoes, Jamaica, St. Christopher's, Antigua, Nevis, Montserrat, &c. Reduced into Engliſh Money, By a Series of Tables ſuited to the ſeveral

Exchanges between the Colonies and Britain, adapted to all the Variations that from Time to Time have, or may happen. With Tables reducing the current money of the Kingdom of Ireland into Sterling, and the contrary, at all the Variations of Exchange. Also, a Chain of Tables for the interchangeable Reduction of the Currencies of the Colonies into each other. And many other useful Tables relating to the Trade in America. By J. Wright, Accomptant. The Third Edition. *London:* J. Smith, MDCCLXV. *lxix and* 326 *pp. Old calf.* 8*vo.* (6s. 6d. 2910)

WYETH (JOSEPH). Remarks/ on/ Dr. Bray's Memorial, &c./ With Brief Obfervations/ On fome Paffages in the Acts of his Vifitation/ in/ Maryland,/ And on his/ Circular Letter to the Clergy there ;/ Subfequent to the faid Vifitation./ By Jofeph Wyeth./ *London,* Printed and Sold by T. Sowle, in White-Hart-/Court in Gracious-ftreet, 1701./ 51 *pp.* 4*to.* (10s. 6d. 2911)

WYNKELMANN (HANS JUST). [*Engraved title*] Hans Juft/ Winkelmans/ Americanifcher/ Neuer Welt/ Beschreibung/ Gedruckt zu Oldenburg/ 1664./ [*Printed title*] Der/ Americanischen/ Neuen Welt/ Befchreibung,/ Darinnen deren Erfindung, Lager, Natur, Eigenfchaft,/ Sitten, Barbarey, und unerhörte Graufamkeit der Einwohner, Thier, Vögel,/ Fifchen und anderer; Beneben einer wunderbaren Schifffart und Reife Be=/fchreibung nach Brafilien Hans von Staden, bürtig aus Homburg in Heffen ;/ Was er vor felzame wunderbare Länder und wilde Leute gefehen ; Was er in=/nerhalb acht Jahren ausgeftanden, und wie der högfte Gott ihn aus fo Vielfal=/tiger grofer Gefahr errettet habe &c. Mit vielen nachdenklichen Fragen/ und nothwendigen Figuren ausgezieret und zu=/fammen getragen/ Durch Hanf Juft Wynkelmann./ Gedruckt zu *Oldenburg* bey Henrich=Conrad Zimmern,/ Im Jahr Chrifti 1664./ 8 *prel. leaves; viz. Engraved and printed titles,* 'Dem Hochwürdigen, Durchleuchtigen, Hoch=/gebornen Fürften und Herrn,'/ 1 *page*; 'Als Alexander,' *etc.* 4 *pp*; 'And den mit Stand und Verftand/ Hochgeneigten Lefer./ 5 *pp*; 'Ordnungs=Regifter der Capiteln,' 2 *pp*; *Folded sheet, a portrait of the Author; Text* 228 *pp*;

Portrait of the Author, 1 *page;* ' Register,' 11 *pp.*
Oblong 4to. (2*l.* 12*s.* 6*d.* 2912)

WYNNE. A General History of the British Empire in America. Containing, An Historical, Political, and Comercial View of the English Settlements; including all the Countries in North-America, and the West-Indies, ceded by the Peace of Paris. In Two Volumes. By Mr. Wynne. *London,* W. Richardson and L. Urquhart, MDCCLXX. *Two Volumes.* Vol. I. *Title ; Contents vi pp ; Introduction, pp. iii-viii; text* 520 *pp. With map.* Vol. II. *Title, vi and* 546 *pp. Half calf.* 8*vo.* (12*s.* 6*d.* 2912*)

WYTFLIET (CORNELIUS). Descriptionis/ Ptolemaicæ/ Avgmentvm./ Siue/ Occidentis Notitia/ Breui commentario/ illustrata/ Studio et opera/ Cornely Wytfliet/ Louaniensis./ *Lovanii/* Tijpis Iohannis Bogardi/ Anno Domini M.D.xcvII./ *Engraved title,* 3 *prel. leaves,* 19 *maps ; followed by Text* 191 *pp ; List of maps,* 1 *page. First Edition. Pigskin. Folio.* (1*l.* 11*s.* 6*d.* 2913)

WYTFLIET (CORNELIUS). Descriptionis/ Ptolemaicæ/ Avgmentvm./ siue/ Occidentis Notitia/ Breui commentario/ illustrata, et hac fe=/cunda editione magna/ sui parte aucta/ Cornelio Wytfliet Louanienfi/ auctore./ *Lovanii/* Tijpis Gerardi Riuij/ Anno Domini. CIƆ. IƆ. XCIIX./ *Engraved title,* 3 *prel. leaves and* 19 *maps ; followed by Text,* 191 *pp. List of Maps,* 1 *page. Folio.* (1*l.* 11*s.* 6*d.* 2914)

IMENEZ (Francisco). Las Historias del Origen de los Indios de esta Provincia de Guatemala, traducidas de la lengua Quiché al Castellano para mas comodidad de los Ministros del S. Evangelio. Por el R. P. F. Francisco Ximenez, cura Doctrinero por el Real Patronato del Pueblo de S. Thomas Chuila. Exactamente segun el texto Español del Manuscrito original que se halla en la Biblioteca de la Universidad de Guatemala, Publicado por la Primera vez, y aumentado con una introduccion y anotaciones por el D^r. C. Scherzer. A expensas de la Imperial Academia de las Ciencias. *Londres*: Trübner & Co. 1857. *xvi and 216 pp. Unbound. 8vo.* (8*s*. 6*d*. 2915)

YALE-COLLEGE subject to the General Assembly. *New-Haven:* Printed by Thomas and Samuel Green. M,DCC,LXXXIV. 44 *pp.* 8vo. (7s. 6d. 2916)

YONGE (F.) A View of the Trade of South-Carolina, with Proposals Humbly Offer'd for Improving the fame. [*London.* 1722.] *Privately printed.* 16 pp. *Half mor.* 8vo. (7s. 6d. 2917)

ARATE (Augustin). Le Histoire/ Del Sig. Agostino/ di Zarate/ Contatore et Consigliero/ del l'Imperatore Carlo V./ Dello Scoprimento et Conqvista del Perv,/ nelle quali ſi ha piena & particolar relatione delle coſe ſucceſſe, in quelle bande,/ dal principio fino alla pacificatione delle Prouincie, ſi in quel che tocca/ allo ſcoprimento, come al ſucceſſo delle guerre ciuili occorſe/ fra gli Spagnuoli & Capitani, che lo conquiſtarono./ Nvovamente di Lingva Castigliana Tradotte/ Dal. S. Alfonso Vlloa./ Con Privilegio./ In *Vinegia* appresso Gabriel/ Giolito de' Ferrari./ MDLXIII. 8 *prel. leaves; viz. Title, the reverse blank;* 'All' Illvstriss. Signore il S. Gvido Brandolino Conte di Valdemarini,' *etc. 3 pp;* 'Tavola,' 11 *pp; Text 294 pp; in Italics. Vellum. 4to.* (3*l.* 3*s.* 2918)

ZARATE (Augustin). [*First title*] The/ Discoverie and Conqvest/ of the Prouinces of Perv, and/ the Nauigation in the South/ Sea, along that Coaſt./ And alſo of the ritche Mines/ of Potosi./ [*Woodcut of*] · The · Riche · Mines · of · Potossi ·/ ¶ Imprinted at London by Richard Ihones. Febru. 6. 1581./ *The reverse blank.* [*Second title*] ☙ The ſtrange and/ delectable Hiſtory of the/ diſcouerie and Conqueſt of the/ Prouinces of Peru, in the/ South Sea./ And of the notable things which/ there are found: and alſo of the bloudie/ ciuill vvarres vvhich there hap=/pened for gouernment./ Written in foure bookes, by/ Auguſtine Sarate, Auditor for/ the Emperour his Maieſtie in the/ ſame prouinces and firme land./ And alſo of the ritche/ Mines of Potoſi./ Tranſlated out of the Spaniſh/ tongue, by T. Nicholas./ Imprinted at *London* by Richard/ Ihones, dwelling ouer againſt the/ Fawlcon, by Holburne bridge. 1581./ *Within*

a woodcut border of figures, the reverse blank. ' 30 To the Right Ho-/nourable, Maifter Thomas Wilson,/ Doctor of the Ciuill Lawe, and one/ of the principall Secretaries, to the/ Queenes moft excellent Maieftie.'/ 6 *pp. signed* 'Thomas Nicholas,' *in Roman type.* 'To the Reader,' 6 *pp. in black letter : Text, black letter, in* 89 *leaves,* 1 *to* 12, *and* 89, *not folioed ; folios* 16, 17, 28 *and* 19, *for* 17, 18, 19 *and* 20 *; with woodcuts on the reverse of folios* 16, 20, 46, 58, 85. 'The difcovery of the ritche Mynes of/ Potofi & how captaine Carauajell toke into his power,'/ *woodcut the same as on the first title,* 3 *pp.* 'The Table of the Chapters,' 3 *pp. Red morocco extra, by Bedford.* 4to. (10*l.* 10*s.* 2919)

ZARATE (Augustin de). Histoire/ de la/ Découverte/ et de la/ Conquete/ du/ Perou./ Traduite de l'Efpagnol/ D'Auguftin de Zarate,/ Par S. D. C./ A *Amsterdam*,/ Chez J. Louis de Lorme, Libraire fur/ le Rockin, à la Liberté./ M.DCC./ *Two Volumes.* Tome Premier. 19 *prel. leaves, and* 307 *pp. Frontispiece, plates and map at pp.* 4, 8, 12, 16, 34, 36, 54, 114, 130, 149, 153, 290. Tome Second. 3 *prel. leaves, and* 408 *pp. Old calf.* 12*mo.* (10*s.* 6*d.* 2920)

ZARATE (Augustin de). Histoire de la Découverte et de la Conquete du Perou. Traduite de l'Efpagnol D'Auguftin de Zarate, Par S. D. C. A *Paris,* Par la Compagnie des Libraires. MDCCXVI. *Two Volumes.* Tome Premier. 20 *prel. leaves and* 360 *pp. Frontispiece, plates and map, at pp.* 5, 10, 15, 20, 29, 41, 43, 64, 133, 155, 176, 177, 185, 340. Tome Second. 4 *prel. leaves and* 479 *pp. Fine copy. Old calf.* 12*mo.* (10*s.* 6*d.* 2921)

ZARATE (Augustin de). Histoire de la Découverte et de la Conquête du Perou. Traduite de l'Efpagnol D'Auguftin de Zarate, Par S. D. C. A *Paris,* Rue S. Jacques, Chez Michel Guignard, près la Fontaine S. Severin, à l'Image S. Jean, M.DCCXVI. *Two Volumes.* Tome Premier. 20 *prel. leaves, and* 360 *pp. Frontispiece.* Tome Second. 4 *prel. leaves and* 479 *pp.* 12*mo.* (10*s.* 6*d.* 2922)

ZARATE (Augustin de). Histoire de la Découverte et de la Conquête du Perou. Traduite de l'Espagnol D'Aguftin de Zarate, Par S. D. C. A *Paris,* Par la Compagnie des Libraires. M. DCC.

XLII. *Two Volumes.* Tome Premier. 20 *prel. leaves and* 360 *pp. Frontispiece, plates and map at pp.* 5, 10, 15, 20, 29, 41, 43, 64, 133, 155, 176, 177, 185, 340. Tome Second. 4 *prel. leaves and* 479 *pp. Old calf.* 12*mo.* (10*s.* 6*d.* 2923)

ZARATE (AUGUSTIN DE). Histoire de la Découverte et de la Conquête du Perou, Traduite de l'Espagnol D'Augustin de Zarate, Par S. D. C. A *Paris*, Par la Compagnie des Libraires. M. DCC. LXXIV. *Two Volumes.* Tome Premier. *xl and* 360 *pp. Frontispiece, plates and map at pp.* 5, 10, 15, 20, 29, 41, 43, 64, 133, 155, 176, 177, 185, 340. Tome Second. *viii and* 479 *pp.* 12*mo.* (10*s.* 6*d.* 2924)

ZENGER (JOHN PETER). The Tryal of John Peter Zenger of New-York, Printer, Who was lately Try'd and Acquitted for Printing and Publishing a Libel againſt the Government. With the Pleadings and Arguments on both Sides. *London*: J. Wilford, 1738. *Title and* 32 *pp. Half morocco.* 4*to.* (7*s.* 6*d.* 2925)

ZENGER (JOHN PETER). The Tryal of John Peter Zenger, of New-York, Printer, Who was lately Try'd and Acquitted for Printing and Publishing a Libel againſt the Government. With the Pleadings and Arguments on both Sides. The Second Edition. *London*: Printed for J. Wilford, 1738. *Title and* 32 *pp. Half morocco.* 4*to.* (7*s.* 6*d.* 2926)

ZENGER (JOHN PETER). The Tryal of John Peter Zenger, of New-York, Printer, Who was lately Try'd and Acquitted for Printing and Pubilshing a Libel againſt the Government. With the Pleadings and Arguments on both Sides. The Fourth Edition. *London*, J. Wilford, 1738. *Title and* 32 *pp.* 4*to.* (7*s.* 6*d.* 2927)

ZENGER (JOHN PETER). The Case and Tryal of John Peter Zenger, of New-York, Printer, Who was lately tryed and acquitted for Printing and Publishing a Libel againſt the Government. With The Pleadings and Arguments on both Sides. *London:* J. Wilford, 1750. 60 *pp. Half morocco.* 8*vo.* (5*s.* 6*d.* 2928)

ZENGER (JOHN PETER). The Trial of John Peter Zenger, Of New-York, Printer: Who was charged with having printed and publifhed a Libel againſt the Government; and acquitted. With a Narrative of his case. To which is now added, being never printed before, the Trial of Mr. William Owen, Bookseller, near Temple-Bar, Who was alſo Charged with the Publication of a Libel againſt the Government; of which he was honourably acquitted by a Jury of Free-born Englifhmen, Citizens of London. *London:* J. Almon, MDCCLXV. 59 pp. *Half morocco.* 8vo. (4s. 6d. 2929)

ZENO (CATERINO). De i Commentarii del/ Viaggio in Perfia di M. Caterino Zeno il K./ & delle guerre fatte nell' Imperio Perfiano,/ dal tempo di Vffuncaffano in quà./ Libri Dve./ Et dello scoprimento/ dell' Ifole Frislanda, Eslanda, Engrouelanda, Efto/tilanda, & Icaria, fatto fotto il Polo Artico, da/ due fratelli zeni, M. Nicolò il K. e M. Antonio./ Libro Vno./ Con vn disegno particolare di/ tutte le dette parte di tramontana de lor fcoperte./ Con gratia, et Privilegio./ In *Venetia/* Per Francefco Marcolini. MDLVIII./ *Title, the reverse blank;* 'Al Reverendiſsimo/ Monsignor M./ Daniel Barbaro/ Eletto Patriarcha/ D'Aqvilegia./ Francefco Marcolini. Vmilferuo.'/ 2 pp. 'Proemio de l'Avtore/ ne i dve Libri de' com-/mentarii del Viaggio in/ Perfia & delle guerre Perfiane/ di M. Caterino Zeno il/ Caualliere,'/ 6 pp. 'Errori,' 1 page. *Text commencing on the reverse of folio 5, and ending on folio 58; on the reverse, the Printer's device.* With 'Carta da Navegar de Nicolo et Antonio Zeni Fvrono in Tramontana Lano. M.CCC. LXXX.' *Russia.* 8vo. (10l. 10s. 2930)

ZENO (CATERINO). *Another copy, wanting the map.* 8vo. (2l. 12s. 6d. 2931)

ZIMMERMANN (E. A. W. DE). Essai de Comparaison entre La France et Les Etats-Unis de L'Amérique Septentrionale, par rapport à leur sol, à leur climat, à leurs productions, à leurs habitans, à leur constitution, et à leur formation progressive. Par Mr. E. A. W. de Zimmermann, Conseiller de Cour et Professeur à Brunsvic, de l'Académie de Petersbourg; Goettingen; Bologne; de la Société Linn. de Londres, etc. Traduit de l'Allemand et Enrichi de Développemens et de Notes par l'Auteur méme. Tome I. à *Leipzig,* Chez Reinicke et

Hinrichs./ 1797. *viii and* 494 *pp. List, and Division, etc.* 4 *pp. Old calf.* 8*vo.* (4*s.* 6*d.* 2932)

ZISNEROS (JOSEPH DE). Difcvrfo/ qve en el infigne/ Avto de la Fe, celebrado en/ efta Real cuidad de Lima, aueinte y tres de/ Enero de 1639. años :/ Predico el M. R. P. F. Ioseph de Zisne-/ros, Calificador de la fuprema, y general Inquificion, Padre de la S. Pro-/uincia de la Concepcion, y Comiffario general en todos eftos Reynos/ del Pirù, y Tierrafirme, del Orden de N. P. S. Francifco./ Dirigido/ al Exmo Señor Don Lvis Geronymo de/ Cabrera y Bobadilla, Conde de Chincon, Virrey, Gouerna/ dor, y Capitan General de los Reynos del Pirú, y Tierrafir-/ma, Gentilhōbre de la Camara de fu Mageftad, y de fu Ilaue/dorada, de los Confejos de gnerra, y eftado, Comēdador/ del campo de Critana, del ordē de Santiago./ Impreffo en *Lima* por Geronymo de Contreras, año 1639./ [*Colophon.*] Con licencia./ Impresso/ en Lima por/ Geronymo de/ Contreras, Im-/pressor de libros, fron-/tero de la Cruz de gradas,/ Año de 1639./ 5 *prel. leaves, viz. Title in a metal type border, and woodcut of arms, the reverse blank*; 'Aprobacion del M. R. P. M. F. Iuan de Ribera Prouincial,' *etc.* 3 *pp. signed* 'Fr. Iuan de Ribera.' 'Dedicatoria,' 4 *pp. signed* 'Fr. Iofeph de Zifneros Comiffario general.' *Text in* 15 *folioed leaves. Calf extra.* 4*to.* (1*l.* 11*s.* 6*d.* 2933)

ZURLA (PLACIDO). Il Mappa Mondo di Fra Mauro Camaldolese Descritto ed Illustrato da D. Placido Zurla dello stess' ordine *Venezia* 1806. 164 *pp. With 2 plates. Large Paper.* 4*to.* (1*l.* 1*s.* 2934)

Laus Deo.

www.ingramcontent.com/pod-product-compliance
Lightning Source LLC
Chambersburg PA
CBHW020309240426
43673CB00039B/751